MOOCs AND OPEN EDUCATION AROUND THE WORLD

Edited by Curtis J. Bonk, Mimi M. Lee,
Thomas C. Reeves, and
Thomas H. Reynolds

Routledge
Taylor & Francis Group

NEW YORK AND LONDON

First published 2015
by Routledge
711 Third Avenue, New York, NY 10017

and by Routledge
2 Park Square, Milton Park, Abingdon, Oxon OX14 4RN

Routledge is an imprint of the Taylor & Francis Group, an informa business

Library of Congress Cataloging in Publication Data
MOOCs and open education around the world / edited by Curtis J. Bonk,
Mimi M. Lee, Thomas C. Reeves, and Thomas H. Reynolds.
pages cm
Includes bibliographical references and index.
1. MOOCs (Web-based instruction) 2. Open learning. 3. Distance education.
I. Bonk, Curtis Jay.
LB1044.87M64 2015
371.33'44678—dc23
2014048370

ISBN: 978-1-138-80740-2 (hbk)
ISBN: 978-1-138-80741-9 (pbk)
ISBN: 978-1-315-75110-8 (ebk)

Typeset in Bembo
by Swales & Willis Ltd, Exeter, Devon, UK

Printed and bound in the United States of America by Edwards Brothers Malloy
on sustainably sourced paper.

"Bonk, Lee, Reeves, and Reynolds accomplish a tremendous task in bringing together dozens of key international leaders to discuss the efforts of open education and MOOCs. Numerous social technologies are open and mostly free thereby providing us the opportunity to connect with others in ways that globally transform our relational and organizational values. It was only natural that we would see this movement impact education. The authors deliver a diverse perspective on these phenomena discussing not only where we have been and where we are going in higher education, but providing us practical information to guide our research and instruction. Moreover, they do not shy away from the challenges and realities of these trends; instead, they offer the reader a critical perspective too. If you want a comprehensive look at the state of higher education and technology today, this is the book to get."
—*Tanya Joosten, Director, eLearning Research and Development, Academic Affairs, and Co-Director, National Research Center for Distance Education and Technological Advancements, University of Wisconsin-Milwaukee*

"For over twenty years you can count on the fact that if you've visited the frontiers of online learning, you will have encountered Dr. Curt Bonk. He and his colleagues, Mimi Lee, Tom Reeves, and Tom Reynolds, have done it again here! This volume represents the best thinking and ultimate compendium of opinion on online learning's latest manifestation . . . MOOCs."
—*Herb Hilderley, Managing Partner, Paxen Publishing LLC*

"After MOOCs took the world by storm in 2012, more sober-minded onlookers concluded that their impact may not be what the breathless adulation they first received indicated. This book cuts through these perspectives to offer a comprehensive look at the promise and peril of MOOCs, as it delves deep into the complicated issues underlying them through a variety of perspectives from different authors."
—*Michael Horn, Co-Founder and Executive Director, Education, Clayton Christensen Institute, and author of* Disrupting Class: How Disruptive Innovation Will Change the Way the World Learns *and* Blended: Using Disruptive Innovation to Improve School

"Open educational resources, practices, and their poster child—MOOCs— deliver a digital learning dividend to billions of learners globally. Bonk, Lee, Reeves, and Reynolds have assembled a 'who's who' of expertise in this quickly emerging field, each of whom shares their insights into the means to both improve and reduce the cost of learning."
—*Terry Anderson, Professor, Athabasca University, Canada, and author of numerous books including* Theory and Practice of Online Learning

"Curt Bonk and his colleagues again stir the world in thinking about where open education is going . . . and why. This book is a tour de force collection of both

thought and insight for the numerous evolving paths, perils, and potential gleaned from early experiences with MOOCs and the many forms of open education."
—*Bradley C. Wheeler, Vice President for IT, CIO, & Professor, Indiana University*

"A long awaited book which reveals controversies surrounding MOOCs and some debates and critical analysis of these controversies; the strengths of open education and how when both these concepts are combined innovatively, they result in greater learning impact for a technological diverse community. A must have, must read, and must analyse book for more impactful understanding!"
—*Abtar Kaur, Dean, School of E-Education, Hamdan Bin Mohammed Smart University, Dubai, UAE*

"A most authoritative examination of MOOCs and their implications for education in the world from some of the finest leading voices in the field! A must-read for anyone interested in emerging trends in technology and education."
—*Yong Zhao, Professor, Presidential Chair, and Director, Institute for Global and Online Education, College of Education, University of Oregon*

"Massive open online courses (MOOCs) and open educational resources have a great deal of potential to transform the world of corporate training and learning here in Korea too. Few managers, however, have specific ideas or strategies about how to surf this gigantic wave and leverage it. This book shows a clear path for strategic moves to all corporate learning professionals who want to shift to a new era of empowered employee learning."
—*Mijin Cho, Vice President of Leadership Develop Group at Hyundai Motor Group University*

"The world really needs *MOOCs and Open Education Around the World*. It is extremely important for academics, practitioners, administrators, and leaders to understand fully the phenomenon that is the MOOC in order to make the right decisions in considering their design, development, and delivery. This book, edited by some of the foremost scholars in our field, provides a full account of MOOCs and open education. It answers all the pressing questions while offering the necessary guidance to make informed and sensible decisions. In addition, it provides a definitive source of timely and salient information for the countless people for whom MOOCs are of interest and value, and, as such, it has my highest recommendation."
—*Professor Ron Oliver, Deputy Vice-Chancellor for Teaching, Learning and International, Edith Cowan University, Western Australia*

"Now that MOOC's have become part of Higher Education delivery landscape all over the world, we are fortunate that Curt Bonk, Mimi Lee, Tom Reeves, and Tom Reynolds have marshalled an extensive social network of leaders in the use of technology in education to give us a thorough review of their impact as well as potential future contributions. The experiences drawn from such diverse

backgrounds are invaluable to anyone interested in the globalisation of education. In addition, the views and ideas offered on implications, concerns, and opportunities make this book a highly valuable resource for those charged with understanding how open educational resources, MOOCs, and other forms of distance learning all fit together. My colleagues and I in the UK have extensively used Bonk's strategic advice before and I am pleased to offer congratulations on yet another unquestionably insightful and yet practically based book."
—*Nigel Banister, Chief Global Officer, Manchester Business School, UK*

"This edited collection provides a comprehensive account of current practice and the possibilities afforded by MOOCs and open education approaches. Curt Bonk and his colleagues present a broad range of views sharing practice and theory from researchers and practitioners who have led the way in designing and evaluating accessible education. I love this book! It is a great addition for everyone interested in rising to the challenge of meeting the demands of the learners of today and the future."
—*Denise Kirkpatrick, Deputy Vice-Chancellor and Vice-President (Academic), University of Western Sydney, Australia*

"In the midst of rapid transformation, where past and current concepts, paradigms, and systems converge to create a new innovation resulting in significant disruptions, a compass and a map would be highly useful to make better sense of what is happening. Fortunately, this book serves as just such a map to venture into this emerging world of MOOCs. While the MOOC is relatively new in rendition, it is not so new in origin ('Massive,' as in the wide availability of textbooks; 'Open,' as the Web and the Internet; 'Online,' as in distance education and eLearning; 'Courses,' as in organized instruction). This book will help join more dots, connect to other pictures, and consolidate a new baseline of understanding. As history has demonstrated, when this happens, new philosophical and technological outcomes will result."
—*Daniel Tan, Group Chief Learning Officer, Taylor's Education Group, Malaysia*

"Anyone who is in the field of educational technology and/or online learning has an opinion about MOOCs and the so-called 'MOOC Revolution.' Curt Bonk and his colleagues, Mimi Lee, Tom Reeves, and Tom Reynolds, have provided us with an outstanding book, capturing the thoughts of leaders and experts on this timely subject. The book takes you from skeptics to supporters, while including case studies from around the world. Whether you are currently offering MOOCs, taking a MOOC, or unsure of their impact on education, this is a must-read."
—*Darcy Hardy, Associate Vice President, Enterprise Consulting at Blackboard Inc.*

"The irrepressible Professor Curt Bonk has now focussed his mind, and the minds of his esteemed colleagues, on the impact of MOOCs and Open Education not just in the USA but around the world. By taking an open view of what MOOCs

are and by including the wider dimensions of Open Education practice, this book provides a real insight that will be a useful support for anyone who is studying the principles or practice of Open Education. The book is well timed as many of the early adopters have learnt the lessons from MOOCs and Open Education and these lessons will inform the next generation of educators and learners in the Open Education environment. Clearly, this is the 'must read' book on the subject."
—*Haydn Blackey, Director of the Centre for Excellence in Learning and Teaching, the University of South Wales, UK*

"This fascinating collection of stories, use cases, and research studies underscores the dramatic and transformative impact that comes from opening the walls of the institution and removing restrictions on how we share our work. Kudos to Drs. Bonk, Lee, Reeves, and Reynolds for inspiring so many experts from the newly emergent land of open education. Whether working in massive courses or from essential open frameworks for action, openness leads to transparency, transparency to trust. From trust, there are no limits as to what is possible."
—*Ellen D. Wagner, Chief Research and Strategy Officer, Predictive Analytics Reporting (PAR) Framework, Inc., and Partner and Senior Analyst for Sage Road Solutions, LLC*

"The concept of the MOOC has probably been the most discussed and debated topic in education during the past eight years. Despite some concerns about the actual benefits, the quality, and the business model of MOOCs, hundreds of new MOOCs are being developed and offered every day. Yet, not much literature can be found that reports on the phenomenon comprehensively. In response, this book offers critical reflections and reports on the development and practice of MOOCs around the world. It will give the readers a comprehensive view on both the benefits of, as well as the issues around, MOOCs that still need to be addressed to make it contribute significantly to the notion of open education."
—*Tian Belawati, Rector, Universitas Terbuka, Indonesia, and President of the International Council for Open and Distance Education, 2012–2015*

"Just as MOOCs stormed the world only a few years ago, Bonk, Lee, Reeves, and Reynolds have brought the world of open education scholars together for a thoughtfully diverse book about the potential for open education globally. This book, thankfully, gives homage to the relatively longer history and backdrop of distance and open education, which, as the authors note, has been building over many years and is capped by the extraordinary opportunity and publicity granted by the coming of MOOCs. Kudos to the editors and authors for their broad geographic, historical, and conceptual perspective."
—*Richard T. Hezel, Founder and Chairman, Hezel Associates, LLC*

To all the inquisitive, informal, nontraditional, and educationally disadvantaged learners around the world who can benefit from innovative learning alternatives and options. May this book help open a few new doors and windows for you.

CONTENTS

FOREWORD 1

The Role of MOOCs in the Future of Education

George Siemens

Few trends in education over the past half-century match the sudden arrival of massive open online courses (MOOCs). In a span of only a few years, MOOCs have received tremendous coverage in mainstream media, traditional academic conferences and journals, and blogs and social media. Following their popularization in the fall of 2011, MOOCs were the subject of unprecedented hype as CEOs of technology startups and university presidents shared the stage in outproclaiming each other about the ways in which traditional higher education was dead and the new guard had arrived.

The CEO of Udacity, Sebastian Thrun, an early MOOC provider that has since transitioned to corporate training, declared that in 50 years, there would only be 10 universities and Udacity would be one of them (Leckart, 2012). Compounding these bold proclamations, and drawing frustration from learning scientists, Thrun stated that they had discovered the 'magic formula' for learning (Carr, 2013). Government officials eagerly embraced the rhetoric, hoping to find leverage to minimize the impact of dramatic state-level defunding of higher education. California proclaimed new opportunities to cut costs and increase student success by engaging with MOOC providers (Hattori, 2013). University leaders were not isolated from these events; they woke up suddenly with new anxieties when the president of University of Virginia was fired (and then later reinstated) for being too slow to react to new trends (Rice, 2012). Top tier systems like Harvard and MIT responded with a $60 million investment in edX (MIT News Office, 2012); a new MOOC provider that arose as an alternative to Coursera and similar offerings.

As both participants and observers in this much-publicized higher education circus, academics were challenged to respond. The first substantive faculty response to MOOCs was from the philosophy faculty at San Jose State University who declared that open online courses were an attempt to dismantle departments and public education (San Jose State Philosophy Department Faculty, 2013). Was their world really crumbling? Can 200,000 students really be taught by one professor, a few teaching assistants, and some clever algorithms?

The narrative of the fall of 2011 to the early part of 2014 was overwhelmingly favorable to these notions of dramatic and substantial change. Pundits and theorists declared that the long-awaited disruption of higher education had arrived. Many of them hoped that it would confirm Peter Drucker's declaration that big university campuses would not survive 2027 (Lenzner & Johnson, 1997). Consulting firms that had previously ignored the drab world of higher education now eagerly contributed to the conversation of change, vying for stage time with a motley mix of academics, venture capital firms, and government officials.

From the perspective of early 2015, this stage of MOOC intoxication now embarrasses. The promised transformation of higher education failed to arrive. MOOCs ended up raising as many questions as they provided answers. Once some of the data of early MOOCs were published, it became clear that systemic change was delayed. Along the way, the flaws of MOOCs were eagerly dissected—high dropout rates, limited social interaction, heavy reliance on instructivist teaching, poor results for underrepresented student populations, and so on. More consequentially, change was coming for something altogether different than a single trend like MOOCs. MOOCs reflected trends rather than drove them; notably, the growing range of knowledge and learning needs of individuals in a society experiencing rapid, almost violent, change.

While the MOOC conversation is only beginning, two important concepts require attention when considering longer-term scenarios for higher education:

1. MOOCs are largely a supply-side answer to decades-long demand-side increase in learning.
2. MOOCs are not the critical trend; on the contrary, it is the complexification and digitization of higher education that is the alpha trend.

MOOCs were never about higher education. They were a response to larger societal needs related to education and training (see, for example, Chapter 28 from Ferguson, Sharples, & Beale, this volume). These same needs drove the development of information access tools like Google search, Wikipedia, and social media. In effect, learning at the start of the globally connected 21st century requires different tools and different methods for building knowledge. Everything moves more quickly in a networked world.

Consider the SARS outbreak of 2003. In a connected world, disease travels more quickly. So does information, as indicated by the rapid response of medical researchers to identify the virus causing SARS. While science often moves in multi-year cycles of peer review research and publication, identifying and understanding how to deal with SARS was a critical emergency. In a span of only a few months, the identification of the coronavirus enabled medical professionals to explore treatment and offer solutions. The speed of this research was only possible in a connected, networked, and online world.

Individuals and society require these same processes of connected learning. Industries change overnight, often taking with them the security of employment. As noted by Michael Keppell in Chapter 26 (this volume), learning, constant learning, defines all aspects of life today, whether the target of learning is a college degree, promotion at work, or simply understanding the world. Universities have traditionally played the educative role in society. Unfortunately, the learning and knowledge needs of society now require more than four years of higher education. Simply stated, in their current form, universities are mismatched to the structure and architecture of knowledge, including the pace of development. As a direct consequence, learners have sought to meet their needs through online learning, social media, and Web communities such as Stack Exchange. Higher education now faces the urgency of re-architecting itself to better serve the needs of society and modern learners.

The need to re-architect higher education is urgent. Universities have become increasingly complex. Student profiles are changing as the average entrance age increases, gender balances shift toward females as majority participants (OECD, 2013), and the traditional full-time university student is no longer in the majority (Davis, 2012). The umbrella of universities is expanding, serving a broader population with diversified needs. In response, as alluded to earlier, higher education is complexifying and many existing narratives of the *idea of the university* are being broadened to include previously unattended populations.

The digitalization of all aspects of modern life represents additional trends influencing learning. Higher education has a long history of expanding to respond to new learner populations. As noted in the Preface to this book, distance education and the development of open universities in the 1960s enabled second-chance access to formal education. As the Web grew in prominence, universities began experimenting with online and blended learning. These efforts were often relegated to a faculty of extension or some similar department. MOOCs, in contrast, have increased the pace of digitization for many faculties. Top tier universities have launched new departments and vice provost positions dedicated to learning innovation.

Additionally, MOOCs and other digital forms of learning serve another key benefit; namely, there are now seemingly infinite trails of data around learner interactions that can be used for research. Instead of being confined to only faculty members of education departments, digital learning research now cuts horizontally across university departments. It is not uncommon to see special issues of academic journals sharing results from previously isolated academic disciplines.

MOOCs may well be a term that fades from view in the near future. But that is not consequential. What is significant is that MOOCs effectively opened the door to new ways of thinking and operationalizing innovations in education.

MOOCs play an important role in understanding what education is becoming by revealing the current state of digital learning and the university in general. MOOCs, in this sense, are both a mirror and a lens for understanding the scope of change in learning.

This book, *MOOCs and Open Education Around the World*, reflects the research and thinking of the most prominent and influential academics and researchers in the field(s) of distance, digital, online, and open learning. The reader is presented with a rich image of the depth and nature of changes now well underway, including openness, faculty professional development, quality assurance, student success, and corporate learning. The zeitgeist of learning in modern society is captured in the process.

The expert curation of leaders in digital learning, Curt Bonk, Mimi Lee, Tom Reeves, and Tom Reynolds, captures the legacy of this highly momentous time of learning innovation. The potential of digital learning to provide access to new opportunities has long been known by researchers and practitioners in distance and online education. The editors of this unique volume offer a splendid overview of the state of learning—what is known, what learning is becoming, and what it means in practice. While the tremendous pace of innovations in education can be daunting at times, this book provides the basis for understanding the unprecedented opportunities available to individual academics, universities, and societies to remake themselves in a knowledge age.

The long-heralded learning revolution is at the doorstep. Future generations will benefit from the shape and structure of learning that is now being created. Prudent guides and thoughtful dialogue are required to ensure that learning remains a liberating and enlightening process in the service of a better society and greater opportunities for all.

 **George Siemens** researches technology, networks, analytics, and openness in education. Dr. Siemens is the Executive Director of the Learning Innovation and Networked Knowledge Research Lab at the University of Texas, Arlington. He has delivered keynote addresses in more than 35 countries on the influence of technology and media in education, organizations, and society. His work has been profiled in provincial, national, and international newspapers (including the *New York Times*), radio, and television. His research has received numerous awards, including honorary doctorates from Universidad de San Martín de Porres and Fraser Valley University for his pioneering work in learning, technology, and networks. Dr. Siemens is a founding member and first President of the Society for Learning Analytics Research (http://www.solaresearch.org/). He has advised government agencies in Australia, the European Union, Canada, and the United States, as well as numerous international universities, on digital learning and utilizing learning analytics for assessing and evaluating productivity gains in

the education sector and improving learner results. In 2008, he pioneered massive open online courses (sometimes referred to as MOOCs). He blogs at http://www.elearnspace.org/blog/ and on Twitter: gsiemens.

References

Carr, D.F. (2013, August 19). Udacity CEO says MOOC "magic formula" emerging. *Information Week*. Retrieved from http://www.informationweek.com/software/udacity-ceo-says-mooc-magic-formula-emerging/d/d-id/1111221.

Davis, J. (2012, October). *School enrollment and work status: 2011. American community survey briefs*, 11–14. US Department of Commerce, Economics and Statistics Administration: United States Census Bureau. Retrieved from http://www.census.gov/prod/2013pubs/acsbr11-14.pdf.

Hattori, K. (2013, January 14). Governor Jerry Brown, Udacity announce pilot program for $150 classes, *EdSurge*. Retrieved from https://www.edsurge.com/n/2013-01-14-governor-jerry-brown-udacity-announce-pilot-program-for-150-classes.

Leckart, S. (2012, March 20). The Stanford education experiment could change higher learning forever. *Wired Magazine, 20*. Retrieved from http://www.wired.com/2012/03/ff_aiclass/all/.

Lenzner, R., & Johnson, S.S. (1997, March 10), Seeing things as they really are. *Forbes, 159*(5), 122–128. Retrieved from http://www.forbes.com/forbes/1997/0310/5905122a.html.

MIT News Office. (2012, May 2). MIT and Harvard announce edX. *MIT News*. Retrieved from http://newsoffice.mit.edu/2012/mit-harvard-edx-announcement-050212.

OECD. (2013, October). How are university students changing? *Education Indicators in Focus*. Retrieved from http://www.oecd.org/edu/skills-beyond-school/EDIF%202013--N%C2%B015.pdf.

Rice, A. (2012, September 11). Anatomy of a campus coup. *The New York Times*. Retrieved from http://www.nytimes.com/2012/09/16/magazine/teresa-sullivan-uva-ouster.html?pagewanted=all.

San Jose State Philosophy Department Faculty. (2013, May 2). An open letter to Professor Michael Sandel from the Philosophy Department at San Jose State U. *Chronicle of Higher Education*. Retrieved from http://chronicle.com/article/The-Document-Open-Letter-From/138937/.

FOREWORD 2

Open(ing up) Education for All . . . Boosted by MOOCs?

Fred Mulder

A foreword to a book can be expected to highlight some of the terms and issues included in its title. Given the thought-provoking and promising title *MOOCs and Open Education Around the World*, that is exactly what I will attempt to do. Two major, long-term developments will be described, one towards open education and the other towards online education, in which the recent emergence of the MOOCs is to be placed. "Open" and "online" are then combined into one reference model for Open Education with five components, the 5COE model. It is in the 5COE model wherein MOOCs can also be profiled. Finally, I will underline the distinctive value of using the expression "Opening up Education" (which goes with a dynamic flavor) on top of the (static) term "Open Education."

Towards Open Education

The first major development towards open education goes back to the 19th century when the University of London started its system of correspondence education, offering learning opportunities at a distance from the university premises. And in the mid-20th century, the predecessor of the current University of South Africa (UNISA) was given a new role as a distance education university. The real breakthrough, however, came with the start of the Open University in the UK around 1970. During the next four decades, this successful initiative was followed up in many countries in Europe and around the world, leading to major operations reaching out to many learners who were not being served by the regular university system. In quite a few countries, for example, China, India, and Turkey, we now find so-called mega-universities enrolling millions of students.

The qualifier "open" in the name "open university" can stand for various attributes, including: (1) open entry (no formal requirements), (2) freedom of time, (3) freedom of place and (4) freedom of pace, (5) open programming (i.e., curriculum variety in size and composition), and (6) open to all people and target groups (i.e., a heterogeneous population, of all ages, and in different contexts; generally involving some type of combination of study with a job or domestic or care tasks). There are no open universities that are fully open in all these six degrees or forms of openness. In fact, there is a large diversity in institutional profiles among open universities. But certainly, by their nature and mission, open universities score much higher than regular universities on classical notions and the above attributes of openness. Note, however, that the increasing blending of educational delivery approaches is blurring the boundaries of open and traditional universities.

Digital Openness Flanking the 'Classical' Openness

This increasing attention toward the word "open" in education is also being influenced by the digital openness that has emerged during the last two decades and flanked the classical notions of openness in education. Forms of digital openness were initiated by the 2001 OpenCourseWare (OCW) move of MIT making available all its courses for free on the Internet. UNESCO was quick in recognizing the enormous potential of this concept for its "Education for All" ambition and marked the movement a year later by coining the term Open Educational Resources (OER) (UNESCO, 2002). Simply put, these are learning materials that are online and available at no cost to anybody: learners, teachers, and institutions. OER can be (re)used, revised, remixed, and redistributed, which is facilitated by so-called open licensing (Wikieducator, 2014). OER and OCW are members of a family of digital openness that has its roots in the Open Source movement (for software) and includes other forerunners like Open Access (for scientific output) and Open Content (for creative works). Meanwhile this family has expanded in other areas like Open Data, Open Science, Open Innovation, Open Practices, and Open Policies.

Such open education trends, terms, and initiatives have significantly changed the world of higher education: new and highly innovative players have entered the field of open education in the midst of traditional players who are often struggling with strategic dilemmas associated with OER. These two worlds, however, are coming closer through blended models. Two relevant international milestones meanwhile are impacting developments around open education and OER: (1) The Cape Town Open Education Declaration (Shuttleworth/OSF, 2008), and, more recently, (2) the Paris OER Declaration (UNESCO/COL, 2012). The Cape Town Declaration is dedicated to a vision to go beyond OER and calls on commitment to pursue and promote the broader concept of Open Education. It has 2,727 signatories, by far most of them individuals. The Paris OER Declaration maintains a focus on OER specifically, and was adopted by the World OER Congress held at UNESCO in Paris on June 20–22, 2012. Its ten recommendations to states around the world range from "Foster awareness and use of OER" to "Encourage the open licensing of educational materials produced with public funds." Clearly, these open education movements are driven by values like equity, inclusion, diversity, quality, and efficiency.

Towards Online Education

The second major development, the one towards online education, was initiated in the 1950s with the advent of new technologies and media to be used in education. Radio and later television, recorded audio and video, computer applications and animations, computer-based learning, intelligent tutoring systems, and automated testing, were all being utilized in education. But generally such technologies never became mainstream. At best, each of these educational delivery mechanisms was viewed as an interesting or useful additive to regular education. The most transformative technological impact emerged in the 1990s with the advent of the Internet, which offered powerful forms of communication and interaction deemed essential for education. We have entered the digital era with the ever-growing opportunities in online learning services, virtual learning activities, and, of course, digital learning materials.

Since the emergence of the Internet, technological capacities have evolved with increasing rapidity in terms of the speed, interactivity, and potential reach of new technologies and online platforms. Digital materials are reproducible under almost no cost. Broadband has given us the opportunity to reach learners in every corner of the world. With 2.7 billion people already having online access, such resources represent a powerful potential for educating the people of this planet.

Massive Open Online Courses

A very strong and rather sensational push came in 2011 when the first massive open online courses (MOOCs) were offered that were truly massive. In actuality, the first MOOCs had come from Canada a few years prior in 2008. They were of a different type, striving more for fundamental openness than to have a massive audience. They were labelled cMOOCs, distinguishing them from the so-called xMOOCs initiated in 2011 by American Ivy League universities. MOOCs, especially xMOOCs, have boomed since then, in large part, due to the fact that the first movers were top American universities like Stanford University and MIT. At the time, significant venture capital was brought in, the media hyped the movement, and politicians spoke out very favorably about MOOCs. Expectations were extremely high in the beginning; indeed, many claimed that it would revolutionize or even disrupt higher education (e.g., Barber, Donnelly, & Rizvi, 2013; Boxall, 2012). Recent developments mitigate, to some degree, these projections into the future and may ultimately result in the normalization of the movement. But, howsoever this movement will proceed, MOOCs are definitely a relevant change agent influencing higher education today.

Meanwhile it is no longer possible to cover MOOCs adequately with one definition. As shown by the chapters of this book, there already is much variety in terms of MOOCs and several derivatives like distributed open collaborative courses (DOCCs), leading to different categories of MOOCs. Without a doubt, MOOCs are courses that differ from OER and online learning materials by offering online learning services, including learning communities, automated self-testing, peer review, and certificates of different kinds, although generally not for credit. In addition, unlike static online documents, MOOCs are quite often based on video lectures plus facilitated interaction or discussion forums.

Regarding massiveness, we already observe major differences in scale that may significantly increase with the rapid expansion in the number of MOOCs. With respect to openness, MOOCs have an open entry on the Internet at no cost. With MOOCs, there is freedom of place, but generally there is no open licensing policy. In addition, most courses in a MOOC environment run in a fixed or predeterminate schedule, and the content is only available during that schedule for registered users (not for institutions).

"Open" and "Online" Combined in One Reference Model with Five Components

I have argued that it is useful to make a distinction between the two major developments in terms of change, namely towards open education and towards online education. Let us now proceed with an attempt to combine them in one overarching reference model, thereby reducing the overlap and emphasizing the convergence. Such an approach was deemed highly necessary having observed that the frequent use of the term open education generally lacks a clear and solid description of what is meant by it. The same problem holds for online education. Unfortunately, as noted below, Wikipedia does not assist in an exploration of the terminological jungle (Wikipedia, 2014).

Open education is a collective term to describe institutional practices and programmatic initiatives that broaden access to the learning and training traditionally offered through formal education systems. The qualifier "open" of open education refers to the elimination of barriers that can preclude both opportunities and recognition for participation in institution-based learning. One aspect of openness in or "opening up" education is the development and adoption of open educational resources.

Institutional practices that seek to eliminate barriers to entry, for example, would not have academic admission requirements. Such universities include The Open University in Britain and Athabasca University in Canada. These programs are commonly distance learning programs like e-learning, MOOCs and opencourseware, but not necessarily. Where many e-learning programs are free to follow, the costs of acquiring a certification may be a barrier, many open education institutes offer free certification schemes accredited by organisations like UKAS in the UK and ANAB in the USA where others offer a badge.

The Wikipedia description lacks a good level of overall clarity, analytical value, and practical utility. To Wikipedia's defense, however, it stipulates that open education is a collective term. This observation—that it is a catch-all type of concept—begs for an analytical and practical framework to be used as a reference model. My colleagues and I have developed such a framework which we call the "5COE model" and is overarching not only for open education but also for online education (Mulder, 2012; Mulder & Janssen, 2013). Recently, we have offered a more refined version (at present, only available in Dutch; see Mulder & Janssen, 2014). 5COE stands for "Five Components for Open Education." The model contains three components on the supply side and two components on the demand side of education, which are required to fully specify Open Education in a broad scope, incorporating also its online instrumentation.

The first supply-side component of the 5COE model is ***Educational Resources***. With the qualifier "Open" added to it, this stands for OER. While OER was already described, for completeness we would like to refer here to an internationally recognized definition (UNESCO/COL, 2012):

> Open Educational Resources are teaching, learning and research materials in any medium, digital or otherwise, that reside in the public domain or have been released under an open license that permits no-cost access, use, adaptation and redistribution by others with no or limited restrictions.

Educational Resources by themselves do not fully comprise education. Along these same lines, Open Educational Resources do not comprise all aspects of open education. Additional, complementary components are required.

Component 2 (on the supply side) is ***Learning Services***. With the qualifier "Open" added to "Learning Services," this term can be abbreviated to OLS. OLS stands for a wide range of online and virtual services which are meant for tutoring, advice, meetings, feedback, communities, teamwork, presentations, consultation of sources, navigating the Internet, testing, examining, etc. In contrast to OER, OLS may be available free of charge or at a cost.

The third component (on the supply side) is ***Teaching Efforts***. With the qualifier "Open" added in, the term becomes "Open Teaching Efforts" or OTE. The concept of OTE relates to the human contribution to the educational content or experience being provided (that generally has to be paid for). This contribution includes the efforts of teachers, instructors, trainers, developers, and support staff in their various roles, in a professional, open, and flexible learning environment and culture.

It is not sufficient to view education solely from the supply side. There needs to be a match with the requirements on the demand side.

Component 4 (on the demand side) is ***Learners' Needs***. When we add "Open to," this term becomes "Open to Learners' Needs" which is abbreviated to OLN. This first demand-side component of the 5COE model refers to the wish of learners for education that is affordable, doable, interesting, of good quality, and that also generates benefits for them. Learners' desire for openness may also relate to the "classical" openness (open entry, freedom of time, place and pace, open programming, and open to people and target groups) as well as to facilitating lifelong learning (e.g., recognition of prior learning or practical experience, credentialing, and bridging between informal learning and formal education).

The fifth and final component (second one on the demand side) is ***Employability & Capabilities Development***. When we add "Open to" to this term, it can be abbreviated as OEC. In effect, OEC implies that education can be expected to suit the changing society, to prepare for the labor market, and to be effective on the pronounced role of knowledge, innovation, and globalization. Moreover, education should offer scope for new (21st-century) skills, critical thinking, creativity, ethics, and responsibility, as well as for personal growth and citizenship.

We are using the umbrella term "Open Education" (OE) with its five components, mentioned earlier, to embrace both open and online education. The diagram in Figure i.1 illustrates the 5COE model.

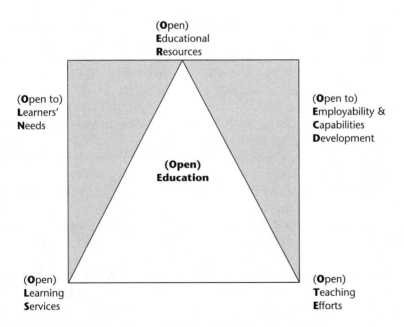

FIGURE I.1 Education and open (including Online) education in five components (The 5COE Model)

Open and Online Is a Profile Choice with Much Room for Diversity

We all know that there does not exist a single ideal model for education. This perspective, of course, also holds for open (and online) education. Stated another way, Open Education should not be considered a new doctrine for all to follow or to use exclusively.

There is no reason for all higher education institutions and organizations to aim at 100 percent openness in all five components. On the contrary, each institution can choose its own specific profile in terms of the degree of openness in those five components. Universities of applied sciences and vocational institutions and colleges, for example, can be expected to be more interested in OEC (Open to Employability and Capabilities development) than research universities. Universities with a MOOCs or open education-related strategy will emphasize OLS (Open Learning Services) much more than traditional universities staying away from the use of MOOCs and open education. In terms of OLN (Open to Learners' Needs), universities catering to lifelong learners and part-time studies like OUs will out vie mainstream universities which are primarily focused on young adult learners (e.g., 18 to 22-year-olds) and full-time studies. University colleges cherishing small-scale education (such as seen in the Cambridge/Oxford model) will likely have a stronger focus on OTE (Open Teaching Efforts) than comprehensive universities with large-scale operations. Finally, the cMOOCs initiated in Canada can be said to be 100 percent OER-based, whereas xMOOCs such as those hosted by edX, Coursera, and NovoEd, and offered by many prestigious universities in the United States, are still far from that level. Furthermore, to date, MOOCs generally are very supply-driven; consequently, they do not score highly on the two demand-side components of the 5COE Model, namely, OLN and OEC.

The diverse profile among institutions regarding their degree of openness here in the early portion of the 21st century is being mirrored through a better serving of the characteristics, circumstances, and needs of the highly diverse people and target groups in society; such individuals increasingly aspire for greater access to higher levels of education. Naturally, the opening up of education to whatever degree provides relevant mechanisms to facilitate this long-standing need of learners and societies. And it also generates a series of potential benefits, even when this takes place through a blending of approaches that vary in their degree of openness (e.g., online combined with on-site).

We can say that the tendency towards opening up education in all five components should be applauded whenever realized. However, our appreciation of the OER component should be more than just applause, but embracement. My colleagues and I in the OER world strongly argue that 100 percent OER is what all institutions and teaching staff should aim for. We contend that major benefits will appear regardless of institutional identity, learning philosophy, target groups, and educational sector. In fact, governments should embrace OER as a "no-regret" option, since OER can serve—quite remarkably—all three governmental responsibilities for education; that is, to promote and ensure accessibility, quality, and efficiency, at the same time (Mulder, 2013).

Open(ing Up) Education for All, Boosted by MOOCs?

It is time to reflect back on the title of this foreword and make some concluding remarks . . .

1. MOOCs are definitely a significant change agent in higher education. They mark a breakthrough of the powerful merger of two major long-term developments, towards open education and online education, respectively.
2. There is a strong need for an analytical and practical framework for the container concept and term Open Education that can be used as a reference model for all those occurrences of the words "open" and "online" in education, learning, and teaching. The proposed 5COE ("Five Components for Open Education") model is intended to serve this goal. This model contains three supply-side and two demand-side components. In line with the goals and premises of this particular book and the assortment of chapters which you are about to read, the 5COE model can be applied to position and profile a wide variety of open and online educational initiatives and projects of whatever size and scope, including MOOCs.
3. The foreword's title refers to "Open(ing up) Education," in part, to indicate a need to change the common expression "open education" to now verbalize it as "Opening up Education." That change, while rather subtle, is highly important since it underlines the dynamics of the processes and strategies involved. Moreover, it accounts for the diversity of educational opportunities and experiences that people increasingly desire. Not all aspects of education should be equally open, with an exception of the educational resources for which it can be argued that full openness (or OER in a broad sense) is beneficial for all learners, teachers, educational institutions, and governments. In this regard, I "openly" express my thanks to Iiyoshi and Kumar (2008) who were likely the first ones to introduce the expression "Opening up Education." Along these same lines, I wish to compliment the European Commission for using this expression as an umbrella title for a highly significant initiative launched in September 2013 (European Commission, 2013). This particular program addresses two major goals, namely: (1) to innovate teaching and learning for all through ICT; and (2) to reshape and modernize EU education through OER.
4. In the foreword's title, I explicitly incorporated UNESCO's "Education for All" mission by amalgamating it with "Opening up Education." Through this terminology, it is hoped that the reader will recognize the ultimate goals

that could be assigned to the global movement of OER, Open Education, Opening up Education, and MOOCs as well. There is much to be delighted about with the arrival and expansion of the MOOCs, including the media attention and politicians' interest that they have generated as well as the promises that they provide. But the real measure from learners, teachers, educational institutions, and societies at large would be whether and how the MOOCs will boost "Opening up Education for All" on a global scale, cherishing diversity. And that remains to be seen.

As you browse through the pages of this book, *MOOCs and Open Education Around the World*, you will be drawn into an inspiring tour d'horizon. The editors have succeeded in bringing together contributions from a broad spectrum of themes, perspectives, and backgrounds while maintaining an appropriate level of overview and connection. With this comprehensive volume, you can learn from examples of MOOC providers in different countries as well as from case studies on pedagogy, quality, innovation, lifelong learning, and learning for development. At the same time, your impending chapter readings will take you beyond current norms and practices and allow you to dive into historical developments, fundamental matters, considered opportunities, and perspectives for the future.

What all these chapters share is the carrying concept of openness, albeit with differences in scope and significance. This foreword is an endeavor to cross-cut the various contributions to this book with one leading question: "To what extent do the practices and experiences related to MOOCs and open education described in this book on the one hand, and the reflections and models of MOOCs and open education provided on the other hand, contribute to an integrative view on and way forward towards truly opening up education for all?" I will let you decide as you read through the remaining pages and chapters of this book. Feel free to write to me with your personal perspectives and thoughts.

 **Fred Mulder** holds a UNESCO/ICDE Chair in OER at the Open University of The Netherlands (OUNL). Previously, he was OUNL Rector for more than a decade. He is actively involved in OER initiatives and policies at the national level, by UNESCO, the OECD, and the EU. He is chairing the first pan-European MOOCs initiative called OpenupEd which was launched in April 2013 by EADTU (i.e., the European Association of Distance Teaching Universities). In addition, he is leading the Global OER Graduate Network. Mulder has received a Royal decoration (2007) for his work in Lifelong Learning, the ICDE Individual Prize of Excellence (2012) for his efforts in OER, and the Leadership Award for OpenCourseWare Excellence (2014).

References

Barber, M., Donnelly, K., & Rizvi, S. (2013). *An avalanche is coming: Higher education and the revolution ahead.* IPPR, London. Retrieved from http://www.ippr.org/assets/media/images/media/files/publication/2013/04/avalanche-is-coming_Mar2013_10432.pdf.

Boxall, M. (2012, August 8). MOOCs: A massive opportunity for higher education, or digital hype? *The Guardian.* Retrieved from http://www.theguardian.com/higher-education-network/blog/2012/aug/08/mooc-coursera-higher-education-investment.

European Commission. (2013). *Opening up education: Innovative teaching and learning for all through new technologies and open educational resources.* Brussels, Belgium. Retrieved from http://eur-lex.europa.eu/legal-content/EN/TXT/?qid=1389115469384&uri=CELEX:52013DC0654.

Iiyoshi, T., & Kumar, M.S.V. (Eds.) (2008). *Opening up education: The collective advancement of education through open technology, open content, and open knowledge.* MIT Press. Retrieved from http://mitpress.mit.edu/sites/default/files/titles/content/9780262515016_Open_Access_Edition.pdf.

Mulder, F. (2012). *Open educational resources in opening up education.* Presentation at the EU Ministerial Conference in Oslo, December 9–11, 2012. Retrieved from http://ministerialconference2012.linkevent.no/F%20Mulder%20parallel.pdf.

Mulder, F. (2013). The logic of national policies and strategies for open educational resources, *International Review of Research on Open and Distance Learning, 14*(2), 96–105. Retrieved from http://www.irrodl.org/index.php/irrodl/article/view/1536/2518.

Mulder, F., & Janssen, B. (2013). Opening up education. *Trend Report OER 2013,* SURF SIG OER, Utrecht (NL), pp. 36–42. Retrieved from http://www.surf.nl/binaries/content/assets/surf/en/knowledgebase/2013/Trend+Report+OER+2013_EN_DEF+07032013+%28HR%29.pdf.

Mulder, F., & Janssen, B. (2014). Naar OER-onderwijs voor iedereen, *Thema,* No. 1, pp. 6–13. Retrieved from https://www.surfspace.nl/media/bijlagen/artikel-1577-fb40e5fc2692d2522a3fdc9d992f958a.pdf.

Shuttleworth Foundation/Open Society Foundation (Shuttleworth/OSF). (2008). *The Cape Town Open Education Declaration.* Retrieved from http://www.capetowndeclaration.org/.

UNESCO. (2002). *Forum on the impact of open courseware for higher education in developing countries.* Final report, UNESCO, Paris. Retrieved from http://unesdoc.unesco.org/images/0012/001285/128515e.pdf.

UNESCO/Commonwealth of Learning. (UNESCO/COL) (2012). *2012 Paris OER Declaration.* Retrieved from http://www.unesco.org/new/fileadmin/MULTIMEDIA/HQ/CI/CI/pdf/Events/Paris%20OER%20Declaration_01.pdf.

Wikieducator. (2014). *Defining OER.* Retrieved from http://wikieducator.org/Educators_care/Defining_OER.

Wikipedia. (2014). *Open education.* Retrieved from http://en.wikipedia.org/wiki/Open_education.

PREFACE

Actions Leading to *MOOCs and Open Education Around the World*

Curtis J. Bonk, Mimi M. Lee, Thomas C. Reeves, and Thomas H. Reynolds

A Half-Century of Opening Up Education

Many readers of this volume may regard Open Education as a relatively new term, but anyone who studied to be a teacher in the early 1970s will recall being assigned to read books with the simple title *Open Education* (cf. Hassett & Weisberg, 1972; Nyquist & Hawes, 1971). Many of the ideas promoted in these books were not unlike some of the concepts and goals associated with contemporary conceptions of "open education." Terms like student-centered, interdisciplinary, project-oriented, individualized development, and the like were pervasive in this earlier literature.

One major difference between the idea of "open education" 50 years ago and the current conceptions of "open education" reflected in the two forewords and 29 chapters found in the eight different parts of this volume is that the former focused primarily on early childhood education. In contrast, today's conception of "open education" is most often, albeit not exclusively, promoted in the context of postsecondary or higher education, or any form of adult learning in general. Another obvious difference is that 50 years ago Web-based technologies did not exist to provide revolutionary ways of opening up educational opportunities for young as well as older learners spanning the globe.

The open education movement in schools of a half-century ago failed miserably; in fact, the classroom walls that were torn down to implement it were soon put back up. A primary reason for this failure was that opponents were able to focus attention on superficial aspects of the movement and distract potential adopters from open education's substantive qualities. As Altwerger, Edelsky, and Flores (1987) explained, "open space was substituted for openness of ideas, [and] learning centers for learning-centeredness. The final irony is that [open education] was judged a failure even though (because of the distortions) it was never implemented on any broad scale" (pp. 9–10).

One of the main reasons behind our endeavor for this book is that we hope to see today's open education movement escape the fate of so many previous attempts to enhance learning and teaching through innovative educational practices (cf. Haas & Fischman, 2010; Mettler, 2014; Tyack & Cuban, 1997). Massive open online courses (MOOCs), for instance, are presently experiencing more than a little criticism, and though much of it is quite thoughtful, some is the result of MOOCs simply being the most widely publicized component of the open education movement during the past few years (cf. White, 2014; Wildavsky, 2014). While posing questions and concerns about the MOOC movement can be useful, hasty denouncements need to be replaced with extended analyses, global discussions, and thoughtful reports.

In any case, the MOOC phenomenon, once lavishly praised in publications such as the *New York Times* and *The Economist*, has more recently become the subject of critical stories across the popular press. Gais (2014) quotes Ben Wildavsky, director of higher education studies at the Rockefeller Institute of Government in New York, as saying, "If 2012 was the year of the MOOC, it wasn't too long until what some call 'MOOC hype' gave way to 'MOOC hate.'" Similarly, Audrey Watters noted in her widely quoted Hack Education blog that while 2012 was the year of the MOOC (Pappano, 2012), 2013 was the year of the anti-MOOC (Watters, 2013). To address such concerns, we decided to bring together in this book a representative and rigorously edited sample of the ideas and experiences of the scholars and practitioners working on the frontlines of the open education movement.

Anyone conducting a Google Scholar search using the terms "MOOC and education" or "Open Educational Resources" (OERs) will encounter a nearly endless listing of documents, blog posts, and news stories. Clearly, the proliferation of MOOC- and OER-related material argues convincingly for a book-length resource to synthesize the myriad, and still emerging and evolving, perspectives of MOOCs and open education around the world. As part of these efforts, it is vital to document how such new forms of educational delivery provide hope for a brighter future for the disadvantaged and those too often trapped on the less privileged side of the digital divide. At the same time, it is also critical to discuss where they fall short. We trust that this book fulfills such needs, but we recognize that these are volatile topics and additional perspectives will come forth quickly.

Perhaps the most important reason that we collaborated on this edited book is that each of us is committed to the principles of the open education movement. We also share an optimistic perspective about the realization of these ideals. Although the aforementioned open education movement in K-12 schools largely failed shortly after its introduction in the early 1970s, another form of open education, the "open university," was introduced around the same time and has thrived. James (1971) described The Open University of the

United Kingdom as a "new phenomenon," but also acknowledged the inspiration of the open university idea "by developments in the United States, South Africa, Australia, Russia, and other countries" (p. 32). Today, nearly 60 open universities around the world enroll more than 17 million students (Guri-Rosenblit, 2012; Lockwood, 2013; Wikieducator, 2014); in fact, a few of them, Indira Gandhi National Open University in India, Anadolu University in Turkey, and Allama Iqbal Open University in Pakistan, alone have enrollments that reach into the millions.

As scholars and activists, we believe that education provides the essential foundation for enabling everyone on the planet, regardless of their gender, age, beliefs, wealth, or social status, to make the best use of their core human rights to personal happiness and fulfillment as well as the liberty to choose their own learning paths. We concur with Johnstone (2005) who wrote, "Education is a fundamental human right. It is the key to sustainable development and peace and stability within and among countries, and thus an indispensable means for effective participation in the societies and economies of the twenty-first century, which are affected by rapid globalization." We believe that the vast majority of likely readers of this book already share these ideals.

Purpose and Goals

Even though the e-learning opportunities provided by MOOCs and OERs continues to proliferate globally, little attention has been placed on how individual regions and countries are taking advantage of such technology-enabled learning. The possibilities for significant educational change, and perhaps even transformation, in developing and underdeveloped countries has been widely discussed and promoted. Also widely endorsed is the notion that e-learning is providing new educational opportunities for adolescent youth and young adults in the workplace as well as fostering professional development among more established older learners around the planet. The emergence of new forms of blended learning as well as the arrival of MOOCs and other forms of OERs have made e-learning front page news across all continents and societies (Bonk, 2009; Bonk & Graham, 2006).

As new digital forms of informal and formal learning proliferate, however, there is an increasing need to better understand how people in different regions of the world are implementing educational delivery innovations such as MOOCs and OERs. Even more importantly, educators, researchers, politicians, and countless others want to grasp what the outcomes of these initiatives are and how they can be improved. And, when combined with the current tidal wave of e-learning announcements and changes, those fostered by MOOCs and open education have caused institutions and organizations to grapple with issues of accreditation, credentialing, quality standards, innovative assessment, and learner motivation and attrition, among numerous other areas of concern. Each passing week, it seems that there is a major report or announcement concerning one or more of these topics.

In response to these issues, this book project explores, probes, and documents an array of unique implementations of MOOCs and open education in particular institutions and organizations as well as across regions and nations. We have invited contributions from thoughtful leaders and innovators whose research and practice have helped establish the movement toward opening up education using MOOCs and OERs. Fortunately, the vast majority of these scholars not only quickly agreed, but met our challenging timeline.

Many of the book contributors have been long-standing proponents of the open education movement. Most of them have been experimenting at the outer edges of traditional learning technology. They may have designed and taught a MOOC or perhaps crafted and disseminated one or more highly valuable open educational resources. Others have tested a unique MOOC platform or system, written strategic plans for their institution or organization on MOOCs and open education, or conducted research and evaluation of MOOCs and open education contents. Their stories and insights capture the present state of open education around the world. Hopefully, their ideas will inspire untold others to engage in this movement.

The contributors to this book focus on the various opportunities, as well as the dilemmas, presented in this new age of technology-enabled learning. What are the different delivery formats, interaction possibilities, assessment schemes, and business models? And what are the key controversies or issues that need to be discussed and addressed. In response, the various chapter authors explain an assortment of specific MOOC and open education trends and issues in their respective locales, share key research directions and findings, and provide suggestions and recommendations for the near future. They also detail their personal experiences and stories related to MOOC offerings and open education developments.

While we are aware that two book forewords and 29 chapters cannot offer a full accounting of all the MOOC and open education initiatives currently underway around the planet, we believe that many important goals for this volume were met. Listed below are ten of the key goals that we had in compiling this particular book, *MOOCs and Open Education Around the World*:

Ten Goals

1. Help the reader better understand the range of MOOC initiatives and open education projects currently underway around the planet.
2. Understand how MOOCs and open educational resources are impacting learners in different ways around the world. This goal includes obtaining a better grasp of the potential global impact of MOOCs and open education.
3. Highlight pressing issues and controversies where there presently is passionate debate.

4. Reflect on and plan for near-term possibilities, obstacles, and trends related to MOOCs and open education.
5. Gain insights into emerging trends in e-learning as well as future plans and visions, especially as they relate to MOOCs and informal or self-directed learning.
6. Learn how culture interacts with e-learning and open education across regions of the world.
7. Emotionally connect to the stories, experiences, pilot testing situations, etc., of those who have attempted a MOOC or developed significant open educational resources.
8. Grasp the challenges and barriers facing different organizations and institutions as well as entire countries in implementing MOOCs and other forms of e-learning and open education.
9. Learn from some of the key instructors, trainers, researchers, administrators, government officials, instructional designers, entrepreneurs, consultants, and others involved in the MOOCs and open education movement. We intend for the reader to get a sense of who some of the key players currently are in this space as well as what issues they are attempting to address.
10. Realize that many of the questions, criticisms, possibilities, and opportunities related to MOOCs and open education are global issues. While the contributors to this book represent diverse regions of the world, they have much in common in terms of their concerns, goals, initiatives, challenges, problems, and successes.

We hope that the readers of this book will attain many, if not most, of these goals as well as those that they carry with them. If any seem unfulfilled upon completion, we encourage the reader to contact one of us or one of the other book contributors with his or her questions and concerns as well as his or her own personal stories and insights.

Audiences and Stakeholders

As you will quickly discover upon turning the pages of this book, MOOCs mean different things to different people. You will also read assorted connotations about the meaning and value of open education. In terms of MOOCs, some view them as a vital way to diversify one's student base. For others, the emphasis is on the creation of global learning communities that share ideas, resources, and best practices. Still others view MOOCs as a tool for expanding access to education. Importantly, several of the contributors to this volume insightfully critique aspects of MOOCs, such as the use of the term "open" by MOOC vendors who restrict access to their course content to a set time period and platform and further limit it to those who actually enroll. You will also discover quite disparate views and problems related to assessment and accreditation of MOOCs and open educational contents.

In the midst of the wide array of MOOC and open education arguments and debates, new acronyms are proliferating in this wondrous world of MOOCs. For instance, you might have already read about cMOOCs (testing the theoretical and practical viability of connectivist-styled learning), xMOOCS (highlighting massive quantity of throughput with thousands of students in some cases), pMOOCs (experimenting with problem or project-based learning), BOOCs (big open online courses), MOOD (massive open online discussion) (Watters, 2013), SPOCs (small private online courses), and, most recently, PD-MOOCs (related to professional development for teachers and other professionals) (Davis, 2014). In this book, the reader will also learn about distributed open collaborative courses or DOCCs. Still other forms of MOOCs and MOOC derivatives are now targeting remedial education, advanced placement, and many other crucial niche areas.

Suffice to say, we hope that this book starts a dialogue about how MOOCs and open education might accelerate access to education by those living in poverty or without adequate access to traditional educational resources as well as for those coveting a move up in their careers or starting a new one. The time is ripe for such a conversation since the open education movement will only gain in significance with each passing year. This book might also shift common discussions about MOOCs and open education from technology and information access issues toward learning-related ones. Educators and learning professionals as well as politicians, information technology (IT) managers, and other educational stakeholders need to grasp that, from an educational standpoint, the Web has become a hub for testing, demonstrating, and evaluating new learning tools, formats, and ideas. MOOCs are just the latest instantiation of the trend toward Web-based teaching and learning.

This book can provide fresh ideas and information to university and college instructors, K–12 educators, corporate executives, administrators and IT managers, researchers, trainers, instructional designers, graduate students, and anyone interested in emerging trends in education; especially those related to open education and learning technology. In particular, this book can be valuable to higher education administrators and instructors as well as corporate, government, and military trainers who are interested in making sense of the recent research on MOOCs and open education as well as enhancing their understanding of key issues related to the design of open educational contents and courses. Instructors and instructional designers in higher education settings might find this book handy in special topic courses and seminars. At the same time, university deans and those in provost offices might use one or more chapters, or perhaps even the entire book, for faculty retreats and strategic planning sessions.

We are hopeful that this book will appeal to higher education administrators struggling with issues of where to place valued resources. In fact, IT managers in various educational sectors might use it for long-range planning and forecasting meetings and reports. Training managers in corporations or government agencies might also take advantage of the stories, ideas, and examples from the book to help justify their open education initiatives and strategic plans. All of these individuals will likely want to take advantage of these trends in a fiscally responsible, efficient, and strategically beneficial way.

A unique synthesis on MOOCs and open education will help administrators and staff from learning and teaching centers on college campuses to train relevant personnel for a wealth of online and open teaching delivery methods and approaches now possible. There are many hesitant, wary, reluctant, and resistant instructors, tutors, and staff on college campuses today as well as in schools and corporate and military environments. This book can provide a starting point from which to design training materials and supports related to MOOCs and open education. The many stories and experiences detailed in this book might also serve to inspire others to engage in a MOOC, either as an instructor or as a learner. Finally, politicians reading or accessing this book will discover that there are countless new possibilities for enhancing the learning of individuals across the lifespan in their respective communities and regions of the world. Many free and open access resources are now available for their citizens (Bonk, 2009). It is time to take advantage of them.

What Happens in Vegas Sometimes Becomes a Book

It is important to point out that the impetus for this book came from a one-day pre-conference symposium titled "MOOCs and Open Education Around the World" that the four of us editors organized before the commencement of E-Learn 2013. For those not familiar with the event or organization, E-Learn is an international conference that occurs each year in October or November and is run by the Association for the Advancement of Computing in Education (AACE). The 2013 pre-conference symposium took place in Las Vegas and attracted over 100 participants as well as two excellent keynote speakers, Paul Kim and George Siemens. Encouraged by the enthusiasm generated at the E-Learn symposium, we decided to undertake editing this volume, which not only includes chapters from both symposium keynote speakers, but also from more than 60 other scholars working at the cutting edge of MOOCs and open education around the world.

The book starts with chapters that look back at the history of open and distance education and offer unique insights and critiques into current trends and events. Some of these opening contributors also discuss the opportunities provided by MOOCs and open education as well as current implementation efforts. Other chapters and sections address teaching issues, instructional design and quality standards, and administrator opportunities as well as dilemmas. Near the end of this volume, several authors pose questions and highlight unique possibilities on the horizon for MOOCs, open education, and related educational innovations. We recommend that you reflect, both individually as well as with your students, colleagues, and work teams, on the pressing questions and concerns offered in each section of the book. You will also discover a plethora of advice, lessons learned, and interesting future trends illuminated in every chapter.

Across the 29 chapters and eight parts of this book you will find deliberations on credentialing policies, instructional design practices, learner-related issues, administration and management decisions, quality assurance standards, mobile and ubiquitous learning delivery, emerging technology tools for MOOCs (and their viability), and much more. Some chapters and sections will appeal to different audiences. Instructors will likely identify with the contributors who discuss instructional design ideas and offer guidelines related to them. Administrators will find value in the decision making that went into developing particular courses, programs, or special learning content for this more open or free educational world. They will undoubtedly be interested in the results as well.

Proponents of educational trends such as MOOCs and open education continue to face a series of roadblocks and extended criticism, much of it rightfully so, from established as well as newly formed educational institutions and organizations. Many corporate and higher education administrators are ignoring these learning delivery innovations, while others simply want more information. To help clarify such issues, the reader of this book is offered a diverse array of viewpoints—some chapters being authored by academic scholars in the field of educational and instructional technology, whereas others are from founders of companies or non-profit organizations. Still other chapters were written by administrators and managers who have helped lead the way toward innovative program designs and delivery options.

Geographically speaking, the countries represented in this volume include Australia, Canada, Germany, Kenya, India, Ireland, Japan, Malaysia, Indonesia, the Netherlands, New Zealand, the Philippines, South Africa, the United Kingdom, and the United States. For those who question whether 15 countries adequately represent what is happening in the MOOCs and open education space around the planet, we need to point out that the chapter authors discuss innovative projects, unique partnerships, ground-breaking policies, and other collaborative initiatives taking place in dozens of other countries. For instance, there are 18 charter member governments in Africa taking part in the African Virtual University (AVU) and 53 partner institutions across 27 countries. Suffice to say, when combined, the geographic impact of the various chapter contributors to this book is quite immense.

In response to those who are concerned with the impact of MOOCs and open education on underrepresented populations or with diverse learners, we have specifically targeted several prominent contributors who provide data and accounts of what is occurring with less privileged populations or in less developed parts of the world. For instance, in addition to the AVU, mentioned above, readers of this volume will learn about unique mobile learning projects sponsored by the Commonwealth of Learning (COL) as well as a couple of strategically designed MOOCs from the World Bank Institute. Many other chapter contributors have made concerted efforts to offer educational services and resources to those who would not ordinarily benefit from courses or programs offered by their institution or organization.

Of course, as free and open Web resources and tools for learning become accessible by larger portions of the global population, the locations and affiliations of the authors, organizations, or institutions are increasingly less indicative of where the impact is taking place. As you will soon discover, in fact, those enrolled in or taking advantage of the MOOC, OER, and OpenCourseWare (OCW) offerings that volume authors have taught, designed, or evaluated undoubtedly come from all parts of the globe.

Before we close, we feel compelled to mention that this book is actually our second such collaborative effort. Three of the editors of this book (Bonk, Lee, and Reynolds) organized a similar symposium at the E-Learn conference in 2008, also held in Las Vegas. That symposium was focused on the state of e-learning in Asia, and yielded a special issue of the *International Journal on E-Learning* (Bonk, Lee, & Reynolds, 2009) as well as a print-on-demand book. Reeves (2009), also an editor of this book, served as a discussant at the 2008 symposium and contributed the concluding article of that special issue. Additionally, several authors of that first volume, including Melinda Bandalaria from the University of the Philippines Open University (UPOU), Sanjaya Mishra, now with the COL, and Zoraini Wati Abas, formerly of the Open University of Malaysia (OUM), and now with the Universitas Siswa Bangsa Internasional—The Sampoerna University in Jakarta, Indonesia, also contributed to that earlier symposium and book project. In the coming years, we hope to reconvene the participants of the two symposia we have coordinated, and, in the process, meet many of you at the next such special conference event whether in Las Vegas or some other location on this planet.

Acknowledgments

There are many people to thank for helping to bring a comprehensive book project such as this one to fruition. First, we gladly acknowledge the trust that Gary Marks, Founder and Executive Director of AACE, had in the four of us to allow us to organize the E-Learn 2013 preconference symposium on "MOOCs and Open Education Around the World" that led to this particular book. Gary, one of the most humble and innovative people in the domain of educational technology, has had an enormously positive impact on the field for more than three decades. Thanks to him and all the staff at AACE who are always helpful in making these kinds of events successful.

We also appreciate the varied, genuine, and thoughtful contributions and ideas of the more than 100 scholars from around the planet who assembled in Las Vegas that October for the symposium. We massively learned from interacting with each of you. Several of these participants have since separately authored papers on MOOCs and open education, which will appear in a special issue of the *International Journal on E-Learning* in early 2015 (Lee, Bonk, Reynolds, & Reeves, in press). Thanks again to Gary Marks and AACE for the opportunity to coordinate that special issue. We have been working on both of these "MOOCs and Open Education" projects—this edited book and the special journal issue—simultaneously, with different material appearing in each one.

Second, we wish to thank the authors of this book. The 29 chapters and two book forewords in this distinctive volume have been penned by some of the foremost scholars and practitioners involved open education today. Given the more than 60 chapter authors or contributors, however, there are too many highly talented individuals to single out here. With each chapter going through several rounds of extended peer review, we got to know all of these people quite well. During the peer review process, it was vital that the communication channels between the four book editors and the respective chapter authors be highly responsive, collaborative, and flexible in order for the *MOOCs and Open Education Around the World* book to be completed in a timely fashion. We feel quite fortunate, indeed, that all the authors were open to our suggested edits, modifying their contributions when it seemed the right thing to do, and sticking to their metaphorical guns when they believed it was warranted. We have enjoyed working with each of them and learning about their MOOC and open education projects, desires, and experiences. They all are fantastic new friends.

We encourage readers to peruse the bio sketches for all the contributors to this volume found at the end of each chapter. We hope that the addition of a picture for each contributor along with their brief bios will help you discover many personal connections both now as you read parts or all of this volume as well as when you might encounter one or more of these contributors at a conference, summit, meeting, or some other situation. As you read the chapters, you will discover that this is a quite impressive group.

Third, we thank Alex Masulis, Daniel Schwartz, and the highly professional team at Routledge. They have provided invaluable guidance and held us to our deadlines firmly, yet kindly.

Lastly, we thank our friends and colleagues from around the world for their informational supports and encouraging comments related to this huge MOOCs and open education project as well as our families (including our animal companions) for sacrificing time with us while we worked on this book.

As we close, the four of us feel quite humbled and immensely fortunate that, through the preconference symposium, special journal issue now in press, and, most importantly, this particular book, we have had a chance to contribute in a small way to what some may eventually call the most significant movement of the 21st century; that is, the genuine opening up of education in its many unique and exciting formats and disguises.

Curtis J. Bonk is Professor of Instructional Systems Technology at Indiana University and President of CourseShare. Drawing on his background as a corporate controller, CPA, educational psychologist, and instructional technologist, Bonk offers unique insights into the intersection of business, education, psychology, and technology. A well-known authority on emerging technologies for learning, Bonk reflects on his speaking experiences around the world in his popular blog, *TravelinEdMan*. In 2014, he was named the recipient of the Mildred B. and Charles A. Wedemeyer Award for Outstanding Practitioner in Distance Education. He also has authored several widely used technology books, including *The World Is Open*, *Empowering Online Learning*, *The Handbook of Blended Learning*, *Electronic Collaborators*, and, most recently, *Adding Some TEC-VARIETY* which is free as an eBook (http://tec-variety.com/). His homepage contains much free and open material (http://php.indiana.edu/~cjbonk/) and he can be contacted at cjbonk@indiana.edu.

Mimi M. Lee is Associate Professor in the Department of Curriculum and Instruction at the University of Houston. She received her PhD in Instructional Systems Technology from Indiana University at Bloomington in 2004. Her research interests include global and multicultural education, theories of identity formation, sociological examination of online communities, issues of representation, and critical ethnography. Mimi has published research on STEM related online teacher education, cross-cultural training research, interactive videoconferencing, opencourseware, and qualitative research. She may be contacted at mlee7@uh.edu.

Thomas C. Reeves is Professor Emeritus of Learning, Design, and Technology at The University of Georgia. Professor Reeves has designed and evaluated numerous interactive learning programs and projects. In recognition of these efforts, in 2003 he received the AACE Fellowship Award, in 2010 he was made an ASCILITE Fellow, and in 2013 he received the AECT David H. Jonassen Excellence in Research Award. His books include *Interactive Learning Systems Evaluation* (with John Hedberg), a *Guide to Authentic E-Learning* (with Jan Herrington and Ron Oliver), and *Conducting Educational Design Research* (with Susan McKenney). His research interests include evaluation, authentic tasks for learning, educational design research, and educational technology in developing countries. He can be reached at treeves@uga.edu and his homepage can be found at http://www.evaluateitnow.com/.

**Thomas H. Reynolds** is currently a professor of Teacher Education at National University in La Jolla, California, where he researches design of online learning environments, standards-based online assessment, and innovations in e-learning. Before coming to National University, he served on faculty at Texas A&M University after earning his PhD in Curriculum and Instruction at the University of Wisconsin-Madison. Professor Reynolds has twice served as a Fulbright Scholar—2010 in Colombia where he researched open education resources and 1998 in Peru where he lectured on Web-based learning and technology-enhanced instruction. His present activities and responsibilities include projects in Colombia, coordination of an e-teaching and learning master's degree specialization, and leadership in online quality assurance and online course review and development for National University. He can be contacted at treynold@nu.edu.

References

Altwerger, B., Edelsky, C., & Flores, B.M. (1987). Whole language: What's new? *The Reading Teacher, 41*(2), 144–54.

Bonk, C.J. (2009). *The world is open: How Web technology is revolutionizing education.* San Francisco, CA: Jossey-Bass.

Bonk, C.J., & Graham, C.R. (Eds.) (2006). *Handbook of blended learning: Global perspectives, local designs.* San Francisco: Pfeiffer.

Bonk, C.J., Lee, M.M., & Reynolds, T.H. (Eds.) (2009). Special issue: A special passage through Asia e-learning. *International Journal on E-Learning, 8*(4), 438–85.

Davis, M. (2014, June 4). Summer professional development with MOOCs. *Edutopia.* Retrieved from http://www.edutopia.org/blog/summer-pd-moocs-matt-davis.

Gais, H. (2014). Is the developing world 'MOOC'd out'? The limits of open access learning. *Al Jazeera America.* Retrieved from http://america.aljazeera.com/opinions/2014/7/mooc-education-developingworldivyleave.html.

Guri-Rosenblit, S. (2012). Open/distance teaching universities worldwide: Current challenges and future prospects. *EduAkcja. Magazyn edukacji elektronicznej,4*(2), 4–12. Retrieved from http://wyrwidab.come.uw.edu.pl/ojs/index.php/eduakcja/article/viewFile/80/83

Haas, E., & Fischman, G. (2010). Nostalgia, entrepreneurship, and redemption Understanding prototypes in higher education. *American Educational Research Journal, 47*(3), 532–62.

Hassett, J.D., & Weisberg, A. (1972). *Open education.* Englewood Cliffs, NJ: Prentice-Hall.

James, W. (1971). The Open University: A new phenomenon. *Educational Technology, 11*(7), 32–3.

Johnstone, S.M. (2005). Open educational resources serve the world. *EDUCAUSE Quarterly, 28*(3), 15. Retrieved from http://www.educause.edu/ero/article/open-educational-resources-serve-world.

Lee, M.M., Bonk, C.J., Reynolds, T.H., & Reeves, T.C. (Eds.) (in press). Special issue: MOOCs and Open Education. *International Journal on E-Learning*.

Lockwood, F. (Ed.). (2013). *Open and distance learning today*. New York: Routledge.

Mettler, S. (2014). *Degrees of inequality: How the politics of higher education sabotaged the American dream*. New York: Basic Books.

Nyquist, E.B., & Hawes, G.R. (Eds.). (1971). *Open education*. New York: Bantam Books.

Pappano, L. (2012, November 2). The year of the MOOC. *The New York Times*. Retrieved from http://www.nytimes.com/2012/11/04/education/edlife/massive-open-online-courses-are-multiplying-at-a-rapid-pace.html?pagewanted=all&_r=0.

Reeves, T.C. (2009). E-Learning in Asia: Just as good is not good enough. *International Journal on E-Learning*, *8*(4), 577–85.

Tyack, D., & Cuban, L. (1997). *Tinkering toward utopia: A century of public school reform*. Boston, MA: Harvard University Press.

Watters, A. (2013, November 29). Top ed-tech trends of 2013: MOOCs and anti-MOOCs. *Hack Education*. Retrieved from http://hackeducation.com/2013/11/29/top-ed-tech-trends-2013-moocs/.

White, B. (2014). Is "MOOC-Mania" over? In S.K.S. Cheung, J. Fong, J. Zhang, R. Kwan, and L.F.K wok (Eds.), *Hybrid learning. Theory and practice* (pp. 11–15). Cham, Switzerland: Springer International Publishing.

Wildavsky, B. (2014). Evolving toward significance or MOOC ado about nothing? *NAFSA: Association of International Educators*. Retrieved from http://www.nafsa.org/_/File/_/ie_mayjun14_forum.pdf.

Wikieducator (2014). *Handbook of open universities*. Retrieved from http://wikieducator.org/Handbook_of_Open_Universities.

PART 1
MOOCs and Open Education
Historical and Critical Reflections

As indicated in the Preface and the respective Forewords by George Siemens and Fred Mulder, we are in the midst of an unprecedented growth in innovative approaches to distance education. Never before in history have so many people been engaged in the development, delivery, research, and evaluation of learning that is not confined to a specific time, location, and instructor of record. Today's technologies provide learners with increasing opportunities to participate and learn from a distance in an interactive and often highly collaborative manner. As the contributors to this book describe in their various chapters, MOOCs and open educational resources are making all forms of distance education more salient and accessible than ever before.

It would be a relatively easy task, therefore, to assemble a compilation of contributors and chapters that simply discussed success stories and opportunities related to MOOCs and open education. Despite the obvious conclusion that might be drawn from the title of this book, however, we do not take MOOCs and open education as a given, and we recommend that others do not do so either. Clearly, there is much that is left to be sorted out about MOOCs and OERs with respect to their acceptance, credibility, quality, assessment, learning outcomes, and much more. Schools, universities, and corporate, government, and military training centers should not endorse MOOCs simply because they exist and are receiving much fanfare and, in some cases, substantial funding. Indeed, MOOCs have arisen so quickly that many of their most enthusiastic proponents seem to have forgotten or ignored the history of distance learning and earlier educational technology developments that led to MOOCs in the first place.

We attempt to provide some balance to the conversation regarding MOOCs and open education by starting this book off with a section addressing many complex challenges and issues in terms of the sheer idea of "MOOCs and Open

Education Around the World." We hope that the chapters included in this opening part of the book will offer the necessary starter fuel for potential class, committee meeting, and town hall debates about MOOCs and open education. We readily admit that three chapters cannot adequately portray the numerous problems, criticisms, barriers, and constraints related to MOOCs and open education today. During the coming decade, many of you will undoubtedly find yourselves confronting dozens of additional issues that we did not have the space to include in this book. As a result, we encourage the reader to browse through the remaining 26 chapters that follow Part 1 and make note of other key questions and concerns.

In the first chapter of this book, David Wiley, Co-founder and Chief Academic Officer of Lumen Learning, explores the damage done to the idea of "open" by MOOCs given that some MOOC vendors do not allow the reuse of content found in their MOOCs. Wiley also discusses the harm done to the idea of "ownership" by modern content companies. He then advocates for a return to a strengthened idea of "open" that ameliorates both problems. Finally, he describes an open education infrastructure on which the future of educational innovation depends. As such, this chapter is a vital and compelling introduction to critical discussions and reflections related to MOOCs and open education around the world.

In the second chapter, Karen Head from the Georgia Institute of Technology raises additional concerns related to the design and delivery of MOOCs. As you explore her chapter, you will notice that she contends that we need to pay attention to more than just content and delivery. Beginning with a broad consideration of the canon as it relates to course design, Professor Head describes a case study of the first-year writing course she taught as a MOOC. In her chapter, she argues against single-provider models and discusses ways MOOCs might be used to leverage the advantages of large student enrollments to make such gigantic open online courses more diverse and inclusive.

In the third and final chapter of this part, Kumiko Aoki of the Open University of Japan discusses how the incorporation of MOOCs and open education may depend on prevailing government policies, norms, expectations, and experiences. As she points out, technology adoption in education is relatively slow in Japan in contrast to what many people outside of the country may have imagined given its rich history in consumer electronics and computing technology. Aoki describes various historical developments of distance learning and open education in Japan from social and cultural vantage points. She also discusses the unique characteristics of the Open University of Japan as a distance open education university. In effect, this chapter illustrates the struggles and efforts of the Open University of Japan, and by extension similar open universities around the world, to offer online education within particular sociocultural contexts.

1

THE MOOC MISSTEP AND THE OPEN EDUCATION INFRASTRUCTURE

David Wiley

In this brief piece, I explore the damage done to the idea of "open" by MOOCs as well as the damage done to the idea of "ownership" by modern content companies. I then advocate for a return to a strengthened idea of "open" that ameliorates both problems. Finally, I describe an open education infrastructure on which the future of educational innovation depends.

MOOCs: One Step Forward, Two Steps Back for Open Education

MOOCs, as popularized by Udacity and Coursera, have done more harm to the cause of open education than anything else in the history of the movement. They have inflicted this harm by promoting and popularizing an abjectly impoverished understanding of the word "open." To fully appreciate the damage they have imposed requires that I lightly sketch some historical context.

The openness of the Open University of the UK, first established in 1969 and admitting its first student in 1971, was an incredible innovation in its time. In this context, the adjective "open" described an enlightened policy of allowing essentially anyone to enroll in courses at the university—regardless of their prior academic achievement. For universities, which are typically characterized in metaphor as being comprised of towers, silos, and walled gardens, this opening of the gates to anyone and everyone represented an unprecedented leap forward in the history of higher education. For decades, "open" in the context of education primarily meant "open entry."

Fast-forward 30 years. In 2001, MIT announced its OpenCourseWare (OCW) initiative, providing additional meaning to the term "open" in the higher education context. MIT OCW would make all the materials used in teaching its on-campus courses available to the public, for free, under an "open license." This open license provided individuals and organizations with a broad range of copyright-related permissions: anyone was free to make copies of the materials, make changes or improvements to the materials, and to redistribute them (in their original or modified forms) to others. All these permissions were granted without any payment or additional copyright clearance hurdles.

While there are dozens of universities around the world that have adopted an open entry policy, in the decade from 2001 to 2010, open education was dominated by individuals, organizations, and schools pursuing the idea of open in terms of open licensing. Hundreds of universities around the globe now maintain opencourseware programs. At the same time, the open access movement, which found its voice in the 2002 Budapest Open Access initiative (http://www.buda pestopenaccessinitiative.org/), has worked to apply open licenses to scholarly articles and other research outputs. Core learning infrastructure technologies, including Learning Management Systems, Financial Management, and Student Information Systems, are created and published under open licenses (e.g., Canvas, Moodle, Sakai, and Kuali). Individuals have also begun contributing significantly to the growing collection of openly licensed educational materials, like Sal Khan, who founded the Khan Academy.

While all this is occurring, governments and charitable organizations like the William and Flora Hewlett Foundation are pouring hundreds of millions of dollars into supporting an idea of open education grounded in the idea of open licensing. In fact, the Hewlett Foundation's definition of "open educational resources" (OER) is the most widely cited:

> OER are teaching, learning, and research resources that reside in the public domain or have been released under an intellectual property license that permits their free use and re-purposing by others. Open educational resources include full courses, course materials, modules, textbooks, streaming videos, tests, software, and any other tools, materials, or techniques used to support access to knowledge. (Hewlett Foundation, 2014)

This funding, combined with a range of other nonfinancial incentives, have catalyzed the development of a huge mass of OER. According to Creative Commons (2014), there were over 400 million openly licensed creative works published online as of 2010, and many of these can be used in support of learning.

Why is the conceptualization of "open" as "open licensing" so interesting, so crucial, and such an advance over the simple notion of open entry? In describing the power of open source software enabled by open licensing, Eric Raymond (2000) wrote, "Any tool should be useful in the expected way, but a truly great tool lends itself to uses you never expected." Those never expected uses are possible because of the broad, free permissions granted by open licensing. Adam Thierer (2014) has described a principle he calls "permissionless innovation."

On my blog, *Iterating toward Openness*, I have summarized the idea by saying that "openness facilitates the unexpected" (Wiley, 2013). However you characterize it, the need to ask for permission and pay for permission makes experimentation more costly. Increasing the cost of experimentation guarantees that less experimentation will happen. Less experimentation means, by definition, less discovery and innovation.

Imagine you are planning to experiment with a new educational model. Now imagine two ways this experiment could be conducted. In the first model, you pay exorbitant fees to temporarily license (never own) digital content from Pearson, and you pay equivalent fees to temporarily license (never own) Blackboard to host and deliver the content. In a second model, you utilize freely available open educational resources delivered from inside a free, open source learning management system. The first experiment cannot occur without raising venture capital or other funding. The second experiment can be run with almost no funding whatsoever. If we wish to democratize innovation, as von Hippel (2005) has described it, we would do well to support and protect our ability to engage in the second model of experimentation. Open licenses provide and protect exactly that sort of experimental space.

Which brings us back to MOOCs. The horrific corruption perpetrated by the Udacity, Coursera, and other copycat MOOCs is to pretend that the last 40 years never happened. Their modus operandi has been to copy and paste the 1969 idea of open entry into online courses in 2014. The primary fallout of the brief, brilliant popularity of MOOCs was to persuade many people that, in the educational context, "open" means open entry to courses which are not only completely and fully copyrighted, but whose Terms of Use are more restrictive than those of the BBC or the *New York Times*, as revealed in the following language from the Coursera website:

> You may not take any Online Course offered by Coursera or use any Statement of Accomplishment as part of any tuition-based or for-credit certification or program for any college, university, or other academic institution without the express written permission from Coursera. Such use of an Online Course or Statement of Accomplishment is a violation of these Terms of Use.

The idea that someone, somewhere believes that open education means "open entry to fully copyrighted courses with draconian terms of use" is beyond tragic. Consequently, after a decade of progress has been reversed by MOOCs, advocates of open education once again find ourselves fighting uphill to establish and advance the idea of "open." The open we envision provides just as much access to educational opportunity as the 1960s vision championed by MOOCs, while simultaneously enabling a culture of democratized, permissionless innovation in education.

An "Open" Worth the Name

How, then, should we talk about "open" in the educational context? What strengthened conception of open will protect ownership and promote innovation? I believe we must ground our thinking in the idea of open licenses. Specifically, we should advocate for "open" in the language of the 5Rs. "Open" should be used as an adjective to describe any copyrightable work that is licensed in a manner that provides users with free and perpetual permission to engage in the 5R activities:

1. Retain—the right to make, own, and control copies of the work (e.g., download, duplicate, store, and manage).
2. Reuse—the right to use the work in a wide range of ways (e.g., in a class, in a study group, on a website, in a video, etc.).
3. Revise—the right to adapt, adjust, modify, or alter the work itself (e.g., translate it into another language).
4. Remix—the right to combine the original or revised work with other open works to create something new (e.g., incorporate the work into a mashup).
5. Redistribute—the right to share copies of the original work, your revisions, or your remixes with others (e.g., give a copy of the work to a friend).

These 5R permissions, together with a clear statement that they are provided for free and in perpetuity, are articulated in many of the Creative Commons licenses. When you download a video from Khan Academy, some lecture notes from MIT OpenCourseWare, an article from Wikipedia, or a textbook from OpenStax College—all of which use a Creative Commons license—you have free and perpetual permission to engage in the 5R activities with those materials. Because they are published under a Creative Commons license, you don't need to call to ask for permission and you don't need to pay a license fee. You can simply get on with the business of supporting your students' learning. Or you can conduct some other kind of teaching and learning experiment—and you can do it for free, without needing additional permissions from a brace of copyright holders.

How would a change in operational definition of "open" impact the large MOOC providers? If MOOC providers changed from "open means open entry" to "open means open licenses," what would the impact be? Specifically, if the videos, assessments, and other content in a Coursera or Udacity MOOC were openly licensed, would it reduce the "massive" access that people around the world have to the courses? No. In fact, it would drastically expand the access enjoyed by people around the world, as learners everywhere would be free to download, translate, and redistribute the MOOC content.

Despite an incredible lift-off thrust comprised of hype and investment, MOOCs have failed to achieve escape velocity. Weighed down by a strange 1960s-meets-the-internet philosophy, MOOCs have started to fall back toward earth under the pull of registration requirements, start dates and end dates, fees charged for credentials, and draconian terms of use. It reminds me of the old joke, "What do you call a MOOC where you have to register, wait for the start date in order to begin, get locked out of the class after the end date, have no permission to copy or reuse the course materials, and have to pay to get a credential?" "An online class."

Despite all the hyperbole, it has become clear that MOOCs are nothing more than open entry online courses—not the innovation so many had hoped for. Worse than that, because of their retrograde approach to "open," MOOCs are guaranteed to be left by the wayside as future educational innovation happens. It is simply too expensive to run a meaningful number of experiments in the MOOC context.

Where will the experiments that define the future of teaching and learning be conducted, then?

Content as Infrastructure

The Wikipedia (2014) entry on infrastructure begins:

> Infrastructure is the basic physical and organizational structures needed for the operation of a society or enterprise, or the services and facilities necessary for an economy to function. It can be generally defined as the set of interconnected structural elements that provide a framework supporting an entire structure of development.
>
> The term typically refers to the technical structures that support a society, such as roads, bridges, water supply, sewers, electrical grids, telecommunications, and so forth, and can be defined as "the physical components of interrelated systems providing commodities and services essential to enable, sustain, or enhance societal living conditions" (Fulmer, 2009). Viewed functionally, infrastructure *facilitates* the production of goods and services . . .

What would constitute an education infrastructure? I don't mean technologies like learning management systems. I mean to ask, what types of components are included in the set of interconnected structural elements that provide the framework supporting education?

I can't imagine a way to conduct a program of education without all four of the following components: (1) competencies or learning outcomes, (2) educational resources that support the achievement of those outcomes, (3) assessments by which learners can demonstrate their achievement of those outcomes, and (4) credentials that certify their mastery of those outcomes to third parties. There may be more components to the core education infrastructure than these four, but I would argue that these four clearly qualify as interconnected structural elements that provide the framework underlying every program of formal education.

Not everyone has the time, resources, talent, or inclination to completely recreate competency maps, textbooks, assessments, and credentialing models for every course they teach. As in the discussion of permissionless, democratized innovation above, it simply makes things faster, easier, cheaper, and better for everyone when there is high-quality, openly available infrastructure already deployed that we can remix and experiment upon.

Historically, we have only applied the principle of openness to one of the four components of the education infrastructure I listed above: educational resources. In fact, I have been arguing that "content is infrastructure" (Wiley, 2005) for about a decade now. More recently, Mozilla has created and shared an open credentialing infrastructure through their open badges work (Mozilla, 2014). But little has been done to champion the cause of openness in the areas of competencies and assessments.

Open Competencies

I think one of the primary reasons competency-based education (CBE) programs have been so slow to develop in the US—even after the Department of Education made its federal financial aid policies friendlier to CBE programs (Fain, 2014)—is the terrific amount of work necessary to develop a solid set of competencies. Again, not everyone has the time or expertise to do this work. Because it's so hard, many institutions with CBE programs treat their competencies like a secret family recipe, hoarding them away and keeping them fully copyrighted (apparently without experiencing any cognitive dissonance while they promote the use of OER among their students). This behavior has seriously stymied growth and innovation in CBE in my view.

If an institution would openly license a complete set of competencies, that would give other institutions a foundation on which to build new programs, models, and other experiments. The open competencies could be revised and remixed according to the needs of local programs, and they can be added to, or subtracted from, to meet those needs as well. This act of sharing would also give the institution of origin an opportunity to benefit from remixes, revisions, and new competencies added to their original set by others.

Furthermore, openly licensing more sophisticated sets of competencies provides a public, transparent, and concrete foundation around which to marshal empirical evidence and build supported arguments about the scoping and sequencing of what students should learn.

Open competencies are the core of the open education infrastructure because they provide the context that imbues resources, assessments, and credentials with meaning—from the perspective of the instructional designer, teacher, or program planner. You don't know if a given resource is the "right" resource to use, or if an assessment is giving students an opportunity to demonstrate the "right" kind of mastery, without the competency as a referent. For example, an extremely high-quality, high-fidelity, interactive chemistry lab simulation is the "wrong" content if students are supposed to be learning world history. Likewise, a credential is essentially meaningless if a third party like an employer cannot refer to the particular skill or set of skills its possession supposedly certifies.

Open Assessments

For years, creators of OER have declined to share their assessments in order to "keep them secure" so that students won't cheat on exams, quizzes, and homework. This security mindset has prevented the sharing of assessments.

In CBE programs, students often demonstrate their mastery of competencies through "performance assessments." Unlike some traditional multiple-choice assessments, performance assessments require students to demonstrate mastery by performing a skill or producing something. Consequently, performance assessments are very difficult to cheat on. For example, even if you find out a week ahead of time that the end of unit exam will require you to make 8 out of 10 free throws, there's really no way to cheat on the assessment. Either you will master the skill and be able to demonstrate that mastery or you won't.

Because performance assessments are so difficult to cheat on, keeping them secure can be less of a concern, making it possible for performance assessments to be openly licensed and publicly shared. Once they are openly licensed, these assessments can be retained, revised, remixed, reused, and redistributed.

Another way of alleviating concerns around the security of assessment items is to create openly licensed assessment banks that contain hundreds or thousands of assessments—so many assessments that cheating becomes more difficult and time consuming than simply learning.

The Open Education Infrastructure

A completely open education infrastructure, which can support extremely rapid, low-cost experimentation and innovation, must be comprised of at least these four parts:

- Open credentials.
- Open assessments.
- Open educational resources.
- Open competencies.

This interconnected set of components provides a foundation that will greatly decrease the time, cost, and complexity of the search for innovative and effective new models of education (while providing benefits for informal learning as well). From the bottom up, open competencies supply the overall blueprint and foundation. Once established, open educational resources offer a pathway to master those competencies. Third, open assessments provide the opportunity to demonstrate mastery of the competencies, Finally, open credentials—which point to both the competency statements and results of performance assessments—certify to third parties that learners have, in fact, mastered the competency or sets of competencies in question.

When open licenses are applied up and down the entire stack—creating truly *open* credentials, *open* assessments, *open* educational resources, and *open* competencies, resulting in an *open* education infrastructure—each part of the stack can be altered, adapted, improved, customized, and otherwise made to fit local needs without the need to ask for permission or pay licensing fees. Local actors with local expertise are empowered to build on top of the infrastructure to solve local problems. And they can do so, freely.

Creating an open education infrastructure unleashes the talent and passion of people who want to solve education problems but lack the time to reinvent the wheel and rediscover fire in the process.

"Openness facilitates the unexpected." We can't possibly imagine all the incredible ways people and institutions will use the open education infrastructure to make incremental improvements or deploy novel innovations from out of left field. That is precisely why we need to build it.

A firm commitment to openness, grounded in the 5Rs and open licenses, is a powerful expression of humility and faith in humanity. A commitment to openness acknowledges our belief that others will have ideas even better than our own, and demonstrates that we are willing to do everything in our power to support them in implementing those more powerful ideas. Because in the end, what we really care about is students learning—not petty squabbles over who gets credit.

David Wiley is Chief Academic Officer and Co-founder of Lumen Learning, an organization dedicated to increasing student success and improving the affordability of education through the adoption of open educational resources by middle schools, high schools, community and state colleges, and universities. He is also currently a Shuttleworth Fellow, Education Fellow at Creative Commons, and an adjunct faculty member in Brigham Young University's graduate program in Instructional Psychology and Technology. Dr. Wiley has received an NSF CAREER grant and was a Nonresident Fellow in the Center for Internet and Society at Stanford Law School as well as a Peery Social Entrepreneurship Research Fellow in the Marriott School of Business at Brigham Young University. As a social entrepreneur, Dr. Wiley has founded or co-founded numerous entities, including Lumen Learning, Degreed, and the Open High School of Utah (now Mountain Heights Academy).

References

Coursera. (2014). Terms of Use. Retrieved from https://www.coursera.org/about/terms.

Creative Commons. (2014). Metrics. Retrieved from https://wiki.creativecommons.org/Metrics.

Fain, P. (July, 2014). Experimenting with Aid. *Inside Higher Ed.* Retrieved from https://www.insidehighered.com/news/2014/07/23/competency-based-education-gets-boost-education-department.

Fulmer, J. (2009). "What in the world is infrastructure?". *PEI Infrastructure Investor* (July/August): 30–2.

Hewlett Foundation. (2014). Open educational resources. *Education.* Retrieved from http://www.hewlett.org/programs/education/open-educational-resources.

Mozilla. (2014). OpenBadges. Retrieved from http://openbadges.org/.

Raymond, E. (2000). *The cathedral and the bazaar.* Retrieved from http://www.catb.org/esr/writings/cathedral-bazaar/cathedral-bazaar/index.html#catbmain.

Thierer, A. (2014). *Permissionless innovation: The continuing case for comprehensive technological freedom.* Arlington, VA: Mercatus Center at George Mason University. Retrieved from http://mercatus.org/sites/default/files/Permissionless.Innovation.web_.v2_0.pdf.

von Hippel, E. (2005). *Democratizing innovation.* Cambridge, MA: MIT Press. Retrieved from http://web.mit.edu/evhippel/www/democ1.htm.

Wikipedia. (2014). Infrastructure. Retrieved from https://en.wikipedia.org/wiki/Infrastructure.

Wiley, D. (2005). Content is infrastructure. *Iterating toward Openness* [Web log post]. Retrieved from http://opencontent.org/blog/archives/215.

Wiley, D. (2013). Where I've been; where I'm going. *Iterating toward Openness* [Web log post]. Retrieved from http://opencontent.org/blog/archives/2723.

2

THE SINGLE CANON

MOOCs and Academic Colonization

Karen Head

I have a confession. I really hate *Moby Dick*. In fact, I'm not a fan of Melville's writing at all. If pressed to teach something by Herman Melville, I would concede to "Bartleby the Scrivener," but frankly, I'd prefer not. As someone who holds a PhD in English with a focus on American writers, this confession may sound like sacrilege. After all, Melville is a canonical figure. Nonetheless, he would not be in the canon at all if it were up to me. Unless a course is specifically about Melville, I can happily find other authors whose work is representative of the same period in American Literature.

Despite my dismissal of such a major American author, I can sleep well at night precisely because I know that there are many other instructors who will include Melville's work in the courses they design. That's one of the wonderful things about the diverse higher educational system in the United States—instructors have many ways in which they can meet course objectives. Even if an instructor prefers a particular writer, a certain curricular resource, or a specific method, the canon remains a challenge he or she must face each time he or she designs or redesigns a course—the primary challenge always being the question of what an instructor will exclude rather than what he or she includes.

The struggle to make good choices is especially difficult in general education courses that are often surveys of periods or themes, where certain canonical standards have been established. No matter the curricular choices, if someone held a national reception for students who just finished a 19th Century American Literature survey course, each one of those students should be able to discuss key themes, issues, and problems of the period. Ideally, however, those students would be able to do so by using different references. And in having conversations with each other, they would discover an even broader understanding of the period.

Cultural Challenges for MOOC Design: A Case Study

As I have been writing about my experiences as the lead-instructor for one of the first Massive Open Online Courses (MOOCs) to attempt teaching First-Year Writing (a project funded by the Bill and Melinda Gates Foundation to investigate how MOOCs might respond to general education needs), I have continually been troubled by ideas of exclusivity in the highly publicized MOOC instructor pool, and, by extension, the limited number of approaches to teaching any subject presented as a MOOC. Here the canon becomes doubly problematic. First, there is the problem I have already defined—a narrowing of the many ways instructors might teach any course in American universities. Second, there is an exponentially challenging problem of bringing our American courses to the world and facing the dilemma that a narrow American view constitutes a new form of colonialism.

In our MOOC on first-year writing, the design team spent many hours considering the diverse backgrounds of the students who might enroll. Given the enrollment in other MOOCs, we knew to expect a large international contingent of students, and we wanted to be considerate of their cultures. Early on, we made the decision to caution students that a native fluency in English would be essential for success in the course, and we included this warning prominently in our pre-launch advertising video. We were sorry not to be able to accommodate individuals who lacked English capabilities; because several members of our team have at least limited backgrounds as English-Language-Learner (ELL) instructors or tutors, we recognized that we did not have the extensive resources needed to support the special needs of non-English speakers. As someone who began her ELL work at the age of six, when I gave up my summer to attend school to help young Vietnamese refugees learn English, I care deeply about ELL instruction, but I also understand how special and demanding this instruction can be.

One interesting outcome of our MOOC was that we had a group of Russian students who translated everything on our course site for Russian speakers. Fortunately, we had a postdoctoral fellow in our department who speaks fluent Russian, so we were able to confirm that the translations were appropriate. While having students do these translations wasn't the same as a fully vetted ELL pedagogical course plan, it did offer some inclusiveness we had not anticipated, and we were happy for it. However, having a group of students who are both willing and qualified to do this work is not something a course instructor can reasonably expect.

We were particularly aware and concerned that with only one exception every member of our team was white—our videography consultant is an African-American, but he was always positioned behind the camera. Our instructional team is not exceptional. A review of the faculty photos on the Coursera website (2014) shows mostly white faculty members. Because many of our team members have lived in other countries, and some team members are representatives of marginalized communities (for example, we had LGBT and disabled team members), we were keenly aware that our team would appear as rather homogenous. Consequently, we had many planning meetings to consider (and debate) everything from the clothes any of our online presenters would wear to whether a visual might include offensive symbols to choosing audio resources with a minimum of difficulty for understanding accents or dialects.

Ultimately, we had nearly 27,000 students, located on every continent except Antarctica, some representing cultures about which we had little knowledge, like Bahrain, Madagascar, and Nepal. Despite our best efforts to be inclusive, we often failed to anticipate the ways we, without noticing at all, privileged American culture. For example, during one of our Google Hangout discussion sessions, we wanted to review some key points about a reading assignment. It became quickly apparent that one of our students from Turkey did not seem fully aware of the author's (Martin Luther King, Jr.) background. I decided to mention Gandhi and the student began to better understand our conversation.

On another day, we had some students express concern over an audio recording of an essay by David Sedaris. We had, in the planning stages, hesitated to use the recording because it contained a bit of profanity. Students didn't so much express offense, but rather confusion. Even though we required fluency in English as a course prerequisite, both profanity and humor are highly idiomatic—something we should have considered. At the very least, we could have provided a listening guide with some information about how Sedaris's style and language choice function.

We also found it challenging to address one of the prevailing canonical traditions in our field—that student essays often become course texts. It is not impossible, but it was impractical to review all the student work in a MOOC with thousands of participants to find samples that could be used as course texts. Since all writing tasks in the course were evaluated via peer evaluation, the course instructors were not the ones who were offering the primary evaluation. As a result, we lost another point of access to include student work that could have offered more diverse texts to consider.

Apart from the issue of what texts our team chose, we also found tangential issues related to the perception of some students that we were imposing certain cultural views. One of the liveliest forum discussions initiated by students was a debate about whether my clothing choices were appropriate. Even this debate reflected issues of colonialism, with one student expressing anger that I would wear something that looked "Indian"—"Is she trying to seem ethnic?" he asked. Another student defended my clothing choice as fashionable. She wrote quite a commentary about women's fashion.

I had given much thought to what I would wear in the video lectures modules, carefully choosing items that would be modest and inoffensive, but that would also look colorful on video. I also made the very conscious choice not to cover my head. I wanted to be considerate, but I also wanted to portray myself in ways that honestly reflected who I am. The forum debate demonstrated the need to be ever vigilant when attempting to work with students from such a wide range of cultural traditions.

MOOCs and the Limitations of Exclusivity

Proponents of MOOCs might argue that if American universities are providing courses for free via MOOCs, then no one should complain about the design and content choices made by the instructor. This is a likely argument given the rhetoric from the original MOOC platform providers and other MOOC proponents that was touted as part of their marketing plans. As MOOCs attracted media attention, there was an intense focus on elite American universities providing their special brands of education to domestic and foreign masses—magnanimous, indeed, given the extremely limited number of students who ever have the opportunity to attend these highly prestigious schools. However, prestige should never be a substitute for thoughtful pedagogy.

Even after the more recent addition of massively open courses from some larger American state research universities to those offered by the elite (and mostly private) universities, the rhetoric has continued to focus on elitism while simultaneously promoting a kind of egalitarianism. The message is that very prestigious (generally, American) institutions will provide free and excellent courses to anyone interested in learning. Still, there are only a limited number of "providers" of courses, and these providers have been specially chosen not because these institutions necessarily have the best instructors but because those instructors happen to be part of the instructional staff of one of these elite schools.

As I have contended, "No matter the institution, there is a very plain argument: Some instructor at some school is the best person to teach some subject. People who believe in a best instructor model would likely argue that there is no need to have hundreds of different approaches to teaching a given subject. However, this argument does not account for the vast knowledge base available in many subjects" (2014). Such a model also does not account for vast cultural differences and considerations that must be part of the design of courses meant for students outside the traditional American university systems, or, for that matter, for the diverse set of students enrolled in American universities.

The responsibilities and challenges inherent in curriculum design have always been a point of debate. Using traffic signals as a metaphor, Lauter (1991) explains,

> Schools, whatever else they do, help establish and transmit our society's cultural signals, those determinative red and green lights. Indeed, one way of understanding the curriculum is as an elaborate set of signals directing students onto the various tracks they will likely follow throughout their lives.

Given that curriculum design has such broad implications, why would such a single provider model be appealing? From a domestic perspective, over the last few years almost every institution of higher learning in the United States has faced declining budgets, whether from state and federal funding cuts or from declining private donations or from diminishing endowments or a combination of all these things. Without doubt, instruction is a key component in determining the cost of higher education, but that cost has been steadily declining while administrative and support service costs are rapidly increasing. According to a recent Bain report,

> Boards of trustees and presidents need to put their collective foot down on the growth of support and administrative costs. Those costs have grown faster than the cost of instruction across most campuses. In no other industry would overhead costs be allowed to grow at this rate—executives would lose their jobs. As colleges and universities look to areas where they can make cuts and achieve efficiencies, they should start farthest from the core of teaching and research. Cut from the outside in, and build from the inside out. (Denneen & Dretler, 2012, p. 5)

Nevertheless, many critics point to cutting costs in higher education instruction as the most important strategy. Given this criticism, what better way to do this than have selected instructors who are the designated content providers? In this model, students would obtain content information from a single MOOC provider—eliminating the need for each university to employ similar content instructors.

Despite the pedagogical challenges with such a model, the least of which would be a lack of direct access to the content instructor who has prepared the course, having only a limited number of (or even worse, only one) instructors for a particular course means that the canon of resources, methods, processes, and approaches for that course will be necessarily limited to the knowledge, experience, and preferences of the designated instructors. If we subscribe to the precedent of only one instructor for each course, the information in such courses will quickly become the new canon. While there may be generally accepted universal goals, there remain many other considerations, examples, experiments, and models that, depending on which combination of these resources are chosen, offer a variety of student experiences within the basic structure of overall outcomes in any course.

Given my initial comments about preferences, if I became the recognized MOOC instructor for 19th Century American Literature, Melville, as one example, would not be part of the curriculum for that course. As I have argued,

> The implications for such a "one size fits all" course approach reach far beyond the classroom. Having a variety of experiences means that when a group of people is working together on a team, perhaps designing a new building, they will more diversely understand the array of possibilities. Limiting content by limiting the number of instructors means limiting possibilities of what students might learn. If we do not consider the loss of a varied curriculum, we will narrow the entire educational experience into what only a small number of people privilege. (2014)

The rhetoric around MOOCs often lends itself to the single provider model and supports a more general move toward limiting canons and of privileging only certain ways of thinking. Domestically, we can see this as part of the discussions about establishing common core materials. More expansively, a move to limit canons by way of single provider models also becomes a political and cultural issue.

One of the problems is a dual focus on providing an education that simultaneously prepares students for jobs. As corporate recruiters and managers, as well as legislators, clamor for graduates with specialized, or even compartmentalized, skills, proponents have lauded MOOCs as particularly well suited to provide such training. The tension between whether a university education should be seen as only a jobs-training program is not a new one, and the canon has always been a big part of that tension. As Lauter (1991) argues,

> Educational institutions always seem to be caught between two prepositions, "in" and "to." Part of our mission is to instruct students in various disciplines, in history, in literature, in physics. But at the same time, we are expected to orient students to the world outside the classroom, to its creation and recreation in the work they will perform and the ideas they will evolve. I find a tension in these prepositions between the voices of the past and the visions of the future.

So much of the rhetoric surrounding MOOCs reflects the tension between past and future. The use of words like *disruption* and *innovation* highlight this tension. Lauter (1991) elaborates his argument by explaining how the tensions between *in* and *to*, as well as the tensions between *past* and *future,* are false ones, and that "the bodies of knowledge we teach" are constructed based on how we feel the past might form a foundation for the future. Lauter contends,

> Any educational program must focus on a small selection from the vast storehouse of human experience. What gets selected is neither accidental nor inevitable, but is determined, I am suggesting, by an implicit vision of what students "ought" to know to live in the world they will inhabit.

Apart from what students *ought* to know for their jobs, epistemologies are further complicated by cultural, and sometimes nationalistic, considerations. Recently in the United Kingdom, Education Secretary Michael Gove decided that there were too many American Literature works on the General Certificate of Secondary Education (GCSE) (Molloy, 2014). Having common educational goals and required outcomes is not necessarily a problem, but having a strict model of texts and methods for attaining those goals and outcomes could prove to further a sense of nationalist, even isolationist, fervor. Additionally, a narrowly focused canon can produce curricular materials that are thoroughly out of context for certain populations.

Political and Cultural Implications of a Single Canon

Canons have always represented a kind of censorship, privileging certain works over others. The balance between Matthew Arnold's philosophical ideal that society should seek "to make the best that has been thought and known in the world current everywhere" and a patent acknowledgment that we can never really define "the best" because it is not, to use a Shakespearean phrase, "an ever-fixed mark," is at the very core of balanced and evolving curricular design. My use of quotes by Arnold and Shakespeare are illustrations of just how ingrained canonical ideas, texts, and methods can become. Yet, despite the widely acknowledged importance of a writer like Shakespeare, nationalistic and political motives could move the world toward more narrow views. If Gove can force a dismissal of American works, then any other country's ministers could decide to dismiss Shakespeare as too English. Consequently, if a single country's representatives, or a select group of country's representatives, become the canonical representatives of what they believe should be taught in courses and those courses become the preferred ones, then we have a new form of colonization: academic colonization.

The challenge of providing resources that can be massively disseminated is that almost exclusively it is Western institutions or companies that provide the primary mechanisms for deployment. This currently overriding Western influence within MOOCs and open education further complicates the issue because a culture can create a dominant canon without regard to other cultures, or as Kennedy explains about the canonical distinctions in art, it is our various notions of "genius and greatness" that prevents inclusiveness. Instead, we build canonical hierarchies that bear "little relationship to the way most people experience art in today's globalized, disparate, multicultural world (Kennedy, 2010).

While it is true that such academic colonization already exists and has existed for many years, the proliferation of information via MOOCs or similar platforms will be categorically and exponentially more influential. As noted in the quote below, Miranda Kennedy (2010) argued in the *World Policy Journal* that in some areas things have been changing:

> Art and literature can no longer be said to center on the European or white experience, when the fast-growing, highly educated populations of China and India resonate as loudly as the voices of immigrant populations in the U.S. and Europe.

While I agree that there have been improvements toward inclusiveness in the academic literary canon, the dominant cultural themes in many foundational courses in the United States remain exceedingly Western in focus. For example, as a graduate student, I was the instructor for a sophomore survey course in World Literature, which was really Western Literature—even course names carry certain canonical elements. The curriculum for that course was almost entirely prescribed—my job was to use an assigned textbook and oversee a fixed set of assignments.

One time when I was leading a discussion on Nathaniel Hawthorne's short story, "Rappaccini's Daughter," I was trying to explain the concept of allusion by pointing out that forbidden plants as central garden fixtures relate to the Garden of Eden. Over half of my students were from China. It took me several minutes to realize they didn't have the Christian Sunday-School Curriculum as part of their cultural literacy. While Kennedy's argument that there are "fast growing, highly educated populations" expanding canonical boundaries, single-provider MOOC models (that is Western-made MOOCs) could function like massive numbers of academic missionaries—returning the world to an established and singularly validated literacy.

Advantages of Fully Open MOOC Platforms

If MOOC proponents truly seek to offer the best educational opportunities to the world, they will have to open these platforms to a wide variety of institutions and instructors. Expanded MOOCs that are entirely open could include a multitude of approaches and contexts, thereby exploding the notion of traditional canons in any discipline. Creating such expanded or open MOOCs could be one of the most important developments in pedagogical design. As Brown (2010) contends,

> We need to understand the factors on which we base our pedagogical canons—our collective curricular choices—in order to preserve and assert our power to determine what students should learn. . . . The factors that underlie admission to pedagogical canons include extrinsic variables (tradition and inertia, recognition, importance for groups and individuals, and availability) and intrinsic factors (place in literary history, informative content, aesthetic superiority, and ability to entertain or move the reader). Knowing these factors, we can determine which criteria should be most important for our own group of learners.

As someone who had the opportunity to be a MOOC instructor, I recognize the need to include a larger pool of instructors from a wider range of institutions. And by becoming more highly critical about our course designs as well as by fully recognizing the ways each of us (consciously or unconsciously) perpetuates particular cultural hegemonies, we can consider ways to leverage MOOCs to broaden rather than narrow the canon in any academic field. Such broadening of the MOOC curricula and accepted practices, instructional approaches, and cultural participants will produce generations of students who are trained in a multitude of theoretical perspectives and practical techniques. These individuals will address (and hopefully solve) problems from a variety of modes. If expansion fails to occur, we risk a dangerous kind of single-mindedness that could significantly diminish innovation and limit problem solving in every sector of our lives.

There are many ways we work across institutions and cultures to reach common goals: one way is to be more inclusive of the large number of students who enroll in our courses—incorporating their differing views and experiences should be an integral part of any course's resources. The diversity of our students is one of the great strengths of MOOCs or similar platforms. Finally, we cannot accept single-provider models, such as those highly prevalent today; that will only limit students and what they can learn.

 Karen Head is Director of the Communication Center at the Georgia Institute of Technology, and an assistant professor in the School of Literature, Media, and Communication. Her research areas focus on writing and communication theory and pedagogical practice. In 2012–13, she was part of the GT team awarded a Gates Foundation Grant to develop one of the first MOOCs focused on college writing. She has published several articles about that experience.

References

Denneen, J., & Dretler, T. (2012). *The financially sustainable university?* Bain Briefs. Retrieved from http://www.bain.com/Images/BAIN_BRIEF_The_financially_sustainable_university.pdf.

Brown, J.L. (2010). Constructing our pedagogical canons. *Pedagogy: Critical approaches to teaching literature language, composition, and culture, 10*(3), 525–53.

Coursera. (2014). Meet our partners. Retrieved from https://www.coursera.org/about/partners.

Head, K. (2014). The hidden costs of MOOCs. In S. D. Krause, & C. Lowe (Eds.), *Invasion of the MOOCs: The promises and perils of massive open online courses.* Anderson, SC: Parlor Press. Retrieved from http://www.parlorpress.com/pdf/invasion_of_the_moocs.pdf.

Kennedy, M. (2010, September). A non-inclusive canon. *World Policy Journal, 27*(3), 3–7. Retrieved from http://wpj.sagepub.com/search/results?fulltext=a+non-inclusive+canon&submit=yes&journal_set=spwpj&src=selected&andorexactfulltext=and&x=0&y=0.

Lauter, P. (1991). *Canons and contexts.* New York: Oxford University Press.

Molloy, A. (2014, May 25). Michael Gove "axes" American classics including To Kill a Mockingbird from English literature GCSE syllabus. *The Independent.* Retrieved from http://tinyurl.com/mhu8rrv.

3

MOOCs AND OPEN EDUCATION IN JAPAN

The Case of the Open University of Japan

Kumiko Aoki

Introduction

Japan is a technologically advanced society and has a reliable telecommunications infrastructure. Therefore, people outside of Japan naturally assume that there is advanced use of information and communication technologies (ICT) in education throughout the country. However, the technology adoption in education, including higher education, is relatively slow in Japan. According to a recent survey conducted by Toru Iiyoshi and his colleagues and published by Kyoto University (Kyoto University, 2014), slightly less than 40 percent of higher education institutions in Japan have offered any form of e-learning and just 57 percent of institutions have implemented university-wide learning management systems (LMS). In addition, less than a half of the higher education institutions in Japan have any institution-wide strategies for e-learning or the use of ICT. In fact, most such efforts are attributable to individual teaching staff who usually manage them in addition to their face-to-face teaching responsibilities.

Even though the adoption of ICT in education or online education in Japan is generally lagging behind those other developed nations, the term, MOOCs, or "massive open online courses," has had a widespread and strong influence on stakeholders in higher education in Japan. In October 2013, a consortium of universities and corporations in Japan established the Japan Open Online Education Promotion Council, also known as "JMOOC" (JMOOC, 2013), as a means to promote the spread and use of MOOCs and open education in Japan. This consortium started to offer three MOOC-related courses in April 2014. As a result, the results of these efforts are unfolding during the time of this writing. In addition, JMOOC is planning to offer 15 more courses from all different universities in Japan by the end of 2014.

Prior to the establishment of JMOOC, the two most reputable national universities in Japan, Tokyo University and Kyoto University, had joined the two well-known U.S. initiatives of MOOCs, Coursera and edX, respectively (Kyoto University, 2013; Tokyo University, 2013). As a sign of interest in MOOCs from Japan, more than 30,000 people registered for the first Coursera course offered by Tokyo University, "From the Big Bang to Dark Energy," in September 2013. Seven months later, about 18,000 people registered for the first edX course offered by Kyoto University, "Chemistry of Life," in April 2014.

Even in Japan where online education offerings are still rare and e-learning usually refers to the transmission of lecture videos online, MOOCs cast some stir among many higher education institutions who had not seriously considered online education as part of their future strategies. As such, they opened up eyes not just to the potential of MOOCs, but to more modest blended and fully online course and program offerings as well.

In terms of open education in Japan, the Open University of Japan (OUJ) (referred to as "*Hoso Daigaku*" in Japanese, meaning "broadcasting university") has broadcasted university-level lecture programs on its television channels as well as radio stations for 30 years to anybody in Japan who has television or radio sets to receive the signals. Considering its mission of providing higher education services to those who have missed or are missing the opportunities to attend regular on-campus university education, it seems natural for the OUJ to provide MOOCs, but the road to online offerings has been rocky within OUJ as well.

This chapter describes various historical developments of distance education and online distance education in Japan from social and cultural perspectives. It also discusses the significance of different forms of distance learning in Japan, both domestically as well as globally.

Historical Context of Distance Higher Education in Japan

It is safe to say that the history of open education in Japan parallels the history of distance education in Japan. More specifically, distance education was developed in Japan as an alternative means to educate people who otherwise would have had no access to higher education. However, in comparison to the history of higher education, it is only in relatively recent times that distance higher education, or correspondence higher education, was officially recognized or accredited in Japan (Aoki, 2006).

It was in 1950 that correspondence programs or distance learning programs were officially authorized to offer credits by the Japanese Ministry of Education, thereby enabling recognized Japanese institutions to offer degrees to their students at a distance. According to the Higher Education Council in Japan, this was the beginning of distance higher education in Japan. Since then, the Japanese Ministry of Education has maintained two separate accreditation systems or the University Establishment Standards: one for traditional on-campus institutions and the other for correspondence distance education.

Back then, although those distance education programs had been officially accredited to offer degrees, 30 credits of the 124 credits required to obtain a bachelor's degree had to be earned through face-to-face classes (i.e., formal schooling). In March 1998, this requirement to earn the minimum of 30 credits through face-to-face classes was relaxed. At that time, the Japanese government decided to allow those 30 credits to be earned through synchronous mediated communication such as videoconferencing. About 13 years later, in March 2001, the government allowed the students to earn those 30 credits through interactions on the Internet. This decision made it possible to earn degrees solely at a distance without ever visiting the physical campus or associated learning center(s) for the first time.

At about the same time, graduate programs through correspondence education began to be officially recognized. In fact, four graduate distance education programs were established in 2002. One year later, in 2003, doctoral programs through distance education were beginning to be recognized. Originally, distance education programs were considered secondary to the regular on-campus programs mostly because of the fact that most distance education programs have open admission policies and allow any qualified individuals to enroll in their courses without entrance examinations. Nevertheless, the widespread notion that distance education programs are secondary in status to the traditional residential programs in their academic rigor has not yet totally disappeared. Fortunately, these negative perceptions are slowly changing, in part, due to the fact that traditional on-campus universities have begun to offer distance education programs.

Throughout the history of distance higher education and open education in Japan, the Open University of Japan (OUJ) has been playing a unique role. The following section will explain its history and current practices.

The Open University of Japan: The Massive Higher Education Provider in Japan

The Open University of Japan (OUJ) was established in 1983. Until 2007, it was known in English as the "University of the Air." Modeled after the Open University in the UK, which combined broadcast lectures with correspondence texts and visits to local centers, OUJ began its instruction via television and radio broadcasts in April 1985. In Japan, the idea of establishing a university which utilizes broadcasting as its instructional medium was first conceived by the Minister of Education in 1967. However, it took more than ten years for the idea to be actually implemented due to an assortment of political issues.

Before OUJ was actually established, the National Center for the Development of Broadcast Education (later called the "National Institute of Multimedia Education" or NIME) was established in 1978 as a body to conduct research and experiments in preparation for the establishment of OUJ. The Center conducted an extensive pilot study to identify the needs of learners for such a university.

A few years later, the Ministry of Education presented the bill to establish the Open University of Japan to Japan's bicameral legislature, known as the "National Diet." The bill passed the Diet in 1981, and, as stated earlier, the OUJ was established in 1983.

In terms of the sheer number of students, the OUJ has been the largest in the country for many years. Currently, there are more than 83,000 students enrolled in the university, while the total number of students who are enrolled in distance higher education programs in Japan is about 212,000 (MEXT, 2014). In other words, about 40 percent of all the current distance higher education students in Japan are the students of OUJ.

What is particularly unique about OUJ is that, since its inception, the university has owned and operated an over-the-air broadcast television and radio station to deliver its instructional programs. Such instructional broadcasting services means that not only registered students, but anybody who can receive the broadcasting signals can watch or listen to its instructional programs. Therefore, it can be argued that OUJ has provided open education since its inception. However, as noted earlier, its transition to online education has been rather slow due to many regulatory, organizational, and cultural reasons.

The main educational model of OUJ has not really changed for the past three decades since its establishment in 1983. In fact, the first fully online programs are only now being designed and will be offered starting in April 2015. Part of the reason for the delay is that the two pillars of the OUJ educational system have been (1) broadcast programs accompanied by textbooks, and (2) face-to-face classes at its study centers. Student assessments for all the broadcast courses are done by final exams held at local study centers.

The Internet has been utilized for those broadcast courses in the form of discussion forums and mid-term assignments in addition to placing the streaming video/audio of the broadcast lecture programs online. However, the forums have never been a key part of the assessment or student learning activities. Not too surprisingly, then, student participation in the forums is usually minimal or non-existent. There has been a system for students to ask questions online; however, those questions are initially sent to the administrative office and then transferred to a teacher, if necessary. As a consequence, there always has been a significant lag between the time the student posts a question and the time they receive an answer. In other words, OUJ has offered open education in Japan since 1983, but it has never been either fully online nor has it been completely interactive. Instead, it has primarily relied on instructor- and content-centered instruction over any learner-centered or interactive activities.

As the idea of MOOCs has spread like a buzzword among various higher education institution stakeholders in Japan, it has also fostered momentum within OUJ to seriously consider and implement online education. It is important to point out that this movement toward online courses and programs did not just simply happen at OUJ after the widespread recognition of MOOCs in the world.

In reality, online education had been in the subject of discussion and debate for several years. However, those attending these discussions had never gained the internal consensus needed to obtain approval for the introduction of online education at OUJ. Top management had always used the following two excuses for not seriously considering offering online education at OUJ: (1) financial difficulties, and (2) student characteristics. The following section focuses on the second of these reasons.

OUJ is legally classified as a private university; nevertheless, more than half of its revenue comes from the government. As part of this funding, the management of OUJ is overseen by two key government ministries: (1) the Ministry of Education, Culture, Sports, Science and Technology (MEXT), and (2) the Ministry of Internal Affairs and Communications (MICA). The former ministry has jurisdiction over its university education and the latter ministry oversees its broadcasting system. No other university in Japan is overseen by two ministries since they do not have broadcasting licenses. In contrast, the mission of OUJ is stipulated as being the provider of university-level instructional programs over the air. Unlike the other Japanese campuses, heretofore, the OUJ receives its subsidy from MICA to operate and maintain its broadcasting station.

Consequently, the top management of the OUJ has always been afraid of losing the revenue source by shifting its instructional delivery mode online. This situation has also made it difficult for the university to allocate its budget to anything other than operating and maintaining its broadcasting station. Suffice to say, broadcasting programs are quite costly and take up the major portion of the OUJ budget to produce and deliver.

The second reason that had been used to justify not offering online courses is the characteristics of OUJ students. These tend to be much older than those found in other universities in Japan where a majority of students are of traditional college-age. Over 60 percent of the students at OUJ are in their 40s or older. In addition, as OUJ has the mission to provide higher education to anybody who possesses a high school diploma or the equivalent, OUJ has been reluctant to offer any online courses since many of the current OUJ students lack the means and skills to access online courses.

The two reasons discussed above had always been used to block any serious consideration of offering online courses at OUJ. However, in 2013, partly influenced by the popularity of MOOCs as a concept in Japan and partly due to management changes experienced during the previous year, the university began to earnestly reflect on the possibility of offering online courses. As a sign of this sudden interest, a working group was established to discuss ways to introduce online learning to both students and instructors. Besides the two most apparent reasons for the lag in implementing online learning at OUJ, mentioned above, there were many other hidden obstacles, including political and social ones, which needed to be overcome before the OUJ could actually realize online education.

The focus of the debate was the way to justify the credit hours. Japanese laws related to the OUJ stipulate the two kinds of courses that it could offer: (1) broadcasting courses, and (2) schooling (face-to-face) courses. In terms of broadcasting courses, each course is accompanied by print material which is specifically written for the course. These courses, naturally, also include broadcasting (television or radio) programs consisting of fifteen 45-minute programs. Studying with the print material comprises one credit and watching the broadcasting programs comprises another credit, amounting to a total of two credits per course. In order for a student to earn the two credits, the student must pass the final exam which is held at study centers all over Japan.

In contrast to a broadcasting course, a schooling course comprises one credit, for which students have to attend face-to-face classes held at a study center. These face-to-face classes are usually offered on the weekend. A student can earn one credit by attending the two-day class on the weekend.

Even though the national law set forth by MEXT makes a vague mention that one credit must consist of 45 hours of learning activities, in reality, a one-credit course usually means a 45-minute face-to-face class per week over the 15-week period – regardless of how much students actually study or learn. Online courses are a totally new category at OUJ. As a result, nobody knows how to count the numbers of credit hours in online courses. For most OUJ faculty and staff members, in fact, it is difficult to think of credit hours in terms of student activities or some other measure other than hours since credit hours have been considered mostly in terms of the length of lectures.

In regular on-campus courses and schooling courses, this change to online instruction may not be as troubling an issue since what constitutes a class is primarily up to the instructor in charge of the course. As with universities in many other countries, there usually is no central authority to actually check what's going on inside each classroom. However, at OUJ, all the broadcasting courses are centrally managed and examined by a university-wide committee and confirmed by the faculty assembly. Such mandated procedures allow no room for spontaneity or flexibility in assigning learning activities. Therefore, it will require a significant transformation of OUJ policies and practices if online courses are to be considered the equivalent of broadcasting courses or schooling courses.

In the course of discussion, it was agreed that there will basically be two kinds of online courses: (1) courses which are primarily set up for delivering information, and (2) courses for encouraging knowledge construction among students. It was easy for most faculty members at OUJ to have a relatively clear image of what the former courses look like as those online courses differed little from current practices of delivering broadcast lectures. Given these similarities, they could focus simply on what to present or talk about. However, it was considerably more problematic for them to conceive of the latter courses as they rarely see and interact with students except those whom they advise for thesis projects. Designing, creating, running, and assessing more learner-centered or constructivistic types of courses involving greater interaction with students would be extremely difficult for them without actually experiencing such approaches firsthand.

Offering online courses at OUJ is also a major challenge not only for faculty members but also for clerical and administrative staff as the entire university system has been set up exclusively for offering broadcast courses over the air and face-to-face courses at local study centers. When the shift to online courses and programs commenced, there were no human resources available for producing, designing, creating, implementing, running, and maintaining online courses. To make matters worse, none would be hired. In fact, the entire online instructional system has to be thought out and created in a time of declining financial revenues due, in part, to a decrease in the number of students attending college in Japan, and, in part, to the decreasing size of governmental subsidies that OUJ was receiving.

In Japan, there is no career track equivalent to the professional tracks in universities found in the United States. For instance, there are two categories of staff at a Japanese university: (1) academic staff, and (2) administrative staff. The administrative staff usually change their positions every three to four years on average. For example, those who have been working for the accounting office or department may be assigned to work for student support services after three years. In other words, it is a culture where specialists are rarely fostered within a university; hence, much professional work needs to be outsourced. This human resource system has to be reconsidered if any university in Japan, and not just OUJ, is serious about offering a substantial number of online courses and programs.

What Open Education Means for OUJ and Japan?

As described above, the broadcast lecture programs produced by OUJ can be viewed by anybody in Japan who can receive the broadcasting signals. By allowing such unfettered access, OUJ has been in a unique position as a long-standing open education provider in Japan. However, OUJ is far from being positioned as a prominent provider of open education in a global sense. Even though the end products of the OUJ are open to viewing domestically, they are neither sharable nor reusable.

Another constraint in terms of open access is that the educational products of the OUJ are not viewable outside Japan. In addition, though "open education" underlies the basic philosophy of the institution and should help to promote innovation and change in educational practices, OUJ has been impervious to changes during the past three decades. As noted in this chapter, it still operates in the educational model of teacher-centered knowledge transfer. It is definitely time for a change. It is plausible that MOOCs – and online learning, in general – may spark such a change or perhaps even a transformation.

As an island country with a unique language, the Japanese people tend to be isolated from the rest of the world in terms of education and the exchange of ideas. Furthermore, the Confucian tradition of respecting authorities and the Japanese culture of maintaining ostensible harmony, called *wa*, also pose a significant barrier to teaching and learning. The free flow and exchange of ideas and discussions is just not that commonly experienced or expected. Therefore, open education is truly called upon to actively facilitate innovations in pedagogy while infusing learners with multiple ideas and perspectives. Open education should be learner-centered rather than teacher-centered. Open education should provide learners with opportunities to make decisions about their own learning, to work at their own pace, to follow their own style, to learn from experiences, to share ideas with peers, and to learn collaboratively.

OUJ has been bestowed with the mission of educating the people of Japan with as little restriction as possible. Television and radio may have been the effective means to achieve such a mission before the age of the Internet and Web 2.0. However, those mediums, while still important to some, have become inadequate in educating the majority of Japanese people in this highly digital and global age. The whole system and organizational structure built around producing contents based on old mediums has to be reconsidered. For instance, the mediums of instruction or teaching and learning should be diverse. The more diverse means of teaching and learning that we can provide, the more effective we will be in including people with different backgrounds and needs.

It is hoped that MOOCs will play a significant role for stakeholders in Japanese higher education in the near future. MOOCs, and other forms of educational delivery that will emerge in the coming decades, will help these individuals to realize that we now live in a vastly different era from the dawn of distance learning in Japan back in 1950 as well as the start of the OUJ in 1983. Clearly, the traditional practices of teaching and learning need to be seriously reconsidered not only in terms of pedagogy, but also in the sense of institutional structures and resource allocations.

Kumiko Aoki is Professor of Informatics and Professor in the Center of Open and Distance Education at the Open University of Japan. Previously she was Associate Professor at the National Institute of Multimedia Education (NIME), Japan, from 2004 to 2009, Assistant Professor of Communication at Boston University from 1998 to 2003, and Assistant Professor of Information Technology at Rochester Institute of Technology from 1995 to 1998. She received her PhD in Communication and Information Sciences from the University of Hawaii at Manoa in 1995. Drawing on her interdisciplinary and transcultural background, she spoke at international conferences and published articles both in Japanese and in English on the topics ranging from distance education, e-learning, learning design, cross-cultural collaborative learning, and tele-collaboration.

References

Aoki, K. (2006). Distance learning programs and schools in Japan: From correspondence learning to e-learning. *Proceedings of the World Conference on E-Learning in Corporate, Government, Healthcare, and Higher Education* (Vol. 2006, No. 1, pp. 1802–6), Chesapeake, VA: Association for the Advancement of Computing in Education (AACE).

JMOOC (2013). *About JMOOC.* Japan Open Online Education Promotion Council and JMOOC. Retrieved from http://www.jmooc.jp/en/about/.

Kyoto University. (2014). *Koutou Kyouiku Kikan niokeru ICT no Rikatuyou nikannsuru chousakennkyuu [Research Report concerning the Use of ICT in Higher Education Institutions].* Submitted to the Japanese Ministry of Education, Culture, Sports, and Technology.

Kyoto University. (2013, May 21). *Nihon de Saisho ni edX no konso-shiamu ni sannkashi-mashita* [Participating in the edX consortium as the first Japanese university]. Retrieved from http://www.kyoto-u.ac.jp/ja/news_data/h/h1/news7/2013/130521_1.htm.

MEXT (Ministry of Education, Culture, Sports, Science and Technology). (2014). Table 30. *Gakko Kihon Chousa [Basic Survey of Schools].* Retrieved from http://www.e-stat.go.jp/SG1/estat/List.do?bid=000001054433&cycode=0.

Tokyo University. (2013, February 22). *Tokyo Daigaku to Coursera (U.S.) ga Daikibo Koukai Online Koza (MOOC) Haishin ni kannsuru Kyotei wo teiketu* [Establishment of the treaty between Tokyo University and Coursera for offering MOOCs] [Press release]. Retrieved from http://www.u-tokyo.ac.jp/public/public01_250222_j.html.

PART 2

Open Education Opportunities Now and On the Horizon

The second part of the book explores various views, policies, and initiatives related to openness. Although MOOCs have received the lion's share of public attention during the past few years, open education resources and open courseware may actually be utilized far more extensively across educational sectors. Unlike MOOCs, which typically entail an extensive personal or institutional commitment or undertaking, open education resources and services can be utilized in a much more modest or even fleeting way. As such, they typically require far less instructional risk and resource commitment than MOOCs. Open educational resources can find their way into a course as a minor component or be used for specific situations or contexts. They might also be targeted programmatically or system-wide as a tool to reduce or alleviate costs or offer novel forms of course flexibility and access. Their appeal, therefore, might come from the course instructors, learners or trainees, course designers, or from the administrators or government officials approving the budgets.

One of the most long-standing open resources in education is MERLOT (Multimedia Educational Resources for Learning and Online Teaching). MERLOT is unique in providing extensive and informative peer reviews for many of the resources it lists. In Chapter 4, the executive director of MERLOT, Gerard Hanley, discusses how MOOCs and open education can be used to address a number of higher education needs without radically disrupting the ecosystem. As a pioneering resource in open educational services for its 128,000 members, MERLOT has continuously developed its community, resources, and services and tools to provide free and open teaching and learning environments for teachers and learners from "K to gray." In addition to managing nearly 50,000 indexed open educational resources, many of which are peer-reviewed, it sponsors or hosts journals, newsletters, conferences, white papers, content recognitions and awards, and community discussions. At the end of his chapter, Hanley includes a useful appendix of the Web tools and resources now available through MERLOT. Anyone reading this chapter will quickly realize that since its inception in the late 1990s, MERLOT has enabled educational institutions to deliver quality, customized, and affordable access to much needed learning resources and tools.

In Chapter 5, Carina Bossu from the University of Tasmania, David Bull from the University of Southern Queensland in Australia, and Mark Brown from Dublin City University in Ireland discuss some of the findings of a centrally funded research project that investigated the state of play of open educational resources (OER) in higher education in Australia. According to participants of a study they conducted, the use of OER has the potential to lead to new pedagogical practices, improve the quality of educational learning materials, and promote and increase access to education. Importantly, the chapter presents a "Feasibility Protocol," which not only is a key outcome of this project, but can also lead to the widespread adoption of open educational practices for the delivery of higher education in Australia and beyond.

In the third and final chapter of this part, Laura Czerniewicz and her colleagues at the University of Cape Town in South Africa provide an illuminating overview of open education. Open scholarship activities and projects have taken place in several guises over the past few years in South Africa with huge implications for anyone in higher education. To help others who may wish to replicate their efforts, Czerniewicz and her colleagues describe how these projects and activities in Cape Town have been loosely connected, driven by champions, and enabled by external grant funding. Open education practices and advocacy work has been firmly grounded in a collegial institutional culture, with several interesting concomitant implications. The year 2014, for instance, saw the organic growth of various open education initiatives at the University of Cape Town, including an institutional commitment to a holistic open access policy and the launch of a repository curating both open educational resources and research.

4

MOOCs, MERLOT, AND OPEN EDUCATIONAL SERVICES

Gerard L. Hanley

The appearance of massive open online courses (MOOCs) may seem sudden. But for those who have been laboring in the vineyard learning to use technology to create and distribute content, mediate pedagogical interaction, and facilitate the business processes of education, MOOCs are just a next branch in the ongoing evolution of Open Educational Resources (OER). This evolution can be traced back to when open learning objects crawled from the primordial technological sea in the mid-1990s and continued evolving with the OpenCourseWare (OCW) and Open Textbooks (OT) initiatives in the early 2000s. Most recently, we have seen the emergence of MOOCs (see Figure 4.1).

Educators welcomed each of these OER species happily and without much threat to the ecosystem of higher education. But at this early stage of the MOOC evolution, there are different reactions. Optimists see synergy in the "open online" features of MOOCs. Open online is perceived as a panacea for expanding access to affordable learning. In addition, many view MOOCs as a test-bed for developing new pedagogical techniques. They can also enable global learning

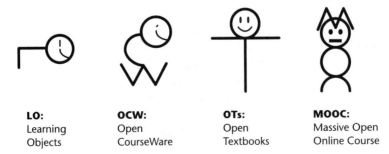

LO:	**OCW:**	**OTs:**	**MOOC:**
Learning	Open	Open	Massive Open
Objects	CourseWare	Textbooks	Online Course

FIGURE 4.1 MOOCs as a recent evolution of OER

communities to create knowledge together. Pessimists liken MOOCs to an invasive species that will destroy institutions by usurping the accreditation of learning, demobilize and devolve faculties by the star-system of instructors, and dilute learning to a fast-food, virtual drive-by experience.

The potential benefits and threats to academic quality, student outcomes, institutional integrity, and administrative processes are still emerging. However, the features of the MOOC that have made them distinctive from the other types of OER are the services integrated with the content. MOOC platforms for organizing and delivering the multimedia content integrated with the social media tools for engaging individuals and various assessment and analytic tools provide feedback on learning and teaching. This combination of services that manage the content delivery within a design for learning has some substitutability with online courses delivered by accredited higher education institutions. Through the open enrollment provided by MOOCs, these services have been increasingly recognized as valuable to many learners, teachers, and institutions.

Higher education institutions can leverage the availability of MOOCs to produce benefits for their institutions, faculty, and students in a number of ways (Hanley, 2013), including:

1. **Reducing Costs of Instructional Content** for their own courses by having students use the MOOCs in a "flipped classroom" pedagogy. The MOOC curriculum becomes the students' homework and the in-class time is spent with more socially engaging and active learning experiences.
2. **Supporting Outreach and College Readiness**: Prospective students can experience college-level, online learning at no financial cost. The institution can provide access to instructional experiences that underserved communities might not have available in their high schools. The MOOCs, however, would have to be embedded in a suite of student support services which frequently exist within the institution's outreach programs.
3. **Determining Acceptance of Transferable Courses:** Students already transfer their credits to another institution with a validated transcript from a trusted institution. Institutions have their policies and practices to address course articulation requirements. Applying these policies and practices to MOOC courses should not be a wholly foreign business process for most institutions.
4. **Reducing Costs of Workforce Development Certificate Programs**: Institutions have existing self-supported/extended education programs targeted to workforce needs. Given that they need to reduce operational costs, using MOOCs to add valued curriculum at low costs can be an effective strategy.
5. **Providing Credit for Prior Learning by Exam**: Institutions have existing policies and procedures for awarding academic credit by examinations with scores required for credit earned. Advance Placement Tests,

International Baccalaureate Exams, and College Level Entrance Program are examples where students get academic credit for prior learning, whether through MOOCs or other independent learning experiences. Streamlining the existing processes for obtaining college credit by exam while maintaining academic standards could benefit both institutions and their students.

In summary, higher education can blend MOOCs into their educational eco-system without major disruptions and expand its ability to serve growing and diverse student needs for alternative modes of instruction.

Open Educational Services and MERLOT

MOOCs are one class of "Open Educational Services" (OES). Simply put, OES are online tools that are free for anyone to use to design their own program of study using OERs or proprietary content. A full range of free and openly available instructional materials available on the Web can be reviewed at MERLOT (Multimedia Educational Resource for Learning and Online Teaching; see Appendix A), along with a suite of free tools to enable learning for everyone. With its birth by the California State University in 1997, MERLOT captured the evolution of OER materials and processes and simultaneously evolved its OES as well.

Back in 1997, the California State University (CSU) system had over 350,000 students and over 30,000 faculty. At that time, we had to design a service for finding and using the emerging learning objects that would be easy to use, would leverage the widespread yet uncoordinated development of academic technologies, and would be low cost to operate. MERLOT became the CSU's open library of free learning resources which was modeled after the 1994 NSF-funded project, "Authoring Tools and an Educational Object Economy" (EOE). This project was led by Dr. James Spohrer and hosted by Apple Computer and other industry, university, and government collaborators. One of the key design requirements for MERLOT was to have a technology service that enables users to contribute directly to a community's collection of online resources. The goal of MERLOT was to enable a "cottage industry" of college and university campuses to develop and distribute academic technology and content in scalable and sustainable ways. MERLOT also intended to support individual faculty members in their development of scalable and sustainable academic technology and high quality educational content (Hanley, 2001; Hanley, Schneebeck, & Zweier, 1998; Schneebeck & Hanley, 2001).

In 1999, the CSU system created an informal consortium with three other state higher education systems (the University System of Georgia, the Oklahoma State Regents for Higher Education, and the University of North Carolina System) to expand the MERLOT collection, conduct peer reviews, and add student-learning assignments. Each system contributed funds to develop the MERLOT software and in-kind support to advance the peer review process. The CSU maintained its leadership of and responsibilities for the operation and improvement of processes and tools and continues to do so.

Today, the CSU system has grown to about 450,000 students and 40,000 faculty. As a result, the need for free, convenient, high-quality, and reliable access to online instructional materials has accelerated. The MERLOT consortium is now composed of over 40 higher education systems, consortia, individual institutions of higher education (representing over 500 campuses), professional academic organizations, other digital libraries, education industries, and over 125,000 individuals to form a community of people who strive to improve the teaching and learning experience through the provision of high-quality online resources. The free and open MERLOT library has over 46,000 free and open online resources, including over 3,300 free and open etextbooks and over 5,500 free and open online courseware. MERLOT's new student-centered portal (see Appendix A) provides easy access to this wide range of OER species.

MERLOT has evolved beyond an open library of materials and directory of individuals to an active, global community voluntarily contributing materials and sharing comments, personal collections, and lesson plans about using MERLOT's resources. MERLOT has 23 editorial boards peer-reviewing the quality of the MERLOT materials. MERLOT has also created over 50 different "Teaching Commons" which are customized websites for specific communities to address their specific educational goals. For example, the CSU system and MERLOT are providing the State of California the "California Open Online Library for Education" (see Appendix A) to reduce the cost of instructional materials for students in the California Community Colleges system, the CSU system, and the University of California system. The CSU's Affordable Learning Solutions initiative (see Appendix A) is another example of customizing MERLOT's OES to support an institutionally strategic priority for reducing the cost of higher education through the use of no-/low-cost, high-quality instructional materials. These websites are open to all so everyone anywhere can use them. In fact, other state higher education systems, such as the University System of Georgia, the State University of New York System, and the Oklahoma State Regents for higher education, have each adopted/adapted MERLOT's OES for their programs through their partnerships with MERLOT (see Appendix A).

With the pervasive changes in learning technologies and associated possibilities, however, there is more to this evolution of services at MERLOT. For instance, in partnership with the Tennessee Board of Regents, MERLOT and the CSU have created a teaching commons that filters the MERLOT collection for mobile apps by platform and grade level (see Appendix A) to support mobile learning initiatives. Second, MERLOT's collaboration with the National Federation of the Blind and the Open Education Consortium has produced a teaching commons focused on improving the accessibility of free and open online resources and services (see Appendix A). Third, the OER for Cancer in

India project (see Appendix A) provides a free and open collection and services focused on cancer education and treatment that can be used by healthcare providers. Fourth, MERLOT Chile is a close collaboration between MERLOT and a higher education system in Chile called INACAP (see Appendix A). As part of these efforts, INACAP delivers free and open access to both Spanish and English-language educational materials to faculty and students that are intended to improve learner digital literacy skills as well as advance their independent learning skills. Significantly, MERLOT's website can be translated into about 90 languages using Google Translate.

Social Media and MERLOT: Open library services that organize online content for people to discover and use are insufficient to support programs for study and learning. Open educational services need to support people freely and openly communicating and collaborating in their teaching and learning. Fortunately, social media have emerged during the past decade to provide such tools. MERLOT Voices (see Appendix A) is an open suite of online community services deploying a customized Ning platform where institutions, organizations, groups, and individuals can engage in synchronous and asynchronous communications, postings, and blogging. MERLOT partners and members are able to leverage MERLOT Voices to immediately engage a community of users with a stable, free, easy-to-use, and familiar platform for its online community-building activities. Membership in MERLOT Voices is free and easy to complete. To augment MERLOT's communication strategy, MERLOT's YouTube channel and Voices complement MERLOT's Grapevine Newsletter, the MERLOT Blog, and its Facebook and Twitter accounts and services (see Appendix A for all of these services and resources). These various forms of social media provide people convenient ways for sharing, communicating, and collaborating.

The above informal social media services are essential for connecting people who share interests, goals, and projects. Within higher education, the formal and traditional "social media" has been the publication of journal articles. This trusted means for communicating has been facilitated by the free access to published works our libraries have provided to millions of faculty members and students. Since 2005, MERLOT has also published an open access, peer-reviewed scholarly eJournal, *MERLOT Journal of Online Learning and Teaching* (JOLT) (see Appendix A). JOLT represents a "social media" for academics sharing research and scholarly activities about online learning and teaching.

Creating OER with MERLOT Content Builder: MERLOT's OES have included its open library, open directory, and open social media. To complete its suite of services, MERLOT provides its members free access to tools to personally author and publish OER at its website. Members of every community need to create and share the products of their community's initiatives and activities. Creating websites is a necessary means for creative authoring and sharing. MERLOT's Content Builder is a free and open access, cloud-based authoring tool that MERLOT members can use to create OER and easily share their

OER with the world (see Appendix A). MERLOT Content Builder can create IMS Common Cartridges with Creative Commons licenses which significantly improve the ability of people to share and use a particular community's collection of OER. The California State University has used MERLOT Content Builder extensively to have its faculty create ePortfolios of their redesigns of courses with technology to improve student learning (see Appendix A). All these Open Educational Services are available free for MERLOT members and form a foundation of capabilities that can be leveraged to achieve institutional goals cost effectively.

The history of the development of OER and OES indicates that MOOC technologies and MOOC-style pedagogy are more than a fad, but less than a revolution. A lasting and substantive transition of online education and digital resources from research and pilot programs to mainstream use in higher education is underway. It is likely that this transition will continue for some time. Clearly, this change process is complex, multidisciplinary, and experimental. Nevertheless, this change is inevitable.

For those individuals, organizations, and institutions who have been involved in MERLOT, OCW, OER, OT, MOOCs and/or other open education initiatives during the past couple of decades or before, the direction is perhaps more clear. MOOCs are simply the latest in this evolution of open educational services. The opening of education for all will continue to unfold and offer intriguing educational opportunities, gifts, challenges, and success stories for educators and learners across the globe. As it does, the open educational services of MERLOT will continue to support the learning and teaching for those who choose to use MERLOT. Ideally, others will find unique ways to incorporate MERLOT in their MOOCs as well as in any new open education initiatives around the world.

Appendix A: Web Resources for MERLOT's Open Educational Services

I. Open Library Services

California Open Online Library for Education, build upon MERLOT's OES: http://cool4ed.org

CSU's Affordable Learning Solutions Initiative: http://affordablelearningsolutions.org

MERLOT Chile—partnership with INACAP (leading higher education system in Chile): http://www.inacap.cl/tportalvp/merlot-chile

MERLOT Homepage/foundation to MERLOT's OES: www.merlot.org

MERLOT's Mobile Apps/Mobile Learning Collection: http://mobileapps.merlot.org

MERLOT, Cal State University, National Federation of the Blind, and the Open Education Consortium teaching commons for improving the accessibility of free and open online resources and services: http://oeraccess.merlot.org

MERLOT's Student Centered Teaching Commons: www.merlotx.org

OER for Cancer in India project, in collaboration with International Network for Cancer Treatment & Research and Open Health Systems Laboratory: http://oercindia.merlot.org

Oklahoma State Regents for Higher Education's Affordable Learning Solutions Initiative: http://affordablelearningok.org

University of New York System's Affordable Learning Solutions Initiative: http://opensunyals.org/

University System of Georgia's Affordable Learning Solutions Initiative: http://affordablelearninggeorgia.org

II. Open Community Services

MERLOT's collection of teaching commons, partner communities, OES for partner communities: http://www.merlot.org/merlot/index.htm?action=communities

MERLOT's Grapevine Newsletter: http://grapevine.merlot.org/

MERLOT's open access, peer reviewed eJournal for Online Teaching and Learning (JOLT): http://jolt.merlot.org

MERLOT Voices, a free online community service: http://voices.merlot.org

III. Open Social Media Services

MERLOT Blog: http://blog.merlot.org/

MERLOT's Facebook Page: https://www.facebook.com/pages/MERLOT-Multimedia-Educational-Resource-for-Learning-and-Online-Teaching/225454444160837

MERLOT News Center: http://www.merlot.org/merlot/index.htm?action=news

MERLOT's Twitter accounts: https://twitter.com/MERLOTOrg

MERLOT's YouTube channel: https://www.youtube.com/user/MERLOTPlace

IV. OER Authoring Services and Guidelines

CSU showcase of faculty ePortfolios created with MERLOT Content Builder: http://courseredesign.csuprojects.org/wp/eportfolios/

Guidelines on using MERLOT's Content Builder/ePortfolio authoring tool: http://taste.merlot.org/Programs_and_Projects/ContentBuilder.html

MERLOT's services to create Personal Collections, ePortfolios, and other OER: http://www.merlot.org/merlot/index.htm?action=contribute

 **Gerard L. Hanley** is the Executive Director of MERLOT (Multimedia Educational Resource for Learning and Online Teaching at www.merlot.org) and Assistant Vice Chancellor for Academic Technology Services for the California State University (CSU), Office of the Chancellor (www.calstate. edu/ats). At MERLOT, he directs the development and sustainability of MERLOT's international consortium of higher education institutions, professional societies, digital libraries, and corporations to provide professional development and technology services to improve teaching and learning. At the CSU, Gerry oversees the development and implementation of system-wide academic technology initiatives serving CSU's 23 campuses with over 22,000 faculty and over 445,000 students. He can be contacted at ghanley@ calstate.edu.

References

Hanley, G.L., Schneebeck, C., & Zweier, L. (1998). Implementing a scalable and sustainable model for instructional software development. *Syllabus, 11*(9), 30–4.

Hanley, G.L. (2001). Designing and delivery of instructional technology. A team-based approach. In C. Barone & P. Hagner (Eds.), *Technology-enhanced learning: A guide to engaging and supporting faculty* (pp. 57–64). San Francisco: Jossey-Bass.

Hanley, G.L. (April, 2013). *MOOCs: So What or SWOT? CSU's use of MOOCs and reflections*. Presentation at the Lumina Workshop on MOOCs and the Public Higher Education System, Atlanta, Georgia.

Schneebeck, C., & Hanley, G.L. (2001). The California State University Center for Distributed Learning. In R.M. Epper & A.W. Bates (Eds.), *Teaching faculty how to use technology: Best practices from leading institutions*. Westport, CT: Greenwood/Oryx Press.

5

ENABLING OPEN EDUCATION

A Feasibility Protocol for Australian Higher Education

Carina Bossu, David Bull, and Mark Brown

Introduction

Since its initial use by the United Nations Educational, Scientific and Cultural Organization (UNESCO) in 2002, the term "Open Educational Resources" (UNESCO, 2002) has been redefined several times to meet the accelerating pace of the movement and to fit with the diverse range of contexts in which it has been applied. According to the OER Foundation (2011):

> Open Educational Resources (OER), are educational materials which are licensed in ways that provide permissions for individuals and institutions to reuse, adapt and modify the materials for their own use. OER can, and do include full courses, textbooks, streaming videos, exams, software, and any other materials or techniques supporting learning.

Also, OER vary in size from full courses to stand-alone learning objects (Butcher & Hoosen, 2014). OER are part of a larger, rapidly growing movement to open up education, which also includes open source software, open access, open learning design, open educational practices, and so forth (Butcher & Hoosen, 2014). Among the drivers behind this movement include the desire to share content and knowledge freely in ways that prevent duplication and encourage economies of scale. In addition, there is a pressing need to increase access to education for a growing and diverse student cohort with minimum restriction (The William and Flora Hewlett Foundation, 2013; Wiley & Gurrell, 2009).

Today, major OER initiatives have reached every continent in the world. Such OER initiatives have not only increased in numbers, but they have also evolved conceptually and ideologically. Examples of this evolution are indicated by terms such as Open Educational Practice (OEP) and Massive Open Online

Courses (MOOCs). According to the Open Educational Quality Initiative (OPAL), "OEP are defined as practices which support the (re)use and production of OER through institutional policies, promote innovative pedagogical models, and respect and empower learners as co-producers on their lifelong learning path" (Open Education Quality Initiative, 2011, p. 12). As MOOCs—and their variations (cMOOCs, xMOOCs, and now pMOOCs)—are explored and defined in other chapters of this edited book, for the purposes of this chapter, we would like to acknowledge that the origins of MOOCs are based on some of OER principles, even though most MOOCs today are "rarely 'open' in the OER sense," they can just be accessed for free (Kelly, 2014, p. 11).

In Australia, there have been some OER and OEP developments and initiatives at national and institutional levels, but most of them have been project based, which tend to discontinue when funding cycles come to an end (Bossu, Brown, & Bull, 2012). Despite myriad such projects and activities initiated by individual proponents or individual institutional departments, OER developments are still not part of the mainstream activities of Australian universities. One of the reasons for the slow pace of implementation could be the lack of national or state-level OER policies and national level funding schemes to support the adoption of OER in the Australian higher education sector (Bossu, Brown, & Bull, 2014a).

As such, this chapter, which explores some of the findings of a research project titled "Adoption, use and management of Open Educational Resources to enhance teaching and learning in Australia" (Bossu et al., 2014a), is an attempt to bring OER into mainstream higher education in Australia. The research project was primarily funded by the Australian Government Office for Learning and Teaching (OLT), which is currently the major funding body for learning and teaching in higher education in Australia. The project started in late 2010 and it was the first of its kind to be focused on OER. Currently, there are several other OLT-funded projects to investigate the application of OER in learning and teaching in Australia.

In addition to presenting our OER research findings, this chapter will also present the "Feasibility Protocol," which is a key outcome of this research project. The Feasibility Protocol is formed by a set of guiding principles that prompt questions and raise issues that should be considered by traditional and distance learning universities and tertiary institutions intending to take advantage of the OER movement. More specifically the protocol aims to assist senior executives and managers to make informed decisions about the adoption of OER and OEP at several levels within their institution.

The Study

This two-year research project involved a comprehensive analysis of the relevant literature regarding OER as well as an examination of institutional and national educational policies and frameworks that enable OER development. The project also included an online survey that was distributed to major higher education professional organisation mailing lists in the Australasian region. Subsequently, interviews were conducted, targeting a diverse range of higher education stakeholders across Australia. Another critical aspect of the project was the organisation of an OER National Symposium held in Sydney. The 2012 Symposium was not only a key dissemination point for this project, but it was also an opportunity for gathering insights and feedback from a diverse range of stakeholders across the higher education sector on the draft of the Feasibility Protocol. Given that context, we report on some of the project findings in the following sections.

Participants

The online survey, distributed through professional organisations mailing lists, resulted in 100 completed responses from across 37 (out of 39) higher education institutions in Australia, with representation from all states and territories in the country, and from all the key stakeholder groups related to this research. There was also a balanced gender distribution amongst the respondents: 48 percent male and 51 percent female (1 percent preferred not to respond to this question). The sample also had a good representation of university stakeholders groups, including senior executives (23 participants), managers (13), educators (28), curriculum designers (14), professional developers (6), library professionals (4) and copyright officers (2). From the 100 survey respondents, 24 agreed to be interviewed. The 24 interview participants were from 18 different Australian institutions.

Current State of Play of OER in Australian Higher Education

The results showed that a good number of survey respondents had been aware of the OER movement from two to five years (41 percent) and rated their knowledge of OER as intermediate (51 percent). However, the majority of participants had rarely or never used OER. As for those who have used OER, learning objects were the most preferred type of resources applied in teaching and learning. Also, most survey participants declared that they were not involved in collaborative OER initiatives either nationally or internationally. However, they indicated that they would like to be involved in such collaborations in the future if the opportunity arises.

At the time, the lack of adoption and participants' limited involvement in OER initiatives could be partly explained by the fact that OER practices and initiatives were not included in the strategic plans of most participating institutions. In the interviews we conducted, participants' level of understanding of OER within the sample group was high. However, it must be taken into account that the interview sample was obtained from volunteers who completed the online survey and were comfortable enough to be questioned about these issues. Thus, a higher level of knowledge and understanding was to be expected.

Most interviewees (62 percent) reported that they used OER for both personal and professional purposes. Unfortunately, few made their resources available, and even fewer specifically created OER content for others to use.

In addition, survey data from the time also revealed that national policies focused on OER could be fundamental in encouraging the development and adoption of OER and OEP across the higher education sector. According to some participants, the Australian government should also support institutions through grants or financial awards. These individuals believed that such financial stimulus could increase the number of OER initiatives and eventually result in a culture of open practices, thereby establishing the agreeable conditions for the OER movement to flourish in Australia (Bossu, Brown, & Bull, 2011).

Institutional policies were considered an important factor to promote the effective use and adoption of OER. According to the participants, educational institutions should develop policies and professional development activities to promote OER awareness and to clarify issues related to intellectual property and quality assurance. They also felt that institutions should also promote and reward OER and OEP activities, such as through institutional performance expectations that are related to career progress and promotion. OER promotion or support could also be exhibited by small financial initiatives.

The importance of such strategies and policies to enhance OEP engagement have emerged in similar studies undertaken in Europe and other parts of the world (Open Education Quality Initiative, 2011; Organisation for Economic Co-operation and Development, 2007). In fact, many studies have alerted institutional policy-makers of existing institutional strategies supporting the adoption of OER. Such research also indicates that these strategies could be implemented through appropriate internal regulations and guidelines (Atkins, Brown, & Hammond, 2007; Downes, 2007; Kanwar, Kodhandaraman, & Umar, 2010).

In terms of the benefits that OER can bring to education and training in Australia, the majority (top five responses) of survey respondents' views were that:

- OER have the potential to increase collaboration within an institution and internationally;
- OER are well aligned with academic traditions involving the sharing and dissemination of knowledge;
- educators can save time and avoid duplication of effort;
- OER can improve the quality of educational materials; and
- OER help to enhance the quality of teaching and learning in higher education.

Respondents believed that OER use is a catalyst for institutional innovation (61 survey responses) and that the use of OER has the potential to lead to new pedagogical practices (58 respondents) within higher education institutions. Interview responses reflected similar trends. Most of the 24 interviewees (i.e., 62 percent) pointed out that social improvements and "access to education for all" are potential benefits of OER movement. Other benefits identified by these respondents included increasing efficiency in time and/or money (50 percent) and the improvement of the quality of teaching resources (42 percent). They indicated that openly licensed teaching materials that are accessible to peer-review processes could only improve in quality. Increasing collaboration was also mentioned by over a third of the respondents as another benefit of OER (37 percent).

When asked to indicate the potential barriers to the use of OER, a majority of survey respondents pointed to the lack of interest in creating and using OER (80 participants). They also mentioned that the poor quality of some OER was problematic (73 participants). Among the other challenges and barriers to the growth of the OER movement in Australia, respondents mentioned insufficient institutional support, as well as the lack of institutional policies to address OER developments. Similarly, common obstacles to OER use, identified by the interview participants, were issues related to intellectual property policies and the lack of a national framework to support OER policy development. Difficulties in changing entrenched academic culture were among the other significant barriers identified.

The Feasibility Protocol

The Feasibility Protocol was conceptualised based on current work in the field and informed by this research, including the survey and interviews conducted with key stakeholders. The Feasibility Protocol (Figure 5.1) prompts questions on four aspects:

- the *Opportunities* involved with the adoption of OER and OEP;
- factors related to the *Challenges* associated with the adoption of OER and OEP;
- *Strategic Directions* that need to be considered for an effective adoption of OER and OEP; and
- some *Policy Recommendations* for higher education institutions in Australia.

With the exception of *Policy Recommendations,* the aspects of the protocol are subdivided into three levels: (1) the first level is focused on the higher education sector as a whole, (2) the second level is related to institutional/organisational issues, and (3) the third concentrates on individuals within educational organisations (mostly staff and students). As for the *Policy Recommendations*, the protocol focuses on organisational, project, and individual levels. For the purpose of this chapter, we will explore and discuss the Feasibility Protocol at organisational levels (for more details on the Feasibility Protocol, see Bossu, Brown, & Bull, 2014b).

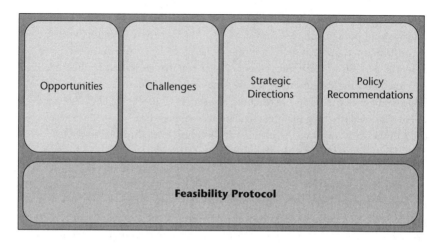

FIGURE 5.1 The Feasibility Protocol

Opportunities Involved with the Adoption of OER and OEP

In keeping with similar research in the field (Open Education Quality Initiative, 2011; Organisation for Economic Co-operation and Development, 2007), this research shows that OER and OEP can bring many opportunities to educational institutions, educators, and traditional as well as non-traditional learners. At an institutional level, OER and OEP can assist in reducing costs, improving quality, and bringing innovation to traditional educational practices (Butcher & Hoosen, 2014; Caswell, Henson, Jensen, & Wiley, 2008; Ehlers, 2011).

The Feasibility Protocol asks senior executives to reflect on the following set of benefits and opportunities of OER and OEP:

- increase institutional reputation through marking and showcasing of educational content as well as raise their international profile and attract more students;
- create opportunities for national and international collaboration with other universities and cooperation with many different stakeholders;
- increase access to education by assisting the alignment of an institution's agendas for social inclusion and widening participation;
- create economies of scale by more efficient content production in terms of time and money (e.g., avoid "reinventing the wheel" and the replication of content); and
- promote innovations and quality in teaching and learning.

Facing the Challenges

Despite the wide range of opportunities that can emerge from the adoption of OEP, educational institutions still face many challenges. They struggle with issues such as resistance to giving away information and knowledge at no cost and free to use and re-use. Intellectual propriety and copyright policies for OEP are also matters that remain ambiguous to educational institutions (Bossu, Bull, & Brown, 2012). Likewise, many questions associated with sustainability and quality of OER and OEP continue to be unanswered and insufficiently researched (Smith, 2013).

The Feasibility Protocol has raised a number of challenges, questions, and issues for educational organisations and their leaders to consider. One of the most significant is the persistence of a traditional academic culture and mindset that represents barriers for the adoption of OEP. Such traditions are steeped in history and may be slow to evolve and embrace a new era of educational delivery. Furthermore, the lack of national and institutional policy enablers supporting OEP need also to be taken into account. If institutional policies and procedures for OEP are non-existent, then there is a need to revise existing ones or develop new policies, especially with regard to content material development to support the adoption of OEP.

In the current climate of global change in the higher education landscape, one cannot ignore the financial concerns of entering the "open" movement. These fiscal considerations challenge the traditional business models of established higher education institutions. Consequently, new business models need to be explored and developed, or existing models adapted, to ensure the sustainability of such initiatives. In order to encourage educational institutions to become involved in open education activities, government bodies and agencies should develop supporting mechanisms such as funding strategies and appropriate policies. In the case of Australia, such strategies could assist the government to effectively achieve some of its wider agenda, e.g., to increase participation and access to education to a more diverse student cohort, to more effectively address the educational needs of working adults as well as those residing in rural and more remote locations, etc. (Bradley, Noonan, Nugent, & Scales, 2008).

Strategic Directions

So far in this chapter we have discussed some of the opportunities and challenges that organisational institutions might face while adopting OER and OEP. The results of this research led to a specific aspect of the Feasibility Protocol that we called "Strategic Directions." Drawing on the above data and the authors' more recent experiences, some of the strategic questions and issues that senior executives should contemplate include:

- *Resourcing*: This item relates to additional investments, such as infrastructure, technology, and personnel, including academic staff development, required for the implementation of an OER initiative; it also concerns the role of this support in promoting the adoption of OER.

- *Innovation*: This item is related to how the adoption of OER can promote institutional "uniqueness and distinctiveness" amongst other institutions across the higher education sector. It also includes ways that OER could be used to meet the expectations of academic staff and students in the use of innovative technologies for learning. Another innovation is related to how OER can be incorporated in the institutional processes for Prior Learning and Assessment Recognition (PLAR).
- *Planning*: This item refers to strategies related to planning including: (1) how institutional consultation with stakeholder groups should be undertaken; (2) the scope of the OER initiative; (3) the institutional purpose of having an OER project; (4) identifying the champions within the institution; and (5) developing dedicated OER policies.

Policies Recommendations for Higher Education Institutions

Another aspect of the Feasibility Protocol was drawn from the analysis of the online publicly available Intellectual Property (IP) policies of Australian universities to determine how these documents address the ownership of course content and educational resources created and developed by their employees (Scott, 2014). This investigation evaluated the scope of these policies and assessed the extent to which they currently support universities and their staff to engage in the development, release, and promotion of OER. As an attempt to initiate discussions and promote solutions, some questions and issues related to university intellectual property and copyright policies are of significance.

Universities wanting to encourage their staff (academic or professional) to engage with OER and OEP, or release existing content under open content licencing, should consider the following recommendations:

- align the desire to encourage OER adoption with current university policy;
- establish employment contracts and reward mechanisms which support the development of content for OER;
- create mechanisms to verify that university content intended for OER release is not already subject to a university commercialisation or other agreements;
- develop guidelines to assist the university employee to make decisions regarding the type of open licences available and under which open licence university developed OER should be badged;
- create university guidelines and processes to ensure that issues of quality and copyright compliance are addressed;
- carefully consider where the university will host OER. Or, alternatively, consider whether the resources might be included in a public repository of OER.

Institutions are understandably concerned when new directions, particularly those as significant and potentially far-reaching as OER. After all, they have the potential to impact upon traditional models of operation and create risks to established practices. Among the Feasibility Protocol's recommendations for risk management strategies at organisational levels are:

- to consider how the university will manage any disputes that may arise about the ownership of the resources;
- to develop policies that address how the institution will respond if it identifies that the resources are being used inappropriately;
- to identify who will carry liability for copyright infringement in university-generated OER—the individual or the university; and
- to build capacity to ensure employees developing OER are aware of the intellectual property and copyright considerations.

Conclusions and Further Remarks

As the demand for openness has grown across all sectors of higher education, OER, OEP and other forms of open education, including MOOCs, have been receiving increasing global attention. Despite some important Australian initiatives, the absence of explicit government policies and incentives appear to be limiting the adoption of OER and OEP in Australia. To date, there have been few internal institutional strategies and policy enablers to encourage universities to pursue OER initiatives to better support current students, attract new ones, and compete against as well as collaborate with other Australian and international institutions. One example of an enabler is the *Technology Enhanced Learning and Teaching White Paper 2014–2018*, developed by the Tasmanian Institute of Learning and Teaching, University of Tasmania (Brown et al., 2013). Thoughtfully designed institutional strategies, as detailed in this particular white paper, can facilitate an organisation's realisation of the full potential of OER and OEP and place Australia amongst the leading countries in this field.

We believe that the Feasibility Protocol is a valuable instrument that could encourage the Australian higher education sector to further develop OER and OEP and be on a par with developments taking place elsewhere. We also believe that this instrument could assist senior executives to make decisions regarding the adoption of OER and OEP, including the issues and questions that they should consider regarding the opportunities, challenges, and strategic directions involving OER. The Feasibility Protocol also prompts questions on highly practical issues related to institutional intellectual property and copyright policies while adopting OER.

Nevertheless, we would like to call attention to the fact that the Feasibility Protocol is not a rigid instrument. Unlike other such frameworks, it can be adapted, changed, and further developed to meet individual university needs. We are well aware that each higher education institution or organisation has unique structures, agendas, cultures, and strategic plans for future and current activities. Ultimately, the usefulness of the Feasibility Protocol will depend on individual institutions and the way that their senior executives make use of it.

Carina Bossu is a lecturer, Learning and Teaching (OEP) with the Tasmanian Institute of Learning and Teaching, at the University of Tasmania, Australia. Her current work and research are primarily focused on Open Educational Resources (OER) and Open Educational Practices (OEP) in higher education; more specifically, she is exploring issues related to learning, teaching, and professional development. Bossu has presented and published widely and is currently involved in several research projects investigating different aspects of OER and OEP in higher education. Contact Carina at carina.bossu@gmail.com.

David Bull is currently the Director of the Open Access College at the University of Southern Queensland. His research interests lie primarily with issues related to equity and access policy in higher education and preparatory program curriculum development. He has extensive teaching and consultancy experience primarily associated with aspects of student diversity in higher education. More recently he has been involved with the "open agenda," pursuing Open Educational Resources (OER) and Open Educational Practices (OEP) activities, supporting the work of the Open Educational Resources university (OERu), and advocating for the widespread adoption of open practices for the delivery of higher education.

Mark Brown is Director of the National Institute for Digital Learning based at Dublin City University (DCU). Before taking up Ireland's first Chair in Digital Learning at the beginning of 2014, Mark was previously Director of both the National Centre for Teaching and Learning and the Distance Education and Learning Futures Alliance (DELFA) at Massey University, New Zealand. Mark has played key leadership roles in the implementation of several major university-wide digital learning and teaching initiatives, including the enterprise-wide deployment of Moodle, the original design and development of the Mahara eportfolio system, and the university-wide implementation of a Massive Open Online Course (MOOC) platform.

References

Atkins, D.E., Brown, J.S., & Hammond, A.L. (2007). *A review of the open educational resources (OER) movement: Achievements, challenges, and new opportunities*. Menlo Park, California: William and Flora Hewlett Foundation. Retrieved from http://www. hewlett.org/uploads/files/ReviewoftheOERMovement.pdf.

Bossu, C., Brown, M., & Bull, D. (2011). Playing catch-up: Investigating public and institutional policies for OER practices in Australia. *The Journal of Open, Flexible and Distance Learning, 15*(2), 41–54.

Bossu, C., Brown, M., & Bull, D. (2012, November). *Do open educational resources represent additional challenges or advantages to the current climate of change in the Australian higher education sector?* Paper presented at the Australasian Society for Computer in Learning in Tertiary Education Conference: Future Challenges | Sustainable Future, Wellington, NZ.

Bossu, C., Brown, M., & Bull, D. (2014a). *Adoption, use and management of Open Educational Resources to enhance teaching and learning in Australia.* Sydney: Australian Government Office for Learning and Teaching. Retrieved from http://www.olt.gov.au/system/files/resources/CG10_1687_Bossu_Report_2014.pdf.

Bossu, C., Brown, M., & Bull, D. (2014b). *Feasibility Protocol for OER and OEP: A decision making tool for higher education.* Sydney: Australian Government Office for Learning and Teaching. Retrieved from www.olt.gov.au/system/files/resources/CG10_1687_Bossu_Feasibility%20Protocol_2014.pdf.

Bossu, C., Bull, D., & Brown, M. (2012). Opening up down under: The role of open educational resources in promoting social inclusion in Australia. *Distance Education, 33*(2), 151–164. doi: 10.1080/01587919.2012.692050.

Bradley, D., Noonan, P., Nugent, H., & Scales, B. (2008). *Review of Australian Higher Education: Final Report.* Canberra, Australian Government.

Brown, N., Kregor, G., Williams, G., Padgett, L., Bossu, C., Warren, V., & Osborne, J. (2013). *Technology enhanced learning and teaching white paper* 2014–2018 (Tasmanian Institute of Learning and Teaching, Trans.). Hobart: University of Tasmania.

Butcher, N., & Hoosen, S. (2014). A guide to quality in post-traditional online higher education. In J. Daniel & S. Uvalic´-Trumbic´ (Eds.). Dallas: Academic Partnerships. Retrieved from http://www.academicpartnerships.com/sites/default/files/Guide-Online HigherEd.PDF.

Caswell, T., Henson, S., Jensen, M., & Wiley, D. (2008). Open educational resources: Enabling universal education. *International Review of Research in Open and Distance Learning, 9*(1), 1–4.

Downes, S. (2007). Models for sustainable Open Educational Resources. *Interdisciplinary Journal of Knowledge and Learning Objects, 3*, 29–44.

Ehlers, U.-D. (2011). From open educational resources to open educational practices. *eLearning Papers, 23.*

Kanwar, A., Kodhandaraman, B., & Umar, A. (2010). Toward sustainable open education resources: A perspective from the global south. *American Journal of Distance Education, 24*(2), 65–80. doi: 10.1080/08923641003696588.

Kelly, A. (2014). Disruptor, distracter, or what? A policymaker's guide to massive open online courses (MOOCs). *Bellwether Education Partners* from http://bellwethereduca tion.org/sites/default/files/BW_MOOC_Final.pdf.

OER Foundation. (2011). *OER Foundation FAQs—What are OERs?* Retrieved from http://wikieducator.org/WikiEducator:OER_Foundation/FAQs/Open_Education_ Resources/.

Open Education Quality Initiative. (2011). *Beyond OER: Shifting focus to open educational practices: Open Education Quality Initiative (OPAL).* Retrieved from https://oerknowl-edgecloud.org/sites/oerknowledgecloud.org/files/OPAL2011.pdf.

Organisation for Economic Co-operation and Development. (2007). *Giving knowledge for free: The emergence of open educational resources.* Paris: Centre for Educational Research and Innovation. Retrieved from http://www.oecd.org/dataoecd/35/7/38654317.pdf.

Scott, B. (2014). *Supporting OER engagement at Australian Universities: An overview of the intellectual property rights, copyright and policy considerations for OER.* Sydney: Australian Government Office for Learning and Teaching. Retrieved from www.olt.gov.au/system/files/resources/CG10_1687_Bossu_OER%20engagement_2014.pdf.

Smith, M. (2013). Ruminations on research on open educational resources. *William and Flora Hewlett Foundation.* Retrieved from http://www.hewlett.org/sites/default/files/OER%20Research%20paper%20December%2015%202013%20Marshall%20Smith_1.pdf (accessed 4 April 2014).

The William and Flora Hewlett Foundation. (2013). White Paper: Open educational resources—Breaking the lockbox on education (pp. 33). *The William and Flora Hewlett Foundation.* Retrieved from http://www.hewlett.org/sites/default/files/OER%20White%20Paper%20Nov%2022%202013%20Final.pdf.

UNESCO. (2002). *Forum on the Impact of open courseware for higher education in developing countries. Final Report.* Paper presented at the Forum on the Impact of Open Courseware for Higher Education in Developing Countries. UNESCO, Paris, July 1–3.

Wiley, D., & Gurrell, S. (2009). A decade of development. *Open Learning: The Journal of Open, Distance and e-Learning, 24*(1), 11–21. doi: 10.1080/02680510802627746.

6

OPEN EDUCATION AT THE UNIVERSITY OF CAPE TOWN

Laura Czerniewicz, Glenda Cox, Cheryl Hodgkinson-Williams, and Michelle Willmers

Introduction

The open education agenda at the University of Cape Town (UCT) has been framed holistically: open education resources (OER) have been a central part of a networked vision which has seen them closely aligned with open access, open research, open data, and other open practices. Unlike certain universities, where the open mission was driven from the highest echelons, at UCT the original impetus came from the middle levels of the institution, in the Centre for Educational Technology. Since the earliest foray into the terrain, a broad view of openness has located the scholar at the center of relationships with other scholars, with students, and with the community beyond the university. This vision has been sustained, despite taking circuitous routes, some of which were determined by the availability of funding. Along the journey of the last eight years since 2007 (see Figure 6.1), partnerships have been forged, committees have been negotiated, a policy has been approved, and a sustainable way forward for open education and open scholarship at the university has been mapped.

The very first "open" project in the Centre for Educational Technology (CET), Opening Scholarship (http://www.cet.uct.ac.za/OpeningScholarship), acknowledged that open activities were already taking place at UCT and brought these into focus by producing twelve case studies from the university, four of which focused on research dissemination, five on teaching and learning, and three on social responsiveness. These institutional reports, together with national and international scans, various seminars, and conference papers, demonstrated the extent of existing activities and identified areas of potential activity going forward. Initially funded in 2007 by the Shuttleworth Foundation, a significant role-player in supporting open activity at UCT, this project led to a decision to build a directory of OER created by UCT staff and students.

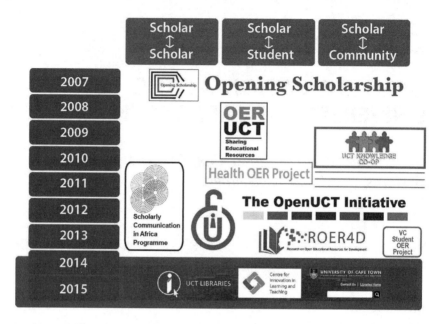

FIGURE 6.1 The openness journey at the University of Cape Town (UCT)

Funded again by Shuttleworth for 2008/9, the OER UCT project work has continued up to the time of writing; when funding ended, some of the work became part of a CET staff member's job description. The initial funding provided the capacity to work with academics in stimulating the development of OER, to navigate licensing, and to curate content. It was also instrumental in surfacing the underground network of open "champions," committed academics whose sharing practice often predated the Internet. In the course of this initiative, a nascent community and a very granular approach to sharing emerged—the model being one of sharing scholarly "objects" rather than solely modules or coursework. While this granular sharing strategy was an unusual approach at the time, there was an authentic desire to share on the part of academics. Such genuine sharing resulted in a wide array of objects being made available under the auspices of OER, but what was essentially open scholarship more broadly.

Outside of the Centre for Higher Education Development, the UCT Faculty of Health Sciences in 2009 became one of eight partners involved in the formation of the African Health OER Network, co-facilitated by OER Africa and the University of Michigan. Funded by the William and Flora Hewlett Foundation, the network provided resources for the conversion of teaching resources to OER. Since the funding ended, the OER health work within the UCT has been incorporated into the work of the Education Development Unit. Fortunately, such work continues unabated today.

The OpenUCT Initiative (OUI), founded in 2011 with a grant from the Andrew Mellon Foundation, was in a sense the culmination of all the open initiatives that preceded it. The extent to which it was a cross-university project is indicated through its structure as a Special Project in the Office of the Dean of the Centre for Higher Education Development (CHED), with a reporting line to the Deputy Vice Chancellor for Research as well as to the Deputy Vice Chancellor for Teaching and Learning. The OUI engaged intensively with both the academic community and university management, operating as a key intermediary in navigating the path to institutionalised open sharing practice. Exploring the continuum between open education and open research, it conceptualised and developed the OpenUCT institutional repository, which has been scoped as a dynamic sharing environment created to reflect and make available the wealth of scholarship produced at UCT.

Effectively a small project-within-a-project using grant funding, the OpenUCT and the OER teams have run a small grants programme whereby academics could apply and use funds to buy in student help or other expertise in order to prepare existing materials or create new materials to share as OER. These very small grants, each of less than $1,000, have proved an effective mechanism for converting resources to open licenses. Through the issuance of 64 grants in a three-year period, they have enabled dozens of educators to share their teaching beyond the limitations of their classrooms.

In 2013, another effective small project saw funding from the Vice Chancellor's Strategic Fund given to employ students to assist academics in adapting their teaching materials for sharing as OER. This project places student facilitators within each of the faculties and tasks them with identifying good teaching resources which would be valuable to OER. The outputs here have ranged in type and discipline and provided rich bottom-up resources known to be excellent in practice.

As open scholarship aligned with the open education work, the 2010 Scholarly Communication in Africa Programme (SCAP) (http://www.scaprogramme.org.za), funded by the International Development Research Centre (IDRC), must be included in this review because of its support for open approaches. In addition, the intersection of research and teaching was evident in its work, which focused on infrastructure development and the investigation of scholars' practices. The programme operated at the nexus of research and educational technologies—the two areas united by the imperative to curate, archive, and share open content beyond traditional research outputs via platforms that are interoperable and sustainable in the long term.

One of the most recent initiatives is the "Research into OERs for Development" (http://roer4d.org/) initiative hosted by the Centre for Innovation on Learning and Teaching (CILT) and launched in 2013. Funded by the IDRC and UKAid, this project aims to provide evidence-based research from a number of countries in South America, Sub-Saharan Africa, and Southeast Asia with the primary

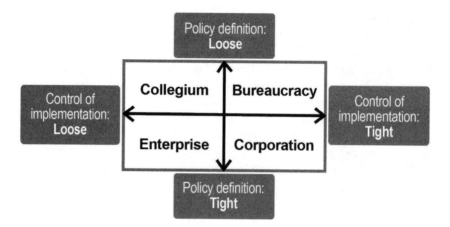

FIGURE 6.2 McNay's taxonomy of institutional cultures

objective of improving educational policy, practice, and research in developing countries through a better understanding of the use and impact of OER.

Assumptions and Approaches

Assumptions

While the work described above may seem ad hoc or organic in its manifestation, it has all been underpinned by a shared set of assumptions and values, based on an understanding of the culture in which open education practices are to be inculcated. The University of Cape Town is typical of many research universities falling neatly into what McNay (1995) describes as the collegium (see Figure 6.2).

This type of organisation is characterised by a loose institutional policy definition, informal networks, and departmental/individual decision-making and innovation. The organisational response is "laissez faire" with few targeted policies or processes (Rossiter, 2007). In effect, the core value of collegium is autonomy with organisational expectations being defined in terms of freedom from external controls (Yee-Tak, 2006).

This understanding has transferred into approaches to building open education at the university by taking the time to make arguments and negotiate genuine buy-in. While slower in the short term, in the long term, ownership means that academic practices change in a sustained way. This approach is also aligned with the notions of academic freedom and academic agency. In addition, it translates into systems which allow and enable maximum individual control. Linked to this is the principle of maximum flexibility which sees the types of resources to be shared as dynamic and as granular as possible. Rather than being regulatory and restrictive, the intention has been to create as enabling and seamless an environment as possible, minimising fuss and bureaucracy, while still maintaining standards which would ensure maximum preservation and discoverability.

Advocacy activities have, therefore, been critical to networks and communities within and across disciplines. Such activities, naturally, also provide spaces for OER champions to influence their colleagues. Workshops and seminars have been conducted on demand (e.g., a request from a department or special interest group) and have been woven into existing staff development activities through faculty structures and existing programmes. In the Health Sciences, for example, presentations are given in individual departments to advance an understanding of OER among educators. The first-year students, for example, learn about OER in workshops. In addition, increased opportunities to solicit resources where possible occur during key events like the Global Open Education Week (held annually in March) and Open Access Week (held annually in October).

Various forms of social media have been used to create a presence and awareness of the OpenContent directory at UCT. The OpenUCT website (http://openuct.uct.ac.za) includes a blog about everything open, including OER and OpenContent. An OpenUCT Twitter account is used to promote new content added to the directory or share interesting links and news related to the OER movement. Certain content posted to Twitter has also found its way into Facebook, which seems to indicate that some of the content has gone viral on a small scale. Conference presentations made available on Slideshare indicate added interest through impressive views and downloads.

International representation is also used as a way to profile UCT OpenContent with UCT an active member of the global Open Education Consortium (OEC), and members of the UCT OpenContent team attending and presenting at conferences hosted by the consortium.

Evolving e-Infrastructure, Evolving Practice

The Open Content Directory

On February 12, 2010, the UCT OpenContent directory (http://opencontent.uct.ac.za) was launched with six resources contributed by UCT academics. By June 2014, ongoing advocacy had resulted in 343 resources being added to the OpenContent directory. Of these, 91 resources were added during 2013; substantially more than in the previous years (2012: 59 resources; 2011: 73 resources). A word of caution is required regarding these numbers, however: although the directory might officially contain approximately 350 resources, some of these resources are complex, consisting of multiple downloadable documents—these granular resources amount to well over 1,000 downloadable items. With the principle of maximum flexibility in place, a diversity of content types has been accepted in various forms, including PowerPoint presentations, PDFs, and electronic books, and a large collection of podcasts, webpages, and videos having also been added.

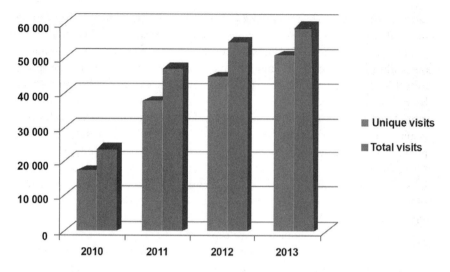

FIGURE 6.3 Growth trajectory of visits to the OpenContent directory (2010–2013)

In terms of contributions by the various faculties, Humanities is the top contributor, with 93 resources; this is followed by 87 from the Centre for Higher Education Development, and 81 resources from the Faculty of Health Science.

Overall site visits have increased steadily since 2010. In fact, the total number of site visits reached 220,000 in June 2014. The location of total site visitors also changed over this period—from just over 50 percent coming from South Africa in 2012 to ~41 percent in 2013, indicating a growing international audience for UCT's OpenContent. As shown in Figure 6.3, the number of visits and unique visits has increased every year.

Especially exciting has been the recognition received in various forms. For instance, two UCT academics (Matumo Ramafikeng and Gina Ziervogel) have been the recipients of awards for excellence in OpenCourseware in the face of hundreds of other nominations. And in 2014, a UCT academic and practicing General Surgeon, Juan Klopper received a prestigious award for individual excellence and contribution to open education. A more indirect form of recognition arose from an opportunistic synergy of an OER developed for a series of Occupational Therapy lectures being identified as a suitable journal article (Ramafikeng, 2013). This latter example was a pleasing illustration of the emergent possibilities that arise out of the "open movement" in general and the potential overlap between OER and Open Access in particular.

From OER to Open Scholarship

Throughout all the years of OER activity at UCT, there was an implicit ambition to incorporate the OER collection as a foundational component of the new repository content. An additional goal has been to continually grow open scholarship practice by utilising the new OpenUCT platform as a means to upscale the curation and preservation of resources. The OpenContent directory was the principal platform for accessing open scholarship from UCT in the period February 2010 to July 2014. At that point, all the content contained in the directory was transitioned to the OpenUCT repository. The strategy of moving away from a directory-type platform to an institutional repository infrastructure was in line with the imperative to institutionalise the ownership of the e-infrastructure, ramp up the curation of resources, take steps to ensure the long-term preservation of content, and promote the role of the institution as publisher or disseminator of its own content.

The new OpenUCT repository, launched in July 2014, is a customised open source repository software instance that allows for the integrated management of research and educational resources. Its manifestation comes at a time not only of great change in global practice, but also at a time of great change in local governance structures and systems. Key stakeholders such as UCT Libraries, the Research Office and Information, the Centre for Innovation on Learning and Teaching (CILT), and Communication Technology Services (ICTS) are all being challenged to transform rapidly and stay abreast with the latest technologies and international developments in content sharing. This pressure is intensified by the need for the institution to stay relevant, competitive, and visible in the increasingly competitive higher education environment.

It is intended that the OpenUCT repository will not only enable the sharing of UCT scholarship with the world, but will also promote open education practice within the institution. While it is anticipated that many of the resources generated and shared will have application across the fields of research, teaching and learning, and community engagement, specific provisions have been made to be able to describe, search by, and harvest teaching- and learning-oriented content. It is envisioned that as e-infrastructure evolves, teaching and learning practices will too. The challenge for the OER agenda will be to ensure that it continues to enjoy equal curatorial representation in the institutional context, which is strongly biased towards research as far as formal systems and reward mechanisms are concerned.

A Research-Based Understanding

In addition to infrastructural development or advocacy work, there has always been a parallel commitment to research. Chief among those research interests was determining how OER was playing out at UCT—especially in a policy vacuum that lasted until June 2014. Encouraging master's students to focus their dissertations on OER uptake issues was one successful strategy. At the time of this writing, four students in the MEd Information Communication Technology programme had undertaken (or were undertaking) relevant research. In particular, they were examining: (1) student perceptions of the reuse of digital educational materials; (2) the adoption of open Mathematics and Science textbooks; (3) the reasons UCT academics had decided to contribute to the OpenContent directory, and (4) the success of the UCT Vice Chancellor's OER adaptation project in its stated goals of supporting lecturers in sharing their teaching and learning materials with the help of student facilitators. In addition, doctoral students have been directed to investigate some of the more tricky theoretical explanations for the adoption or non-adoption of OER.

Other strategies entail encouraging institutional research on OER at UCT as well as inter-institutional OER research with UCT and its OER partners. One institutionally-focused study investigated the role of senior students in adapting teaching and learning materials as OER (Hodgkinson-Williams & Paskevicius, 2012a, 2012b, 2013). Based on the Health OER Inter-Institutional Project (with Ghana and Michigan), one study documented the growth of OER in the Faculty of Health Sciences (Mawoyo, 2012), another posited a sustainable inter-institutional collaborative framework for OER (Ng'ambi & Luo, 2013) and a third generated understandings on initiating and sustaining OER in African contexts (Harley, 2011). A cross-institutional survey showed that the majority of UCT students were overwhelmingly positive about using OER (Hardin, Hodgkinson-Williams, & Cox, 2011).

Finally, UCT has joined and is playing a central role in a Global South research study on the adoption and impact of OER in educational institutions in South America, Sub-Saharan Africa, and South East Asia (ROER4D). Still in its inception phase, this ambitious project aims to provide in-depth analysis of OER creation, awareness, use, and distribution across all three regions through a combination of regional surveys, case studies, and action research studies (Hodgkinson-Williams & Arinto, 2014).

Policy Engagement

Over the past few years, the university's senior echelons have made important symbolic commitments to the open agenda. In 2008, a Deputy Vice Chancellor signed the Cape Town Open Education Declaration which drew extensive media attention. This declaration was built on "the belief that everyone should have the freedom to use, customize, improve and redistribute educational resources without constraint." Three years later, the UCT Vice Chancellor signed the Berlin Declaration which sought "to realize the vision of a global and accessible representation of knowledge [where] the future Web has to be sustainable, interactive, and transparent."

In 2014, two events marked the culmination of this organic era of change and growth: (1) the approval by UCT Council of an Open Access Policy (available at http://uct.ac.za/downloads/uct.ac.za/about/policies/UCTOpenAccessPolicy. pdf) and (2) the commitment of UCT Libraries to being the home for open online content going forward. In terms of the latter, many open education and open access project activities are becoming mainstreamed into existing and new positions in the library. Such activities are not too surprising given that the UCT library has been quite explicit in its support of both research and teaching resources. In fact, the UCT library is the formal owner of the Open Access Policy, working closely with UCT's Research Office and the Centre for Innovation in Learning and Teaching.

The policy foundation for an ongoing emphasis on open education resources is evident in the new policy which notes: "The widespread availability of open education resources, open content, open courses, etc. from the global north is both an opportunity and a concern as there is an equally urgent need for local teaching and learning resources to be made freely available online."

Scholarship is understood to take multiple forms which cut across research, teaching, and learning. UCT not only encourages that all of these be made available, it also provides the enabling conditions for the stewardship, preservation, and discoverability of this content. More specifically, the policy states that "The University encourages Employees and Students to make all forms of works of scholarship available . . . This includes (but is not limited to) essays, books, conference papers, reports (where permitted by a funder of the research leading to the report), educational resources, presentations, scholarly multi-media material, audio-visual works and digital representations of pictorial and graphical materials."

In the more common fashion of open access policies around the world, the policy requires UCT authors to deposit journal articles. At the time, students are now required to deposit the final versions of their theses and dissertations in order to graduate. It is this high-profile inclusion of and support for open educational resources that distinguishes the policy from that of other institutions and organisations.

Going Forward

After seven years of project-based activities and ad hoc individual activities by academics quietly getting on with good work, the University of Cape Town's work in open education has culminated in an open access policy that supports open education broadly and the mainstreaming of open education in the university library. This is the realisation of the vision expressed eight years ago in the Opening Scholarship project; a vision which sought to find ways of grappling with granular, composite content of all kinds (including research and teaching) and of ensuring sustainability while integrating with institutional infrastructure.

The open education agenda at UCT has come full circle. At the same time, it is a new beginning—one which will see open education and OER having to assert themselves and stay on an institutional agenda which now includes the rise of open data and research data management as well as a nascent open research agenda.

The mainstreaming of this open education movement and the series of OER and open scholarship initiatives within UCT bodes well in terms of sustainability, particularly as the OER approach aligns neatly with a granular, semantic future.

Dangers exist in the forms of enterprise content management and research management systems that do not integrate teaching components. Such emerging systems amplify the ongoing tensions regarding the value and legitimacy of teaching in research-intensive universities. The contradictions are ongoing, just as they are in universities throughout the world. Even though the initial policy battles have been won, transforming policy intentions into practice is never straightforward. That said, the solid work of the last decade at the university augurs well for the scalability and sustainability of open education at the University of Cape Town for the foreseeable future.

 **Laura Czerniewicz,** researcher, educator, advocate, and strategist, is Associate Professor and the Director of the University of Cape Town's Centre for Innovation in Learning and Teaching (CILT). In addition, she recently headed the university's OpenUCT initiative. Having previously worked in educational publishing, Professor Czerniewicz was the founding director of the Centre for Educational Technology. She has research interests in student and academic digitally-mediated practices, in open education and scholarship, and in learning technology as a field.

 Glenda Cox is a lecturer in the Centre for Educational at the University of Cape Town. Glenda Cox's portfolio includes: curriculum projects, "Teaching with Technology" innovation grants, open education resources, and staff development. Her key research area related to identifying why academic staff choose to share or not share their teaching resources as open educational resources. One of her main passions involves uncovering the innovative ways staff incorporate technology into their teaching. She believes that showcasing staff at the University of Cape Town who are excellent teachers is of great importance, both in traditional face-to-face classrooms and in the online world.

 Cheryl Hodgkinson-Williams is an Associate Professor in the Centre for Innovation in Learning and Teaching (CILT) at the University of Cape Town (UCT), South Africa. She holds a PhD in computer-assisted learning and has taught and supervised in the field of information communication technologies (ICTs) in education since 1998. Her particular research interests include online learning design, electronic portfolios, open education, the adoption and impact of open educational resources (OER), and massive open online courses (MOOCs). She is Principal Investigator of the IDRC-funded international Research on OER in the Global South (ROER4D) project.

 **Michelle Willmers** has a background in academic and scholarly publishing. She was previously a senior team member in the Shuttleworth Foundation OER UCT initiative. She was also programme manager of the IDRC Scholarly Communication in Africa Programme (SCAP), a four-country research and publishing initiative aimed at increasing the visibility of African research. She is currently the project manager of the OpenUCT initiative.

References

Cartmill, E.T. (2013). *Viewing the use of open educational resources through a community of practice lens: A case study of teachers' use of the Everything Maths and Everything Science open textbooks.* Unpublished MPhil minor dissertation, University of Cape Town. Retrieved from http://uctscholar.uct.ac.za/PDF/98798_Cartmill_ET.pdf.

Cox, G. (2013, December 8). *A model of the interplay between academic agency, institutional structure and open culture in the contribution and non contribution of Open Educational resources.* PhD research presentation GO-GN seminar in Cape Town. Retrieved from http://www.slideshare.net/GO-GN/ph-d-proposal-presentation-cape-townglencox.

Czerniewicz, L., Cox, G., Hodgkinson-Williams, C.A., & Doyle, G. (2012). *From project to mainstreamed in a constrained environment: Towards openness at the University of Cape Town.* Cambridge OCW Conference, April 16–18. Retrieved from http://www.slideshare.net/laura_Cz/openness-at-the-university-of-cape-town.

Hardin, J., Hodgkinson-Williams, C.A., & Cox, G. (2011). *OCW use and production by faculty and students: An inter-institutional comparison.* OCWC Conference, Cambridge Massachusetts, May 4–6, 2011. Retrieved from http://www-personal.umich.edu/~hardin/Talks/OCWC2011/OCWC2011-V0.5.pdf.

Harley, K. (2011). Insights from the Health OER Inter-Institutional Project. *Distance Education, 32*(2), 213–27.

Hodgkinson-Williams, C.A., & Paskevicius, M. (2012a). The role of postgraduate students in co-authoring open educational resources to promote social inclusion: A case study at the University of Cape Town. *Distance Education, 33*(2), 253–69.

Hodgkinson-Williams, C.A., & Paskevicius, M. (2012b). Framework to understand postgraduate students' adaption of academics' teaching materials as OER. In A. Okada (Ed.), *Open educational resources and social networks: Co-learning and professional development.* London: Scholio Educational Research & Publishing.

Hodgkinson-Williams, C.A., & Paskevicius, M. (2013). "It's not their job to share content": A case study of the role of senior students in adapting teaching and learning materials as open educational resources at the University of Cape Town. *E-Learning and Digital Media, 10*(2), 135–47. Retrieved from http://dx.doi.org/10.2304/elea.2013.10.2.135.

Hodgkinson-Williams, C.A., & Arinto, P. (2014). *Open education for a multicultural world: A report from the Research on Open Educational Resources for Development (ROER4D) project in the Global South.* OCWC 2014 Conference, Ljubljana,

Slovenia, April 25, 2014. Retrieved from http://www.slideshare.net/ROER4D/roer4-d-hodgkinson-williams-arinto-ocwc-2014-33930519.

Mawoyo, M. (2012). *Growing an institutional health OER initiative: A case study of the University of Cape Town.* Regents of the University of Michigan and Saide. Retrieved from http://www.oerafrica.org/resource/growing-institutional-health-oer-initiative-case-study-university-cape-town.

McNay, I. (1995). From collegial academy to corporate enterprise: The changing cultures of universities. In T. Schuller (Ed.) *The changing university.* Buckingham: Society for Research into Higher Education and Open University Press.

Ng'ambi, D., & Luo, A. (2013). Towards a sustainable inter-institutional collaborative framework for open educational resources (OER). In R. McGreal, W. Kinuthia, & S. Marshall (Eds). *Open educational resources: Innovation, research and practice* (pp. 223–39). Commonwealth of Learning, Athabasca University. Retrieved from https://oer-knowledgecloud.org/sites/oerknowledgecloud.org/files/pub_PS_OER-IRP_web.pdf#page=249.

Paskevicius, M. (2011). *Student perceptions of the reuse of digital educational materials: A case study of the social outreach group SHAWCO.* Unpublished MPhil minor dissertation, University of Cape Town. Retrieved from http://uctscholar.uct.ac.za:1801/webclient/StreamGate?folder_id=0&dvs=1405127427526~602.

Ramafikeng, M. (2013). *True stories of open sharing: From Cape Town OER to Spanish journal article, Matumo Ramafikeng.* Video interview. Retrieved from http://stories.cogdogblog.com/oer-to-journal/.

Rossiter, D. (2007). Whither e-learning? Conceptions of change and innovation in higher education. *Journal of Organisational Transformation and Social Change, 4*(1), 93–107.

Yee-Tak, W. (2006). *Student expectations in the new millennium: An explorative study of higher education in Hong Kong.* Unpublished Dissertation, Ludwig-Maximilians-Universität, Munich, Germany.

PART 3

Researching and Evaluating Notions of MOOCs and Openness

In any emerging field or discipline, a refrain commonly heard is "What does the research say?" Such interest in the research is especially germane when in the midst of a potentially paradigm-changing revolution or transformation such as the one in which we presently find ourselves in relation to MOOCs and open education. Consequently, in the third part of this book, several research and evaluation chapters are presented that attempt to provide insights into the effectiveness of MOOCs and open education.

The first chapter in this section, from Markus Deimann, Alexander Lipka, and Theo Bastiaens at FernUniversität in Hagen, Germany, encourages reflection on the history of distance education and what it offers to those advocating or utilizing MOOCs. The authors link the comparatively recent discourse on MOOCs to the much older and richer theoretical tradition of distance education. As they appropriately point out, to date, the research and practice on distance education has received scant attention from MOOC researchers even though there is a rich history that can be tapped into to enhance the efficiency and results of MOOC initiatives. Deimann, Lipka, and Bastiaens also illustrate how MOOCs can be utilized within a distance education ecosystem. To that end, these authors present data-based comparisons of a traditional distance education course and two different types of MOOCs offered recently by their university in Germany. Finally, they discuss what those advocating MOOCs can learn from distance education and offer several useful instructional recommendations.

Anyone interested in alternatives to edX, Coursera, NovoEd, Udemy, Udacity, and other North American MOOC providers can turn to Chapter 8. In this chapter, Hartnett, Brown, and Wilson team up to explore a MOOC-related venture call Open2Study developed by Open Universities Australia (OUA) (see https://www.open2study.com/). These researchers report lessons from the design, implementation, and evaluation of Open2Study at Massey University. Not only is this MOOC venture unique, but in 2013, Massey was New Zealand's first university to adopt an enterprise-wide MOOC platform. The authors explain why Massey University decided to enter the MOOC space while simultaneously outlining some of the distinguishing features of Open2Study. This chapter reports lessons learned from the experience "down under" and concludes with a number of questions relevant to the wider international context and the future of the MOOC movement as a whole.

In the third and final chapter of this part, researchers from the University of Edinburgh provide an overview of their MOOC endeavors since they first entered the fray back in 2012. At first, Jeff Haywood, Amy Woodgate, and David Dewhurst discuss the decision to be the first university in the UK to venture into MOOCs when they partnered with Coursera back in 2012. Given that the University of Edinburgh is now the largest MOOC provider in the UK, with over one million enrollments, it was simultaneously a bold and a successful move. In terms of quality, the University of Edinburgh took a centrally coordinated approach to course design and development, with strong technical, pedagogical, and financial support for academic teams. These efforts were backed up by formal course approval and quality assurance processes. Accordingly, they have gathered consistent longitudinal data about their MOOC participants and the associated learning and retention outcomes. This ongoing research and evaluation effort is helping the University of Edinburgh understand how to design and implement their MOOC efforts as well as to develop MOOCs in collaboration with other universities. In the end, this chapter focuses on the potential benefits MOOCs can bring to a university, and the kinds of return on investment that they can deliver.

7

STRANGE BEDFELLOWS?!

What Can MOOCs Learn from Distance Education?

Markus Deimann, Alexander Lipka, and Theo Bastiaens

The explosion of Massive Open Online Courses (MOOCs) in 2012 represents a landmark case in the history of educational technology because never before has there been so much interest by political, economical, and educational stakeholders. Many major media outlets have accompanied the emergence of MOOCs and contributed to the hype by coining catchphrases such as "The Campus Tsunami" (Brooks, 2012).

However, such claims should be put into perspective. In fact, as the title of this chapter suggests, MOOCs are closely linked to the distance education (DE) community. Interestingly, the English Wikipedia article on "distance education" refers to MOOCs as "a recent development in distance education" (Wikipedia, 2014). Some scholars argue that MOOCs do nothing more than to reinforce old beliefs about what it means to reach and teach the masses. By contrast, DE has built a reputation dating back to the 18th century with many different learning approaches being tested. Over the centuries, such research and experimentation has resulted in a huge body of knowledge on how people learn in this special setting (Moore & Kearsley, 1996).

While for the past five years, the emergence of MOOCs has arrived on the general educational landscape with much fanfare and impact, DE has surprisingly been completely excluded from the general conversation. Unfortunately, the MOOC debate mostly takes place outside of DE. It can be considered as a development of face-to-face teaching universities discovering the world of mass education at a distance. Therefore, there has not as yet been a systematic investigation concerning the potential of DE models and practices for MOOCs. It is the purpose of the present chapter to bring about an informed conversation between these two "strange bedfellows."

In what follows, we first review DE with regard to the factors that have contributed to its constitution as an academic discipline. In the second part, we will discuss how MOOCs can be utilized within a DE ecosystem and present empirical data from: (1) a traditional DE course at the FernUniversität in Hagen, Germany, and (2) two MOOCs offered by the same university. Finally, we will discuss what those advocating, developing, or evaluating MOOCs can learn from DE.

Introduction: MOOCs Invading the Territory of Distance Education

Much of what occurred in the aftermath of opening up traditional courses at Ivy League colleges in the United States to the "world" could leave the DE community cold given the catchy headlines of mass media. Furthermore, the MOOC approach is based on a rather reductionist understanding of the role that technology can play in education, i.e., digital technologies are perceived as neutral instruments that can fulfill any educational goal because they are totally in the power of the user (Hamilton & Friesen, 2013). A striking example for this kind of instrumentalism is Peter Norvig's TED talk on "The 100,000 student classroom" in which he argues that "while the subject matter of the class is advanced and modern, the teaching technology isn't" (Norvig, 2012). Norvig then goes on to claim that technology is able to emulate the pedagogical principle of one-on-one tutoring without acknowledging the "hidden production of technology" (Knox, 2013), i.e., the complex ways of how technology is produced and used, some aspects of which may not always benefit the learning process.

In contrast to the "revolutionary" emergence of MOOCs, DE has seen an evolutionary progress from its very beginning in the mid-19th century which has given rise to the development of different models and conceptualizations—yet one factor has remained constant: "Adult, distance, and continuing educators have always led the movement to take education to the student rather than requiring the student to come to the education" (Hoskins, 2013, p. 189). Typically, those models have been classified either in terms of the underlying technology (Garrison, 1985) or pedagogy (Anderson & Dron, 2011) in order to reflect the most distinctive characteristics of DE, many of which have a direct correspondence to the problems MOOCs are currently facing. Therefore, we suggest DE should be taken much more seriously as a valuable and inspiring source.

Three Generations of Distance Education

As one of the foundations for the understanding of DE, Garrison (1985) proposed his "Three generations of technological innovations in distance education" model, which is based on a strong technological determination (see Table 7.1).

As can be seen, every shift has triggered a form of "outsourcing" of certain pedagogical functions to the realm of technology such as during the first shift "when it was realized that educational interaction need not be face-to-face but could be mediated via correspondence" (Garrison, 1985, p. 241).

TABLE 7.1 Generations of distance education and the shifts of technology (Garrison, 1985)

Generation of Distance Education	Technological Means	Shift
correspondence	printed materials, postal system	F2F → mediated communication
telecommunications	electronic transmission of communication (radio, telephone)	personalization of interaction and communication two-way communication
computer (multimedia)	computer-assisted learning	mediated communication → mix of interaction and independence

Although technological innovations have accelerated over the last decades, the three generations outlined in Table 7.1 are basically still in existence. Yet this narrow, technology-driven perspective of distance education has been criticized and a more holistic approach has been suggested which is considered to be "a middle ground between either technological or pedagogical determinism" (Anderson & Dron, 2011, p. 81). More precisely, as Anderson and Dron point out, it is assumed that whereas technology will help create the music and even establish the beat to it, it is pedagogy that will define the moves. Stated another way, technology frames the opportunities for pedagogy in DE.

While the reliance on the power of technology constitutes a major similarity between DE and MOOCs, they both differ significantly in terms of the theoretical validation of the pedagogical assumptions (Daniel, 2012). Moreover, from its beginning, DE has been supported through theoretical reflections which had a great influence on the professionalization of the field. DE theories focus on crucial aspects of learning such as interaction and feedback and have managed to generate a unique body of knowledge that help to structure programs, courses, and materials. Ultimately, DE has been conceptualized as a "system sui generis" (Peters, 2010) or as an operating system of its own with a special emphasis on the modes of industrialization.

Certainly it would be unfair to expect the same amount of theoretical depth from the MOOC debate. Nevertheless, it does raise the question why the field of DE has not been heavily consulted or referenced given that they both conduct the same business.

DE and MOOCs: Distant Siblings with a Joint Future?

From an emancipatory standpoint, MOOCs and DE are both based on the belief that technology-enabled instruction can surmount socio-economic barriers of education so that virtually everybody with the desire and willingness to study can enter a course. However, this humanistic stance carries the danger of downplaying other important conditions or factors such as cultural capital (Bady, 2013). The overriding focus on technological access to open content has become increasingly apparent as several studies reveal the lack of digital learning skills as the main causes of learner failure to complete the course (e.g., Christensen, Steinmetz, Alcorn, Bennet, Woods, & Emanuel, 2013). In this regard, the massive attraction of MOOCs, which has been triggered by the reputation of Ivy League universities, is highly problematic. A key issue of this general fascination with MOOCs is that it shifts the attention away from conditions determining the effectiveness of distance learning. Once again, technology trumps pedagogy.

MOOCs have yet to spark much debate within the DE community. Worse, a literature review from Liyanagunawardena and her colleagues (Liyanagunawardena, Adams, & Williams, 2013) points out that there is only limited coverage in academic journals of the subject of online and distance education. A comprehensive review of MOOCs undertaken by Sir John Daniel (2012) while at the Korea National Open University (KNOU) provides one of the few examples in which a distinguished DE scholar undertakes a systematic analysis of MOOCs. Despite these various problems and issues, the MOOC hype has pushed aside many prevailing negative connotations that learning at a distance is inferior to face-to-face education. The same accusation had been used in the past to devalue DE with the result of increased theorization on DE (Perraton, 1987).

Against this background, it can be concluded that the field of DE is in an advantageous or safe position because of its outstanding accomplishments in theory and practice over a period of more than one hundred years. Yet there are several political and economical developments that have the potential to render the established DE system moot. More precisely, there is strong pressure from governments and political heads targeted at educational institutions and urging them to "open up" their materials and admission procedures (Castaño Muñoz, Redecker, Vuorikari, & Punie, 2013). Thus, it seemed warranted for us to experiment with MOOCs within the DE ecosystem. Such experimentation can put the various claims about MOOCs and open education into an empirical perspective.

Empirical Grounding: Two Instances of MOOCs and One DE Course

The "strange bedfellows" metaphor introduced with the title of the chapter begs the question as to what are the key differences and similarities of MOOC and DE courses. In order to shed some light on this issue, we present three data-enriched course descriptions with a focus on the following aspects of these courses: demographics, goals and design, content, enabling technologies, and activity trends.

The #iddg13 MOOC: Interdisciplinary Discourse on the Digital Society

Early in the summer of 2013 the Department of Instructional Technology & Media conducted the FernUniversität's first ever MOOC; a four-week-long "Interdisciplinary Discourse on the Digital Society."

Content: The MOOC was inspired by the ongoing trend of digital technologies pervading society. This topic was addressed from multiple perspectives: Week 1 revolved around a highly salient issue from the domain of education: Is it possible to identify the existence of a new generation of university students, intimately familiar with digital media, and, if so, does it require new ways of teaching? Week 2 focused on an issue drawn from the domain of economics: How can businesses harvest and leverage Web-based collective intelligence for their value-creation processes? In the third week, the essential role of Internet access for the conduct of everyday life was considered from a Science of Law perspective. Finally, Week 4 explored digital certificates and their implications for trust in Internet-based communications as it is being discussed in the area of Computer Science.

Goals and design: The course's goal was twofold. One aim was to increase DE students' awareness of the exceptionally broad impact on society of digitalization-based trends. The second key goal was to explore some of the challenges these developments posed from multiple scientific points of view. To this end, students were required to watch a 10- to 15-minute long videocast for each problem in which a professor in the respective field gave a non-technical introduction. At the end of the video, he or she set a task for the students to work on in the ensuing discussions. All videos were accompanied by Web-based resources intended to establish a common conceptual basis and to provide some starting points for further investigations. One week of discussion time was allotted to each problem. After two-thirds of each week, a feedback video was posted in which the respective professor commented on the preceding debate and gave some insights into what a solution to the task could have looked like.

Enabling technologies: The learning management system Moodle served as the main hub for the presentation of content, course discussion, and the linking or embedding of external resources. Additionally, the course deployed and encouraged the exploratory use of a number of supporting social media tools: *YouTube* was used as a hosting service for all videocasts which were embedded in the Moodle environment. *Twitter* was used to allow MOOC-related microblogging via the #iddg13 hashtag. Noteworthy Web resources and student products from each week were exhibited on *Scoop.it*, a content curation tool. Additionally, a number of students used their own blogs, podcasts, slidehosters, or Google+ groups as outlets for their contributions.

Demographics: The course was open to all 85,000 students of the FernUniversität in Hagen. However, it was dedicated solely to this specific audience, of which a total of 1,426 enrolled. A voluntary survey (N=73) administered online at the end of the MOOC suggests that there was nearly equal representation of males and females. The mean age of the respondents was 41 years (SD=9.5). About one-third (32 percent) were in their 4th semester of study and came principally from programs in Educational Science (42 percent) and Psychology (12 percent). The remaining proportion was made up of smaller groups from over a dozen of other programs offered at the FernUniversität.

Activity trends: Student participation, as indicated by the number of forum posts during each of the four weeks, started comparatively strongly, with 504 posts in Week 1. Thereafter, it declined and stabilized at around one-third of that number, with 178, 109, and 146 posts in the three subsequent weeks. The number of views of each of the introductory videos may be seen as a rough measure of at least receptive participation. In this study, the number of views declined from 676 to 516 to 301, and to 246 views with each successive week for the content presentation video. A similar decline in views applied in the case of the feedback videos (466, 283, 146, and 97 views, respectively, over the four weeks). Both measures, therefore, approximate an exponential decay curve. On average, each participant created 0.9 posts. Another noteworthy, yet expected (Jordan, 2014), fact is that of the 1,426 inscribed students, only 42 (3 percent) lasted to the very end of the course and handed in a final reflective essay in order to obtain a certificate of participation.

The #exif13 cMOOC: Discover the Island of Research

A few weeks after the #iddg13 course, the authors of the #iddg13 MOOC joined forces with the Department of Educational Science at the FernUniversität to conduct another MOOC called #exif13—Discover the Island of Research.

Content: The course revolved around Research Methodology on an introductory level. Its content presentation was loosely aligned with the basic steps of the empirical research process. Episode 1 focused on the most basic question: "What does 'working scientifically' mean?" Episode 2 introduced viewers to conceptual basics and strategies for literature search. The third episode settled on the issue of what a good research question is—and why it is needed. The next installment extended this topic and relayed to the viewer what it takes to come up with a methodologically sound answer to a research question. The subsequent episode zoned in on the role of statistics in answering research questions. The end of the course wrapped things up and gave some pointers with regard to the process of writing a scientific paper.

Goals and design: The course aimed to provide a non-technical introduction to the subject matter in the format of a cMOOC (Siemens, 2005). The #exif13 MOOC merged connectivist ideas for interaction design with a re-imagining of educational TV for content presentation (Vogt & Deimann, 2013): Seven weekly episodes of educational TV were produced with each show hosted by two educational scientists, who invited a different expert each week to present and discuss key issues in scientific research. Leveraging the affordances of Twitter, viewers of the livestream were able to pose questions or comments and get real-time answers from the experts. At the end of each episode, viewers were invited to engage actively in the presented lines of reasoning by working on research-related tasks and then sharing their results with the community. Drawing on connectivist ideas, participants had to self-organize their learning and their interactions making use of whatever Web-enabled tools they saw fit.

Enabling technologies: In place of a central learning management system, a number of Web tools were deployed to serve as functional substitutes. The Twitter account associated with the MOOC (twitter.com/exif13) served as the focal point for all activities. For instance, it supplied links to the live streams of new episodes and posts from the exif13-makers. Afterwards, broadcasts of the episodes were made available on YouTube. Participants primarily used a Google+ group to reflect on each episode. A few participants also posted on their own private blogs and created YouTube videos in response to #exif13 episodes. In addition, a Web-based bibliography was created and collaboratively filled with entries relevant to each episode.

Demographics: In contrast to the #iddg13 MOOC, the #exif13 cMOOC addressed an open-ended population. Due to the openness of the format (i.e., no registration, no tracking, etc.), it proves difficult to assess the number and the composition of participants. However, traces left by the Web-enabled tools can be analyzed to arrive at some rough estimates of participant demographics. For instance, based on the number of followers on Twitter (190) and the number of views on YouTube (ranging from 2,994 to 570), we conservatively estimate the cMOOC to have had somewhere between 190 and 570 regular participants.

Activity trends: As with the #iddg13 MOOC, it was possible to identify a roughly exponential decline on measures of participation: The first of the seven videos generated around 3,000 views, while the last one created only 570 views. Counting the posts per course phase in the #exif13 Google+ group—a measure of more active participation than simply viewing a video—also reveals a decline of activity with course duration. Week 1 started with 73 participant posts made in Google+. This number dropped to 43 and 49 posts made in the second and third weeks of the course, respectively. And beginning with the fourth week, contributions were down to 9, 27, and 13 posts for each of the remaining three weeks.

Distance Education Course: "Teaching and Learning in the Knowledge Society"

To allow for some comparisons with the two MOOCs, we now outline a course that represents what DE had been like at FernUniversität long before the recent hype over MOOCs. We chose to analyse the first module of the university's master's program "Education and Media—eEducation"—a course with the title: "Teaching and Learning in the Knowledge Society."

Content: The main topics of the course are foundational and application-oriented theories relevant to the field of e-learning (e.g., the paradigms of learning, some basics of instructional design and technology, strategies for assessment of teaching and learning, etc.). Weblogs as aids for reflective learning are treated as one field of application.

Goal and design: The course, which lasted for four months, strives to prepare the students for subsequent modules by establishing some common ground. It combines reading assignments with tasks that require the students to apply what they have learned using blogs, Wikis, and a portfolio. Grading is based on a final paper which requires students to scientifically conceptualize their blogging activities against the backdrop of select theories from the course.

Enabling technologies: The primary vehicles for content delivery were textbooks, parts of which were also accompanied by vodcasts. Asynchronous interaction, such as discussions and tutor feedback, took place on Moodle. The e-portfolio used was Exabis (a Moodle plugin). For the blogging activities, students could use either a university-hosted Wordpress installation or any private blogs that they already owned. The Wiki used was Mediawiki.

Demographic: The course had approximately 200 participants, mainly in the age group of 25 to 45. As is typical with students at FernUniversität, the majority of these students were studying on a part-time basis, mostly in addition to a regular occupation. Around two-thirds of the students in the course were female.

Activity trends: The main observable indicator of participation was student forum posts. Interestingly, forum participation for this course did not reveal as steep an exponential decay as had taken place in the two MOOCs. Instead, it showed only a modest decline during later phases of the course (posts per course unit: 178, 422, 22, 310, 116, 117, and 125 across the seven units). The average number of posts per student was 6.3. One has to bear in mind, however, that—in contrast to the participation in the MOOCs—many learner posts were created simply because of course requirements. It was only after all intermediate course requirements had been fulfilled, that students could take the final exam. Around 30 percent of the enrolled students did take the final, which is on the lower end of completion rates found in the program (ranging from circa 30 percent up to 60 percent).

MOOCs and DE Courses at FernUniversität in Review: Only Non-significant Differences?

When described at this grain size or level of activity, MOOCs and DE courses appear to have a number of similarities: Both present to-be-learned information to large groups and require students to engage in it in some way. In addition, both delivery formats deploy partially overlapping sets of distance media to enable content delivery and interaction. One difference worth noting, however, is that the attrition rate experienced in the two MOOCs was substantially higher than in the DE course. In addition, the per capita participation (e.g., the number of on-topic posts per person) in the latter was also between two and five times higher and somewhat less variable over time. This finding suggests that being part of a structured DE master's degree program changes the incentive structure for the participants and discourages the lurking behavior that tends to be common with MOOCs.

Conclusions: What Can MOOC Developers and Providers Learn from Distance Education?

Our experience suggests that grounding the design in instructional principles and striving for structure in terms of pacing, content presentation, assignments, and interaction design is preferable to low-structure approaches (e.g., a cMOOC).

With regard to media selections, using a plethora of Web tools can work. However, it seems beneficial to establish clear roles for each tool selected and adhere to a clear centerperiphery distinction. We recommend preselecting one medium as the central hub and assigning a peripheral role to all others. Such an approach allows for an easier integration of all contributions made to the course and helps to maintain learner orientation within the course. As far as choices of goals, contents, and assignments for courses are concerned, linking them in some way to the professional or everyday lives of the learners and having them apply their knowledge there, can help with motivation and depth of processing.

While this chapter only touched upon a number of selected similarities and differences between MOOCs and DE courses, there is clearly more to the story. Further investigation of the historic and future relations between these "strange bedfellows" could be a worthwhile endeavor for future research.

Markus Deimann was a Research Assistant in the Department of Instructional Technology and Media from May 2006 to August 2013. Since September 2013, he has been Assistant Professor (Akademischer Rat) and has completed his studies of Educational Sciences and Political Sciences at the University of Mannheim. He has also been working as Research Assistant on the Project "Multimedia-based Distance Study Medical Computer Science" at the Ilmenau University of Technology and at the University of Erfurt. In addition, he has been Visiting Scholar at the Florida State University, Tallahassee (USA) for one year. In 2011, he was a Scholarship Holder at the Open University (UK) for three months.

Alexander Lipka is a Research Assistant with the Department of Instructional Technology & Media at FernUniversität in Hagen, Germany. He holds a Diploma in Education from the University of Münster, Germany. His research interests include instructional media choice, Cognitive Task Analysis, and domain-general instructional principles. His current line of research examines how implementing instruction with social media influences the way learners traverse learning event spaces. Contact: alexander.lipka@fernuni-hagen.de.

 **Theo Bastiaens** is Full Professor at the Institute for Educational Science and Media Research of the Fernuniversität in Hagen, Germany. In addition to this appointment, he is part-time professor of Educational Technology at the Open University of the Netherlands. Bastiaens' specific research interest is in Instructional Design and E-learning. He has published extensively in these areas.

References

Anderson, T., & Dron, J. (2011). Three generations of distance education pedagogy. *International Review of Research in Open and Distance Learning, 12*(3). Retrieved from http://www.irrodl.org/index.php/irrodl/article/view/890/1663.

Bady, A. (2013, May 15). The MOOC moment and the end of reform. *The New Inquiry.* Retrieved from http://thenewinquiry.com/blogs/zunguzungu/the-mooc-moment-and-the-end-of-reform/.

Brooks, D. (2012, May 3). The campus tsunami. *New York Times.* Retrieved from http://www.nytimes.com/2012/05/04/opinion/brooks-the-campus-tsunami.html?_r=0.

Castaño Muñoz, J., Redecker, C., Vuorikari, R., & Punie, Y. (2013). Open Education 2030: planning the future of adult learning in Europe. *Open Learning: The Journal of Open, Distance and e-Learning, 28*(3), 171–86.

Christensen, G., Steinmetz, A., Alcorn, B., Bennet, A., Woods, D., & Emanuel, E.J. (2013). *The MOOC phenomenon: Who takes massive open online courses and why?* Working Paper, University of Pennsylvania, Philadelphia, PA. Retrieved from http://papers.ssrn.com/sol3/papers.cfm?abstract_id=2350964.

Daniel, J. (2012). *Making sense of MOOCs: Musings in a maze of myth, paradox and possibility.* Seoul: Korea National Open University. Retrieved from http://www.tonybates.ca/wp-content/uploads/Making-Sense-of-MOOCs.pdf.

Garrison, D.R. (1985). Three generations of technological innovation in distance education. *Distance Education, 6*, 235–41.

Hamilton, E., & Friesen, N. (2013). Online education: A science and technology studies perspective/Éducation en ligne: Perspective des études en science et technologie. *Canadian Journal of Learning and Technology, 39*(2). Retrieved from http://www.cjlt.ca/index.php/cjlt/article/view/689.

Hoskins, B.J. (2013). The changing face of distance education. *The Journal of Continuing Higher Education, 61*(3), 189–90.

Jordan, K. (2014). Initial trends in enrolment and completion of massive open online courses. *International Review of Research in Open and Distance Learning, 15*(1), 133–60.

Knox, J. (2013). Five critiques of the open educational resources movement. *Teaching in Higher Education, 18*(8), 1–12.

Liyanagunawardena, T.R., Adams, A.A., & Williams, S.A. (2013). MOOCs: A systematic study of the published literature 2008–2012. *International Review of Research in Open and Distance Learning, 14*(3), 202–27.

Moore, M., & Kearsley, G. (1996). *Distance education: A systems view.* Belmont, CA: Wadsworth Pub. Co.

Norvig, P. (2012). *The 100,000-student classroom.* Retrieved from http://www.youtube.com/watch?v=tYclUdcsdeo.

Perraton, H. (1987). Theories, generalisation and practice in distance education. *Open Learning: The Journal of Open, Distance and e-Learning, 2*(3), 3–12.

Peters, O. (2010). *Distance education in transition: Developments and issues.* Oldenburg: BIS-Verlag der Carl von Ossietzky Universität Oldenburg.

Siemens, G. (2005). Connectivism: A learning theory for the digital age. *International Journal of Instructional Technology and Distance Learning, 2*(1). Retrieved from http://www.itdl.org/Journal/Jan_05/article01.htm.

Vogt, S., & Deimann, M. (2013). *Educational TV reloaded: Production of the cMOOC Discover the Island of Research (#ExIF13).* Hagen: FernUniversität in Hagen. Retrieved from http://deposit.fernuni-hagen.de/2969/.

Wikipedia (2014). *Distance education.* Retrieved from http://en.wikipedia.org/wiki/Distance_education.

8

MOOCs DOWN UNDER

Insights from the Open2Study Experience

Maggie Hartnett, Mark Brown, and Amy Wilson

Introduction

The massive open online course (MOOC) movement continues to attract attention from futurists, popular media, and senior administrators concerned with the future of higher education. There are even predictions MOOCs are a metaphorical avalanche that will totally transform higher education (Barber, Donnelly, & Rizvi, 2013). While millions of people have registered to participate in xMOOCs through platforms such as edX, Coursera, and FutureLearn, much of the literature on the learner experience and the institutional drivers for developing free online courses remains in the academic blogosphere. Although more serious research and literature reviews are beginning to appear (e.g., Department for Business, Innovation and Skills, 2013; Hollands & Tirthali, 2014; Jacoby, 2014; Liyanagunawardena, Adams, & Williams, 2013; Selwyn & Bulfin, 2014), the maturing MOOC landscape can still be described as *messy* and the subject of considerable debate.

There have been numerous claims and counterclaims made about the promise and perils of MOOCs in today's new global higher education environment (Krause & Lowe, 2014). On the one hand, MOOCs are claimed to challenge the privileged nature of knowledge in traditional universities and address the problem of meeting increasing demand for higher education, especially in the developing world. In this regard, the new openness movement is seen as a real game changer (Daniel, 2012). On the other hand, a growing number of critical commentators point to low completion rates and regard the growth of MOOCs as a clever marketing ploy by elite universities (Selwyn, 2014). Peters (2013) argues, amongst other things, that MOOCs reflect a new academic labor policy for globalized universities, an expression of Silicon Valley values, and a kind of entertainment media. For some, the MOOC is just another neo-colonialist tool reproducing privilege through a hidden curriculum (Barlow, 2014).

Set against these claims, this chapter describes the Open2Study (www.open-2study.com) platform and explains the rationale and strategic drivers behind the MOOC initiative at Massey University. Massey was the first university in New Zealand to join an international MOOC platform on an enterprise-wide level. We briefly share examples from the design of Massey's first three courses and then reflect on key lessons. More specifically, the chapter reports a number of preliminary findings from the implementation and formal evaluation of the Massey experience, including participation data and different stakeholder perceptions. Finally, mindful of the international context, we conclude with a number of questions relevant to the future of the MOOC movement and higher education more generally.

Description of Open2Study

Open2Study is a lesser-known MOOC platform developed and maintained by Open Universities Australia (OUA). The platform currently has a stable of 11 Australian partner universities along with a handful of international providers, and almost 50 free courses. The core principle underpinning Open2Study is that "learning is life-long and should be accessible by all." As of July 2014, Open2Study reported that people in over 221 countries had registered to undertake at least one free online course (Open2Study, 2014). Since the launch of Open2Study in March 2013, by the beginning of July 2014, there had been, in total, almost 400,000 registrations from over 200,000 individuals.

Open2Study courses (subjects) are packaged in four-week blocks (see Figure 8.1). Each subject is divided into four modules, designed to be studied over the

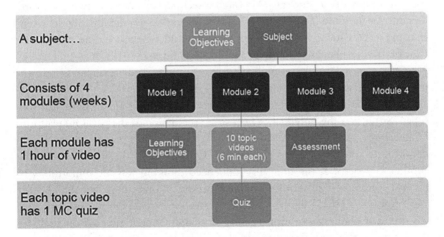

FIGURE 8.1 Basic design of an Open2Study subject

duration of a week. In turn, each module is divided into up to ten topics, covering a different aspect of the overall module theme. The course makes extensive use of video where the Subject Matter Expert (SME) explains the content. Each week, a member of Open2Study's Social Learning and Community Team posts a question or a discussion topic in the classroom forum. Notably, the SME who developed the course is not expected to lead these discussions. At the end of each topic, learners receive a multiple-choice pop quiz or a simulator exercise to help them test their learning. The pop quizzes and simulators do not contribute to the final grade—instead they are intended to be formative.

Each module ends with an assessment of the information covered in that module. The assessments open one at a time, each week, and stay open until the end of the course. Participants get three attempts at every assessment and need an overall average grade of at least 60 percent to pass the course. Upon successful completion, learners are able to download a certificate of achievement along with their final grade.

Massey's Rationale

When Massey was approached to join Open2Study in February 2013, the University's Senior Leadership Team weighed up potential benefits. At the time, some of the perceived benefits included enhancing Massey's reputation as New Zealand's pre-eminent distance education provider and world leader in online learning. Massey has five QS Stars for Teaching from the educational benchmarking agency Quacquarelli Symonds and is one of the highest-ranking major distance education providers in the Southern Hemisphere. The opportunity to join Open2Study was also seen as a way of promoting Massey's signature platforms in key areas of world-class expertise and to showcase the university to prospective international students. Although a secondary benefit, drawing on early literature at the time, MOOCs were also perceived to potentially support retention and learner success by helping prospective students to select the right course (Carson, Kanchanaraksa, Gooding, Mulder, & Schuwer, 2012). In a similar vein, MOOCs were seen to have some value in promoting student readiness in learning how to be an effective online learner.

Another important consideration for Massey in the decision to join Open2Study was the potential to help shape the design of the MOOC platform. Unlike more established MOOC platforms, as an anchor partner, there was an opportunity to influence the direction of Open2Study's development. Finally, another key factor at the time that influenced thinking was the opportunity to foster a culture of innovation in online learning and teaching. Notably, Weller and Anderson's (2013) digital resilience metaphor taken from the field of ecology influenced the innovation agenda as Massey sought to position itself for the future in the new digital world. Membership of Open2Study was seen as a way of helping Massey increase its capacity and capability for offering high-quality online courses throughout the world. In this regard, the decision to join Open2Study was part of a much larger strategic development to establish a new Massey University Worldwide brand, which was formally launched by the New Zealand Minister of Tertiary Education in February 2014.

Massey's aforementioned rationale for joining the Open2Study initiative can be compared and contrasted with assorted reasons that other institutions detail in a recent study of MOOC expectations and reality (Hollands & Tirthali, 2014). Notably, similar to the goals of Massey, in this study, 65 percent of institutions report that "extending reach and access" was a key reason for offering MOOCs, followed by 41 percent acknowledging the value of "building and maintaining their brand." In addition, "promoting innovation" (38 percent) in online learning and teaching appears to be a common theme for both Massey and the institutions involved in Hollands and Tirthali's research. However, while "improving economics" (38 percent) and "supporting research on teaching and learning" (28 percent) were also cited as drivers, these were not identified as a rationale for Massey's decision to partner with Open2Study.

Massey's Courses

In the latter half of 2013, Massey developed three online courses (also called subjects) in the Open2Study platform in the areas of:

- Agriculture
- Emergency management
- Indigenous cultures.

After several months of development and a full week of filming in Melbourne, Australia, the first subject in the area of Agriculture was officially launched in November 2013. Massey chose the subject of Agriculture for three main reasons. First of all, based on QS rankings, Massey is acknowledged as one of the top 20 universities in the world in this field. Second, it was consistent with the university's mission of promoting access and development. Such access was deemed especially critical in agriculture due to a rapidly growing population. With this growth, the world has a food shortage problem, and enhanced and sustainable agricultural practices are crucial to our future. And, third, a member of staff with experience in online teaching and learning was available at relatively short notice to develop the course. In effect, this course would be offered in an area of expertise where resources, both content and human, were available and where there was a dire need for this knowledge.

The subject, eventually called "Agriculture and the World We Live In," explored how agriculture feeds the world: a study of farms, farmers, and the

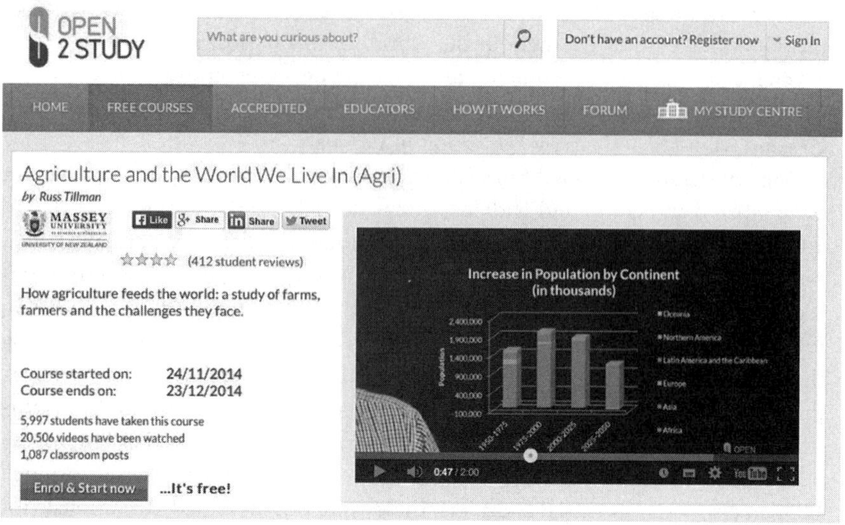

FIGURE 8.2   Open2Study website for Open2Sudy course, "Agriculture and the World We Live In"

challenges they face (see Figure 8.2). In terms of design, a notable feature of the course was the use of an iPad by the instructor to engage learners through a series of interactive videos. This technique was an example of how Open2Study was attempting to avoid the passive delivery of information following more traditional uses of video for teaching. Each video was designed as a short interactive learning experience supported by relevant online readings and resources.

The first iteration of the course attracted over one thousand learners. Notably only 55 percent of these learners actually started the online course, with 23 percent of the original total number of registrations successfully completing the subject. This figure meant that the completion rate for people who actually started the course was over 40 percent. There were 1,498 discussion posts during the first iteration of the course. For this cohort, 78.0 percent of the registered participants came from an overseas location, while 22.0 percent were from Australia. The top three overseas source countries consistently across Open2Study subject offerings were the United Kingdom, the United States, and India.

Massey's second online subject was in the area of Emergency Management, where it has considerable expertise. This area was chosen for two reasons: (1) staff working in the area had advanced skills in online teaching and already offered a fully online postgraduate program, and (2) there is a significant skill shortage in the area of Emergency Management, especially in the developing world, as demonstrated by a number of recent natural disasters including major earthquakes and tsunamis. The first iteration of this online subject was offered in January 2014 and participation data followed a similar trend to that observed on other Open2Study courses.

The third subject was in the area of Indigenous Studies, which was first offered in February 2014. This course was noteworthy for the way it was jointly developed by two universities. The University of Tasmania collaborated with Massey by exploring the histories of Maori, Aboriginal, and Torres Strait Islanders. This collaboration was an example of an unexpected outcome of the Open2Study experience. In effect, partner institutions began to share their experiences after a face-to-face meeting of Open2Study partners in March 2014. Once again, the participation data for the Indigenous Studies course were similar to other Open2Study offerings. Notably, participation data for all courses are openly available from the Open2Study website.

Evaluation Process

In December 2013, the university engaged a small team of staff to formally evaluate the Open2Study experience utilizing a qualitative approach. Ethical approval for the evaluation was obtained from the university's Human Ethics Committee prior to commencement of the research. In-depth qualitative data were gathered through staff interviews (conducted in April 2014), that included course lecturers, academic development staff, and online/distance learning managers involved in the initiative. Lessons learned that are presented here draw on staff interview data that were collected after the development of the three courses in the initiative. The interview procedure asked staff to talk about their experiences, particularly in terms of the benefits and challenges of the project. While the interviews were conducted with a small number of staff (N=8), this number represented an overall participation rate of 80 percent of the key people involved in the project. These interviews, then, provide some useful feedback on the pilot both in terms of affordance and challenges.

Lessons from the Experience

This section identifies just a handful of the more strategic lessons that have so far emerged from the Massey Open2Study experience.

Workload and Time

The biggest challenge, mentioned by all of the participants involved in the development of Open2Study courses, was the amount of work required. The work aspect, however, was only part of the issue. The volume of work, coupled with the tight timeframes in which to complete the design of the courses, resulted in significant difficulties for staff. Typically, course development was on top of already full teaching and research workloads. Deadlines were particularly strict because they were dependent upon the Open2Study asset production team being available within a specific time slot. Typically, each subject was assigned just one week to complete the filming of videos which, in itself, imposed a tight time-frame. Added to this highly time-bound schedule, the differing expectations of academics, who were unfamiliar with the production process and what actually needed to be done, resulted, in some cases, in a lack of understanding of the scale of the task. As one participant reported:

> There were phases that we thought were going to take this long, and actually, because we had a fixed in-date . . . it meant bulges in terms of capacity, so we had to kind of increase the hours . . . that we could make available.

The inflexibility of the video development process also caused difficulties. Even when materials and resources had been adapted from previous online usage, issues with the resolution of images or the format of files meant they could not be used when filming the videos. In other words, the academic staff fronting the videos could not refer to resources, images, or diagrams on screen whilst they were being filmed. This necessitated the restructuring of course content which, in turn, required the re-writing of scripts prior to filming, a further time-consuming process.

Not All MOOCs Are Created Equal

The breadth and depth of the content covered in each subject also had implications for staff workloads. In one case, it was problematic because the MOOC content went way beyond what was typically covered in the academic's existing program. Other academics found course development required a fine balance of giving a taster to learners with sufficient content but, at the same time, was not unmanageable in such a short course and did not impact on their own courses. As one of the participants observed, "it was really a delicate balance of giving people enough for them to get some tangible benefit for having engaged and gone through the course." The differing experiences of the Massey staff during the design phase based on unique discipline challenges suggests that even when following a tightly structured template, not all MOOCs are created equal.

Requires Strategic Oversight

The university's strategic drivers of increasing visibility, attracting new enrolments, and the ability to build capacity to offer larger-scale course offerings were endorsed by participants in this investigation. As this participant indicated, "one of the reasons we were doing this was to learn about how you could design courses more effectively in an online space." Raising the academics' profile both within their institution and externally was also highlighted. Another participant commented that "the benefits are, I think, that we have increased our profile, we are getting really good feedback." Some indicated that the MOOC courses also provided good visibility for their own courses and programs. They were even hopeful that it might expand their university course offerings, as reported by the following participant: "It could be a way in to a course that you might do as a front piece to enrolling into a post-grad programme."

But for successful implementation to occur, strategic oversight is required. This guideline was mentioned by one of the participants who had overall responsibility for the initiative: "[when] it started becoming more real I needed to project manage it." The need for oversight was also apparent in the different experiences described by the academics involved in developing the subjects. For instance, the Emergency Management specialists worked as a team to develop their offering. One team member was responsible for overseeing the project and ensuring the team met regularly to verify that development was progressing and to address any issues that arose. This approach was identified as having a positive effect on the experience of the whole team and, to a certain extent, their perception of how successful the development process had been. As one of the participants stated, "you get to develop quite a close relationship with a team like that."

Not Exactly Disruptive

Staff experiences also suggest that the Open2Study initiative has been one of ongoing development rather than disruption. Several participants commented on how the knowledge and skills gained could be extended to benefit their teaching within the university courses and programs for which they have responsibility. There was also a greater understanding about what was possible in a larger-scale online course. As this participant stated:

> I think they're really useful tools, particularly with the distance teaching we do. Massey has a natural . . . involvement in this sort of teaching and we have some capacity and capability. I think we could build that even further.

The developmental perspective reflected in this comment is not so surprising given that the structure of the Open2Study courses most closely resemble the xMOOC model underpinned by a combination of behaviorist and cognitivist approaches (Conole, 2013; Kop, 2011) where participants receive knowledge via pre-prepared modules (e.g., video tutorials, quizzes, etc.) developed by experts in the field. While the basic design of Open2Study could hardly be described as disruptive or transformative, the Massey experience was useful in helping to understand the potential of xMOOCs.

A Work in Progress

At this stage, these are admittedly only preliminary findings. Further analysis of the data as well as additional data collection is necessary, especially to monitor the uptake and implementation lessons beyond any Hawthorne Effect. But what is apparent, even at this early stage, is that more discussion with academics about what the development process entails is needed prior to the creation of any future courses. As one participant remarked when asked what advice he/she would give to someone embarking on a similar project:

> Not to take it on unless you've got a decent period of time that you can pull all this together, and then what funding will be available, what sort of support will be, and have that upfront. Because they said we had support but there wasn't any, and in the end I had to, I had to find support for me.

In other words, successful implementation requires targeted training and professional development for participating staff—even those who have previous online course design experience. Such professional development needs to ensure for scalability and succession planning that there is sufficient capacity and capability across an organization without the overreliance on particular individuals.

Wider Questions

Mindful of the wider international context, based on the authors' experience coupled with our data, we conclude this chapter with a number of deeper questions about the future of the MOOC movement:

- How do you measure the benefits?
- What is the real cost of developing MOOCs?
- What is the most sustainable business model for MOOCs?
- What role will MOOCs play in the future accreditation of degree programs?
- To what extent are universities missing out if they are not innovating with MOOCs?
- How will MOOCs help to reshape the nature of online/distance education at a national and international level?
- How can MOOCs help to serve the type of higher education system we want to create in the future?

Conclusion

In conclusion, the Open2Study experience at Massey University resulted in considerable publicity within New Zealand and provided a platform for the university's Senior Leadership Team and several academics to gain first-hand experiences of MOOCs. Where the initiative goes from here remains to be seen as discussions around a sustainable business model are ongoing and the flow-on effect of students enrolling in for credit university courses are yet to be determined.

What is clear is that the experience has had a significant impact on the staff involved; particularly, by broadening their thinking about the value of high-quality media objects in online courses. In this respect, these experiences reflect those of Hollands and Tirthali (2014, p. 7) who state, "There is no doubt that the advent of MOOCs has precipitated many institutions to consider or revisit their strategy with respect to online learning, whether at large scale or small." That said, based on the experience down under reported in this chapter MOOCs have yet to live up to the metaphor of an avalanche, which is going to fundamentally transform higher education forever.

Maggie Hartnett is a researcher and lecturer within the Institute of Education at Massey University, New Zealand, in the areas of e-learning and digital technologies. Her research focuses on the intersection of technologies and pedagogies and their influence on learners' and teachers' experiences, motivation, engagement, and behavior in a variety of online, distance, and blended learning contexts. Her research interests include motivation and engagement in digital environments, teaching and learning with digital technologies, support for digital learners, digital places and spaces for learning, and electronic portfolios and mobile technologies. Maggie's research interests are not confined to formal learning settings.

Mark Brown is Director of the National Institute for Digital Learning based at Dublin City University (DCU). Before taking up Ireland's first Chair in Digital Learning at the beginning of 2014, Mark was previously Director of both the National Centre for Teaching and Learning and the Distance Education and Learning Futures Alliance (DELFA) at Massey University, New Zealand. Mark has played key leadership roles in the implementation of several major university-wide digital learning and teaching initiatives, including the enterprise-wide deployment of Moodle, the original design and development of the Mahara e-portfolio system, and the university-wide implementation of a Massive Open Online Course (MOOC) platform.

Amy Wilson teaches at Massey University in the Masters in Education (e-learning) program. Dr Wilson has developed online and blended courses and worked with teaching staff. Her interests are in MOOCs, professional development, learning design, and e-portfolios. From 2005 to 2008, she was a Convener of the eLearning Forum of the Institutes of Technology and Polytechnics in New Zealand. In this role, she facilitated international online conferences and served on national e-learning projects. In 2005–6, Dr Wilson was selected for the Flexible Learning Leaders in New Zealand, a professional development scholarship awarded to emerging leaders in the tertiary e-learning sector.

References

Barber, M., Donnelly, K., & Rizvi, S. (2013). *An avalanche is coming: Higher education and the revolution ahead.* London: Institute for Public Policy Research.

Barlow, A. (2014). Just another colonist tool? In S. Krause & C. Lowe (Eds.), *Invasion of the MOOCs: The promise and perils of massive open online courses* (pp. 73–85). San Francisco: Parlor Press. Retrieved from http://www.parlorpress.com/pdf/invasion_of_the_moocs.pdf.

Carson, S., Kanchanaraksa, S., Gooding, I., Mulder, F., & Schuwer, R. (2012). Impact of opencourseware publications on higher education participation and student recruitment. *The International Review of Research in Open and Distance Learning, 13*(4), 19–32.

Conole, G. (2013). MOOCs as disruptive technologies: Strategies for enhancing the learner experience and quality of MOOCs. *RED—Revista de Educación a Distancia, 39.* Retrieved from http://www.um.es/ead/red/39.

Daniel, J. (2012). Making sense of MOOCs: Musings in a maze of myth, paradox and possibility. *Journal of Interactive Media in Education, 3.* Retrieved from http://jime.open.ac.uk/2012/18.

Department for Business, Innovation and Skills (2013). *The maturing of the MOOC: Literature review of massive open online courses and other forms of online distance learning.* BIS Research Paper Number 130.

Hollands, F. M., & Tirthali, D. (2014). *MOOCs: Expectations and reality. Full report. Center for Benefit-Cost Studies of Education.* Teachers College, Columbia University. Retrieved from http://cbcse.org/wordpress/wp-content/uploads/2014/05/MOOCs_Expectations_and_Reality.pdf.

Jacoby, J. (2014). The disruptive potential of the Massive Open Online Course: A literature review. *Journal of Open, Flexible and Distance Learning, 18*(1), 73–85.

Kop, R. (2011). The challenges to connectivist learning on open online networks: Learning experiences during a massive open online course. *The International Review of Research in Open and Distance Learning, 12*(3). Retrieved from http://nparc.cisti-icist.nrc-cnrc.gc.ca/npsi/ctrl?action=rtdoc&an=18150443&lang=en.

Krause, S., & Lowe, C. (2014). *Invasion of the MOOCs: The promise and perils of massive open online courses.* San Francisco: Parlor Press. Retrieved from http://www.parlorpress.com/pdf/invasion_of_the_moocs.pdf.

Liyanagunawardena, T.R., Adams, A.A., & Williams, S.A. (2013). MOOCs: A systematic study of the published literature 2008–2012. *International Review of Research in Open & Distance Learning, 14*(3), 202–27. Retrieved from http://www.irrodl.org/index.php/irrodl/article/view/1455/2531.

Open2Study (2014). *Community dashboard: Our student numbers.* Retrieved from https://www.open2study.com/community-dashboard.

Peters, M. (2013, August 17). Massive Open Online Courses and beyond: The revolution to come. Retrieved from http://www.truth-out.org/news/item/18120-massive-open-online-courses-and-beyond-the-revolution-to-come.

Selwyn, N. (2014). *Digital technology and the contemporary university: Degrees of digitalisation.* London: Routledge.

Selwyn, N., & Bulfin, S. (2014). The discursive construction of MOOCs as educational opportunity and educational threat. *Final Report.* Retrieved from http://www.moocresearch.com/wp-content/uploads/2014/06/C9130_Selwyn-Bulfin-MRI-final-report-publication-report.pdf.

Weller, M., & Anderson, T. (2013). Digital resilience in higher education. *European Journal of Open, Distance and e-Learning, 16*(1), 53–66. Retrieved from http://www.eurodl.org/materials/contrib/2013/Weller_Anderson.pdf.

9

REFLECTIONS OF AN EARLY MOOC PROVIDER

Achievements and Future Directions

Jeff Haywood, Amy Woodgate, and David Dewhurst

The Origins and Development of MOOCs at the University of Edinburgh

The University of Edinburgh was an early entrant into offering MOOCs. In only two years, it has developed an extensive portfolio of free and open content and educational activities. We first partnered with the US Coursera platform in 2012. A year later, in 2013, we joined the UK FutureLearn. While this early decision to offer MOOCs and establish ourselves at the leading edge had distinct advantages for the university, it came with the added challenge of having to reach some difficult choices early: 'What should our steady-state, including our MOOC sustainability, look like?', and 'What sort of future do we envisage for our open education, in the short and the longer terms?' Our decisions, and those of our fellow early adopters, may provide a path to follow for later adopters. The questions we asked, such as deciding whether to join in and how to support MOOC design and delivery, should be informative and illuminating to others. We, and several other universities, have published reflections on various stages of the MOOC experiences (MOOCs @ Edinburgh Group (2013); Hollands & Tirthali (2014)).

From the start of our MOOC adventure, we have been clear on why we are offering them. Over the past 20 years, the University of Edinburgh has built up a reputation for innovative use of technology in education. Without a doubt, offering MOOCs helps us to enhance that standing. We also have a strong focus on outreach and MOOCs offer us a way to reach new audiences, including those in more disadvantaged settings. Moreover, given that the universities offering MOOCs in 2012 were our international peers and research partners, the potential for wider collaborations was evident. We could also see that producing and teaching MOOCs was fun and stimulating for the faculty who were involved.

Another major reason for our involvement in the MOOC experience was that the emerging MOOCs space provided an opportunity for exciting educational

R&D which could benefit the whole university while supporting its overall research agenda. To be effective, therefore, it was important that the processes were transparent and open. We have recently explored our processes for early decision-making in detail (Haywood & MacLeod, 2015) and have also reported on our MOOC development process, our recruitment statistics, and our learner demographics (MOOCs @ Edinburgh Group, 2013; Harrison, 2014).

Briefly, we see that our MOOC learners are mostly well educated, in the age range 25–45, and come from all over the world. However, this generalisation hides significant differences such as the fact that some of our MOOCs attract more young learners and some attract fewer highly educated learners. Figures 9.1 and 9.2 show the age and qualification patterns of the learners from our first six MOOCs. These patterns in recruitment appear to be generally stable over the early iterations of each course, although there are also some signs of change; for example, the number of younger learners in the Astrobiology course grew appreciably.

As of August 2014, the University of Edinburgh had 18 MOOCs that have been offered on one or more occasions. By August 2015, we expect to have 30

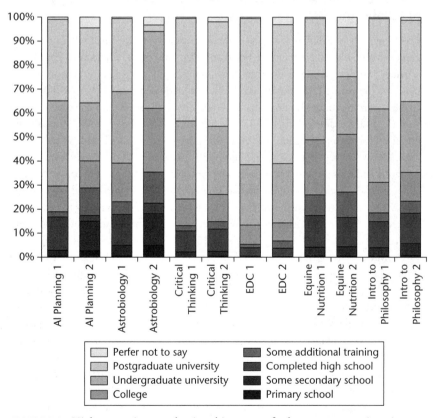

FIGURE 9.1 Highest previous academic achievement for learners on two iterations of six Edinburgh MOOCs (January 2013–January 2014)

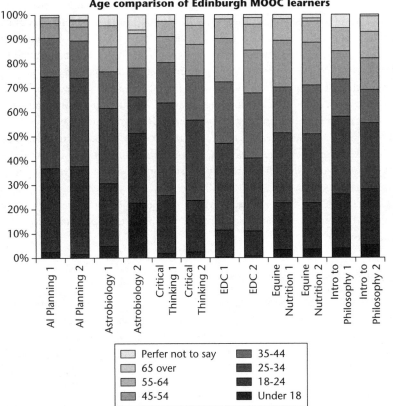

Age comparison of Edinburgh MOOC learners

FIGURE 9.2 Profile of ages of learners on two iterations of six Edinburgh MOOCs (January 2013–January 2014)

MOOCs available, with none having closed. All Edinburgh MOOCs have a minimum lifespan of three years. Hence, we can safely predict that the *earliest* point for us to 'gracefully' cease offering MOOCs would be mid-2018, i.e., six years from the initial decision to join Coursera.

To reach this stage has required significant institutional investment. Throughout 2012, a regular question from the media, and from those of our colleagues considering developing MOOCs, was: 'What does it cost to develop a MOOC?' A consensus has emerged that the 'lifetime cost' of a single MOOC is approximately US$50,000, excluding start-up costs and associated senior staff time (although we found the latter to be crucial to extract the maximum value from the initiative) (Haywood & MacLeod, 2015). Thus, we estimate that an investment of US$1.5 million to US$2 million over six years will be required to develop and support our projected portfolio of MOOC courses. This investment has funded a new dedicated video production service (facilities and staff). It has also provided the resources needed for a small central team in the Vice Principal's Office to manage the operational relationship for the MOOC platforms, support the academic teams, and ensure high-quality outputs. Importantly, it also funds the initial salary and training costs of the teaching assistants on each MOOC. Additional resources came from the Academic Schools who provided their faculty time 'free' (a significant investment estimated at 30 faculty working days per MOOC), and committed to supporting their MOOCs for three years or, in effect, three iterations.

Although the total investment is relatively modest compared to the annual turn-over of the university (US$1.3 billion per annum), it is still significant. Naturally, we needed to ensure a return on that investment (ROI) of funds that could have been used in many other ways. Fortunately, the university has benefitted considerably; in fact, in some important respects, the benefits have been different to those originally anticipated. It is for this reason that support to continue developing new MOOCs remains high.

In this chapter, we will explore the ROIs and other benefits of our MOOCs. We will also summarise what we expect to be doing in the open education area over the next few years.

Returns on Investment

Figure 9.3 shows the different ROIs that might be realised by a university from the investments made in MOOCs. In this section, we shall discuss some of the most important ROIs to the University of Edinburgh in light of the evidence gathered to date that has enabled us to be confident that sufficient returns are being made.

New Experiences for Experienced Online Teachers

Several of our early MOOC teams were already well acquainted with teaching online. They found the experience of 'designing for the unknown learner' both stimulating and scary (MacLeod, Haywood, Woodgate, & Sinclair, 2014). None of them had previously taken such an open and hands-off approach with thousands of learners. In contrast, they had always worked with tutor:learner ratios of around 1:25. These new experiences stimulated a rethinking of online pedagogies and, as a result, other courses taught online have simultaneously benefited from the influence of MOOCs. For instance, some have used MOOCs as part of on-campus programmes, and MOOC videos for on-campus classes. One particularly novel development has been the use of MOOCs as courses taught by other institutions, something which is quite rare for traditional education. For example, the 'Critical Thinking' MOOC has been used in Rwanda (Bartholet, 2013) as well as in a Gates Foundation-funded experiment by the University of Maryland State System (Griffiths, Chingos, Mulhern, & Spies, 2014). It is now also being used in an international collaboration (see below).

Online Newbies and Appetite for Further Online Education

In the early days of our MOOC initiative, we knew there would be interest in developing a MOOC from a few faculty. At the same time, we were unsure just

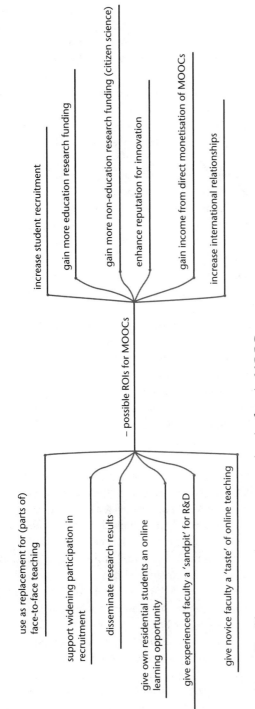

FIGURE 9.3 Possible returns on investment to a university from its MOOCs

use as replacement for (parts of) face-to-face teaching

support widening participation in recruitment

disseminate research results

give own residential students an online learning opportunity

give experienced faculty a 'sandpit' for R&D

give novice faculty a 'taste' of online teaching

– possible ROIs for MOOCs

increase student recruitment

gain more education research funding

gain more non-education research funding (citizen science)

enhance reputation for innovation

gain income from direct monetisation of MOOCs

increase international relationships

how many others might wish to be involved, especially as the amount of work involved became clear. However, a 'queue' of faculty teams quickly formed from all areas of the university who wished to explore open online courses. During the early adopter phase, everything was new and faculty members and support teams learned together. Today, we have a well-honed process in place that supports faculty from the initial idea stage through to delivery and to repeat runs. With this process in place, we can simultaneously manage approximately ten MOOCs at various stages of development. Colleagues at other universities report similar developments, e.g., the MOOC Factory at École Polytechnique Fédérale de Lausanne (EPFL—http://moocs.epfl.ch/mooc-factory).

The support process involves an early discussion between our central admin and course production teams with interested faculty, so that we can better understand their thinking and begin to inform them about what will be involved. We have not used a formal proposal and application process. Instead, we prefer an iterative dialogue approach as it enables us to shape the MOOC design before it 'gels' in a faculty member's mind. We recommend small teams of faculty (perhaps three or four) to encourage self-support and knowledge sharing and also to spread the workload and scheduling. The head of their school must formally agree to make the MOOC a school responsibility and then run it a minimum of three times over a three-year span. They must also agree to submit a 'light touch' business plan that we require for all MOOCs.

We help the academic team with course and instructional design. In addition, we provide access to the video and multimedia production services and are responsible for all the administration duties associated with the chosen MOOC platform (Coursera or Futurelearn). We also pay for the teaching assistants for the first iteration of a MOOC and for their modest involvement in course construction. Importantly, we train everyone involved in the MOOC process. The support described is managed from within a central service (i.e., 'Information Services') and involves the University of Edinburgh's academic development unit. We have actively supported a community of practice by ensuring that, insofar as possible, new entrants learn from more experienced MOOCers, and also from their newbie colleagues.

Initially, control over which MOOCs are released as well as the overall quality control rested firmly with the central team. This decision to centralise MOOC administration and quality control was made in recognition that the risks were high, especially in the early months. This 'grip' is now being eased as we gain confidence in our procedures and outcomes.

The institutional investment in MOOCs has enabled us to support faculty members from almost all subject areas and disciplines at the University of Edinburgh, many of whom had never before been involved in fully online learning (although, of course, all have used technology with on-campus classes). These have been successful and exciting experiences for such faculty as they have gained knowledge about course design, online education, and open education. Some are now using their MOOC materials with their residential classes, whereas others have begun to create online master's degree programmes to add to the university's existing portfolio of online degrees (which number around 50 as of August 2014).

This effect has not been limited to the faculty teams involved; it has often caused a wider discussion within a particular school about online education. To broaden that experience, sometimes a school decides it wishes to offer more than one MOOC. We have also seen a small, but very important positive impact on the career prospects for faculty members and teaching assistants involved in MOOCs.

Sparking a Debate about Digital Education

From the outset, we have maintained a strong dialogue with the governance processes of the university as well as with faculty interested in educational innovation. Our governing board, University Court, was involved in the initial decision to join Coursera and to offer MOOCs. Fortunately, it has maintained its interest and support since that adoption. As a result, the MOOC project reports into the governance of the university through a high-level committee called the 'Knowledge Strategy Committee,' thereby engaging senior members of faculty and administration in the debate. Senatus Academicus, our top-level academic governance body, has discussed online education and MOOCs as part of its business. From the outset, MOOCs have been subjected to a formal course approval and quality assurance (QA) process, which has been a light version of the QA process employed for traditional, credit-bearing, courses. Initially, the course approval process was led by a vice principal (that is, a member of the university senior management team), but now, as the level of confidence rises, it is beginning to be devolved to the academic schools to manage themselves, as they do for traditional courses.

All these actions have led to a vigorous debate about MOOCs and also about online education more broadly. Although some members of the university have expressed legitimate concerns about costs, reputational risk, and sustainability, the debate has generally been in favour of a well-managed expansion of the number and diversity of MOOCs on offer. There is also encouragement to learn and disseminate as much as we can from the experience.

MOOCs and Research: Citizen Science/Communities

One unexpected development has been that some faculty now regard MOOCs as a part of their personal research. We have seen grant proposals funded that promise MOOCs as part of the outputs, both as simple dissemination and impact enhancements, and also as part of the research process (i.e., 'citizen science'). An example of the latter was in behavioural economics, where a large audience was sought, via a MOOC, to participate in an analysis of European dietary choices. Similarly, for their MOOC, the astrobiologists have created a large international community of people interested in research into life on other planets. More recently, a MOOC on Scottish Independence, 'Toward Scottish Independence? Understanding the Referendum,' offered by the School of Social and Political Science, not only provided valuable data for the citizens of the United Kingdom, but also engaged others in the analysis. It seems likely that such examples will grow as faculty members become aware of the new possibilities offered to them to engage in research with very large numbers of MOOCs learners, that, until now, they would have found it difficult, if not impossible, to reach.

Enhanced International Collaborations

From the outset, we have seen participation in MOOC platforms as a route to strengthening existing partnerships with peer universities and to forming new ones. Some concrete examples of this have already emerged:

- Working with our existing partners in the global alliance Universitas 21 (see http://www.universitas21.com/), one of our existing MOOCs will be used as a closed online course (i.e., a SPOC or 'Small Online Private Course') with students from around 15 universities worldwide learning together online.
- Our MOOCs have been franchised to other universities (e.g., the University of Maryland State System), and we have learned from their experiences.
- Our strong relationships with many top European universities are leading to explorations around joint MOOC creation, targeted toward areas such as academic staff development and research methods.
- We share learner analytics and course design data with many of our partners. That sharing enables us to help our own faculty improve their MOOC design and delivery.

Impacts on Student Recruitment

Reports in the press and elsewhere suggest that the purpose of MOOCs for many universities has been to promote traditional (and fee-paying) education—this has not been a core objective for Edinburgh nor for our MOOC partner institutions with whom we have discussed this issue. Clearly, if MOOCs do result in more qualified students enrolling at the University of Edinburgh that would be a welcome development. However, with an annual intake of around 7,000 students, to make a significant difference, MOOCs would have to be extremely effective marketing tools, and probably designed primarily for that purpose.

Given this situation, we have attempted to ensure that our MOOC learners are aware of our other MOOC offerings and other related online and on-campus degree programmes, though this has not been a 'hard sell.' As part of these efforts, on our university website, we have placed MOOCs in the same area as our taught online master's courses, since prospective online learners may be interested in either or both formats.

There is evidence of a small number of direct 'conversions' from MOOCs to online degree programmes. While such conversions are just beginning, it is likely that MOOC learners (and particularly their families) are more aware of Edinburgh's courses as a result of MOOCs. There has been a generalised enhancement of our reputation for innovative online education amongst potential students. Others have also reported some direct conversion (e.g., Grainger, 2013).

Enhancing the University's Reputation

Among the major objectives for our entry into MOOCs has been to enhance the university's reputation for innovation in learning and teaching. Fortunately, there is good evidence that this has been achieved; in particular, in Europe.

Since July 2012, when we announced our partnership with Coursera, staff from the wider MOOC team have presented at major conferences, seminars, and invited sessions about technology in higher education. These invitations have come from a wide range of organisations and individuals, including the European Commission, university alliances and mission groups, quality assurance agencies, and numerous university officials (including finance directors who are interested in the cost–benefit analyses related to MOOCs). While the rate of invitations has not slowed over time, the nature of the events has 'matured' as the reality of MOOCs has become clearer and some of the hype has subsided. There has been substantial attention from the UK government and its agencies, and from within Europe (particularly from the European Commission), as a consequence of our early adoption of MOOCs. This interest has led to the provision of some research funding as well as opportunities to influence policy towards online education. Our early MOOCs covered diverse topics, at a time when the focus of most MOOCs was in topics related to computer science and technology. This diversity of MOOC topics attracted some very influential 'learners' who wanted to explore MOOCs and also see what our university was doing in this space. As far as we can determine, their experiences in these MOOCs were of high quality. Such positive experiences will continue to enhance our reputation for some time.

Colleagues from many organisations and other universities have visited us to learn more about our MOOC experiences over the past couple of years. We have been able to share our experiences with them as well as to learn from theirs. Many of these visits have offered explorations and collaborations that are likely to bear fruit over the coming years.

It is now quite common for interviewees for both junior and senior faculty posts to make reference to Edinburgh's MOOCs during their interviews. Although hard to evidence unequivocally, it does appear that our activities in this area have led some individuals to apply to work for the University of Edinburgh. And, most certainly, many are thinking about innovation in learning and teaching as part of their preparation for an interview.

Ever since we began our e-learning provision for residential students back in the 1990s, we have had a research strand running alongside it that has both learned from and informed the appropriate use of technology in support of credit-bearing courses. This research has continued as we have added fully online taught master's programmes, and now MOOCs, to our portfolio. These efforts have resulted in further publications, research collaborations with partner universities, doctoral and master's studentships, grant applications, and modest funding.

What Next?

As we come to the end of two years as MOOC providers, we are now facing up to some difficult questions and options. Our thinking in this area is illustrated in Figure 9.4.

Given the cost of MOOCs, how many should we hold in our overall portfolio? We will soon have 30, but should we stop there or increase to, say, 100 or even 300? Should we offer all of them together, just some of them in any single year, or should we 'retire' a MOOC after three or four years (based perhaps on first–in–first-out, or those with lowest success on some measure)? Should we balance our portfolio between Coursera and FutureLearn, or are there good reasons for using a particular platform for a particular MOOC? How do we cover the costs of repeat offerings? Will a slicker production system reduce costs? Is it time to cease central funding and leave that to the schools? What action do we take when a key faculty member retires or leaves for another (perhaps MOOC-offering) university? Lastly, can we find ways to use our MOOCs more purposefully towards achieving the original goal of widening participation and outreach?

We do not currently have answers to all of these questions, but our internal discussions have suggested a few possibilities. For example, it is unlikely that we shall create more than about 50 MOOCs from central funding, although research grant-funded MOOCs might push the final number higher. A total of 50 MOOCs represents approximately two per school. At present, there are no signs that schools have set their sights on more; indeed, at some point, the opportunity costs begin to outweigh the gains. There is some evidence that paid-for value-added items such as certificates might generate enough income to cover the modest costs of teaching assistants. Moreover, options such as offering MOOCs as on-demand, untutored courses might enable us to remove current limits on the frequency of repeat runs. A self-paced MOOC may also solve the problem of faculty who 'lose interest' after a short time. To take just one example, a key faculty member, who had led one of our first MOOCs, has now moved on. In that instance, we negotiated an arrangement that that MOOC will be offered again; however, we have yet to formalise that informal arrangement to cover future instances.

Significant thought and effort is being focussed on how we reach audiences, such as younger learners and those in disadvantaged settings. One attempt has been to develop MOOCs with a wider appeal, such as our new Football MOOC, produced by the School of Education and designed for young adults. Similarly, a joint venture with Universidad ORT in Uruguay to create Spanish and English versions of one of our MOOCs (i.e., basic computing and app development) targeted at teenagers is also underway. Developing MOOCs to support local communities is also a priority. For instance, we are working with our students in their regular volunteering scheme to provide support to people in Edinburgh who wish to study online but need help in getting going.

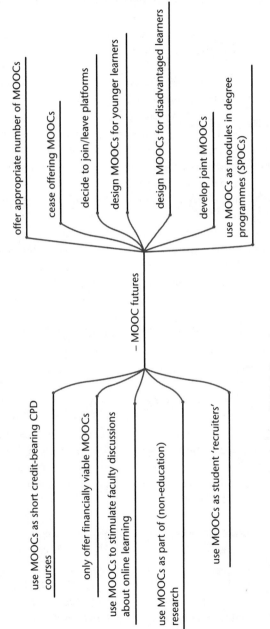

FIGURE 9.4 Options for universities in future uses of MOOCs

Even though some aspects of MOOC production and administration have become more routine and formalised, the future still looks quite exciting and fun. Ideas from our faculty continue to flow in; although some stretch the limits of what we can presently offer, we will continue to support them because it will be from such explorations that creative insights and vital research into the wider digital education agenda at the University of Edinburgh and other institutions will emerge.

Jeff Haywood is Vice-Principal Knowledge Management, CIO and Librarian at the University of Edinburgh. He is head of the university's integrated Information Service, offering a wide range of services in Library, IT, Technology-Enhanced Learning and Classroom Technology. Jeff leads many major university-wide initiatives, including the substantial expansion of taught online distance master's degrees and Massive Open Online Courses (MOOCs). As Professor of Education and Technology in the university's School of Education, his research interests are in the development of strategies for the effective use of ICT in education at institutional, national, and international levels. He is currently academic lead on a European Commission study of EU government options for modernising HE using technology. Jeff is a past member of the JISC Board and past Chair of the eLearning Task Force for the Coimbra Group. He is currently a member of the Scottish Government's ICT for Excellence Group which is designing the next-generation digital learning environment for Scottish schools.

Amy Woodgate is the Project Manager of Edinburgh University's Online Learning Special Projects, based within the Vice Principal's Office of Information Services. She is responsible for the expansion of the university's online learning portfolio through strategic investment projects, including the Distance Education Initiative—fully online master's programmes—and Massive Open Online Courses.

David Dewhurst has a life sciences background and over 25 years of teaching experience. He is Professor of e-Learning, Director of Educational Information Services in Medicine and Veterinary Medicine, and academic lead of a university-wide distance education initiative. His research in technology-enhanced learning (TEL) is internationally renowned. David has over 250 peer-reviewed publications, significant grant income, several PhD students, and he has also directed major educational projects in Africa and Eastern Europe. Notable prizes include a prestigious Queen's Anniversary Prize for Higher and Further Education in 2005 for 'The Virtual Hospital Online' and the Doerenkamp-Zbinden Foundation International Prize for Animal free Research in 2006.

References

Bartholet, J. (2013, July 17). Free online courses bring 'magic' to Rwanda. *Scientific American.* Retrieved from http://www.scientificamerican.com/article/free-online-classes-bring-magic-rwanda/.

Grainger, B. (2013). *Massive open online course report.* University of London International Programmes. Retrieved from http://www.londoninternational.ac.uk/sites/default/files/documents/mooc_report-2013.pdf.

Griffiths, R., Chingos, M., Mulhern, C., & Spies, R. (2014, July 10). *Interactive online learning on campus: Testing MOOCs and other platforms in hybrid formats in the University System of Maryland.* Retrieved from http://www.sr.ithaka.org/research-publications/interactive-online-learning-on-campus.

Haywood, J., & MacLeod, H. (2015). To MOOC or not to MOOC? University decision-making and agile governance for educational innovation. In P. Kim (Ed.), *Massive open online courses: The MOOC revolution.* New York: Routledge.

Harrison, L. (2014). Open UToronto MOOC Initiative: Report on second year of activity. Retrieved from http://www.ocw.utoronto.ca/open-utoronto-mooc-initiative/.

Hollands, F. M., & Tirthali, D. (2014, May). *MOOCs: Expectations and reality.* Center for Benefit-Cost Studies of Education, Teachers College, Columbia University. Retrieved from http://cbcse.org/wordpress/wp-content/uploads/2014/05/MOOCs_Expectations_and_Reality.pdf.

MacLeod, H., Haywood, J., Woodgate, A., & Sinclair, C. (2014, February). Designing for the unknown learner. *Proceedings of EMOOCs: European MOOC Stakeholders Summit 2014* (pp. 245–8). Lausanne, Switzerland. Retrieved from http://emoocs2014.eu/sites/default/files/Proceedings-Moocs-Summit-2014.pdf.

MOOCs @ Edinburgh Group (2013, May10). *MOOCs @ Edinburgh 2013—Report #1.* Retrieved from http://hdl.handle.net/1842/6683.

Morris, N. (2014). *What have we learned from MOOCs.* University of Leeds report. Retrieved from: http://www.slideshare.net/NeilMorris2/oer-and-mooc-strategy-university-of-leeds-hea-cll.

Shah, D. (2014). *Penn reaches 2.3 million students, plans to offer 20 more courses.* University of Pennsylvania MOOCs Report. Retrieved from: https://www.class-central.com/report/penn-2-3-million-students/.

Waters, J.K. (2013). Stanford's online strategy. *Campus Technology,* 2013, pp. 22–6. Retrieved from: http://online.qmags.com/CPT0113/default.aspx?pg=22&mode=1#pg22&mode1.

PART 4
Thoughts on the Quality of MOOCs and OER

Nearly every conversation about the various forms of educational delivery offered at a distance eventually turns to questions of quality. It does not matter if that discussion involves the use of the telephone, radio, audiotapes, television, correspondence courses, satellites, videoconferencing, or some type of computer technology, content and course quality will need to be addressed before widespread acceptance can be garnered. As part of this process, there will be research funding announcements, special conferences and summits, new guidelines and recommendations, and college courses and workshops that will emerge about quality related to that new form of delivering education. Such is definitely the case with MOOCs and open education today. To help the reader understand what is presently occurring in this regard, Part 4 of this book offers three views or insights related to quality.

The first chapter in this section, contributed by Karen Swan and her research team at the University of Illinois Springfield, discusses the development and validation of an innovative tool called "Assessing MOOC Pedagogies" (or AMP). The AMP tool can be used to characterize the pedagogical approaches taken in MOOCs along ten dimensions. Preliminary testing of AMP on some 20 different MOOCs demonstrated high inter-rater reliability for this new instrument and the facility of AMP to reveal distinct pedagogical patterns within MOOCs. For example, key patterns found across different content areas were akin to two common metaphors of learning—namely, those related to learner knowledge acquisition or to the reception of content from an expert and learner participation in a highly connected knowledge building and sharing community. A third pattern related to self-regulated learning is also alluded to in this groundbreaking chapter.

Whereas Chapter 10 from Swan et al. focuses on the pedagogical quality in MOOCs, in Chapter 11, Sanjaya Mishra and Asha Kanwar, from the Commonwealth of Learning (COL), explore quality assurance issues for open educational resources (OER). The emergence of the OER movement has provided the COL with a means to promote access to quality educational materials in the developing countries of the Commonwealth (e.g., Namibia, India, Bangladesh, Tanzania, Jamaica, Belize, Rwanda, and Pakistan). While OER provide many distinct advantages to the people in these developing countries, Mishra and Kanwar readily admit that issues of quality remain a chief concern. In response, the Commonwealth Educational Media Centre for Asia (CEMCA), a regional center of the COL located in New Delhi, India, has been engaged in developing guidelines and measures for quality assurance of OER. Several important quality guidelines are presented for OER that employ a framework from COL called TIPS or: (1) Teaching and learning, (2) Information and content, (3) Presentation, and (4) Technology. While Mishra and Kanwar emphasize the need for quality guidelines with frameworks such as TIPS, they simultaneously contend that teachers and learners should be able to use the criteria to decide on the quality of OER based on their differing needs and perspectives. The authors offer recommendations related to training and capacity building, the use of affordable and appropriate technology, and the development of exemplar courses that can promote OER quality.

The third and final chapter of this section comes from a pan-European MOOC project called "OpenupEd." In this piece, Fred Mulder and Darco Jansen describe how OpenupEd combines what they refer to as "classical" notions of openness that have been attached to open universities since the early 1970s with the more recent forms of digital openness now possible via MOOCs and OER. The chapter's leading question is whether MOOCs and OER can play instrumental roles in opening up education for all potential learners across all lands. To that end, Mulder and Jansen perceive a need for the various barriers to learning to be removed. At the same time, they argue that learners should receive incentives towards their success when enrolled in MOOCs and other forms of open education. In total, eleven barriers and three incentives are examined in this chapter. These two European scholars recommend that other MOOC providers utilize the ingredients found in their chapter to adopt a mission of opening up education as a way forward in this new age of open learning.

10

AMP[1]

A Tool for Characterizing the Pedagogical Approaches of MOOCs

Karen Swan, Scott Day, Leonard Bogle, and Traci van Prooyen

Introduction

Since the development of the first Massive Open Online Course (MOOC) pioneered by George Siemens and Stephen Downes of Canada in 2008 (Bousquet, 2012), an explosion of course offerings have emerged in the United States, engendering a great deal of debate (Waters, 2013). MOOCs have come to be viewed by some as the savior of higher education (Friedman, 2013), and by others as the harbinger of its ultimate demise (Vardi, 2012).

Empirical evidence on the effectiveness MOOC pedagogy is hard to find. However, some of the pedagogical strategies used in MOOCs have been consciously adapted from other contexts (Glance, Forsey, & Riley, 2013). Commonly used pedagogical strategies include: lectures formatted into short videos (Khan, 2012; Norvig, 2012); videos combined with short quizzes (Shirky, 2012); automated and peer/self-assessments (Lu & Law, 2012; Stiggins, 2002; Strijbos, Narciss, & Dünnebier, 2010); and online discussions (Darabi, Arrastia, Nelson, Cornille, & Liang, 2011; Li, 2004; Walker, 2007). In addition, "cMOOC's provide great opportunities for non-traditional forms of teaching approaches and learner-centered pedagogy where students learn from one another" (Yuan & Powell, 2013, p. 11).

Because the mainstream media seems to have mistaken MOOCs for online learning in general, and because not all MOOCs are the same, it is increasingly vital to distinguish among them. We believe that finding mechanisms to distinguish among MOOCs or evaluate their underlying components or characteristics should be the first step in the "research, evaluation, and assessment of learning" in MOOCs (see also Reeves & Hedberg, 2014, p. 4). Given that most MOOCs have not been designed to take advantage of the affordances of sophisticated instructional designs or advances in learning technologies (Romiszowski, 2013), we agree with Reeves and Hedberg (2014) that researchers should begin by investigating their designs for learning, with an eye toward how such pedagogies meet the needs of the learners who enroll in MOOCs.

Recent research has uncovered unique characteristics of those who enroll in MOOCs. Many are well educated with a college degree, employed, and reside in developed countries—a far cry from the original and intended audience for free online courses (Christensen, Steinmetz, Bennett, Woods, & Emanuel, 2013; Guzdial & Adams, 2014; Sandeen, 2013). Males are more represented in MOOC courses as well (Christensen et al., 2013). Many of those who enroll in MOOC courses do so in order to take advantage of professional development and continuing educational opportunities, as well as to address their curiosity toward MOOCs and MOOC topics (Christensen et al., 2013; Guzdial & Adams, 2014).

In effect, the typical goals and uses of those enrolled in MOOCs is far different from those learners enrolled in traditional online courses (Roth, 2013). Indeed, emerging research regarding MOOC participants has revealed that many learners stay engaged and are committed to learning without ever taking an assessment nor with any intention of completion (DeBoer, Ho, Stump, & Breslo, 2014; Kizilcec, Piech, & Schneider, 2013; Roth, 2013). These learners have been given a variety of labels including "users," "browsers," "auditors," "registrants," and "samplers" (DeBoer et al., 2014; Kizilcec et al., 2013). Others refer to them as "viewers," "solvers," "all-rounders," "collectors," and "bystanders" (Anderson, Huttenlocher, Kleinberg, & Leskoed, 2014). Such individuals do not generally engage with MOOCs in the same way that they do with traditional online courses in which the assumption is active participation and interaction (Anderson et al., 2014; DeBoer et al., 2014).

In this chapter, the authors describe the development of an instrument, AMP (Assessing MOOC Pedagogies), which characterizes the pedagogical approaches taken by individual MOOCs along ten dimensions. Much has been written about both the pros and cons of MOOCs, but minimal work has been done to empirically review the pedagogical approaches actually taken by specific MOOCs. It should be noted that our goal is to characterize, not evaluate, MOOC pedagogies.

Context

The development of the AMP tool began with work conducted by the American Council on Education's College Credit Recommendation Service (ACE CREDIT) to review MOOCs for college credits. In 2013, the project, which was funded by the Gates Foundation, resulted in ACE CREDIT approving 13 MOOCs for college credit. ACE CREDIT created exams to test content learning for each of the MOOCs it approved—since ACE CREDIT exams can be taken at a relatively small cost, they can thereby considerably reduce the costs of obtaining college credits.

While ACE reviewed MOOCs for content coverage, they subcontracted with the University of Illinois Springfield (UIS) team to develop a tool to categorize the pedagogical approaches taken by the same MOOCs. The research reported in this chapter deals with the development and validation of that tool and preliminary findings concerning its applicability to review the original 13 ACE-approved MOOCs, as well as four non-STEM Coursera MOOCs, one Carnegie Mellon Open Learning Initiative (https://oli.cmu.edu/), and two Saylor (http://www.saylor.org/) courses chosen for comparison purposes.

The AMP Tool

The focus of AMP (Assessing MOOC Pedagogies) instrument is on characterizing the pedagogies employed in MOOCs. It is based on a similar tool developed by Professor Thomas Reeves (1996) of the University of Georgia for describing the pedagogical dimensions of computer-based instruction. Reeves wrote, "Pedagogical dimensions are concerned with those aspects of design and implementation . . . that directly affect learning" (1996, p. 1). His original CBI tool included 14 dimensions focused on aspects of design and implementation that had been shown to directly affect learning. Reviewers were asked to characterize where a particular CBI application fell on a 1 to 10 scale for each dimension.

In adapting Reeves' tool, the UIS team retained 6 of the 14 dimensions: (1) epistemology, (2) the role of the teacher, (3) experiential validity (renamed "focus of activities"), (4) cooperative learning, (5) the accommodation of individual differences, and (6) user role—albeit adapting these to the MOOC context. They also added four other dimensions: (7) structure, (8) the approach to content, (9) feedback, and (10) activities/assessment. The 1–10 scale for each dimension was also reduced to a 1–5 scale after this was found to result in much better inter-rater reliability. Indeed, the researchers iteratively revised the AMP tool through testing its efficacy to provide consistent reviews. In addition to changing the scale, the researchers also developed specific criteria for many of the dimensions to guide reviewers toward common ratings. AMP's ten pedagogical dimensions are described below.

1. EPISTEMOLOGY (1 = Objectivist/5 = Constructivist)

Objectivists believe that knowledge exists separately from knowing; while constructivists believe that knowledge is "constructed" in the minds of individuals. Each perspective leads to different pedagogical approaches—instructionists focus on instruction, instructional materials, and absolute goals, whereas constructivists focus on learning and the integration of learners' goals, experiences, and abilities into their learning experiences. The EPISTEMOLOGY dimension asks reviewers to discern the epistemological thrust of a MOOC from the activities and materials provided.

2. ROLE OF THE TEACHER (1 = Teacher Centered/5 = Student Centered)

Teacher-centered teaching and learning is what it sounds like. A teacher-centered learning environment focuses on firm deadlines, one-size-fits-all, automated grading with little or no human response, and one-way communication. Indicators of student-centeredness include: choice in ways of indicating the acquistion of knowledge, self-paced, generative assessments, and discussions that are responded to and/or graded.

3. FOCUS OF ACTIVITIES (1 = Convergent/5 = Divergent)

Convergent learning is learning that "converges" on a single correct answer. In contrast, in divergent learning, learners explore, and defend, what Judith Langer (2000) called a "horizon of possibilities." The focus of activities is rated 1 if all answers are either right or wrong; 2 if there is more than one path to a single right answer; 3 if there is a balance of convergent and divergent activities; 4 if a majority of questions suggest multiple correct answers; and 5 if most questions can be answered multiple ways.

4. STRUCTURE (1 = Less Structured/5 = More Structured)

The structure dimension describes the level and clarity of structure in the MOOC. Four criteria are provided that indicate more structure: clear directions, transparent navigation, consistent organizations of the units, and the consistent organization of the presentation of the material from unit to unit.

5. APPROACH TO CONTENT (1 = Concrete/5 = Abstract)

The ratings for this pedagogical dimension are not intended to reflect whether the subject matter is abstract or concrete; rather, it examines whether the material is presented in an abstract or a concrete manner. Concrete presentations would include real world examples and activities, whereas abstract presentations are not related to real world applications. Those presentations that fall in the middle include ones which use concrete analogies to make abstract ideas more understandable.

6. FEEDBACK (1 = Infrequent, Unclear/5 = Frequent, Constructive)

The ratings for this dimension focus on the usefulness of feedback provided using four criteria which include whether or not the feedback is: immediate, clear, constructive, and/or personal.

7. COOPERATIVE LEARNING (1 = Unsupported/5 = Integral)

This dimension examines the extent of cooperative learning in the MOOC. The criteria for this dimension include the following: meetups/discussion boards are encouraged, cooperative learning is employed as a teaching strategy, the assessment of collaborative work is evident, and group activities are a main part of the course.

8. ACCOMMODATION OF INDIVIDUAL DIFFERENCES
(1 = Unsupported/5 = Multifaceted)

Although it might be assumed that MOOCs would be accommodating to individual differences among learners, this is not always the case. Some MOOCs make minimal, if any, provision for individual differences, whereas others are designed to accommodate a wide range of individual differences A rating of multifaceted (5) on this dimension would indicate all four of the following criteria—self-directed learning, verbal and written presentations by instructor, opportunities for students to present answers to material in a variety of ways, and universal design—are met.

9. ACTIVITIES/ASSIGNMENTS (1 = Artificial/5 = Authentic)

Brown, Collins, and Duguid (1989) argued that knowledge, and hence learning, is situated in the context in which it is developed; therefore, instructional activities and assessments should be situated in real world activities and problems. They labeled such activities as "authentic" and contrast them with typical school activities which they deemed "artificial" because they are typically contrived. In the AMP context, the evidence of artificial approaches focused on activities and assessments which ask for declarative knowledge, formulas, rules, and/or definitions, whereas authentic approaches might include relevant examples that the instructor works through for the learners, and assessments that regularly involve real world problems.

10. USER ROLE (1 = Passive/5 = Generative)

Hannafin (1992) identified an important distinction between learning environments. He maintained that some learning environments, which he termed "mathemagenic" but that other researchers call "passive," were primarily intended to enable learners to access various representations of content. Other learning environments, called "generative," engage learners in the process of creating, elaborating, or representing knowledge themselves.

The AMP tool also includes fields for identifying the MOOC title, instructor(s), platform/university offering the course, subject area, level/prerequisites, length, and the time required. Using the AMP tool, reviewers are also asked to provide a general description of the MOOC, its use of media, and the types of assessment used in it. In this chapter, however, we will focus on the pedagogical characteristics and the different patterns which distinguish unique pedagogical approaches.

Methodology

After initial revisions of the AMP instrument (which included reducing the scales from 10 to 5 points and adding criteria to some dimensions to make it easier to distinguish between ratings), four independent reviewers surveyed the first 13

MOOCs they were given. Afterwards, they met to see if they could come to consensus on their ratings. Initial inter-rater reliability across measures was above 80 percent on all MOOCs; importantly, the level of agreement increased to 100 percent through consensus as reviewers met and went over their decisions. The MOOC review process and initial findings are described in the following sections.

MOOC Reviews

To date, researchers in the AMP group have reviewed nine Coursera, seven Udacity, one edX, one Carnegie Mellon Open Learning Initiative, and two Saylor MOOCs.

They began by considering 13 MOOCs that were approved for credit by the American Council on Education (ACE). These courses were: *College Algebra, BioElectricity, Genetics, Pre-Calculus,* and *Single Variable Calculus* from Coursera; *Introduction to Artificial Intelligence, Introduction to Computer Science, Introduction to Physics, Introduction to Statistics, Introduction to Parallel Programming, 3-D Modeling* and *HTML 5 Game Development* from Udacity; and *Circuits and Electronics* from edX.

Each set of these first courses received quite similar ratings, although there were some clear differences between platforms. Interestingly, while Coursera MOOCs followed a format that resembles the traditional university lecture-text–testing routine spread over multiple weeks with hard deadlines, Udacity courses all followed a format highly akin to that of the programmed learning approach developed long ago by the well-known behaviorist B. F. Skinner (see, e.g., Holland & Skinner, 1961). Interestingly, Udacity courses accordingly tended to fall slightly more in the middle of the ratings than was the case with Coursera courses. Only one course, Circuits, was available for review from edX, so little can be inferred about that platform; that being said, this one course on Circuits was very much like the Coursera courses in both obvious format and pedagogical ratings.

Whereas Table 10.1 summarizes these numerical findings, Figure 10.1 explores the patterns in terms of pedagogical approaches.

TABLE 10.1 Average ratings for ACE approved courses across platforms

Dimension	COURSERA	UDACITY	EDX
1. Epistemology	1.0	2.4	1.0
2. Role of teacher	1.4	2.0	1.0
3. Focus of activities	1.0	1.9	1.0
4. Structure	5.0	4.9	5.0
5. Approach to content	3.6	3.0	4.0
6. Feedback	2.0	4.3	3.0
7. Cooperative learning	2.8	2.1	2.0
8. Accommodation of individual differences	2.6	3.0	2.0
9. Activities/assessment	2.6	3.3	1.0
10. User role	2.0	3.1	2.0

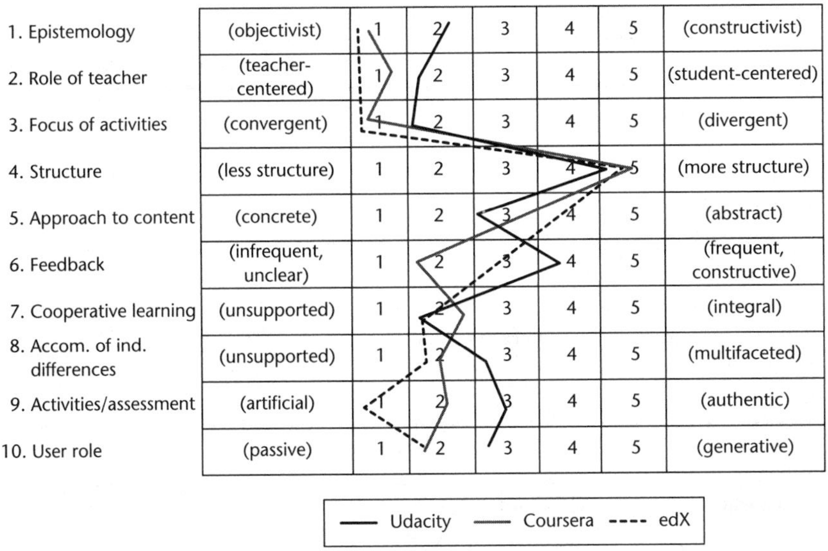

		1	2	3	4	5	
1. Epistemology	(objectivist)	1	2	3	4	5	(constructivist)
2. Role of teacher	(teacher-centered)	1	2	3	4	5	(student-centered)
3. Focus of activities	(convergent)	1	2	3	4	5	(divergent)
4. Structure	(less structure)	1	2	3	4	5	(more structure)
5. Approach to content	(concrete)	1	2	3	4	5	(abstract)
6. Feedback	(infrequent, unclear)	1	2	3	4	5	(frequent, constructive)
7. Cooperative learning	(unsupported)	1	2	3	4	5	(integral)
8. Accom. of ind. differences	(unsupported)	1	2	3	4	5	(multifaceted)
9. Activities/assessment	(artificial)	1	2	3	4	5	(authentic)
10. User role	(passive)	1	2	3	4	5	(generative)

—— Udacity   —— Coursera   ---- edX

FIGURE 10.1   Comparisons of pedagogical approaches across 1 edX, 5 Coursera, and 7 Udacity courses

Because all of the ACE for credit MOOCs were in the STEM disciplines, the researchers decided to move on to investigate some MOOCs in non-STEM areas. More specifically, we considered four Coursera courses in non-STEM subjects, including, (1) *Art and Inquiry*, (2) *Comics and Graphic Novels*, (3) *Jazz Improvisation*, and (4) *The Music of the Beatles*. Interestingly, *The Music of the Beatles'* ratings were very similar to those of the Coursera STEM MOOCs. The ratings for the other three non-STEM MOOCs, however, differed quite substantially from the STEM MOOCs. Table 10.2 compares ratings for the Coursera STEM courses, *The Music of the Beatles*, and the non-STEM courses without *The Music of the Beatles*. Figure 10.2 graphically compares these ratings.

With the exception of *The Music of the Beatles*, the non-STEM Coursera courses tended to be constructivist, more student-centered, and highly divergent, but less structured than their STEM counterparts. Although similar in their approach to content, the non-STEM courses were more personal in that a greater variety of feedback was provided, they were more supportive of cooperative learning, and they were more accommodating of individual assessment choices; in terms of the latter, these non-STEM courses can be regarded as more authentic and more generative.

The comparison of Coursera STEM and non-STEM MOOCs, and the way the Beatles course seems to fit with the STEM and not the non-STEM MOOCs suggests two distinct pedagogical patterns. Interestingly, the two patterns that we observed are related to what Anna Sfard (1998) identified as two metaphors for learning—the acquisition metaphor and the participation metaphor. In the acquisition metaphor, learning is seen as acquiring

TABLE 10.2 Average ratings for Coursera STEM vs non-STEM courses

Dimension	STEM	BEATLES	NON-STEM
1. Epistemology	1.0	3.8	4.7
2. Role of teacher	1.4	2.5	3.0
3. Focus of activities	1.0	3.5	4.3
4. Structure	5.0	3.8	3.3
5. Approach to content	3.6	2.5	2.7
6. Feedback	2.0	3.0	3.3
7. Cooperative learning	2.8	2.8	3.0
8. Accommodation of individual differences	2.6	3.0	3.3
9. Activities/assessment	2.6	3.8	4.7
10. User role	3.0	3.8	4.3

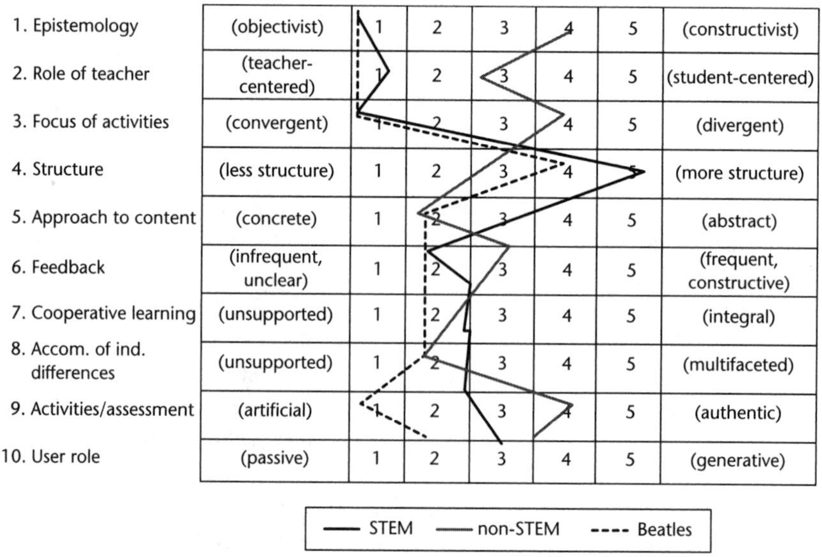

FIGURE 10.2 Comparison of STEM vs non–STEM courses

knowledge from outside the individual. In the participation metaphor, individuals collaboratively construct knowledge. From this perspective, the two patterns we identified in our preliminary findings were most divergent in terms of epistemology; particularly in terms of the key dimensions that follow from epistemology, such as the focus of activities, assessments, and the role of the teacher and student.

To further explore the efficacy of the learning metaphors for describing pedagogical patterns among MOOCs, the researchers decided to review courses offered on additional platforms: *World History in the Early Modern and Modern Eras* and *Introduction to Statistics* offered through Saylor University, and *Probability and Statistics*, offered by the Carnegie Mellon Open Learning Initiative (OLI). While the Saylor *Introduction to Statistics* course seemed to align with the Coursera STEM MOOCs and *The Music of the Beatles* as "acquisition" courses, the OLI MOOC and the other Saylor course seemed most akin to the Udacity MOOCs in that they were "self-directed" courses, suggesting a third metaphor for learning. Three Coursera MOOCs—*Art and Inquiry, Comics and Graphic Novels,* and *Jazz Improvisation*—continued to be categorized as "participation" courses. Table 10.3 compares the ratings of MOOCs falling into these pedagogical categories and Figure 10.3 gives a graphical comparison of these courses. These representations clearly show self-directed MOOCs falling between the acquisition and participatory categories.

In terms of interpreting Table 10.3, "Acquisition MOOCs" included Coursera STEM courses + *The Music of the Beatles* + *Circuits* (edX) + Saylor's *Introduction to Statistics*. "Participation MOOCs" included Coursera non-STEM courses—*The Music of the Beatles* MOOC. "Self-direction MOOCs" included Udacity courses + *World History in the Early Modern and Modern Eras* from Saylor and *Probability and Statistics* from Carnegie Mellon OLI.

Conclusions

Preliminary research suggests that the AMP tool can be used to distinguish between MOOC pedagogical approaches, and that it can do so with high

TABLE 10.3 Average ratings by metaphors for learning*

Dimension	Acquisition MOOCs $n = 8$	Self-direction MOOCs $n = 9$	Participation MOOCs $n = 3$
1. Epistemology	1.0	2.3	4.7
2. Role of teacher	1.4	2.1	3.0
3. Focus of activities	1.0	1.9	4.3
4. Structure	4.9	4.8	3.3
5. Approach to content	3.4	2.8	2.7
6. Feedback	2.2	4.0	3.3
7. Cooperative learning	2.4	1.9	3.0
8. Accommodation of individual differences	2.2	2.8	3.3
9. Activities/assessment	2.2	3.4	4.7
10. User role	1.8	2.7	4.3

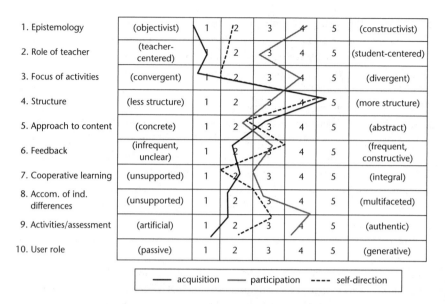

1. Epistemology	(objectivist)	1	2	3	4	5	(constructivist)
2. Role of teacher	(teacher-centered)		2	3	4	5	(student-centered)
3. Focus of activities	(convergent)	1	2	3	4	5	(divergent)
4. Structure	(less structure)	1	2	3	4	5	(more structure)
5. Approach to content	(concrete)	1	2	3	4	5	(abstract)
6. Feedback	(infrequent, unclear)	1	2	3	4	5	(frequent, constructive)
7. Cooperative learning	(unsupported)	1	2	3	4	5	(integral)
8. Accom. of ind. differences	(unsupported)	1	2	3	4	5	(multifaceted)
9. Activities/assessment	(artificial)	1	2	3	4	5	(authentic)
10. User role	(passive)	1	2	3	4	5	(generative)

——— acquisition   ——— participation   ---- self-direction

FIGURE 10.3 Comparison of ratings by metaphors for learning

consistency among raters. Indeed, inter-rater reliability has only improved over time even as the team has sought out different sorts of MOOCs to review. Future work should test whether others can use it with a similar degree of consistency.

In our preliminary MOOC reviews, while finding some differences between the major platforms and/or between disciplinary areas, the most compelling distinctions were between pedagogical approaches that were centered on metaphors for learning; specifically acquisition, participation, and self-direction.

Of particular interest are the self-directed courses as these seem to fit most clearly with the ways most participants actually use MOOCs. Based on an analysis of extensive data retrieved from a prototypical MOOC, for instance, Anderson and colleagues (2014) described five ways users engaged with it, as *viewers* who just watch lectures, *solvers* who just do assignments, *all-rounders* who do both, *collectors* who pick and choose from the materials, and *bystanders* who seemingly do nothing. Of these, only the all-rounders, who make up a very small percentage of those enrolled, behave like typical post-secondary students. Similarly, Kizilcec and colleagues (2014) characterized participants in the three MOOCs as *completers*, *auditors*, *samplers*, and *disengaged learners*. They argued that these clusters suggest that binary, pass/fail models of completion do not work for MOOCs.

Indeed, anecdotal evidence suggests a variety of reasons users engage with MOOCs ranging from simple curiosity to brushing up on a topic to exploring a new subject, and that only a small percentage of those enrolled in MOOCs actually approach them as courses. DeBoer and colleagues (2014) use data from a single MOOC to argue that student behavior in a MOOC is nothing if not idiosyncratic. They argue that typical variables like enrollment, participation, curriculum, and achievement must be reconceptualized for the MOOC environment. The fact that research reveals that users have multiple reasons for, and corresponding patterns of, engaging with MOOCs suggests that MOOCs which fit with the self-direction paradigm may be of the greatest utility. This trend will certainly be explored by our team in the near future.

We expect that MOOCs will become more sophisticated as they evolve. Future work will explore such potential evolution, as well as more courses and differing platforms, including cMOOCs and adaptive structures (DeBoer et al., 2014; Fasihuddin, Skinner, & Athauda, 2013). It further appears that future work will need to further explore self-directed participation models in order to better address the ways in which MOOC learners often access and use MOOC learning platforms (DeBoer et al., 2014).

The rapid growth of MOOCs has presented a pedagogical and design challenge that needs to be addressed as these types of courses continue to be developed at an expanding rate. The need to identify course designs that address student needs and increase student retention without overwhelming instructors is important. Our research in this highly evolving and exciting field is a first step in this direction.

Karen Swan is the Stukel Distinguished Professor of Educational Leadership at the University of Illinois Springfield. Her research is in the general area of technology and learning, on which she has published over 125 journal articles and book chapters and co-edited two books. Her research currently focuses on online learning, learning analytics, and MOOCs. She was awarded Most Outstanding Achievement in Online Learning by an Individual by the Online Learning Consortium, the Distinguished Alumnus Award from Teachers College, Columbia University, and the Burks Oakley II Distinguished Online Teaching Award from UIS. She is a Fellow of the Online Learning Consortium.

Scott Day is Professor and Chair of the Department of Educational Leadership at the University of Illinois at Springfield and holds an Ed.D. in Educational Organization and Leadership from the University of Illinois at Urbana-Champaign. Dr. Day teaches courses on Instructional Leadership and Assessment for Learning Online. The program was awarded the Sloan-C Outstanding Program of the Year in 2010. In 2010, Dr. Day was awarded the Pearson Faculty Award for Outstanding Teaching at the University of Illinois at Springfield. He has published on design-based approaches to improving online courses, using peer review and analytics to develop communities of inquiry in online courses, and, most recently, on pedagogical approaches to massive open online courses (MOOCs).

Leonard Bogle is an Associate Professor in the Educational Leadership program and a University Fellow at the University of Illinois at Springfield where he serves as a Master Teacher Leader (MTL) online instructor. His major areas of interest are in the enhancement of online instruction through the improvement of course design and the analysis of pedagogy as presented in MOOC offerings. He is part of a team that has published three book chapters on these topics and has also taught master's courses in leadership, curriculum design, introduction to research, Capstone projects, Master's Closure projects, organizational dynamics, and teacher evaluation and assessment.

Traci van Prooyen is an Assistant Professor in the Teacher Education Department at the University of Illinois at Springfield. She holds an Ed.D. in Curriculum and Instruction from Illinois State University. Dr. Van Prooyen teaches courses on child development, educational psychology, classroom management, exceptional child, and curriculum, planning, and assessment. In addition to her interests related to online pedagogy, Dr. Van Prooyen's research interests also includes the qualitative aspects of teaching related primarily to dispositions.

Note

1 Portions of this chapter appear in an article in *E-mentor* 2014, *2*(54) and are included here with permission from the publisher.

References

Anderson, A., Huttenlocher, D., Kleinberg, J., & Leskovec, J. (2014). *Engaging with massive online courses*. Paper presented at WWW '14, April 7–11, Seoul, South Korea. Retrieved from: http://cs.stanford.edu/people/ashton/pubs/mooc-engagement-www2014.pdf.

Bousquet, M. (2012, July 25). Good MOOCs, bad MOOCs. *Chronicle of Higher Education*. Retrieved from http://chronicle.com/blogs/brainstorm/good-moocsbad-moocs/50361.

Brown, J.S., Collins, A., & Duguid, P. (1989). Situated cognition and the culture of learning. *Educational Researcher, 18*(1), 32–42.

Christensen, G., Steinmetz, A., Alcorn, B., Bennett, A., Woods, D., & Emanuel, E.J. (2013). The MOOC phenomenon: Who takes massive open online courses and why? Retrieved from http://papers.ssrn.com/sol3/papers.cfm?abstract_id=2350964.

Coursera. (2012a). *Course Explorer.* Retrieved from http://www.cousera.org/.

Coursera. (2012b). Coursera hits 1 million students across 196 countries. *Coursera Blog.* Retrieved from http://blog.coursera.org/post/29062736760/coursera-hits-1-million students-scross-196-countries.

Darabi, A., Arrastia, M., Nelson, D., Cornille, T., & Liang, X. (2011). Cognitive presence in asynchronous online learning: A comparison of four discussion strategies. *Journal of Computer Assisted Learning, 27*(3), 216–27.

DeBoer, J., Ho, A.D., Stump, G.S., & Breslow, L. (2014). Changing "course": Reconceptualizing educational variables for massive open online courses. *Educational Researcher, 43*(2), 74–84.

edX (2012). *EdX.* Retrieved from https://www.edx.org/.

Fasihuddin, H.A., Skinner, G.D., & Athauda, R.I. (2013). Boosting the opportunities of open learning (MOOCs) through learning theories. *GSTF Journal on Computing, 3*(3). Retrieved from http://www.globalsciencejournals.com/article/10.7603%2Fs40601-013-0031-z#page-1.

Friedman, T.L. (2013, January 26). Revolution hits the universities. *The New York Times.* Retrieved from http://www.nytimes.com/2013/01/27/opinion/sunday/friedman-revolution-hits-the-universities.html?_r=0.

Glance, D., Forsey, M., & Riley, M. (2013, May). The pedagogical foundations of massive open online courses. *First Monday.* Retrieved from http://firstmonday.org/ojs/index.php/fm/article/view/4350/3673.

Guzdial, M., & Adams, J.C. (2014). MOOCs need more work; so do CS graduates. *Communications of the ACM, 57*(1), 18–19.

Hannafin, M.J. (1992). Emerging technologies, ISD, and learning environments: Critical perspectives. *Educational Technology Research and Development, 40*(1), 49–63.

Holland, J.G., & Skinner, B.F. (1961). *The analysis of behavior: A program for self-instruction.* New York: McGraw-Hill.

Khan, S. (2012). *The one world school house: Education reimagined.* New York: Twelve.

Kizilcec, R.F., Piech, C., & Schneider, E. (2013). Deconstructing disengagement: Analyzing learner subpopulations in massive open online courses. In *Proceedings of the Third International Conference on Learning Analytics and Knowledge* (pp. 170–9). New York, NY, USA: ACM. doi:10.1145/2460296.2460330.

Langer, J. (2000). *Discussion as exploration: Literature and the horizon of possibilities.* National Research Center on English Learning and Achievement. Retrieved from http://www.albany.edu/cela/reports/langer/langerdiscussion.pdf.

Levin, T. (2013, December 10). After setbacks, online courses are rethought. *The New York Times.* Retrieved from: http://www.nytimes.com/2013/12/11/us/after-set-backs-online-courses-are-rethought.html.

Li, Q. (2004). Knowledge building community: Keys for using online forums. *TechTrends, 48*(4), 24–9.

Lu, J., & Law, N. (2012). Online peer assessment: Effects of cognitive and affective feedback. *Instructional Science, 40*(2), 257–75.

Masterson, K. (2013). Giving MOOCs some credit. *American Council on Education.* Retrieved from http://www.acenet.edu/the-presidency/columns-and-features/Pages/Giving-MOOCs-Some-Credit.aspx.

Norvig, P. (2012). Peter Norvig: The 100,000-student classroom. Retrieved from http://www.ted.com/talks/peter_norvig_the_100_000_student_classroom.

Reeves, T. (1996). *Evaluating what really matters in computer-based education.* Retrieved from http://eduworks.com/Documents/Workshops/EdMedia1998/docs/reeves.html.

Reeves, T.C., & Hedberg, J.G. (2014). MOOCs: Let's get REAL. *Educational Technology*, *54*(1), 3–8.

Romiszowski, A.J. (2013). What's really new about MOOCs? *Educational Technology*, *53*(4), 48–51.

Roth, M.S. (2013, April 29). My modern experience teaching a MOOC. *The Chronicle of Higher Education: The Digital Campus*. Retrieved from http://chronicle.com/article/My-Modern-MOOC-Experience/138781/.

Sandeen, C. (2013). Integrating MOOCs into traditional higher education: The emerging "MOOC 3.0" era. *Change*, *45*(5), 34–9.

Sfard, A. (1998). On two metaphors for learning and the dangers of choosing just one. *Educational Researcher*, *27*(4), 4–13.

Shirky, C. (2012). Napster, Udacity and the Academy. Retrieved from http://www.shirky.com/weblog/2012/11/napster-udacity-and-the-academy/.

Stiggins, R.J. (2002). Assessment crisis: The absence of assessment for learning. *Phi Delta Kappan*, *83*(10), 758–65.

Strijbos, J.W., Narciss, S., & Dünnebier, K. (2010). Peer feedback content and sender's competence level in academic writing revision tasks: Are they critical for feedback perceptions and efficiency? *Learning and Instruction*, *20*(4), 291–303.

Swan K., & Mitrani, M. (1993). The changing nature of teaching and learning in computer-based classrooms. *Journal of Research on Computing in Education*, *26*(1), 40–54.

Vardi, M.Y. (2012). Will MOOCs destroy academia? *Communications of the ACM*, *55*(11), 5. Retrieved from http://cacm.acm.org/magazines/2012/11/156587-will-moocs-destroy-academia/fulltext.

Walker, B. (2007). *Bridging the distance: How social interaction, presence, social presence, and sense of community influence student learning experiences in an online virtual environment*. Unpublished PhD dissertation, University of North Carolina. Retrieved from http://libres.uncg.edu/ir/uncg/f/umi-uncg-1472.pdf.

Waters, J.K. (2013). What do massive open online courses mean for higher ed? *Campus Technology*, *26*(12). Retrieved from http://camputechnology.com/Home.aspx.

Udacity (2012). *Udacity*. Retrieved from http://udacity.com.

Yuan, L., & Powell, S. (2013). MOOC's and open education: Implications for higher education. *Centre for Educational Technology & Interoperability Standards*. Retrieved from http://publications.cetis.ac.uk/2013/667.

11

QUALITY ASSURANCE FOR OPEN EDUCATIONAL RESOURCES

What's the Difference?

Sanjaya Mishra and Asha Kanwar

Introduction

In 1987, the Commonwealth Heads of Government agreed to create a Commonwealth institution to support cooperation in distance education. They made this decision after considering a report entitled *Towards a Commonwealth of Learning: A Proposal to Create the University of the Commonwealth for Co-operation in Distance Learning* prepared by a committee of experts chaired by Lord Briggs. The report proposed the creation of a new institution designed to promote collaboration among Commonwealth countries. It stated that the objectives of this new institution would be "to widen access to education, to share resources, to raise educational quality and to support the mobility of ideas, of teaching, of relevant research and of people" (Briggs, 1987, p. 60). In addition, the Memorandum of Understanding that established the Commonwealth of Learning (COL) included supporting objectives such as "assisting the creation and development of institutional capacity in distance education in member countries"; "assisting the acquisition and delivery of teaching materials and more generally facilitating access to them"; and "commissioning and promoting the adaptation and development of teaching materials." Such statements make it clear that, since its inception, COL has supported the development and sharing of quality distance learning materials.

COL's approach to quality assurance has been threefold: (1) to influence policy at national and institutional levels, (2) to develop resources, and (3) to build the capacity of institutions and individuals in implementing quality assurance (QA) to manage Open and Distance Learning (ODL) systems with efficiency and effectiveness. At present, COL continues its advocacy efforts to ensure that open universities and campus providers share the purpose of all universities. It is true that many open universities see themselves as having a social mission and use more flexible delivery modes, but if judgements are based on fitness for purpose, quality of courses, effective learner support, and student achievement, there is no need for separate QA regulations for ODL activities. COL recognized the importance and the need to assure the quality of ODL provision at an early stage to warrant "parity of esteem" or respect for the degrees offered through ODL.

COL has developed several QA toolkits and publications as well as a QA micro-site with free resources. The *Transnational Qualifications Framework*, developed by COL for mutual recognition of qualifications, is used by the 32 small states of the Commonwealth and the Review and Improvement Model (COLRIM) for quality assurance. Using the framework, institutions assess their respective practices as a step towards external accreditation or as an ongoing process of continuous self-improvement. Recognizing the potential of making learning resources available free of cost as well as free from restrictions on their wider use, COL embraced the Open Educational Resource (OER) movement to promote access and adaptation of teaching materials. In the following section, we discuss the specific features of our QA initiatives for OER.

March of Open Educational Resources

The OER movement began with the emergence of MIT OpenCourseWare, which was announced in the *New York Times* just after the start of the millennium (Goldberg, 2001). Ever since the coining of the term OER, at a meeting at UNESCO in 2002, numerous other OER projects and initiatives have arisen across the globe. It is worth mentioning, however, that COL had been developing learning materials collaboratively and sharing these with its stakeholders even before this time. For example, COL's Science Technology and Maths Programme (STAMP 2000+) modules were developed collaboratively by 140 academics from eight countries in Southern Africa and made available for free use prior to 2001, albeit without any open license. These STAMP 2,000+ modules were developed *by* Africans *for* Africans and within Africa and were uploaded on the World Space satellite for free use by anyone anywhere on the continent. In addition, COL has been involved in many material development projects, including initially supporting the WikiEducator online platform to share materials. Such participation has resulted in many lessons having been learned, including the following (Kanwar, Kodhandaraman, & Umar, 2010):

- While capacity development is necessary, it is also important to ensure buy-in from local partners and to have a clear implementation strategy.
- In spite of the strength of the communities to self-organize and contribute resources, there is a need to put in place a governance structure to steer the project and monitor progress against agreed-upon quality standards.
- Any OER project with a bottom-up participatory approach requires much longer time frames.

In 2012, UNESCO and COL, drawing on the assistance from the William and Flora Hewlett Foundation, organized the World OER Congress at Paris. This event, which was attended by both authors of this chapter, resulted in the Paris OER Declaration (2012). This declaration recommended that governments promote and use OERs. It also encouraged the open licensing of educational materials produced with public funds and reiterated that OERs are teaching, learning, and research materials in any medium, digital or otherwise. These resources are either available in the public domain or released under an open license that enables no-cost access, use, adaptation, and redistribution with either no or only limited restrictions.

We at COL view OERs as (1) free and freely available, (2) suitable for all levels of education, (3) modular, (4) reusable, and (5) online. The assumption here is that OERs would be small reusable learning objects residing in online repositories that institutions would access, adapt, and construct as courses (Kanwar et al., 2010). While the often-cited advantage of OERs is about the exchange of knowledge and South–South and North–South collaboration, it obviously saves both course authoring time and money. We have also witnessed the fact that OERs foster collaborative approaches to content development—unlike the single-author model of textbook writing. Therefore, OERs are a powerful tool to support capacity building in developing countries as well as to assist in improving the quality of the materials due to collaboration. In addition, OERs encourage the preservation and dissemination of indigenous knowledge (Kanwar et al., 2010).

Given that education in most disciplines is context-based, the obvious cost–benefit of OERs is not visible to many teachers and educational administrators. Preliminary research supported by COL on the cost economics of OERs revealed substantial savings in terms of both time and cost (Butcher & Hoosen, 2012). Moreover, there are different levels of understanding in relation to copyright and intellectual property rights issues. There are also issues related to the adaptation of OERs as many teachers and administrators have a "not invented here" syndrome (Johnson, Levine, Smith, & Stone, 2010). Challenges to their adoption still exist, including institutional barriers and the quality of the resources available (Bossu & Tynan, 2011).

OER: Quality Issues

With the rise of social media, there has been a global movement towards collaboration in the development and sharing of content. The fundamental principle is that any materials developed with public funds should be made available free for others to use as required under an open license. Since anyone can adapt the content, many ask questions, such as, who is responsible for the quality of repurposed content? How do institutions ensure the integrity of their credentials? And what is the role of QA agencies?

While there is a growing demand for OERs, many people believe that "free educational resources must necessarily be of poor quality" (Wiley & Gurrell, 2009, p. 19). Quality dimensions, such as accuracy, relevance, currency, and pedagogic effectiveness in terms of learning design, would apply to OERs just as they would to any educational content. Wiley and Gurrell (2009) further argue that despite the issues related to the traditional parameters of quality, the increasing acceptability of OERs is related to the relationship of the user to the resource. This relationship comes from the adaptation and co-creation of the content, which emanates from two basic characteristics of OERs, namely, reusability and openness.

Dhanarajan and Abeywardena (2013, pp. 9–10) found that teachers' lack of ability to locate quality OERs was a leading barrier against reusing OERs. This issue is primarily due to a lack of availability of any mechanism to ensure and assess the quality of OERs. In addition, Nikoi, Rowlett, Armellini, and Witthaus (2011) reported that a few studies have found several important discrepancies between the rising culture of openness and existing approaches to teaching. More specifically, they identified a number of key issues such as a lack of time to adapt OERs, disciplinary differences, cultural issues, and differences in the level of support for OER development emerging as major impediments for academic staff.

Many OER advocates and educators also believe that quality assurance of OERs is contrary to its notion of openness. From this perspective, it is the users who should decide the quality, as a function of purpose. Any a priori assurance of quality would be of no help to the users of OERs. As such, the proponents of this line of thought believe that the user (learner or teacher) is the best judge and knowledgeable enough to make decisions on the quality of the resource. In contrast, educators and thought leaders typically believe that every teaching-learning resource should undergo a rigorous peer-review process to ensure quality. Such an approach definitely slows down the process of OER development, and it creates a structure not needed for the Web 2.0/3.0 world.

The Commonwealth Educational Media Centre for Asia (CEMCA) is the regional centre of COL for the eight Commonwealth countries of Asia. As OER began to become popular, at CEMCA, we recognized the need to develop quality assurance guidelines for OERs covering the two divergent approaches. First, OERs should be user-generated content and inherently open. In effect, it would be detrimental to create formal structures and processes to assure the quality of OERs within QA agencies. Second, we also believe that OERs should be of high quality and appropriate for the needs and contexts of the stakeholders who use and produce them. Thus, we developed a framework to assist the users in deciding the quality of OERs using a range of criteria. We expect that the framework and its criteria can be automated within any repository to help users rate the content by choosing criteria applicable to them. Such an approach would gather ratings from different users to provide information to prospective users of a resource—thereby saving time for both learners and teachers as they navigate the abundance of OERs.

As part of the CEMCA project to develop QA guidelines for OERs, Kawachi (2013) reviewed more than thirty frameworks/lists of criteria for quality assurance in related fields such as e-learning or educational innovations. This review revealed several criteria suitable for the quality assurance of OERs.

As a means of developing our own guidelines, we convened a regional forum and conducted online consultations in order to develop the OER TIPS Framework, Version 1.0 (Kawachi, 2013). The important aspect that emerged from those consultations concerned the unique features of the openness of OERs, and the effect of such features on the quality of courses. Experts agreed that openness brings additional values for making learning materials more accessible to learners with special needs. Openness also offers the localization of content to suit specific linguistic and cultural needs. And, it improves access using open software and technologies. TIPS represents a set of 65 criteria grouped under four broad headings: (1) Teaching and learning, (2) Information and content, (3) Presentation, and (4) Technology. Since the criteria list was lengthy, we conducted further research to develop a consensus using the Delphi technique and Content Validity Ratio (CVR) (Lawshe, 1975) as the statistical anchor to reduce the criteria to a more manageable list. While the work remains in progress, preliminary results reveal a set of 18 criteria using a modified statistical approach to CVR (see Table 11.1).

Our intention is to develop an assessment model using these criteria to help users assess any OER materials by reviewing the criteria or feature using a four-point scale: (1) not visible, (2) shows little evidence, (3) fairly demonstrates this criteria, and (4) very much demonstrates this criteria. The same can also be used by developers of OERs to analyze their actions to assure quality in the process of OER development.

Approaches to Quality OER

In developing countries, the quality assurance of ODL has been a major area of concern over the past five decades, in large part, since face-to-face education is culturally the norm for the elite few. As most of those who are in the educational system have experienced face-to-face forms of instruction, they have a negative disposition towards the ODL system of education. Therefore, the ODL system has always had to place a high importance on quality to maintain parity with face-to-face education systems.

As Dhanarajan (2013) points out, the ODL system is primarily concerned with the learning paradigm, in contrast to the instructional paradigm which is highly salient in the conventional face-to-face system. In the instructional paradigm, the time of learning is constant and there is variation in learning outcomes, whereas in the learning paradigm, time varies and learning outcomes remain constant for all the learners. Emphasizing this transformative change in paradigm has not been an easy task for ODL practitioners—that is, until the emergence of the massive

TABLE 11.1 Quality guidelines for OER (Kawachi, 2014)

T: Teaching and learning processes

Consider giving a study guide for how to use your OER, with an advance organizer, and navigational aids.

Use a learner-centred approach.

Use up-to-date appropriate and authentic pedagogy.

It should be aligned to local wants and needs, and anticipate the current and future needs of the student.

Don't use difficult or complex language, and do check the readability to ensure it is appropriate to age/level.

Provide a way for the student and other teachers to give you feedback and suggestions on how to improve.

I: Information and material content

Make sure that the knowledge and skills you want the student to learn are up-to-date, accurate, and reliable. Consider asking a subject-matter expert for advice.

All your content should be relevant and appropriate to purpose. Avoid superfluous material and distractions.

Your content should be authentic, internally consistent and appropriately localized

Add links to other materials to enrich your content.

P: Presentation product and format

Be sure the open licence is clearly visible.

Ensure your OER is easy to access and engaging.

Present your material in a clear, concise, and coherent way, taking care with sound quality.

Use open formats for delivery of OERs to enable maximum reuse and remix.

Consider suggesting which OER could come before your OER, and which OER could come afterwards in a learning pathway.

S: System technical and technology

Consider adding metadata tags about the content to help you and others later on to find your OER.

Give metadata tags for expected study duration, for expected level of difficulty, format, and size.

Your OER should be easily portable and transmissible, and you should be able to keep an off-line copy.

open online courses (MOOCs) that depend on learning and instruction practices similar to that of the ODL system (e.g., see the chapter from Deimann, Lipka, & Bastiaens in this volume).

While the acceptability of ODL programmes are growing due to their inherent extensive emphasis on quality assurance, adoption, and adaptation of OERs in both the face-to-face and ODL, the situation still has a long way to go to reach its potential. Realizing that mainstreaming OERs in the educational systems of developing countries would require sustained and long-term interventions,

COL has been engaged in promoting the quality of OERs through four different approaches:

- *Appropriate Policy Development:* In order to create an enabling environment for teachers in educational institutions to use and create OER, it is important that appropriate credit is given to the teachers who create educational resources. In many institutions, publication in a peer-reviewed journal gets credit for promotion, whereas the preparation and making of freely available educational materials is recognized only rarely. In response, COL has been working with national governments and institutions to help them develop appropriate policies for OERs. As part of these efforts, COL has developed a national OER policy template as well as an institutional OER policy template for adoption by governments and educational institutions. COL has supported the Government of Antigua and Barbuda in developing a national OER policy, while two open universities in India have adopted the OER institutional policy template. COL/CEMCA has also assisted the Government of India to develop the open licensing policy guidelines for its flagship project entitled the National Mission on Education through ICTs (NMEICT).

- *Capacity Building:* While policy development is necessary, it is not a sufficient condition to foster the development of OERs in a major way. Training on quality and OER development is central to the creation of additional OERs. In the absence of local capacity, OERs will only create consumers of external information or knowledge resources. More substantial gains from OERs are possible if one aligns the available resource(s) with local needs while releasing such content again with an appropriate open license. Therefore, capacity building in relation to OERs, especially among teachers and policy makers, is a key strategy. In addition to holding workshops, COL is also organizing online training and using MOOC platforms to promote the concepts and practices of OERs. Over the years, COL has developed a huge and widely disseminated knowledge base in this area. For instance, as part of the institutional capacity building at Wawasan Open University in Malaysia, CEMCA assisted in the development of a five-module course on OER-based eLearning. The focus of the course is on integrating OER into online programme design and development as a means to bring cost-effectiveness into online learning.

- *Technology:* The availability of affordable technology is essential for teachers to find and create OERs. While technology penetration in educational institutions is a crucial factor in promoting the use of quality OERs, it is vital to educate top management on appropriate technology in developing countries. COL has been working with institutional leaders to facilitate the integration of Information and Communication technologies (ICTs) in education. Strong leadership support and institutional commitment play a significant role in successful ICT integration (Kirkland & Sutch, 2009) and in promoting the use of OERs. A successful ICT leader in education should be able to lead from the front to not only give vision, but also manage change and influence major stakeholder buy-in. COL is also assuming the role of technology innovator and pathfinder by developing appropriate solutions in tune with technological developments. One of the current innovations that COL has been recommending is the use of low-cost servers, named "Aptus," in classrooms and schools. Aptus servers can reduce the cost of Internet access and provide bundled OERs for access to learners at geographically disadvantaged and resource-poor locations.

- *Course Development:* One of the objectives of COL is to commission the development of relevant teaching materials. As an organization promoting the use of OERs, it is important that COL develops such instructional resources and releases them as OERs. To operationalize this goal, COL developed its own institutional OER policy. All the courses developed at COL are released to the community under a CC BY-SA license. The objective of such a policy is to encourage the development of exemplar courses that can be adopted and adapted in the Commonwealth and elsewhere. Such an approach also helps to reduce costs due to the economies of scale. COL has also developed a directory of OERs using different classification tags to help find and use these resources. While the quality of OERs remains a central concern, the goal of this initiative is to collate available content in one place. In true OER spirit, this approach avoids the duplication of efforts. COL is also promoting the development of open textbooks to ensure quality course development.

While the development of quality OERs is necessary, it is not a sufficient condition for its appropriate use. Finding suitable and high-quality OER forms the starting point for the use of available open education content. However, in the absence of appropriate pedagogical interventions, it remains only a textbook, simulation, animation, or other type of learning resource. Content is not enough. Teachers' capacities to use and integrate OER in their classrooms as well as facilitate learning in ODL environments are crucial to the achievement of learning for those who are less privileged or previously lacking access. Using appropriate self-directed learning principles to develop OERs, and then using these OERs to facilitate learning would improve the quality of learning outcomes for untold numbers of learners.

Conclusion

As is clear from the foregoing discussion, an extensive array of OER efforts is currently taking place around the world. We have witnessed many of these efforts first-hand. In fact, the Commonwealth of Learning has been particularly focussed on promoting the use of quality OERs in both face-to-face and ODL institutions. But, the question still remains—what is the difference? How has our approach to quality changed as a result of the availability of educational resources with an open license? And what is the right balance between crowd-sourced OERs and institutionally generated quality-assured OERs?

Unfortunately, we cannot yet offer specific answers to many of these questions. As might be expected, a particular OER may be considered highly valuable by different learners and users from the perspective of their need to take a particular examination or entrance test. However, teachers and other experts may think that the material in question is narrowly preparing the learners only for the examination, and, therefore, is not of high quality.

Naturally, what is deemed good or bad for one individual is not the same in the case of other individuals, especially when it concerns educational resources. Consequently, we can only offer a set of guidelines and a framework to assist both the creators as well as the users of OERs. To us, the major differences that OERs bring to the discourse about quality in the field of open education relates to the acceptance of the need for the localization of such content as well as a greater awareness of the possible learning contexts in which it will be used. The expansion of OER and associated quality guidelines and frameworks concerning its appropriateness and use also raises in salience questions about how it will be used, as well as who ultimately is using the quality criteria and in what ways are they using it. Recognizing that education is about socially constructed knowledge, COL supports the use of OERs by both teachers and students to create new knowledge when using an acceptable framework. As this occurs, the consumers become the producers of content.

Ultimately, we believe that ODL, as well as face-to-face teaching institutions, can leverage the availability of OERs to improve the quality of learning outcomes for all learners. When this happens, teachers will have more time to think about student engagement and eventually create and facilitate highly interactive and engaging learning environments using open technology and resources. Such is the mission of COL.

 **Sanjaya Mishra** is Director of the Commonwealth Educational Media Centre for Asia (CEMCA). A leading scholar in open, distance and online learning in Asia, Dr. Mishra previously served as Programme Specialist (ICT in Education, Science and Culture) at UNESCO, Paris and as Associate Professor of Distance Education at the Staff Training and Research Institute of Distance Education of Indira Gandhi National Open University, India. Dr. Mishra has received the ISTD-Vivekanand National Award for Excellence in Human Resource Development and Training in 2007 and was the recipient of the Indian Library Leaders Professional Excellence Award 2012 and the Prof. G. Ram Reddy Memorial Social Scientist Award in 2013.

 **Asha Kanwar** is the President and CEO of the Commonwealth of Learning (COL), Vancouver, Canada. She is an internationally renowned distance educator who is also known for her pioneering contributions in the area of learning for development. She has made significant contributions to gender studies, especially the impact of distance education on the lives of Asian women. A recipient of several awards, fellowships, and Honorary Doctorates, Professor Kanwar has studied and worked in different contexts, both developing and developed. She received her master's and MPhil degrees from the Panjab University in India and her DPhil from the University of Sussex.

References

Bossu, C., & Tynan, B. (2011). OERs: New media in the learning landscape. *On the Horizon, 19*(4), 259–67.

Briggs, A. (1987). *Towards a Commonwealth of Learning: A proposal to create the University of the Commonwealth for Co-operation in Distance Learning.* London: Commonwealth Secretariat.

Butcher, N., & Hoosen, S. (2012). *Exploring the business case of open educational resources.* Vancouver: Commonwealth of Learning.

Dhanarajan, G. (2013). Open educational resources: A perspective on quality. *EduComm Asia, 17*(3), 2–5.

Dhanarajan, G., & Abeywardena, I.S. (2013). Higher education and open educational resources in Asia: An overview. In G. Dhanarajan & D. Porter (Eds.), *Open educational resources: An Asian perspective* (pp. 3–20). Vancouver, BC: Commonwealth of Learning. Retrieved from http://www.col.org/PublicationDocuments/pub_PS_OER_Asia_web.pdf.

Goldberg, C. (2001, April 4). Auditing classes at M.I.T., on the Web and free. *New York Times.* Retrieved from http://www.nytimes.com/2001/04/04/us/auditing-classes-at-mit-on-the-web-and-free.html.

Johnson, L., Levine, A., Smith, R., & Stone, S. (2010). *The 2010 Horizon Report.* Austin, TX: New Media Consortium.

Kanwar, A., Kodhandaraman, B., & Umar, A. (2010). Toward sustainable open education resources: A perspective from the global south. *The American Journal of Distance Education, 24,* 65–80.

Kawachi, P. (2013). *Quality assurance guidelines for open educational resources: TIPS framework.* New Delhi, India: CEMCA. Retrieved from http://cemca.org.in/ckfinder/userfiles/files/OERQ_TIPS_978-81-88770-07-6.pdf.

Kawachi, P. (2014). The TIPS quality assurance framework for creating open educational resources: Validation. *Paper presented at the 2nd regional symposium on open educational resources: Beyond advocacy, research and policy,* June 24–7, 2014, Penang, Malaysia.

Kirkland, K., & Sutch, D. (2009). *Overcoming the barriers to educational innovation: A literature Review.* Bristol: Futurelab. Retrieved from http://www2.futurelab.org.uk/resources/documents/lit_reviews/Barriers_to_Innovation_review.pdf.

Lawshe, C.H. (1975). A quantitative approach to content validity. *Personnel Psychology, 28*(4), 563–75. Retrieved from http://www.bwgriffin.com/gsu/courses/edur9131/content/Lawshe_content_valdity.pdf.

Nikoi, S.K., Rowlett, T., Armellini, A., & Witthaus, G. (2011). CORRE: A framework for evaluating and transforming teaching materials into open educational resources. *Open Learning: The Journal of Open, Distance and e-Learning, 26*(3), 191–207.

Paris OER Declaration. (2012, June). World OER Congress held at UNESCO. June 20–2, 2012, Paris, France. Retrieved from http://www.unesco.org/new/fileadmin/MULTIMEDIA/HQ/CI/CI/pdf/Events/English_Paris_OER_Declaration.pdf.

Wiley, D., & Gurrell, S. (2009). A decade of development. *Open learning. The Journal of Open, Distance and e-Learning, 24*(1), 11–21.

12

MOOCs FOR OPENING UP EDUCATION AND THE OpenupEd INITIATIVE

Fred Mulder and Darco Jansen

MOOCs' Expansion into a Mishmash

MOOCs have received considerable media coverage since the beginning of 2012. Concurrent with their expansion, confusion swiftly arose around what a typical MOOC would look like and what could be expected as its main added value. In contrasting two different pedagogics, Siemens (2012) introduced an initial distinction between so-called cMOOCs and xMOOCs.

Meanwhile, the MOOC spectrum has become decidedly broad. Within this huge variety, the 'C' generally stands for a 'Course,' while the second 'O' usually refers to 'Online.' But the first 'O,' which should stand for 'Open,' receives myriad interpretations, either justified or questionable. And the 'M,' which is supposed to refer to 'Massive,' can apply to a large-scale operation but, in many cases, this is not the reality.

MOOCs Roots . . .

Moreover, as Mulder notes in the Foreword to this volume, we seem to forget and ignore the essential long-term developments in which the recent emergence of the MOOC is to be placed. The first is the development towards 'Open Education,' which dates back to the 19th century. Open education received a real boost in the second half of the 19th century when the model for open universities emerged and became embraced worldwide.

During the past decade or so, the concept of the open university has received an innovative, digital infusion with the well-documented global Open Educational Resources (OER) movement. The other crucial development towards 'Online Education' was initiated in the 1950s. It was from that time that new technologies and media were introduced in education, starting with radio and television and then moving on to the more recent emergence of personal computers and their wide range of educational applications, from basic computer-based training to intelligent tutoring systems and sophisticated simulations. Each of these cycles of technology failed to become mainstream in education. It was not until the 1990s, with the entry of the Internet, that the power of technology-based communication and interaction became widely available for education. Yet it took more than a decade of often highly cautious and quite hesitant search and experimentation to come to the point of a significant change towards a rich, full, and widespread exploitation of the Internet for educational purposes. Such embracement of learning over the Internet marked a new era filled with the potential for considerable impact from educational technology (Allen & Seaman, 2014).

Back in 2007, it was the ICDE (International Council for Open and Distance Education) which keenly emphasized the possible 'golden combination' of open, flexible and distance learning with OER for the massive educational opportunities that were much needed in developing countries. Moreover, the ICDE also noted that these new modes of learning and teaching were also relevant for emerging economies as well as for matured knowledge-based societies (Mulder & Rikers, 2008). Importantly, the combined power of the 'classical' Open Universities model and the new 'digital openness' was elaborated in the 2011 EADTU (European Association of Distance Teaching Universities) Conference (Mulder, 2011). These reports and conferences have led to a better understanding of what Open Education is about and what it could offer to learners and societies.

Open(ing Up) Education!

OER and MOOCs can be positioned in the broader development of Open Education as described above. The potential of Open Education was strongly marked by the Cape Town Open Education Declaration (Shuttleworth Foundation/OSF, 2008). It is quite remarkable, however, that the frequent reference to the concept of Open Education generally is not combined with a clear and solid description of what this term means. Only recently, an analytical and practical framework has been proposed as a reference model for Open Education. This so-called 5COE model includes OER as just one of five components. Different kinds of MOOCs can be mapped on to this reference model, but, in all cases, these maps show a rather limited coverage across those five components (Mulder, Foreword, this volume; Mulder & Janssen, 2013).

Reference should be made here to the European Commission's initiative, 'Opening up Education' (European Commission, 2013a). Opening up Education was launched in September 2013 as a coordinated European move to innovate learning and teaching through ICT and to modernize education for the full spectrum of learners across all educational sectors through OER (and MOOCs). The overarching title "Opening up Education" signals that not all education is required to be open in all respects (Mulder, Foreword, this volume). This nuanced approach—of no need or wish to be open in any sense—holds for our overall educational system with its wide variety of philosophies and implementa-tions. Within this spectrum of occurrences and approaches to delivering educa-tion, MOOCs offer an exceptional position. Based on the first 'O' in the term, one might expect that openness is the ultimate goal. This issue as to what extent MOOCs do indeed contribute to opening up education is the central question of this chapter. Much of the mainstream MOOCs movement, however, does not seem to be driven primarily by this mission to open up education.

OpenupEd as a Special MOOCs Flavour

It is within the context described above of building on the roots of MOOCs in the 'traditional' world of open learning and education (i.e., the Open Universities), and of embracing the goal to open up education as much as possible, that the OpenupEd initiative emerged. OpenupEd is the first, and, thus far, the only pan-European MOOC initiative. It was launched in April 2013 by EADTU, and communicated in collaboration with the European Commission (European Commission, 2013b). The 11 launch partners in the scheme are based in eight EU countries (France, Italy, Lithuania, the Netherlands, Portugal, Slovakia, Spain, and the UK), as well as in three countries outside the EU (Russia, Turkey, and Israel). Almost all OpenupEd partners are EADTU members. Another ten institutions, again mostly from the EADTU membership, have confirmed that they will also join OpenupEd in the near future.

OpenupEd began with four courses in a wide variety of subject areas. Since the start, each partner has offered courses via its own learning platform and in its home language, if not more. Currently, potential learners can choose from the 11 lan-guages of the partners, plus Arabic. Meanwhile, the number of courses has increased significantly since the fall of 2013. Courses can either be taken at a scheduled period of time or anytime and at the student's own pace. All courses may lead to recogni-tion; for instance, (1) a certificate of completion, (2) a badge, or, (3) most valuable, a credit certificate provided upon formal examination by the partner operating the course (that typically has to be paid for) and which can count towards a degree.

OpenupEd is an open, non-profit partnership offering MOOCs that contrib-ute to open up education—much to the benefit of individual learners and the wider society. The vision is to reach out to all those learners who are interested to take part in online higher education in a way that meets their needs and accommodates their particular situation. OpenupEd is not using nor advocating one single platform for all the partners, because most of them are operating suc-cessfully with their own platforms. Moreover, partners can be involved in other MOOC platforms and portals as well. For example, the Open University has its own MOOC FutureLearn and is a partner of OpenupEd. In effect, OpenupEd embraces a decentralized model where the institutions take the lead and make their own decisions regarding, for example, the number of MOOCs and the subjects that they will offer. They also have control over the types of interactive components embedded in their MOOCs, the language(s) used, and their possible embedding of MOOCs within the curriculum. Indeed, diversity in how institutions approach MOOCs and open education is cherished as an important value in the OpenupEd partnership. Also valued in this partnership is equity and quality. Importantly, the partnership is open to any institution as long as it will embrace the OpenupEd common features and will acquire and keep up with the OpenupEd quality label for MOOCs.

OpenupEd's Common Features

Although there is diversity of institutional approaches, the partnership has agreed on the following framework of eight common features for its MOOCs:

1. Openness to learners
2. Digital openness
3. Learner-centred approach
4. Independent learning
5. Media-supported interaction
6. Recognition options
7. Quality focus
8. Spectrum of diversity.

This framework is not meant to act as a straitjacket; rather it is intended to give guidance on the principles to which we aspire. Therefore, all OpenupEd courses need to conform to these eight features to the degree that the partner considers appropriate and feasible. Given that flexibility, some institutions will conform more than others. Partner institutions, however, should be serious in executing a development plan regarding those features. They need to outline the process they are using towards a fuller perspective with respect to opening up education.

The section below summarizes a series of specific OpenupEd highlights that may serve to help the reader better understand OpenupEd's practice.

Some OpenupEd Highlights

This section focuses on how a decentralized model of MOOC collaboration with modest or light centralized coordination efforts might work while respecting the diversity in (institutional) approaches.

As indicated, OpenupEd aims to be a distinct quality brand embracing a wide diversity of (institutional) approaches to open up education via the use of MOOCs, rather than restricting to one platform, model, or approach as is common of most MOOC providers. As a consequence, OpenupEd partners agreed that the quality process should be one that is tailored to both e-learning and open education. The OpenupEd quality label for MOOCs (Rosewell & Jansen, 2014) is based on the more general E-xcellence label that EADTU has established during the past few years (Williams, Kear, & Rosewell, 2012). The associated institutional benchmarking within OpenupEd is primarily meant to be applied as an improvement tool, comparing institutional performances with current best practices and leading to measures to raise the quality of its MOOCs and their operation. This process is designed to complement both an institutional course approval process, and the ongoing evaluation and monitoring of courses in presentation.

There is considerable diversity in institutional approaches in opening up education through the use of MOOCs which the OpenupEd label fully embraces. As part of this process, OpenupEd partners are integrating the OpenupEd label into their own quality process. Universidad Nacional de Educación a Distancia (UNED) in Madrid, Spain was one of the first OpenupEd partners to provide MOOCs. UNED already had its internal QA process in place but adjusted that to the OpenupEd label. To this end, the proposed set of benchmarks of the OpenupEd label was tested on over 20 different UNED COMA courses in an initial self-evaluation process (Rodrigo, Read, Santamaria, & Sánchez-Elvira, 2014). The research from UNED illustrated that the quality label could be a versatile tool that considers the overall structure and function of each course in terms of a variable set of characteristics. Moreover, they indicated that some additional indicators were found that could improve the benchmarking.

Preliminary results on the OpenupEd quality label stress the importance of research on how MOOCs in different institutional and cultural settings can help with the opening up of education. To this end, OpenupEd partners are collaborating on research and evaluation as well. In terms of quality assurance, the partners felt an urgent need to focus research on the learner perspective. In a funded project called MOOCKnowledge (Open Education (OpenEdu), 2014), questionnaires have been developed on the motivation, intentions, social context, lifelong learning profile, and the impact on study success and career development of MOOC participants. As with the highly flexible and open partnerships of OpenupEd, MOOCKnowledge is intended to be open for use by all MOOC providers and will hopefully lead to many cross-provider and large-scale data collections. At the present moment, OpenupEd partners are translating the questionnaires into their own languages while complementing them with contextualized dimensions of local importance. Once again, this partnership embraces a diversity of approaches within a common (research) framework.

This diversity is also an essential reason why partners of OpenupEd are involved in MOOCs. In essence, the institutional business models range from using MOOCs for reputation and visibility (e.g., student recruitment, increase marketing potential, and reaching new students) to MOOCs as an innovation area (e.g., transition to more flexible and online education, improve teaching, provide viable income through online courses, improve quality of regular offerings, etc.). Moreover, some OpenupEd partners are focussing explicitly on the demands of learners and societies. As such, these partners are strongly dependent on public funding.

Other institutions were experimenting with the unbundling of their education services. One example is that of Università Telematica Internazionale UNINETTUNO in Italy who decided to redesign their regular courses (offered as part of curricula) such that the complete course is offered for free but that MOOC participants have the option to pay for additional services such as tutoring or a formal exam for a credit certificate that may count towards a degree. UNINETTUNO first experimented with this model in early 2013 with only a few MOOCs, but quickly realized that this business model was more profitable than the old one (although there was a fall in the students' fees per course). At the present time, they are offering almost 100 MOOCs based on that model.

Other OpenupEd partners experienced some difficulties regarding governmental legislation. For instance, Moscow State University of Economics, Statistics and Informatics (MESI) was only recently able to offer online courses as a result of a change in Russian legislation in early 2014. Worse, Anadolu University in Turkey, with more than 1.3 million students, is still unable to offer formal credits for complete online courses. As a result, it has experienced some difficulties in providing MOOC participants with a pathway to formal higher education. Nevertheless, they will offer an additional 100 MOOCs by early 2015; however, these will not yet be available with the option for participants to obtain formal credit. In response, OpenupEd partners are working jointly to improve governmental legislation—for example, by benchmarking institutional and governmental strategies on MOOCs.

For further information regarding the OpenupEd initiative, please refer to the portal: www.openuped.eu. This website also functions as a referatory to the OpenupEd MOOCs offered by partner institutions.

Leading Question

Having introduced the roots of MOOCs, the Open Education model, the associated concept of opening up education, and the OpenupEd MOOCs initiative, we will now discuss the leading question of this chapter: "Are MOOCs instrumental to open up education?"

In order to answer this question, it is obviously vital to identify the requirements for opening up education. As noted below, there are two major ones that should be met in order to truly open up education:

1. All unnecessary barriers to learning should be removed, both at the entry into learning and along the learning path.
2. Learners should be facilitated with appropriate incentives to make progress and to succeed in their learning efforts.

We will define MOOCs as "online courses designed for large numbers of participants, that can be accessed by anyone anywhere as long as they have an internet connection, are open to everyone without entry qualifications, and offer a full/complete course experience online for free" (ECO, 2014).

In Table 12.1, we have identified and given a brief description of a series of barriers that MOOCs could remove as well as a set of incentives for progress and success that MOOCs could offer. We also provide our indication of how OpenupEd is performing. Rather than presenting a continuous narrative, we have decided to structure our text into a table in order to maintain an overview. As a result, we suggest using this as a table-to-read as opposed to a table-to-check.

From our observations and perceptions detailed in Table 12.1, we can conclude that the answer to the question: "Are MOOCs instrumental to open up education?" is a "Well, that really depends . . . "

Of the 11 barriers detailed in Table 12.1, several (i.e., Network connectivity, Accessibility to all, and Cultural) will not—or probably cannot—be removed easily by MOOCs and their providers. In the case of four others (i.e., Scheduling, Accessibility over time, Legal, and Quality), it is more or less a matter of goodwill. And the remaining four (i.e., Economic, Entry requirements, Location, and Digital literacy) can be taken away by MOOCs and their providers. The three incentives (i.e., Learner satisfaction, Completion, and Recognition) could all be provided through MOOCs and their providers, although this is certainly not straightforward and requires significant targeted effort. And such effort, in the end, is basically a matter of priority.

From the table, it appears that the 'score' for OpenupEd on the 11 barriers is better or at least equal to what is shown as indicative for the wide variety of MOOC initiatives. Likewise, for the three incentives, OpenupEd seems to be in a slightly better position than many of the other MOOC ventures and initiatives, but yet requiring sustained additional effort. We have decided not to present our perspectives on the performance of other MOOC initiatives like Coursera, edX, Udacity, FutureLearn, MiríadaX, iversity, FUN, and Open2Study, not wanting to take the risk of bias and limited insight.

More Work to Be Done to Open Up Education for All . . .

The previous section may induce an agenda for MOOC providers, but only if they are serious about opening up education. Such an agenda can be derived from the barriers and incentives that need more attention and improvement, according to their own analyses. Speaking for ourselves, OpenupEd intends to continue to strengthen its commitment to the mission of opening up education, in particular, by improving on the weaker ingredients as they appear in Table 12.1 while maintaining the already strong assets.

As part of these efforts, in the section below, we highlight four of the eight common features of the OpenupEd framework, mentioned earlier; in effect, priority is set at four features where the partnership could or should make further progress: (1) digital openness, (2) recognition options, (3) quality focus, and (4) spectrum of diversity.

TABLE 12.1 Opening up education: Barriers to be removed and incentives to be offered by MOOCs, and a "score" for OpenupEd (first the barriers and then the incentives).

Barrier	Could MOOCs remove the barrier?	How about OpenupEd?
Economic	**YES**, all MOOCs offer a course experience without any cost to participants.	**YES.**
Entry Requirements	**YES** (formally), since generally anybody can enter the course.	**YES.**
	This does **NOT** necessarily imply that the course can be taken without any learnt competencies or experience. **Advanced pedagogics and remedial courses** can be **supportive** here.	**Additional support** increasingly offered.
Location	**YES**, the online provision guarantees the freedom of place, learners can be anywhere.	**YES.**
	This does generally **NOT** apply to formal examinations.	**Experimenting** with online examination.
Scheduling	**NO** (general practice), since most MOOCs have a fixed starting moment and a fixed scheme in time.	**Scheduled courses** (part of the provision).
	But in principle it can be a **YES** if participants can start any time and can choose their own scheme (freedom of time and pace).	**Self-paced courses** (the other part of the provision).
Network Connectivity	**NOT AT ALL**, weak or no connectivity is an external and prohibitive barrier for all MOOCs. This applies in particular to countries in the Global South, but is expected to improve significantly in the forthcoming years.	**NOT** really in position to remove this serious external barrier when it occurs (applies to **all MOOCs initiatives**).
Digital literacy	**YES**, digital skills are a condition to participate in a MOOC. And it is quite natural to take away a possible barrier in this respect by offering MOOCs on digital skills; which is increasingly happening.	**Increasingly YES.**
Accessibility Over Time	**PROBLEMATIC** if the course content is only accessible between the start and end date for a scheduled course, which frequently is the case.	**Mostly and increasingly YES.**
	It would be easy, however, to make it a **YES** by providing any-time access.	

(continued)

TABLE 12.1 (continued)

Barrier	Could MOOCs remove the barrier?	How about OpenupEd?
Accessibility to All	**PROBLEMATIC** if courses are provided primarily in English. This is the current situation for most MOOCs, although there are providers operating in other languages (e.g., Spanish) and translation of MOOC content and courses is starting to expand.	**Essentially YES** within the language spectrum of the partners.
	PROBLEMATIC if courses exclude participants from sanctioned countries or if there is an age limit. Occasionally this is the practice.	**YES.**
Cultural	**PROBLEMATIC** if courses are mainly developed in one dominant ('Western') cultural perspective, which typically is the case. This practice affects both the subject matter and the educational method. It could become a **YES** in collaboration with partners from other cultures.	**Essentially YES** with the partners from different cultures leading their own initiatives (with the current focus on Europe).
Legal	**YES**, but only if the course materials are openly licensed (or, in other words, if they are OER). And there are still too many major providers **NOT** having adopted an open licensing policy. Open licensing is directly important for the teaching staff who wish to retain, reuse, revise, remix, and redistribute content (Wiley, 2007, 2014). But indirectly it is also significant for the learners who will benefit more from a richer learning materials space if there are no legal barriers. The OER approach (for learning materials) has similarity with the notions of **open access** (for scientific output) and **open source** (for software).	**Mostly and increasingly YES** with OpenupEd endorsing OER and an open licensing policy. **Open source** is also **preferred** for the MOOCs platforms, although it is **NOT** a general **rule.**
Quality	**YES** (to a certain extent), since MOOCs can contribute to better quality education, which is what learners deserve. With an open licensing policy, chances of raising quality are even better. Generally there is **NOT** a systems guarantee, however, since the QA and accreditation schemes are not yet equipped for MOOCs and OER.	**YES,** since all partners apply their internal QA system to their MOOCs, and are subject to the **OpenupEd quality label** for MOOCs.

Incentive	Could MOOCs offer the incentive?	How about OpenupEd?
Learner Satisfaction	**YES**, but it's a constant challenge to incorporate in the courses: > ingredients to motivate, to entice, to provoke, to raise curiosity, and incite to discovery. > an attractive lay-out varying between text and graphics and including video and animations. > an effective and pleasant ICT-based learning environment. > appropriate and non-obtrusive interaction between learners (and teachers), partly through social media.	**More or less YES** but requires more attention and dedication for further improvement.
Completion	**YES**, but more so if: > dedicated and proven modern online learning pedagogics are used (rather than sticking to classroom-based didactics). > independent learning is the paradigm, with a learner-centred approach. > context sensitivity is being adopted. > the learning can take place step-by-step along chunks and units to be finished.	**Essentially YES** with the partners having a mission and long-standing experience in the areas mentioned.
Recognition	**YES**, MOOCs do offer various recognition options: certificates of participation, badges for specific activities, overall credentials based on a final online test, and full formal credit certificates based on a proctored exam. The last option is the most rewarding and significant, however, is **NOT** at all mainstream. The utmost arrangement is recognition of the **formal credit** as a component in a full **curriculum** (e.g., a bachelor programme), with an ultimate perspective of credit transfer between institutions. We are still **FAR AWAY** from the latter situation.	**YES.** **Increasingly YES** with a fair share of courses offering the **formal credit** option, mostly combined with the opportunity of inclusion in a full **curriculum.**

Digital Openness

- The endorsement of an open licensing policy in the partnership must lead to a larger share of openly licensed courses to ultimately reach 100 percent. (Note: this is related to the barrier *Legal* detailed in Table 12.1.)
- Courses on digital skills should become available in all 12 languages in the partnership. (Note: such an approach directly addresses the barrier *Digital literacy* explained in Table 12.1.)

Recognition Options

- The partnership will intensify its ongoing arrangements towards mainstreaming recognition through formal credit course certificates where the credit value can count for a larger educational programme (e.g., a bachelor degree). This movement is facilitated (at a fee) by the university hosting the OpenupEd MOOC. (Note: this relates to the incentive *Recognition* considered in Table 12.1.)
- Credit transfer among (and possibly beyond) the partnership is an additional (but not so easy) target, where we can build on earlier initiatives and experiences within EADTU. (Note: this is linked to the incentive *Recognition* discussed in Table 12.1.)

Quality Focus

- The OpenupEd quality label for MOOCs (Rosewell & Jansen, 2014) is the first such recognition of its kind to become operational and is intended to encourage quality enhancement for MOOCs and their providers. There is a considerable array of institutional approaches related to opening up education via the use of MOOCs. As indicated, the OpenupEd label accommodates many such MOOC choices. Now, with the availability of the OpenupEd quality label, we expect new partners and possibly other providers to get to apply it, generating experience for further refinement. (Note: this is our response to the barrier related to *Quality* outlined in Table 12.1.)
- The partnership will facilitate the required collaboration in order to harmonize the research and evaluation efforts among the partners, thereby monitoring and analyzing their operations heading to enhanced performance. Different from the centralized MOOC providers where, for example, learning analytics can be applied smoothly, the more decentralized OpenupEd has to explicitly make specific arrangements in this respect among the partners.

Spectrum of Diversity

- While OpenupEd emerged in Europe, its mission could have global relevance and scope, thereby widening the spectrum of diversity. Recently, we have begun to explore the creation of similar initiatives ('OpenupEd alikes') in other regions around the world. They could show basic similarity in intention and approach, but with a flavour and profile that is specific to their region. And they could be interlinked in order to maximize benefits like common branding, sharing expertise and content ('localized'), and facilitating global learners. This discovery tour is a joint effort with UNESCO wherein we are collaborating with our sister organizations in Africa and in Asia (such a collaboration addresses the core of the barrier *Cultural* detailed in Table 12.1).

Finally, in line with what has been noted earlier with the incentive *Learner satisfaction*, it is crucial to underscore the need of more dedication within the various ingredients contributing to the satisfaction of learners.

To Conclude . . .

OpenupEd has explicitly chosen to open up education as the mission of its MOOCs. As we have argued in this chapter, it is a purposeful choice that can generate extensive benefits for learners and the broader society. Will this soon be a stance or perspective of other MOOC providers as well? That, of course, is within their discretion . . .

Fred Mulder holds a UNESCO/ICDE Chair in OER at the Open University of The Netherlands (OUNL). Previously, he was OUNL Rector for more than a decade. He is actively involved in OER initiatives and policies at the national level, by UNESCO, the OECD, and the EU. He is chairing the first pan-European MOOCs initiative called OpenupEd which was launched in April 2013 by EADTU (the European Association of Distance Teaching Universities). In addition, he is leading the Global OER Graduate Network. Mulder has received a Royal decoration (2007) for his work in Lifelong Learning, the ICDE Individual Prize of Excellence (2012) for his efforts in OER, and the Leadership Award for OpenCourseWare Excellence (2014).

Darco Jansen is programme manager at EADTU (the European Association of Distance Teaching Universities). He is responsible for the development of different long-term themes for EADTU (-members) on online education, MOOCs and OER, employability, and open and social innovation (e.g., with small businesses). In addition, he is the coordinator of several European projects. Darco's fields of expertise are in the areas of e-learning, open innovation, educational business development, continuous education, non-/informal learning, and workplace learning. He worked for over 20 years at the Open Universiteit of the

Netherlands. Currently, Darco is the coordinator of the first pan-European MOOC initiative called OpenupEd.

References

Allen, I.E., & Seaman, J. (2014, January). *Grade change: Tracking online education in the United States.* Babson Survey Research Group and The Sloan Consortium. Retrieved from http://www.onlinelearningsurvey.com/reports/gradechange.pdf.

ECO. (2014). E-Learning, communication and open data: Massive, mobile, ubiquitous and open learning. Retrieved from http://ecolearning.eu/wp-content/uploads/2014/06/ECO_D2.2_Instructional_design_and_scenarios_v1.0.pdf.

European Commission. (2013a). *Opening up education: Innovative teaching and learning for all through new technologies and open educational resources.* Brussels, Belgium. Retrieved from http://eur-lex.europa.eu/legal-content/EN/TXT/PDF/?uri=CELEX:52013DC0654&from=EN.

European Commission. (2013b). *Vassiliou welcomes launch of first pan-European university MOOCs.* [Press release IP/13/349]. Retrieved from http://europa.eu/rapid/press-release_IP-13-349_en.htm.

Mulder, F. (2011). *Classical and digital openness in a fascinating blend: Global! . . . institutional?* Presentation at the EADTU Conference, November 3–4, Eskişehir (Turkey). Retrieved from http://oer.unescochair-ou.nl/?wpfb_dl=31.

Mulder, F.R., & Janssen, B. (2013). Opening up education. In R. Jacobi, H. Jelgerhuis, & N. van der Woert (Eds.), *Trend report: Open educational resources 2013*, SURF SIG OER, Utrecht, pp. 36–42. Retrieved from http://www.surf.nl/en/knowledge-and-innovation/knowledge-base/2013/trend-report-open-educational-resources-2013.html.

Mulder, F., & Rikers, J. (Eds.) (2008). *A Golden Combi?!—Open educational resources and open, flexible and distance learning.* Final Report from the ICDE Task Force on Open Educational Resources. Oslo, Norway: ICDE. Retrieved from http://www.icde.org/filestore/Resources/Taskforce_on_OER/OpenEducationalResourcesTaskForceFinalReport.pdf.

Open Education (Open Edu). (2014). *MOOCKnowledge.* European Commission, Joint Research Centre, Institute for Prospective Technological Studies. Retrieved from http://is.jrc.ec.europa.eu/pages/EAP/OpenEduMOOC.html.

Rodrigo, C., Read, T., Santamaria, M., & Sánchez-Elvira, A. (2014). OpenupEdLabel for MOOCs quality assurance: UNED COMA initial self-evaluation. In L. Bengoechea, R. Hernández, & J.R. Hilera (Eds.), *Proceedings of V Congreso Internacional sobre Calidad y Accesibilidad en la Formación Virtual (CAFVIR 2014)* Universidad Galileo (Guatemala), pp. 551–5.

Rosewell, J., & Jansen, D. (2014). The OpenupEd quality label: Benchmarks for MOOCs, *INNOQUAL*, 2(3), 88–100 (Special Issue on Quality in MOOCs). Retrieved from http://papers.efquel.org/index.php/innoqual/article/view/160/45.

Shuttleworth Foundation/Open Society Foundation (OSF). (2008). *The Cape Town Open Education Declaration.* Retrieved from http://www.capetowndeclaration.org/.

Wiley, D. (2007, August 8). Open education license draft. *Iterating toward openness.* Retrieved from http://opencontent.org/blog/archives/355.

Wiley, D. (2014, March 5). The access compromise and the 5th R. *Iterating toward openness.* Retrieved from http://opencontent.org/blog/archives/3221.

Williams, K., Kear, K., & Rosewell, J. (2012). *Quality assessment for e-learning: A benchmarking approach* (2nd edn). Heerlen, The Netherlands: European Association of Distance Teaching Universities (EADTU). Retrieved from http://e-xcellencelabel.eadtu.eu/tools/manual.

PART 5

Designing Innovative Courses, Programs, and Models of Instruction

This part of the book provides a look at innovative courses, programs, and models of instruction incorporating MOOCs and related MOOC spin-offs or derivatives. The chapters in this section introduce groundbreaking ideas for creating communities and entire ecosystems, addressing budgetary concerns, streamlining and enhancing course development, fostering expert collaboration and sharing, and much more. Part 5 also shows how higher education programs of study might be designed around MOOCs and OER at significantly reduced costs and with much higher enrollments. Such opportunities to simultaneously reduce costs while increasing the number of students in the program pipeline should strike a chord with politicians, educators, and members of the media often voicing complaints about the rapidly accelerating costs of higher education as well as with students and parents who have to foot the bill.

In the first chapter of this section, Richard DeMillo, Director of Georgia Tech's Center for 21st Century Universities, discusses the results of unbundling many of the costs of higher education. DeMillo notes that in early 2013, Zvi Galil, Dean of Georgia Tech's College of Computing, announced an online master's degree in computer science based entirely on MOOCs. In this new program, anyone could enroll for free and take these courses. Naturally, in order to satisfy the requirements for a degree at Georgia Tech, a student would first have to be admitted to the highly selective master's program in computer science and pay tuition. However, unlike normal tuition and fees, students would only be charged for those services that were actually used to deliver course content. As DeMillo notes, at program launch, that fee was less than US$7,000, which amounted to a discount of nearly 70 percent. In what many observers proclaimed was a bold experiment, this high-profile program was launched in January 2014. However, Georgia Tech does not look at this degree as a simple experiment. Rather, it is a prototype for an alternative kind of academic program. Like all prototypes, it will be revised and refined over time. However, it currently stands alone as the first of its kind; a unique program that warrants a chronicling of the rationale and institutional decision-making that went into its design and development.

In Chapter 14, Paul Kim from Stanford University and Charlie Chung from Class Central describe their experience with a highly interesting and cutting-edge MOOC, "Designing a New Learning Environment." This MOOC on designing new learning environments attracted more than 18,000 sign-ups from over 200 countries, while generating enthusiastic engagement among those who later participated in it. This course was initially offered in the fall of 2012 with Kim as the instructor and Chung one of the students. It is important to realize that Kim developed this MOOC to explore how MOOCs could help facilitate improvements in global education by identifying future global education leaders, fostering educational innovations, and providing development experiences at scale. Many of the elements that were missing in the MOOC's educational ecosystem and basic technology infrastructure (e.g., pointers to additional resources, timely reposting of events and ideas, personalized feedback, etc.) were supplied by participants who self-organized to collect, catalogue, and share them. This level of emergent voluntarism was made feasible, ironically, by the short duration of this MOOC. In effect, the compressed timeline of the course established the validity of identifying global leaders through such voluntary and collaborative behaviors. As noted in this chapter, a high level of interaction in this particular MOOC supported the potential of MOOCs as a platform to spur new innovations, leadership training, and peer-to-peer support structures. Kim and Chung hold out hope that MOOCs may be utilized to further improve global education and training of the next generation of world leaders and educators.

Whereas Kim and Chung document how technology tools and pedagogical principles can combine to foster a global ecosystem within a MOOC, others, like Charles Severance from the University of Michigan, extend the basic MOOC ecosystem or technology infrastructure offered by vendors like Coursera with unique opportunities for personalized live events. Across some ten MOOCs that he has delivered to date on computer programing and the history of the Internet, Severance has shown that interesting and engaging communities of learners can arise from synchronous experiences with the instructor or other experts, including live, face-to-face meetings in coffee houses, cafés, bookstores, restaurants, and hotel lobbies. As the title of his chapter makes explicit, we can learn from MOOCs by talking to our students. According to Severance, it is both tempting and easy to aggregate all the student data from a MOOC or series of MOOC offerings and come up with an "average" that is well supported by that data and then posted by prominent news media. This chapter, in contrast, takes a different approach by focusing on what he terms "the smallest of small data." Such small data points are derived from his one-to-one conversations with his MOOC students around the planet when he meets up with them. During the past few years,

Severance has travelled to over 30 locations around the world (including Miami, Manila, Mexico City, London, Barcelona, Melbourne, Seoul, Zagreb (Croatia), New York, Quebec, etc.) where he has held face-to-face office hours with his MOOC students. This chapter is particularly valuable in sharing anecdotal stories from those students as a way to add some detail to the large aggregate datasets often gathered about MOOC participant behaviors and results.

In Chapter 16, students are involved in MOOCs in a somewhat different way from that described in the previous two chapters. Using Coursera, Bernard Robin and Sara McNeil from the University of Houston involve their graduate students in the actual development of MOOCs. Using their Webscape design model, their students have assisted with the design and development of two MOOCs; one on Digital Storytelling and the other on Web. 2.0 tools. In this highly authentic project, Robin and McNeil, along with their graduate students, collaboratively designed and developed MOOCs that focused on professional development for K–16 teachers. As a replicable approach, the Webscape model provides a structure or system for small teams of students to work with faculty members who serve as content experts throughout the entire instructional design process, from brainstorming through formative evaluation. Key components and lessons learned in the MOOC design and development process are shared from a faculty member perspective. As such, this chapter should resonate with institutions that have strong instructional design or educational technology programs from which to support their own MOOC design and development projects and initiatives.

The final chapter in this section is written by a team of eight scholars who offer a feminist alternative to MOOCs. Here, Erika Behrmann and her colleagues discuss the creation and evolution of a "Distributed Open Online Course" (or "DOCC") as well as the community that supported it; namely, FemTechNet. Since 2012, FemTechNet, a network of scholars, artists, and students who engage with feminism and technology, has been experimenting with ideas related to the DOCC. As a viable and more socially just alternative to MOOCs, the DOCC embodies six core values: (1) Effective pedagogy that reflects feminist principles; (2) A disruption of the structural status quo within educational institutions; (3) A challenge to the assumption that access to technology guarantees access to knowledge while ameliorating issues of labor in education; (4) An understanding that technoscientific choices are not value–neutral and infrastructure is not simply choosing among consumer products; (5) A recognition of regional and cultural complexities; and (6) An innovative experimentation that enables learning for its multiple stakeholders. As a vital contribution to this book, the chapter discusses the impetus behind the DOCC and argues that, through the embodiment of these values, the DOCC has become a successful replacement for the more well-known MOOC.

13

UNBUNDLING HIGHER EDUCATION AND THE GEORGIA TECH ONLINE MS IN COMPUTER SCIENCE

A Chronicle

Richard DeMillo

Introduction

Georgia Tech's Center for 21st Century Universities (C21U) was originally conceived as a sandbox for experimenting with new educational technologies. Its mission expanded even before it was launched in 2011. A deepening worldwide recession—and with it a loss of revenue for both public and private institutions, a growing student debt crisis, and lagging public confidence in the value of a college degree—had exposed faultlines in higher education that went beyond classroom hardware and software technologies. By sheer coincidence, C21U was launched and empowered to span business, policy, technological, and pedagogical innovation at the exact moment when those fault lines began to fracture.

C21U quickly became a kind of internal think-tank, not a research center in the traditional sense. We knew that there were many research organizations that studied higher education and developed new technologies, but the idea of actually experimenting with institutional form seemed highly novel to us. Whatever was going to happen to American colleges and universities over the coming months and years, Georgia Tech had decided to be in control of its own fate and perhaps serve as a beacon for others. It was a decision that led faculty and administrators at Georgia Tech to an entirely unanticipated experiment that, if successful, might disrupt the business of running universities.

The experiment was an online master's degree in computer science (OMS) based entirely on free delivery using massive open online courses (MOOCs). OMS was designed from the outset to be *open*. Anyone could enroll for free and take courses, but in order to satisfy the requirements for a degree, a student would first have to be admitted to Georgia Tech's highly selective program and pay tuition. However, unlike normal tuition and fees, the OMS would charge students only for those services that were actually used to deliver course content.

At program launch, that fee was less than US$7,000, which amounted to a discount of nearly 70 percent. There were many online master's degrees in computer science, but they all charged students full tuition and none were based on MOOC technology. In order to offer a financially viable program, the designers of this new degree would have to figure out how to unbundle the costs that the university normally passed on to students in the form of tuition and fees. And, in order to offer a quality degree, they would have to maintain Georgia Tech standards in admissions and course offerings.

Replacing videos of traditional fifty-minute lectures with MOOC delivery was itself an innovation. The courses in the OMS program were to be based on mastery learning principles and utilized formative assessment, which is a better pedagogical model. This was an overriding concern for program designers at Georgia Tech and greatly influenced the selection of Sebastian Thrun's Udacity as the distribution platform provider.

The degree was launched in January 2014 to considerable media fanfare and much student interest (Lewin, 2013). What was expected to be a soft launch to a small initial cohort quickly became a full launch as hundreds, and then thousands, of students applied for admission to the OMS program at Georgia Tech. Thousands more bypassed the application process and enrolled for free. At the time of this writing, there is insufficient data to confirm whether this degree represents a successful experiment with institutional form. That analysis will take time.

Georgia Tech, however, does not look at this degree as a simple experiment. Rather, it is a prototype for an alternative kind of academic program. Like all prototypes, it will be revised and refined over time. However, it stands alone as the first of its kind; a unique program that warrants a chronicle of the rationale and institutional decision-making that went into its development.

Commoditized Content

In early 2011, C21U joined Athabasca University's George Siemens and his colleagues in planning a 30-week online course entitled "Change 11;" a MOOC that was intended to showcase technology-induced change in higher education. The course ultimately engaged several thousand enrolled students from around the world in wide-ranging discussions on many emerging and controversial topics related to higher education. While an interesting experience, Change 11 employed a meandering, exploratory style not typically found in Georgia Tech courses. But there was an even more significant issue that none of us could have foreseen: a series of highly popular MOOCs from Stanford and MIT were launched at roughly the same time (Markoff, 2011). Not only was their enrollment a hundred times larger than Change 11, they were more recognizable as courses, complete with homework and exams. Soon after, MIT formed a nonprofit company called edX to develop its MOOCs, while two for-profit companies, Coursera and Udacity, were spun out of Stanford to commercialize the Stanford MOOCs.

C21U began negotiating with Udacity and Coursera. Those agreements were important to a longer-term strategy to make a substantial fraction of Georgia Tech's course catalog available in MOOC format. We believed that, much as commoditized content enabled by the Internet had disrupted industries over the past 20 years, higher education also was headed for a period of disruptive innovation. We were determined to find ways to use it to the benefit of Georgia Tech students.

Many considered MOOCs to be simply a new form of textbook. But MOOCs were entire courses, and if they turned out to be a better or cheaper—even if they were only effective for some courses—they were bound to have an effect on the higher education market. Students (and their parents) would quickly realize they were paying a hefty price for quality instruction that they could get for free online. In turn, college administrators might feel compelled to start unbundling their offerings, which—critics argued—paid unnecessary attention to an expensive, outmoded classroom format that had not changed much over the centuries.

The Shifting Landscape

In May 2013, almost exactly a year after the launch of Coursera, Georgia Tech announced that it would partner with AT&T™ and Udacity to offer a MOOC-based master's degree in computer science for less than US$7,000. The media lit up at the announcement and there was much press coverage. MOOCs had been in the news for over a year, but as many tried to figure out whether this technology really altered the landscape, vocal critics emerged. Problems with individual courses and shrill dissent, became as newsworthy as announcements of a new batch of university partners for Coursera, edX, and newcomers like NovoEd (Empson, 2013).

The OMS announcement seemed to change the nature of the debate. Above-the-fold coverage in the *New York Times* (Lewin, 2013) was followed by *Wall Street Journal* editorials (Belkin & Porter, 2013), and hundreds of broadcast, print, and online articles. President Obama even mentioned it in his speeches (White House, 2013). Most of the coverage zeroed in on the same point: this was a high-risk and highly controversial bet that higher education was going to change radically.

Shortly after the Georgia Tech announcement, I received an email entitled "Shifting Landscape" from Steve Mintz, who directs the Institute for Transformational Learning for the University of Texas System. "The future is here," Mintz wrote. "From now on the pace of change will only accelerate." Mintz is responsible for educational innovation in the massive Texas system and then investing to make them successful. "Anything that really improves learning is interesting to me," he once told me. Mintz then sagely added, "But I suspect that students are going to vote with their feet for digital knowledge."

One of Mintz's colleagues was Israeli computer scientist and Dean of Engineering at Columbia, Dr. Zvi Galil. Columbia's Engineering School had been operating a distance education program called Columbia Video Network (CVN) since the late

1980s. Even though it reached thousands of students, the program was losing money and was slated to be shut down. Galil argued that it should not only be saved, it should convert from videotape distribution to Web-based courses. The turnround was dramatic. Very quickly CVN began generating millions of new dollars.

We Could Be Doing More

By the time Galil was named my successor as Dean of Computing at Georgia Tech, the "Threads" Program—a redefinition of a college degree that allowed students to tailor the undergraduate curriculum to suit their interests and needs (DeMillo, 2011)—had been operating successfully for several years. Although there were pockets of resistance, Threads was widely admired and had been adopted around the world. Galil embraced Threads, but he was also looking for a way make to his own personal mark on education at Georgia Tech. "One of the first things I did," he told me, "was to let everyone know that it seemed to me that we could be doing more."

What shape "more" might take was less clear. Galil was an enthusiastic backer of Georgia Tech's Coursera MOOCs, but he also wanted a clearer vision. "It was wonderful to see hundreds of thousands of new learners drawn to Georgia Tech instructors," he remarked. He had learned at Columbia that eventually someone would have to pay for these courses. According to Galil, "I was also concerned that Georgia Tech's MOOCs were not being offered for credit. I saw what happened at Columbia—too much money was spent on non-credit courses." He was determined to not make the same mistakes. CVN, which led to actual degrees, had been a great financial success—and financial viability was one of Galil's top priorities.

Building a MOOC Faculty

Faculty and administrative backing for the new course format were extremely important, but, their support was not automatic. There were many who wanted to scuttle the new technology before it had a chance to be evaluated. Charges that MOOC providers were out to decimate the ranks of traditional faculty members or that students would be shunted to impersonal and vastly ineffective videos rather than high-quality classrooms were common. Some were worried that large pools of enrolled online students would dilute carefully built brands.

The poor quality of many MOOCs did little to strengthen the hand of early enthusiasts. Despite the founders' interest in pedagogy, Coursera and edX had decided not to enforce instructional standards. Many MOOCs were simply videos of actual classroom lectures. As a result, among the many excellent courses, some were truly awful. Clearly these first-generation products did not fairly represent the potential of the medium. Unfortunately, that message was often lost on skeptics whose arguments depended on a snapshot of the current technology, rather than on its rapid rate of improvement or potential.

When an astute reviewer caught errors in a Udacity course entitled Statistics 101, there was an uproar about the poor quality of MOOCs. Messageboards were flooded with calls to cancel the course. Many argued that problems like this one were the inevitable result of mass-market approaches to education. Whether or not the problems with Statistics 101 were as severe as the critics maintained, that episode highlighted an unanticipated feature of MOOCs: the technology allows instructors to catch and correct errors without going through layers of academic bureaucracy. Within hours of critical articles about Statistics 101 appearing, Sebastian responded with the following statement, "I agree . . . that the course can be improved in more than one way" (Thrun, 2012). He then promised that, unlike traditional courses that are often not revised for years, Statistics 101 would be revised immediately. As he stated, "We are very grateful for any feedback that we receive. These are the early days of online education, and sometimes our experimentation gets in the way of a coherent class" (Thrun, 2012).

There were other bandwagons that critics could jump on. For instance, the fraction of students who successfully completed MOOCs—often less than one percent—seemed alarmingly small. An additional red flag was that males often outnumbered females by wide margins (Christensen & Alcord, 2014), which, some argued, indicated gender bias in the selection of topics, courses, and instructors. Issues like these, left unresolved, might have doomed the idea of credit-bearing MOOCS for institutions like Georgia Tech.

Unlike many other universities, the Georgia Tech online strategy was not being defined by the administration. Instead, faculty would have to make the case to their colleagues if any MOOC experiments were going to be successful. Georgia Tech had built a portfolio of 20 Coursera MOOCs. As part of this process, the MOOC instructors (who had started labeling themselves as "MOOC Faculty") formed an informal community for improving the quality of online teaching.

For instance, computer science professor Tucker Balch was teaching a Coursera MOOC on applied statistics when he noticed that many of the problems identified by MOOC critics were based on anecdotes, not on actual experience (Balch, 2013). Balch took advantage of a new Coursera feature called "Signature Track" under which students who paid a small fee could receive certificates of completion if they performed well in the course. Students did not receive academic credit, but simply paying the fee clearly signaled a commitment to participate. In fact, he found that 99 percent of the signature track students completed the course. This was a startling contrast to the 5 percent completion rates that MOOC critics were typically citing. Even more surprising was that the completion rate for signature track students was nearly 25 percent higher than the full-tuition Georgia Tech students who took the same course on campus. Balch's course offered many other similar surprises.

Other MOOC faculty had noticed differences as well. Knowing of Udacity's experience with Statistics 101, one Georgia Tech professor—reasoning that the ability to change content "on the fly" was an advantage that MOOCs had over traditional courses—reviewed dozens of online forum messages every day, searching for suggestions for how to change course materials. When it was impractical to make all of the changes right away, the instructor promised, "We will definitely take this feedback into strong consideration for the next offering. We [would] like to talk to you offline for more suggestions" (personal conversation, MOOC instructor, August 1, 2014).

Finally, the deeply personal stories that students told affected even tough-minded instructors. Former physician Mark Braunstein, whose MOOC on healthcare informatics drew students from around the world, encouraged his class to communicate with him by e-mail. "The two from Africa are the ones that I'll never forget," he recalled. "One (from Benin) came in almost immediately after the course launched the first time. I had to look up where it is!"

These and other experiences with Coursera had convinced many professors that MOOCs were not only interesting experiments, but were actually a good way to reach an entirely new population of students with a better mode of instruction—one which, incidentally, improved their classroom teaching as well. As stories like these circulated, support for the idea of credit-bearing MOOCs gradually grew at Georgia Tech.

The $1,000 Degree

During one of his many visits to Georgia Tech, Udacity founder Sebastian Thrun mentioned that he thought a high-quality master's degree in Computer Science could be offered for US$1,000 if most of the courses were in MOOC format. Zvi Galil was also in attendance at that meeting. He was intrigued but he also knew that once all of the university's expenses were aggregated, a $1,000 degree was impossible.

It seems like an easy arithmetic problem. First, keep in mind that most public universities or university systems in the United States budget on a per-credit hour basis. State governments typically use a fixed formula to reimburse institutions based on the total number of graduate or undergraduate credit hours taught. For example, the Interactive Distance Education Alliance, a consortium of 20 public universities, publishes a Common Price per credit hour (Great Plains IDEA, 2014). During the 2013–14 academic year, for instance, each credit hour was worth $500 for graduate credits and $350 for undergraduate credits.

While this accounting method is familiar to university budgeting offices, students who try to allocate their personal educational budgets in this way run into immediate problems. Universities charge students to enroll in courses, not to complete credits, and the price that a student pays to enroll in a three-credit graduate course is often not equal to $1,500. There are many ways that this seemingly straightforward calculation can go awry.

It is tempting to view enrolling in and paying for a university class as a commercial transaction in which a service (one three-credit hour course on American

History, for example) is offered for a price determined by the cost of offering the class (the fixed cost of the instructor and assistants plus all the variable costs associated with class size). If that were true, then higher education would constitute what is called a *single-sided market* in which a seller sets a price for a product or service that a buyer is either willing or not willing to pay. In reality, higher education institutions do not work that way.

Universities link more than buyers and sellers of credit hours. For instance, they link buyers and sellers of entertainment services like intercollegiate athletics and performing arts. They also connect public information services like newspapers and radio stations, health services such as university hospitals and clinics, housing and hotel services, parking services, retail stores, food services, and research services. In each of these cases, a university services an independent market need, and, since many of these groups have conflicting interests, there is often competition among them for resources. But since services come and go, universities have developed ways to accommodate new activities and businesses—in essence, allowing them to seamlessly "plug in" to the institutional systems. Universities, in effect, have become *platforms*, which allow many stakeholders to more easily participate in the commerce associated with higher education.

In short, higher education is a *multi-sided market* that connects these groups together, aggregating costs, prices, subsidies, and cross-subsidies. In order for Georgia Tech to offer a $1,000 master's degree, links would have to be broken. Disaggregating costs in this way is a challenge for any platform that uses discounts and cross-subsidies to offer low prices to one side of the market at the expense of another side. Technological innovation often spurs this kind of disaggregation. One consequence is often widespread disruption like the one that has occurred in the news industry, for example, where a downward revenue spiral stemming from a loss of classified advertising revenues threatened the extinction of the local newspaper business (Seamans & Zhu, 2011). This same downward spiral is exactly what can take place in colleges and universities if technological innovations like MOOCs disrupt other sides of the higher education market. If so, the benefits could flow to students. It could conceivably enable a university to offer a lower cost master's degree by disaggregating the costs of participating in a multi-side market.

Not an Experiment

Galil had heard the idea of teaching the world before. His own CVN had greatly expanded the reach of Columbia's engineering program, but it was priced out of reach for most of the world. When Sebastian suggested a $1,000 Master's in Computer Science degree, "I immediately liked the idea," recalls Galil. "But I told him that $1,000 will not do," suggesting $4,000 instead, but even that "was based solely on intuition."

Galil had to let faculty members reach the conclusion that such a plan was a good thing without a lot of interference. As he put it, "I told Sebastian that I will need some time, and I told the faculty that we would only do it if they were behind the idea." The entire process took almost seven months. During this period, Sebastian came to the campus to meet with faculty groups and answer questions. "It turned out this was a very smart move," says Galil. Although there were deeply skeptical critics among the Computer Science faculty, sentiment moved steadily in the direction of approving the degree. Reporters who later acquired minutes of faculty meetings tried to cast unfiltered discussions as rampant dissent, but the facts were very different.

By January 2013, AT&T had provided US$2 million in philanthropic support to underwrite course development. Over the course of several weeks, the outlines of the Online Master of Science degree (OMS) began to emerge. In the end, the program won the support of 75 percent of the faculty. It was supported by both the Tech president Bud Peterson and its provost Rafael Bras. Bras made the final presentation to the Board of Regents of Georgia's University System, who approved the OMS in less than an hour. There were ruffled feathers in some on-campus committees, who thought their voices were not being heard, but the faculty vote was what mattered most.

Galil knew that the degree would cost closer to $4,000 than $1,000, but no one knew exactly how much more since the university had never tried to disaggregate costs before. A finance team was given broad latitude to develop a new cost model. The only criteria were that the courses had to remain free and open to non-Georgia Tech students and that enrolled students should get the benefit of disaggregated costs. One by one, costs were peeled away. OMS students would not need to pay athletic fees. Their use of on-campus facilities would be limited. On the other hand, counseling and support services related to the OMS program should be paid for with OMS tuition as core services for OMS students, not as a charge that was spread across all Georgia Tech students.

In the end, it was the underlying cost of course production and distribution through Udacity that determined the price of the program. Many questions were being asked. For instance, how many students were required for program viability? How many hours of tutoring help would be needed? Who would employ and train teaching assistants? What was the cost of insuring that OMS students received the same high-quality education as residential students? And, after answering such questions, the degree had to be what Provost Rafael Bras called a "full service degree."

Steve Mintz's shifting landscape was real. It was, in one step, a transition from individual non-credit courses to a curriculum that led to an accredited degree. Barack Obama's Council of Advisors on Science and Technology argued that "it could begin the process of lowering the cost of education and lowering barriers for millions of Americans" (Lewin, 2013). But only if it works. Galil, himself, admits that there are many unknowns. "We want to prove that it can be done," he says. "What is important to me is to make a high-quality degree at an affordable price."

The one word that is not used for OMS is "experiment." "An experiment is something you can walk away from," states Tech president Bud Peterson. "We know we cannot walk away from this." Peterson, an engineer, thinks of the OMS as a prototype. "We will tweak it, improve it, redesign it even," he says. In effect, it is the one condition he placed on the program. According to Peterson, "We do not think of this as an experiment. This is a pilot."

Richard DeMillo is an American engineer and computer scientist who specializes in cyber security, software engineering, and educational technology. He is Director of the Center for 21st Century Universities and Charlotte B. and Roger C. Warren Chair of Computer Science and Professor of Management at the Georgia Institute of Technology. He is best known for his pragmatic style of working on technical, business, and policy problems and he has helped guide public and private organizations through times of tumultuous change, including the 2002 Compaq–HP merger and the 1990s divestiture of Bellcore by the Bell Operating Companies. His 2011 book, *Abelard to Apple: The Fate of American Colleges and Universities*, was a seminal work that helped shape the current international conversation about the future of higher education.

References

Balch, T. (2013, November 30). A comparison of online MOOC versus on campus course delivery. *The Augmented Trader*. Retrieved from http://augmentedtrader.word-press.com/2013/11/20/a-comparison-of-online-mooc-versus-on-campus-course-delivery/.

Belkin, D., & Porter, C. (2013, September 26). Job market embraces massive online courses. *Wall Street Journal Online*. Retrieved from http://www.wsj.com/articles/SB1 0001424127887324807704579087840126695698.

Christensen, G., & Alcord, B. (2014, March 16). The revolution is not being MOOC-ized. Students are educated, employed, and male. *Slate*. Retrieved from http://www.slate.com/articles/health_and_science/new_scientist/2014/03/mooc_survey_students_of_free_online_courses_are_educated_employed_and_male.html.

DeMillo, R.A. (2011). *Abelard to Apple: The fate of American colleges and universities*. Cambridge, MA: MIT Press.

Empson, R. (2013, April 15). Stanford's NovoEd brings collaboration and group learning to MOOCs to help fight attrition. *TechCrunch*. Retrieved from http://techcrunch.com/2013/04/15/stanfords-novoed-brings-collaboration-and-group-learning-to-moocs-to-help-fight-attrition/.

Great Plains IDEA. (2014, July 30). *Student costs: Common price*. Retrieved from Great Plains IDEA website http://www.gpidea.org/students/costs/.

Lewin, T. (2013, August 18). Master's degree is new frontier of study online. *New York Times*. Retrieved from www.nytimes.com/2013/08/18/education/masters-edgree-is-new-frontier-of-study-online.html/?pagewanted=all.

Markoff, J. (2011, August 15). Virtual and artificial, but 58,000 want course. *New York Times*. Retrieved from http://wwwnytimes.com/2011/08/16/science/16stanford.html.

Seamans, R., & Zhu, F. (2011, October 5). *Technology shocks in multi-side markets: The impact of Craigslist on local newspapers*. Retrieved from Econ Papers: Working Papers, NET Institute website http://EconPapers.repec.org/RePEc:net:wpaper:1011.

Thrun, S. (2012, September 11). Sebastian Thrun: Statistics 101 will be majorly updated. *Udacity Blog*. Retrieved from http://blog.udacity.com/2012/09/sebastian-thrun-statistics-101-will-be.html#sthash.X7YRxFmR.dpuf.

White House. (2013, August 22). *President Obama speaks on college affordability*. Retrieved from Whitehouse.gov: http://www.whitehouse.gov/photos-and-video/video/2013/08/22/president-obama-speaks-college-affordability.

14

CREATING A TEMPORARY SPONTANEOUS MINI-ECOSYSTEM THROUGH A MOOC[1]

Paul Kim and Charlie Chung

One of the most important things that we need to keep in mind about education is that the various components of an educational system do not operate independently. Rather, they collectively form an interdependent ecosystem (Fullan, 2006; Patterson, 2004) which includes: learners, teachers, families, and pedagogical activities. There are also assessments, certifications, facilities, tools, finances, social norms, and many other factors to consider. To be sustainable, an innovation that makes a significant and lasting difference in education also needs to address other relevant parts of the ecosystem.

As an example, the first author developed the SMILE (Stanford Mobile Inquiry-based Learning Environment) platform, along with colleagues at Stanford University. SMILE offers a unique pedagogy and innovative mobile technology (not reliant on Internet access) that can be implemented in underdeveloped parts of the world. However, the SMILE research and development team had to do more than simply develop the platform. We conducted field workshops, partnered with non-governmental organizations (NGOs) and industry, worked with graduate school researchers, and harnessed volunteer energies in order to try to implement sustainable solutions. During these efforts, we encountered countless challenges and barriers trying to implement just one program. Thus, in order to transform education around the world, we will need a large supply of both innovations and leaders who are striving to address the needs of all of the various educational ecosystems.

The emergence of massive open online courses (MOOCs) on an unprecedented scale (via platforms such as Coursera and edX) was hailed as an avenue for achieving global scale in educational reform (Mahraj, 2012). Although MOOCs represented genuine innovations, it was clear that, in isolation, they would neither revolutionize higher education nor transform the prospects for underserved communities around the world. In their current form, the large MOOC platforms are too dependent on high Internet bandwidth, a lecture-based pedagogy, simplistic assessments, and uncertain business models. But this does not mean that they did not hold promise; in fact, one of the most important characteristics of a sustainable learning technology solution is its capacity to evolve (Wildavsky, Kelly, & Carey, 2011). Thus, a telling indicator of the potential for MOOCs in global education would be how quickly they changed and adapted as they matured.

A MOOC to Experiment in Capability-Building

While observing this MOOC evolution process from a distance, in the summer of 2012, the first author had the opportunity to be on the front lines when he was approached by fellow Stanford Professor Amin Saberi. Professor Saberi developed a new MOOC platform, along with co-founder Farnaz Ronaghi, called Stanford Venture-lab (now known as NovoEd). The Stanford Venture-lab was a unique MOOC platform based on social learning theory and emphasized group projects (Ronaghi, Saberi, & Trumbore, 2014).

Professor Saberi asked Kim to offer a course during the fall of 2012 in the area of educational entrepreneurship. The concept of offering fully online courses was not new to Professor Kim. In fact, he had taught courses such as "Technology in Education" and "Mobile Learning for Developing Regions" since 2002 in various formats, including blended. However, what was unique was the opportunity to offer open access to anyone in the world who wanted to and was able to join, so the offer was accepted. This would be an experiment to see how MOOCs could support various aspects of the global education ecosystem. In particular, the first author was eager to see how MOOCs could help achieve reach and scale, in the following ways:

1. **Identify innovative future education leaders globally**—we will need innovative leaders across the globe, and only a portion of these potential leaders will flow through formal training programs. Thus, if we can help to identify some of them via MOOCs, we could start to help equip these future leaders with some of the information, ideas, and connections that they will need to have an impact.

2. **Achieve the critical mass to boost the number of innovative ideas**— we know that problem-solving is improved when a diversity of people and ideas are involved (Meirink, Imants, Meijer, & Verloop, 2010). Since the various challenges in education around the globe are monumental, we will need to have as many minds and voices as possible engaged in thinking about solutions. Though only a small proportion of these ideas will turn out

to be revolutionary, MOOCs could be a large and globally diverse channel through which to generate ideas.

3.   **Provide training experiences for educators at scale**—educators around the globe have varied training needs, and should have access to ongoing learning opportunities. There are also many non-teacher stakeholders who would benefit from understanding educational concepts in order to best contribute in their roles (de Souza Briggs, 2008). The level and scale of potential impact provided by MOOCs may help fill some of these learning needs.

In the following sections, we will first describe the design of the MOOC and its activities, and then reflect on what we learned relative to the three primary objectives spelled out above.

The Goal of Imagining New Learning Environments

The MOOC, which started in October 2012, was entitled "Designing a New Learning Environment" (DNLE). The focus of the DNLE MOOC was to encourage participants to imagine new education environments and systems; the goal was the same for everyone, whether they themselves were currently operating within educational systems or outside of them. In terms of instructional content, the intent was to forgo a series of long, boring lectures (a goal shared by many professors, but realized by few). To accomplish this objective, the course was designed to show and discuss examples of innovative programs in various educational contexts around the world. The next step was to get participants to think of innovations that might address one or more of the challenges found in their environment or region of the world.

As it happened, the first author wrote the introductory class message from his mobile phone in Newala, Tanzania (Figure 14.1 contains the first portion of the welcome message that was sent at the start of the MOOC). Even in this initial message, the topic of sustainability was brought up, despite it typically being the least thought-through aspect of most educational innovations. Even though it did not occur to Professor Kim at the time, it is possible that the issue of sustainability was simultaneously being asked about the DNLE MOOC itself. Given the short duration of the MOOCs, what level of sustainability could be expected of it, he pondered? In the end, this led to an interesting and important observation related the level of voluntarism in the MOOC, as described later in this chapter.

As with many MOOCs, the first author created a series of short videos for the participants to watch. However, only the first few were akin to lecture-based instruction from an expert, with explanations of foundational concepts in educational psychology such as Bloom's Taxonomy and Vygotsky's ideas about the

Mambo marafiki zangu, karibuni DNLE! (Swahili for: "Hello my friends, welcome everyone to DNLE!")

I am typing this reply from the Mtwara region in Tanzania using my phone. It takes little more time and effort, but I am glad that it is possible so we connect like this. I am here to replicate my SMILE (Stanford Mobile Inquiry-based Learning Environment) project to new schools. It is amazing that I have been able to use either 3G in Dar es Salaam and Edge in most rural villages I have visited–this is a good example of sustainability for the time being (I am enjoying seeing that important discussion starting on the forums). Mobile technology seems quite useful and sustainable here, and I feel that it will only get better.

When we design and implement a learning technology solution, we do so with perceived theoretical value of our solution. As we conduct user case studies or small scale pilot-studies, we can find out a **little** more about the value of our solution. As we conduct larger-scale case studies in a real-world context, we can witness how the real or true value of our solution manifests over time. **No** solution is perpetually sustainable in an ecosystem. Things change, evolve, adapt, mutate, or become extinct over time. Therefore, one of important characteristic of a sustainable learning technology solution is the **capacity to evolve.** Another important matter would be collective and "sustained commitment" from the constituencies of an ecosystem to make a solution sustainable.

One question is *how long should a solution sustain to be qualified as a "sustainable" solution?* I would say it has to do with the intended goal of the constituencies as a whole in an ecosystem.

FIGURE 14.1   First portion of the Designing a New Learning Environment (DNLE) MOOC welcome message

zone of proximal development (ZPD). Other videos focused on showing what it meant to look at an educational need or scenario with the wide lens of viewing its ecosystem (many innovative solutions remain ground-breaking only in research labs, and are often useless when implemented in the real world). We provided examples of various failures and successes, many based on personal experiences. We also had guest lectures representing different stakeholder perspectives in the sphere of education. However, the main focus of the course was not on predefined content; rather, the intent of the course was to have participants work in teams to collaboratively envision new learning environments in the educational contexts of their choosing.

A Global Latent Desire to Innovate

The MOOC clearly touched upon a latent need among people interested in the future of education. With the help of colleagues, we sent a few messages out about the course and posted an introductory video on YouTube a few weeks prior to the course. Interestingly, the response to the course took off via social media (including Twitter, Facebook, LinkedIn, and YouTube). This positive response demonstrated how eager people were to try new ways of learning and collaborating when it comes to improving education.

Over 18,800 students registered for the course from over 200 sovereign states around the world. The gender distribution skewed slightly female (57 percent), and there was a wide age distribution (14 percent were under age 26; 26 percent were aged 26–34; 46 percent were aged 34–54; and the remaining 14 percent were older than 54). A number of the participants were in high school and

middle school. In fact, one youngster who finished the course with a 5 out of 5 peer rating from his team had the following inspiring personal statement on his profile page:

> The idea of teaching needy kids with technology never came up to my mind before . . . Although I am only a middle schooler, I hope that my team and I will create a new learning environment that could change the course of other childrens' [sic] life.

Among the geographies represented were conflict regions such as Syria, Palestine, and Afghanistan. Apparently, even in the most difficult of circumstances, people were trying to improve education in their communities. Some learners were from rural villages with limited access to the Internet. When the course developers saw students joining the course from villages in Tanzania and other African countries as well as towns in Pakistan near the border of Afghanistan, we openly wondered, "How in the world did they even find this course?"

Global Sourcing and Alignment on Innovative Ideas

As mentioned, the Stanford Venture-Lab/NovoEd MOOC platform was designed to focus on team formation and collaboration. With this platform, participants could start a team and then describe their project idea to recruit their peers, or browse existing teams and join one. As part of the NovoEd tool features, at a designated time, participants lacking a team affiliation are automatically assigned to a team via a matching algorithm. When the MOOC commenced, we had 1,336 groups with an average of four or five members per team. Given the retention data and experiences reported by other MOOCs, we expected that participation would drop off over time. In terms of actual numbers, our attrition rate ranged from 10–20 percent each week. By the end of the course, 284 of the original 1,336 teams submitted a final project. This apparent retention metric is misleading since many additional participants were actively engaging in the MOOC beyond the 1,000+ members of these 284 final reporting teams. They just did not submit a final report.

In some cases, school district staffs would join the MOOC together and form groups with a common focus. However, in most cases, teams were composed of complete strangers. This process of forming teams is important in the cultivation of leadership skills (Ladewig & Rohs, 2000; Sobrero & Craycraft, 2008) because in many areas of education aligning people to focus on a particular problem can be more difficult than actually solving it. Having a platform where leaders could emerge by developing a vision and drawing others from around the world to work together on it, allowed for the development of this important skill (see Figure 14.2 for an example of such a solicitation).

-Design Thinking, Learning and Building on Value-

I'm [name], and you are reading this because you want to find a like-minded person to team up with…I believe that education needs to start with helping young people get in touch with what they would really enjoy most doing in life. Most people start a life where they learn that making a living is a primary goal, then that desire can be objectified. Helping them realize what's valuable can help them make the difference between short term gratification and sustainable solutions, between commodity and design, between whim and value and so on. I believe in teaching the principles of a good "information diet" where people actively choose what to assimilate and build on.

The bottom line is, let's see if education can be improved by:
- using design to create engaging interactive environments/platforms
- use technology to create immersive experiences
- use gamification to motivate and collaboration to organize content. I've been interested in game mechanics for a while, applied in marketing and in design.
 - build tools that will help people find and assimilate useful information, like mindmapping tools, personal growth and goals oriented apps.
 - add progress tracking and personal stats
- help people learn and grow, so they can live more fulfilling lives focused on value, not money making

I started with a Bachelor's Degree in Psychology, got a MA in Marketing and became a self taught graphic designer later in life.

Please reply to this introduction if you want to team up with me.

UPDATE
As a result of your amazing feedback, I have started a new post on my "Journal" page where I provide more in depth details related to this initial idea presented in my introduction…thank you for your support! Keep the good energy flowing!

I'll be contacting everybody who left a reply in private as well.

FIGURE 14.2   Group solicitation message from a DNLE MOOC participant

We were also extremely excited to see the cross-national nature of the self-formed teams. Among the top ten group projects (as measured by peer votes), the project teams had an average of seven members from four different countries. This dynamic resulted in a diverse mix of perspectives.

Spontaneous Voluntarism in the MOOC

Although we fully expected that the design of the MOOC platform and course would facilitate a high level of teamwork, we also witnessed additional organizational efforts arise spontaneously that were neither anticipated nor asked for. Various participants would step up and volunteer ways to help enable learning among their peers. Among the examples were the following:

- Much of the learning content was new to some participants, but not to others. Volunteers posted links to external articles or resources that explained some of the concepts in different or more in-depth ways. As part of these efforts, one volunteer created and maintained a glossary of terms for the new vocabulary.

- When the discussion boards became crowded with information, participants took it upon themselves to re-post key information in order to ensure high visibility to those posts.
- One volunteer (a large education company executive), took it upon himself to convert the lecture videos into low-bandwidth versions that would be easier to download in areas of the world with limited Internet bandwidth.
- Participants often evaluated more than the required minimum number of peer assignments, thereby providing additional feedback on the work of others in the course.

The efforts of the DNLE MOOC participants to go above and beyond what was required in order to help each other was recognized by their peers in several ways, including through nominations to a student "Hall of Fame." There was so much assistance provided at various points of the course that it seemed as if we all had been working together so long that we immediately knew what we were supposed to do! This ambience of consistent and timely support occurred despite the fact that we had never met or even had an orientation session together.

How did all of this come about? First, we think scale played a role, as we would not have had this level of voluntarism in a course of 30 or even 100 students. Stated another way, if there are amazing volunteers at a rate of one out of every 50 people, there will only be a couple in a class of 100. But with a course enrolling thousands of participants, there is sufficient critical mass to provide dozens of volunteers who can help with many of the missing aspects of the ecosystem. It is not just a matter of numbers, of course, but also the culture that is shaped for the course. We did not rely solely on personality traits or tendencies of participants to volunteer their support. Instead, we took intentional steps to cultivate such a culture, including the following:

1. **We put course participants in the mindset of seeing themselves as agents of change.** After explaining a few basic ideas and principles related to educational theory, we quickly focused on describing examples of innovative programs (such as mobile technology, community storytelling, agriculture-based games, etc.). Next, we asked participants to think of new innovations. The purpose of this approach was to inspire participants and to get them into the mindset of being education innovators. The trade-off was that many of the resulting ideas may have been pedagogically naïve, or they may have been inadvertent replicas of previously tried solutions. However, the important thing to keep in mind is that if we train educational change agents, they will come up with better ideas as they gain experience. In contrast, if people get bogged down in the intricacies of educational or psychological theory (perhaps better suited to graduate study), it may be difficult later to make the jump to practical applications and real-world implementation. Thus, our measure of success was not the quality of the

specific team projects from the course, but, rather, the number of people who became energized and inspired to imagine and attempt further changes.

2. **We illustrated innovation through diverse examples in order to be as inclusive as possible.** With a widely diverse participant group, it was important to show a rich mix of examples and instances of innovation from around the world. We made an effort to highlight a variety of attempts at innovation—in some cases showing actual footage from various classrooms. This approach had the best chance of providing examples that the audience could relate to. It also helped illustrate the possibilities of innovating in different areas of various educational ecosystems. Given the fact that mobile devices have a wider reach in many parts of the developing world than broadband Internet, we especially wanted to emphasize some of the creative innovations leveraging mobile technologies (International Telecommunications Union, 2014).

3. **We encouraged leadership by cultivating the initial set of self-identified leaders.** From the start of the MOOC, we attempted to establish a flat hierarchy and avoid the standard teacher–student paradigm. Instead of "students," we used the term "fellow innovators," thereby encouraging people to take on an identity as both learners as well as leaders. Such an approach is in tune with the rapid pace of change in our modern world. With a flattened hierarchy and fellow innovator philosophy in place, highly motivated people in the course who are venturing into new learning areas are more likely to contribute to their peers' understanding (Angelaccio & Buttarazzi, 2010; Williams, 2012). Such peer-to-peer contributions may extend well beyond the actual course instructor resources and ideas.

Though we started with a flat hierarchy, a few participants established themselves as leaders early on. We took efforts to recognize and encourage this early leadership by acknowledging their contributions and actively soliciting their feedback as the course progressed. Such efforts to recognize and support these early ad hoc leaders within the DNLE MOOC did not mean that they were established as exclusive leaders. On the contrary, part of their leadership role was to encourage others to step up, offer resources, and be helpful to their fellow participants. In this way, these early leaders modeled leadership for their peers.

There was one very interesting aspect of the DNLE MOOC that probably helped to enable this ecosystem. It is something rarely mentioned as a benefit of MOOCs—namely, its limited duration. Because the course lasted only ten weeks, it was a relatively limited commitment for volunteers to help their fellow learners. We suspect this would have been much less sustainable, for example, if the person who volunteered to convert videos to low-bandwidth formats might have had to do so for six or nine months. With a longer course, it seems likely that fewer people would have volunteered their services, and, thus, additional structures (technology, processes and procedures, teaching assistants, etc.) would have been required. But since the ecosystem of a MOOC tends to be limited to a period of only two or three months, temporary voluntary resources can arise and be sustained. Thus, ironically, the limited temporal nature of the MOOC might allow some of the supporting aspects of this particular type of ecosystem to arise spontaneously and persist for its duration.

We also found that many students continued to interact with others after the course was officially over. This ongoing involvement was not solely an individual phenomenon. Some project teams, surprisingly, continued their collaborations long past the course end date. Even the instructor, Paul Kim, has been involved in collaborative projects with more than a dozen course participants since "finishing" the MOOC. As one example, a group of Oxford MBA students participated in the course and were excited about the SMILE program described in the course. They wanted to become involved in it, and consequently reached out to Professor Kim and collaborated to implement a SMILE program in India as part of their MBA studies. This example was but one of a number of collaborations that were initiated online in the MOOC and which later resulted in improvements to actual educational systems in the real world.

MOOC Exceeding Reasonable Expectations

Much of the debate around MOOCs has been due to the wide gulf between the hype and what is currently achievable. The key to not being disappointed is to not start with unrealistic expectations. Although we were very impressed with the results of the DNLE MOOC, we think that MOOCs, at this point in their development, should be evaluated by their specific tangible results, such as those briefly described in this chapter. Unfortunately, a narrow focus on completion rates has become a replacement for discussion about better forms of evaluation. But even more important than evaluating the "success" of a MOOC is capturing and reflecting on what we have learned from them. In that spirit, we noted a few particularly interesting aspects of the DNLE MOOC, as detailed below:

- The desire to learn about educational innovation and then actually make innovations in education was very strong. This was apparent in the thousands of learners who found this course and invested significant personal time and effort in it (74 percent of whom were working or were full-time students).
- The diversity of learners and the extent to which they interacted via groups and discussions was inspiring. The DNLE MOOC was a highly accessible way to get a worldwide flow of ideas on new ways to improve education among passionate groups of people with common interests.
- The deliverables were impressive for the amount of time spent on them, with many different types of ideas being developed and presented.
- The spontaneous self-organizing activities pursued by volunteers helped overcome the gaps in the learning ecosystem of the course.

Regarding the three specific hypotheses we wanted to test in the MOOC, we saw positive support for each of them.

1. As a channel to identify future education leaders, the MOOC provided an impetus for participants to be proactive, establish a vision, rally a team, and look for ways to support their peers.
2. As a forum to generate innovative ideas, the large scale of the DNLE MOOC allowed for the generation of and exposure to a large number of ideas. A delightful surprise was the extent to which idea-sharing and collaboration occurred across national boundaries.
3. As a way to train a large number of educators, the DNLE MOOC seemed to perform well as a channel to convey basic educational concepts to those who had come from outside the field. In addition, the videos and discussion boards provided a good way to highlight and discuss examples of innovations in different education contexts. It remains to be seen how well suited MOOCs may be for more advanced personal development, but these initial results seem promising.

Since the DNLE MOOC, hundreds of MOOCs have been designed and completed. Some of these MOOCs have tried to facilitate idea generation, innovation, cross-global communication, leadership, and inspiration by example. It remains for those of us involved in these MOOCs, or who are studying them, to compare notes and to develop further conclusions, hypotheses, and ideas regarding how we can further evolve MOOCs to meet the needs of different people and educational systems around the world.

With the DNLE MOOC, we knew at the outset that an innovation in a single component of an educational ecosystem is not sufficient. Nevertheless, we felt that we achieved some measure of a mini-ecosystem. But how? We believe that it was through forming a culture of innovation and collaboration (e.g., establishing a flat hierarchy where course participants were fellow innovators, showing diverse innovation examples, recognizing early leaders, etc.). Also vital was leveraging a MOOC platform that was geared towards project-based learning (e.g., group work, self-selected teams, focus on a final product, etc.). It was in such a project-based learning community where the seeds for a vibrant ecosystem could be formed.

But none of this would have made a difference had there not been a latent group of passionate individuals hungry to make a difference and willing to come together (virtually) to share ideas and collaborate. We learned from each other at a waypoint on our respective learning journeys. At the same time, we also inspired each other to tackle challenges with new innovations. In retrospect, it seems that our shared understanding of the importance of our separate, but related, errands was the key driving force behind this MOOC. This shared understanding helped us to start working together quickly, without fuss or delay.

The DNLE MOOC was spontaneous, self-organizing, and implicitly treasured for its short duration. It was like a firefly that, recognizing its limited time, burned as brightly as it could during its brief lifespan. Hopefully, the DLNE firefly provided some small light for others. We also hope that it left offspring to provide future light and hope through the development of leaders and new learning environments that will bear delicious fruit in the near future.

Paul Kim is the Chief Technology Officer and Assistant Dean of the Graduate School of Education at Stanford University. Dr. Kim served on the Board of Directors of WestEd, the Committee on Grand Challenges in International Development for the National Academies of Science, and the advisory committee for the National Science Foundation's Education and Human Resources Directorate. As founder of Seeds of Empowerment, a non-profit global education incubator for social innovations leveraging mobile technologies, Paul has developed, implemented, and evaluated an array of technology tools for underserved and hard-to-reach communities as a means of addressing literacy gaps. Dr. Kim has implemented various mobile learning pedagogies such as SMILE (Stanford Mobile Inquiry-based Learning Environment) in over 22 countries. He launched a MOOC on designing new learning environments in the Stanford Venture Lab (now called NovoEd) which attracted over 20,000 students from around the world. His involvements in overseas projects include Oman's launch of a new national public university, Deutsche Telekom's global e-learning initiative, Saudi Arabia's national online education initiative, the national evaluation of Uruguay's One Laptop Per Child project, and Rwanda's national ICT planning.

Charlie Chung has a background in management consulting and works in entrepreneurial ventures in the area of his passion; namely, lifelong learning. He works with Class Central (www.class-central.com), a comprehensive MOOC directory, and ZS Associates, a global sales and marketing consulting firm, on a new venture in corporate learning. Charlie holds an MBA from the Ross School of Business at the University of Michigan.

Note

1 Stanford Professor Paul Kim wrote this chapter in collaboration with Charlie Chung, one of the many participants who engaged fully in the MOOC described in this chapter. Both Kim and Chung were inspired by the energy and enthusiasm in the course as they interacted with course participants around the globe. For some, new forms of collaboration continued beyond the course, as was the case with the development of the present chapter.

References

Angelaccio, M., & Buttarazzi, B. (2010). A social network based-enhanced learning system. *Enabling Technologies: Infrastructures for Collaborative Enterprises (WETICE), Proceedings of the 2010 19th IEEE International Workshop,* 94–5. June 28–30, 2010, Larissa, Greece. doi:10.1109/WETICE.2010.59.

de Souza Briggs, X. (2008). *Democracy as problem solving: Civic capacity in communities across the globe.* Cambridge, MA: MIT Press.

Fullan, M. (2006). The future of educational change: System thinkers in action. *Journal of Educational Change,* 7(3), 113–22.

International Telecommunications Union (2014). *ICT facts & figures: The World in 2014.* ICT Data and Statistics Division. Retrieved from http://www.itu.int/en/ITU-D/Statistics/Documents/facts/ICTFactsFigures2014-e.pdf.

Ladewig, H., & Rohs, F.R. (2000). Southern extension leadership development: Leadership development for a learning organization. *Journal of Extension,* 38(3). Retrieved from http://www.joe.org/joe/2000june/a2.html.

Mahraj, K. (2012). Using information expertise to enhance massive open online courses. *Public Services Quarterly,* 8(4), 359–68.

Meirink, J.A., Imants, J., Meijer, P., & Verloop, N. (2010). Teacher learning and collaboration in innovative teams. *Cambridge Journal of Education,* 40(2), 161–81.

Patterson, G. (2004). Harmony through diversity: Exploring an ecosystem paradigm for higher education. *Journal of Higher Education Policy and Management,* 26(1), 59–74.

Ronaghi, F., Saberi, A., & Trumbore, A. (2014). NovoEd, a social learning environment. In P. Kim (Ed.), *Massive open online courses: The MOOC revolution.* New York: Routledge.

Sobrero, P.M., & Craycraft, C.G. (2008). Virtual communities of practice: A 21st century method for learning programming, and developing professionally. *Journal of Extension,* 46(5). Retrieved from http://www.joe.org/joe/2008october/a1.php.

Wildavsky, B.K., Kelly, A.P., & Carey, K. (Eds.). (2011). *Reinventing higher education: The promise of innovation.* Cambridge, MA: Harvard Education Press.

Williams, C. (2012, April). Social learning networks for K12 education. *District Administration.* Retrieved from http://www.districtadministration.com/article/social-learning-networks-k12-education.

15

LEARNING ABOUT MOOCs BY TALKING TO STUDENTS

Charles Severance

Having access to a large amount of activity data in MOOC platforms like Coursera and offering courses to thousands of students naturally leads to applying "big data" analytics in attempts to extract vital bits of knowledge from that vast store of data. There have been countless brilliant papers written with extensive graphs based on millions of data points distilled down to a few lines on a few graphs. As researchers, we are habituated to believe that with enough data and proper analysis, graphs are truth and their conclusions are self-evident.

This article takes the opposite approach and explores different aspects of the MOOC phenomenon through the eyes of individual students. In the course of teaching two MOOCs on Coursera over the past two years with over 350,000 total registered students, I also have traveled to over 25 different locations around the world and had live face-to-face office hours with my MOOC students. Each time, somewhere between one and 15 students showed up and we talked for approximately an hour—usually in a Starbucks or a local café. This chapter summarizes the reflections and conclusions that I have reached from these highly personal interactions—small data at its smallest—namely, one-to-one communications.

Some Background

I have dabbled in media since the late 1970s, working in and on television and radio. During this vast expanse of time, I have always been fascinated with the power and reach of media. In the very early days of the Internet, I viewed it as a way to bring scale to education and training. In many ways, I looked at television programs like *This Old House* and *Bill Nye the Science Guy* as massively consumable educational experiences that found ways to engage viewers and maintain their interest and educate them in a way that did not feel like "education."

But the limitation of these professionally (and expensively) produced programs was that there was no way to build enough materials to meet the real needs of education. For one thing, education was changing constantly. If we produced a 30-minute experience for US$500,000 and then something significant happened to alter or transform a field, it took another US$500,000 to redo the "lecture." For real education to happen the production costs and effort needed to be driven down and the tools for creating and delivering educational content needed to be put in the hands of the teachers so that they could change or update their materials at any time.

In response, I built teacher-oriented tools to enable the production of lecture materials. My first tool, which I called Sync-O-Matic, used RealAudio (and later RealVideo) to deliver audio and synchronized slides over the Web employing 14.4 Kbps modems. I utilized this software to produce a course called "EGR124—Introduction to the Internet," which I taught with completely online streaming audio in the fall of 1997. Over the next 18 months I taught the course on a total of three occasions, switching from streaming audio to streaming video, refining the technology and pedagogy each time I taught the class.

By the fall of 1998, students were telling me that the course was fun, engaging, useful, and convenient—even with no face-to-face interaction. Interestingly, as the students' satisfaction with the course was increasing, I was enjoying teaching the course less and less. It was quite enjoyable to produce the materials and exhilarating to identify and solve the technical problems. But once the course was complete and could pretty much run without me, I started to feel useless. Suffice to say, the students were having fun learning but I was not part of it—I began to feel isolated and lonely. So I decided to do an experiment.

I told the students that we would have one face-to-face meeting in this class to take the midterm examination. My goal was to meet the students at least once so I could get a sense of who they were and what they were getting out of the course. As the students arrived to take the exam, I greeted them and handed one to each of them. What was interesting was that the students knew me well and greeted me as an old friend. After all, they had been watching me and listening to my bad jokes on video throughout the prior eight weeks. Not only did they know much about me by that time, but they also seemed genuinely happy to have me as their friend, mentor, and coach. In stark contrast, to me, they were all strangers. It was as if I had created a unique event wherein I was the center of attention, but I did not know anyone who came to the gathering.

Because of my feelings of isolation, that was the last time I taught that class. I decided that if I were going to enjoy this online teaching experience, I needed to build some type of technology that would allow me to actually "see" my students, get to know them, and learn why they were involved in the course. In the fall of 1998, I wrote a grant to the National Science Foundation Division of Undergraduate Education with a proposal to build a "Facebook for Education." (Note: that was seven years before Facebook was founded and six years before

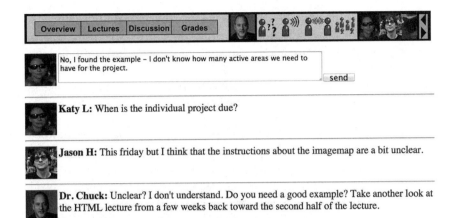

FIGURE 15.1 Proposed asynchronous chat with avatars (1998)

anyone heard of MySpace.) The software featured asynchronous chats with avatars throughout the user interface with presence tracking so you could get a sense
of who was nearby (see Figure 15.1).

While the proposal was not funded, I continued to imagine ways to build better technology to increase the connections between teachers and students as well
as tools that allow students to connect and collaborate with each other. Starting
in 1999, I built a product called ClipBoard-2000 that recorded slides, instructor video, audio, document camera video, and annotations using QuickTime.
ClipBoard-2000 allowed for the production of a synchronized multi-stream lecture in a single QuickTime file; this, in turn, enabled the production of a fully
synchronized lecture in a single file rather than a set of interlinked Web pages
as I had done with Sync-O-Matic. Clipboard-2000 had similar functionality to
popular tools today like TechSmith's Camtasia and other such products. I made
an offer to donate my lecture recording technology to Apple so that it could be
included in their products in 2001; unfortunately, they were not interested.

Starting in 2004, I led the Sakai open source learning management system that
focused on collaboration and connection, instead of simply "managing learning."
Starting in 2008, I became involved in the IMS Global Learning Consortium in
the development of the IMS Learning Tools Interoperability standard that allows
recently popular tools like Piazza to be integrated into any Learning Management
System using standard protocols.

A few years later, in the fall of 2011, Stanford University taught the first three
MOOCs that experienced truly massive enrollment levels of over 100,000 participants each. The MOOC instructors at Stanford used a purpose-built learning
management system and other technologies to achieve this scale. Along with
Princeton, Stanford, and the University of Pennsylvania, my own university—
the University of Michigan—was one of the first four Coursera partners. By

the summer of 2012, I was teaching my first Coursera course titled "Internet History, Technology, and Security" based loosely on the materials that I had gathered when I was hosting a television program about the Internet in the mid-1990s initially called "Internet:TCI" and later renamed "Nuthin' but Net." In April 2014, I launched my second Coursera course titled "Programming for Everybody (Python)," based on a course I taught to incoming graduate students at the University of Michigan School of Information.

Unlike my previous online teaching experiences, with my two MOOCs, Coursera was responsible for improving the underlying software technology. This felt wonderful! In fact, for the first time in decades, I could focus on my teaching and enjoy exploring this new pedagogy, rather than constantly building infrastructure for others to pilot test and send feedback to me to improve the course. So I put my "Tool Builder" hat aside and replaced it with a "MOOC Instructional Experimenter" hat.

My Approach to MOOCs

My approach to developing MOOCs was to give students skills that they could use as building blocks or instructional scaffolding to find their way into other educational experiences. I wanted to make the course something that met the students' needs whatever *their* starting point and advance them along *their* learning arc. My goal was not to teach them everything—but, instead, simply to influence their personal learning arc by opening their minds to new ideas.

In terms of production, I wanted to create a very personal feel to the course material with extensive eye contact and a very close camera shot (see Figure 15.2).

During a lecture recording, I typically drink coffee, make mistakes, tell jokes, wear a costume, or introduce my students to my cat if it happens to come walking into the room. I even leave a few typos in the slides to avoid any sense that

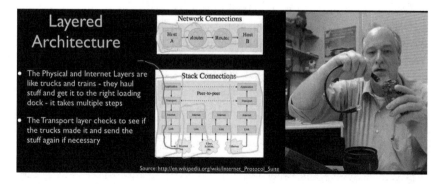

FIGURE 15.2   Internet History, Technology, and Security MOOC on the Coursera platform.

this is "canned" or "perfect." These informal bits are intended to increase intimacy and engagement—like a television talk show or reality program. I wanted each student to feel that while I was lecturing, they were my only focus.

Beyond the format of the recorded lectures, I also put a lot of energy into making the assessments fun and engaging. The Coursera staff coached me to avoid thinking about cheating and focus only on learning. The problem with trying to build assessments that stop people from cheating is that students that want to cheat will defeat any system you might come up with and all of those easily defeated anti-cheating systems become significant barriers to those who are just there to learn.

Both of my Coursera MOOCs were successful in their debut session. During the first time I teach a MOOC, there are lots of small details that need fixing. The second time the course is taught, my team and I find and fix the remaining mistakes. By the third time, the course materials need minimal editing. As a result, most of my focus is increasingly on the pedagogy and the community that is being built in each ensuing session of the course.

Community Teaching Assistants: The Core of the Learning Community

Another impressive Coursera innovation is the use of Community Teaching Assistants (CTAs). I run my MOOCs as learning communities, encouraging discussion amongst the students and making sure that my participation in any of the course discussions is as just another community member rather than the "expert on high." Instead of attempting to quickly answer every question, I let students answer one another's questions and then thank the student that answered the question. Such an approach encourages students to be more self-reliant and self-directed and not to wait for me to provide an answer.

A well-designed learning community does not depend on a single central leader to succeed. When effectively conducted, leaders emerge from the community as it forms and the community builds structure where and when needed.

But sometimes there are students that seem to be natural leaders and mentors. These are the students that Coursera identifies as possible CTAs. In the very first teaching of my MOOC, "Internet History, Technology, and Security," we identified eight students who showed above-average leadership and mentoring skills and invited them to be CTAs for the second running of the course. While we have experienced some turnover in the CTAs, three of those original eight CTAs have stuck with me through ten MOOCs and have become the lead CTAs.

Sue (Northern California), Mauro (Italy), and Mazen (Egypt) as my lead CTAs have become an essential part of my MOOC teaching to this point. When we were building the new version of the "Programming for Everybody" MOOC, they spent endless hours reviewing and improving the materials in the months before the course was launched.

I use teaching assistants (or Graduate Student Instructors (GSIs)) in teaching my on-campus classes and they are all wonderful teachers and mentors. At times, I have invited some of my on-campus teaching assistants (TAs) to be a Community Teaching Assistant in MOOC classes over the summer. While on-campus TAs were excellent in the face-to-face teaching environment, they did not feel as comfortable in the MOOC environment as the CTAs who were recruited from registered MOOC students and were strong participants in one of the sessions of the online course. That difference suggests that these educational environments—residential classes and MOOCs—require quite different instructional support skill sets.

Face-to-Face Office Hours

My goal for the face-to-face office hours was simply to better understand the various contexts where students were taking my courses. In a sense, I viewed them as ad hoc focus groups to help me improve my course. I found that there was an amazing diversity in the reasons that students had for taking the various MOOC courses, as well as the value they were expecting for these courses. The reasons tended to vary significantly according to an individual student's geographical locations. I will recount a few specific observations below from some of these conversations with no attempt to make any claim other than anecdotal comments. This is "small data" at its smallest. In the process, we hear from and attempt to learn about individual students over a cup of coffee or tea.

My first MOOC-related face-to-face office hours were in New York City on July 26, 2012. I had no idea what to expect—it was like a blind date where any of 56,000 people might appear or no one at all. This time, six students showed up and we talked for over an hour. What surprised me was that we talked very little about the course content. Instead, we spent most of the time talking about what MOOCs meant and how education might be changed by MOOCs. Students were extremely curious about what "Coursera" actually was or could become. If you are interested in what happened, you can watch the video of those students and the videos of the rest of the office hours at http://office-hours.dr-chuck.com.

Even though it was less than six months into the MOOC movement, some students were already viewing MOOC classes as a viable substitute for an MBA. Those students had solid jobs in a strong economy with a high demand for their skills. They did not perceive a need to obtain another degree to increase their salary; however, they did feel the need for the kinds of knowledge and skills one receives in an MBA program to open up more options in their career paths.

Back in October 2012, I had my first experience with international office hours in Seoul, Korea. When I arrived, I found out that one of the students in Seoul was enrolling in MOOCs to ease her transition into a master's program in the United States that she would be attending in a few months. Another student was an alumnus of the University of Michigan and wanted to participate in something interesting and reconnect with his alma mater. A third student was taking the class to build his professional skills.

In Barcelona, also in October 2012, nearly all of the students were in their late 20s and already had an undergraduate degree. They saw Coursera as a highly significant and valuable source of education. They thought that Coursera provided those same skills and knowledge as a local master's degree but at no cost. Several of them were taking and completing a five-course load of Coursera classes.

I had office hours in Melbourne and Perth in Australia in June 2013. These office hours had a wider age range than previous ones with some older students who were interested in learning for the sake of learning. In contrast, other MOOC students were unemployed and attempting to get back into the job market through the acquisition of new skills.

At the Hammersmith Tube Station in London later that same month in 2013, the crowd was also highly diverse. However, this time it seemed as though the majority of the students were taking part in MOOC courses to satisfy personal curiosity as well as for personal growth. It was the first office hours where one of my students brought a camera and recorded the actual office hour conversations. Later, I jokingly asked my colleagues in the digital education group at the University of Michigan if they would hire a cameraperson to travel with me so that we could turn the class into a reality show. After briefly reflecting on it, they replied "no."

In my office hours in Slovenia and Croatia near the end of that year, there were only a few attendees but a theme that emerged was a conscious effort to diversify their educational experiences even while pursuing their degree locally. At my Phoenix, AZ office hours, both of the students who showed up were older, highly educated, and already had solid careers. They saw Coursera classes as a great way to go back and learn some things they might have missed along the way because they were overly involved in their careers.

When I held office hours in Salt Lake City in February 2014, only one student showed up but he was extremely interesting and engaging. He was the first student that I had met who had an incredibly dynamic and relaxed approach to his career. He had no formal education but was doing quite well working in a technical company. He was enormously bright and found formal education rather unexciting so he just would self-learn material at the moment he needed it—such as when he had decided to make a career move. Coursera was ideal for him because he could fit needed learning experiences into his spare time at no charge.

By the time I did a follow-up to my earlier office hours in Washington, DC in May 2014, I had launched my second MOOC on Coursera titled "Programming for Everybody." This time I specifically taught a course on the computer language Python for people with neither a math nor a programming background.

While I enjoyed my time in Washington, DC, Seoul, Melbourne, London, and so on, it was my office hours in Miami, FL in June 2014 that tugged at my heartstrings more than any of the other ones. About half of the students were the typical middle-class students who viewed the class as loads of fun and full of potential. In contrast, some of the students—who were a little down on their luck—viewed Coursera as the one source of education that was there for them no matter what. Coursera gave them a path back into their own educational arc. As such, it was an enabling tool for the disadvantaged as well as for those who were seeking employment.

My most recent office hours experience—as of the writing of this chapter— was in July 2014 when in Cambridge, MA near MIT. I have fond memories of it since there was an intense level of energy in the room and about half of the students were mid-career and highly educated. One student was a former MIT professor, whereas another student was a stay-at-home mother who was furthering her education. Nevertheless, the most interesting conversation at the table that day was with a student who had received a non-technical bachelor's degree and desperately yearned for education in a technical field that would allow him to move into a technical career path. That particular conversation made me wish that Coursera had a high-quality series of courses on programming and Web design. The good news was that the other more technically savvy students helped this person find his way to meet-ups so that he could get a better understanding of the highly active technical community nearby which could start him along a path towards a new career. Stated another way, my Coursera MOOC connected him to a community where he could be mentored as well as find additional resources and professional connections.

To date, I have completed more than 25 of these face-to-face office hours for my MOOC courses. Regardless of how many of these office hours I complete, the story will actually never be finished. There will always be something new for me to learn with as well as from my students. The students often thank me for coming and make casual comments that I am so giving of my time. When this occurs, I try to explain that my motivation for conducting these office hours is somewhat selfish. Without face-to-face interactions, I would not know who I was teaching and that would mean I would not know why I was teaching. And if that happened, I would probably stop teaching my MOOCs just like my online course from the late 1990s, mentioned earlier, which lacked this personal connection.

The Voices of the Students in MOOCs

Granted my "office hours" were somewhat unique MOOC experiences that may be unexpected for an instructor. As a means to showcase the possibilities of using face-to-face meetings with MOOC participants, I gave a presentation at the 2014 SXSWedu conference in Austin, Texas titled "The Voices of the Students in MOOCs." Part of my goal was to expose people to the students in these MOOCs. From my interactions with the MOOC students over the preceding

24 months in locations around the world, I knew that their stories were diverse, interesting, and vital to hear.

So I put out a broad call to the 100,000+ students that I had previously taught via a MOOC and asked them to send me a short video of their feelings about MOOCs that I would edit and link together to produce my SXSWedu talk. By using YouTube to collect the incoming videos, I was able to assemble a few perspectives beyond those that I had encountered in my office hours. You can see both the student videos I collected and my SXSWedu presentation (minus my M.C. efforts) at voices.dr-chuck.com.

Several of the additional student motivations that came out of my "Voices" project included:

- Students who recently finished their formal education graduated, and often had landed a good job, but wanted to make sure that learning remained part of their life.
- Students who had requirements for continuing education as part of their career, but often could not attend courses any other way due to geographical or other reasons.
- Students who were excited about the MOOC movement and its potential for social transformation.
- Students who were often enrolling in MOOCs in order to be exposed to cultures other than their own and learn from that experience.

I continue to solicit contributions from students and add new videoclips to my "Voices of the Students in MOOCs" YouTube channel as they come in. If you browse that website and watch one or two of these videos, the ideas of this chapter should come alive for you.

Conclusion

The creation of MOOCs is almost like the plot of a science fiction movie where someone unearths a piece of technology from an advanced civilization and inadvertently activates the device. In a way, we discovered truly large-scale MOOCs in the fall of 2011 when Daphne Kollar, Sebastien Thrun, Andrew Ng, and others opened their courses to anyone with an Internet connection and received an immediate and overwhelming response from millions of people around the world.

In the intervening three years, we have learned how to design more effective MOOCs, though research and experimentation is ongoing. Dozens of additional colleges and universities have made specific decisions to join this movement. At the same time, thoughtful research has been conducted that analyzes vast amounts of data that have been gathered as students participate in MOOCs. Leading universities are even developing strategies around how to best use MOOCs to advance their rankings and brands. Naturally, some faculty members are thriving in this new environment and using MOOCs and open education resources and experiences to advance their careers. In fact, there is report of a professor at Ohio State University who achieved tenure in large part due to the creation and teaching of the highly successful Calculus One MOOC via Coursera.

My own feeling is that the meteoric success of MOOCs and the plethora of readily available data and analysis have blinded us to the fact that we are ignoring the most basic of questions. How do MOOCs make us feel? What is the heart and soul of a MOOC? Why are we here (in a MOOC)? You may come to your own conclusions as you explore other chapters of this book and engage in your own MOOC-related experiences.

I do not believe that the answer to these questions can be found in mountains of data. And I do not think that there is any single answer to these questions. My experience suggests that the students in MOOCs are gaining value from their learning experiences in ways we cannot even begin to imagine. The more I converse with students, the more I see different ways that a MOOC can positively alter the direction of a student's life learning arc. And the more I interact with students, the more I realize that every student's life learning arc is different.

In higher education, we have become quite adept at altering a student's life learning arc by bringing him or her to our campus for four years for an intensive and immersive learning experience at a physical location. But it is clear that we have neither the space nor money to educate everyone in the world needing or hoping for such an educational experience using instructional approaches handed down from the Middle Ages. With MOOCs, a single teacher can affect millions of students' learning arcs. However, until we get a better sense of the real needs of this new population, we will never move beyond a few ten-week learning experiences to finally offer education that learners genuinely need.

I think that the best way to figure out this new educational form is to use the age-old approach of sharing a cup of coffee or tea. However, unlike the Middle Ages, in this highly connected world and increasingly digital education era, MOOC instructors like myself now have the opportunity (and I would say the good fortune) to visit a wide array of physical coffee shops wherein they can personally meet with students from around the world who are participating in their massively open online courses, and, thereby, better understand their diverse needs, expectations, and experiences. Take advantage of it if you can. These students need you!

Charles Severance has a BS, MS, and PhD in Computer Science from Michigan State University. He is currently a Clinical Associate Professor and teaches in the School of Information at the University of Michigan. Charles teaches two popular MOOCs to students worldwide on the Coursera platform: Internet History, Technology, and Security and Programming for Everybody. He is also the editor of the Computing Conversations column in *IEEE Computer* magazine and is the author of the book, *Sakai: Building an Open Source Community*. In addition to viewing media as a personal hobby, Charles has co-hosted several television shows including "Nothin but Net" produced by MediaOne and "Internet:TCI." He has also co-hosted a radio show for 10 years on Internet and Technology.

16

THE COLLABORATIVE DESIGN AND DEVELOPMENT OF MOOCs FOR TEACHER PROFESSIONAL DEVELOPMENT

Bernard Robin and Sara McNeil

Developing MOOCs for Teacher Professional Development

Like many other educators around the world, we have been closely following news and research about MOOCs. In fact, after reading numerous MOOC-related reports and announcements, we became interested in the idea of creating a series of MOOCs for the professional development of K–16 teachers. In 2013, the University of Houston System (UHS) and nine other state universities formed a consortium with Coursera, a MOOC platform developer, to explore the possibilities of using MOOC technology and content to improve completion, quality, and access to higher education. We applied for and received funding from UHS for a three-year period to explore Coursera's delivery platform, investigate how to personalize the curriculum, and analyze huge numbers of student experiences to see which approaches work best. In the coming years, we plan to design, develop, and deliver additional MOOCs that focus on innovative technology tools that K–16 teachers can use in their classrooms to support active student learning.

The overall theme we selected for the six-course MOOC series was *Powerful Tools for Teaching and Learning*. The topics and the proposed delivery dates are: (1) 2014: New Technology Tools for Education and Educational Uses of Digital Storytelling; (2) 2015: Educational Uses of Digital Graphics and Educational Uses of Digital Photography; and (3) 2016: The Design, Development and Evaluation of Presentations and Educational Uses of Digital Video. To help accomplish these goals, the University of Houston adopted the Coursera platform (Coursera, 2014).

The Collaborative Design and Development of Multimedia

In the fall of 2013, we were scheduled to teach *The Collaborative Design of Multimedia* and *The Collaborative Development of Multimedia,* a linked pair of graduate courses that focus on planning and creating interactive multimedia resources on educationally-relevant topics. Linked courses occur when two graduate courses are taught collaboratively, usually by two different instructors who work together so that the content of one course complements the content of the other course. Assignments and final semester projects for the two courses are aligned so the work that is done for one course is connected to the work that is done for the other course (McNeil & Robin, 2013). The main objective of the linked courses is to enable students to engage in a collaborative design process while learning to use multimedia authoring software, and then apply this knowledge in an authentic team-based environment.

We felt that the design and development of the first two MOOCs on digital storytelling and new technologies for teachers could be meaningful projects for these linked courses since it would enable our students to explore many of the same issues related to MOOCs we ourselves had been investigating. Current research studies on MOOCs highlight issues such as the influence of MOOCs on the future of higher education (Billington & Fronmuller, 2013), the effects of MOOCs on teaching and learning (Martin, 2012), the educational problems that MOOCs might solve (Rivard, 2013), gaps in MOOC research (Liyanagunawardena, Adams, & Williams, 2013), and blending face-to-face classes with online MOOC classes (Bruff, Fisher, McEwen, & Smith, 2013). We also felt that the real-world nature of designing and developing a MOOC would be a good problem for our students to investigate as members of a team tasked with designing and developing an instructional product.

At the beginning of the semester, we immersed ourselves with our students in learning as much as we could about MOOCs. All of the students, as well as ourselves, enrolled in different MOOCs that were being taught at that time. During class discussion, we discussed in detail the differences and similarities of these MOOCs. We began trying to answer some basic questions about MOOCs that had been extensively reported in the literature (Abramson, 2013; Kolowich, 2013; Lombardi, 2013; Marshall, 2013). Such questions included: Why would a student want to take a MOOC? Why would a faculty member want to create and teach a MOOC? Why would a university want to offer a MOOC for free?

Along with the students, we spent the next few weeks brainstorming ideas about the content and strategies for the two MOOCs we planned to create. The original content for the two MOOCs would come from traditional courses on digital storytelling and new technologies that are part of our graduate degree programs. The first challenge was compressing and converting the large amount of content covered in a normal 15-week semester to a shorter, "preview" version in a five-week MOOC. The second challenge for the teams was determining suitable assignments. There were a number of issues specific to MOOCs that challenged the students to make design decisions, such as the decrease in student–teacher interaction (Dolan, 2014), students as independent learners (Yuan & Powell, 2013), the assessment of student performance (Guàrdia, Maina, & Sangrà,

2013; Sandeen, 2013), and the typically low completion rate of MOOCs (Daniel, 2012).

During the first part of the courses, the teams identified instructional needs, formulated objectives, wrote content, and created storyboards. In the second part of the courses, the teams began developing specific components, including the topics that would be covered, a preliminary schedule, evaluation criteria, and guidelines for the graphics and interface design. Over the five-month semester, our roles changed from information providers and instructors to facilitators, and, subsequently, to observers as the teams increasingly assumed responsibility for the projects. The structure of the course also diminished progressively over this time period until the students, working in their teams, had complete control over the organization of their team meetings as well as in-class discussions.

The Webscape Model

We coined the term "Webscapes" more than a decade ago (Robin & McNeil, 1998) in conjunction with our work developing a new model for designing Web-based, multimedia-enhanced educational environments. There are five components of the Webscape model (Robin & McNeil, 2015). First, students, faculty and content experts work collaboratively in small teams to design and develop multimedia-rich educational projects. This diverse team composition has played a significant role in the outcome of projects by infusing different social, cultural, ethnic, and educational themes and perspectives into the design and development process.

Second, we use a range of technology tools and resources, including sophisticated multimedia authoring programs, dynamic databases, digital storytelling software, and advanced uses of digital video editing. In the process, students develop a collection of multimedia tools that they can use for a variety of projects as well as the ability to select the best tool for a given situation.

Third, we create actual projects that will be used by real teachers and students, as well as Web visitors from around the world. Instruction and learning occur within the context of a challenging project (Lee & Lim, 2012; Thomas, 2000; Vega & Brown, 2013).

Fourth, Webscape projects use a constructivist, team-based approach to instructional design (ID) developed by Willis (1995). The instructional design process is characterized as reflective and recursive, and the planning is typically non-linear, organic, developmental, and collaborative.

Finally, because the Webscape projects are complex and multifaceted, they often cannot be completed in a single semester. As a result, work on such projects often continues throughout the school year. These five components of the Webscape model, (1) small team collaboration, (2) variety of multimedia and technologies used, (3) real-world projects, (4) reflective, recursive instructional design, and (5) an extended timeline for development, instill a highly engaging and interactive learning environment.

Webscape Model Connections

Small Team Collaboration

From our perspective as instructors, there were numerous challenges in applying the Webscape model to the design and development of the MOOCs. A primary concern was that, although we had a great deal of experience and expertise with the content for the MOOCs we were designing—digital storytelling and new technologies for K-12 teachers, these topics were unfamiliar to most of the students. Consequently, we asked the students to place themselves in the roles of learners who would enroll in the MOOCs and identify what they would expect to learn from such an educational experience. To alleviate the students' anxiety over their lack of content knowledge, we noted that few instructional designers are experts in the content areas of the projects they are asked to develop.

The Variety of Multimedia and Technologies Used

We use cutting-edge, innovative technologies in our Webscapes to push the limitations of what technology can do while maintaining universal access to these resources. In our earliest Webscape projects, many of the students who enrolled in our courses needed to learn basic Web design skills, including how to create and edit Web pages with HTML, how to work with graphics, and how to upload files to a Web server. However, even in the early years, we encouraged students to learn to use advanced technologies, such as QuickTime VR, JavaScript, and streaming video, once they had mastered the basic skills. This constant effort to use some of the most current and innovative technologies has allowed us to typically create educational resources with tools that are state of the art. It has also forced us to examine the most critical issues associated with user interface design as well as consider accessibility and usability for diverse Web audiences.

Real-World Projects

The design process is relatively easy when a student creates a project for themselves. Everything changes when the project is designed and developed by a group. For instance, the level of expectation for the final product is much higher, and the scope of the project usually broadens as a result of multiple ideas and viewpoints. The quality standards are raised as team members contribute their individual perspectives and jointly negotiate project goals and objectives.

We deliberately incorporated "struggle" as a design element in the linked courses. At first, the students floundered a little when we did not provide them with a list of desired goals, checklists of needed materials, or a detailed outline of the content. Students were uncomfortable with this at first, but over the 15 weeks of the semester, they became increasingly confident in their abilities to design and develop materials, to write goals and objectives, and to determine for themselves what materials should be required and how they should be structured. We feel that challenging projects situated in authentic contexts have the potential to provide lifelong skills to students and can enrich and change their mental models. A project that both mirrors complicated tasks encountered in today's workplaces and has an actual application can act as a focus and catalyst for learning.

Reflective, Recursive Instructional Design

The students in these courses had all completed a basic course in instructional design in which they created a simple project using the Dick and Carey model (Dick, Carey, & Carey, 2011). Even though this model has a step called "revise instruction," in our experience, most of the students viewed instructional design as a linear process. In the reflective and recursive instructional design model that we used for these courses, students learned that many decisions in the design and development of the product needed to be revisited, some on several occasions. In fact, they started to realize that refinements and revisions were needed throughout the process. One of the reasons that a MOOC was an excellent topic for a Webscape is that there were no clear right answers or universally accepted model for developing MOOCs (Franka, Meinel, Totschnig, & Willems, 2013; Schrire & Levy, 2012). Students' ideas of the instructional design process changed dramatically after they began designing the MOOCs and incorporating reflection and revision into the design of the project.

Extended Timeline for Development

As indicated earlier, most Webscape projects are so complex and multifaceted that they are often impossible to complete in a single semester. Although the teams made considerable progress in designing the two MOOCs during the fall semester, the actual content materials, such as videos, quizzes, and discussion assignments, were not developed. Instead, the materials development work continued throughout the following spring and summer semesters with five students from the original teams and another student who works in our lab participating in the design process, along with us serving as subject matter experts.

Lessons Learned

As we have embarked on our collaborative effort to design and develop our first two MOOCs, we have gained insight and expertise that we confidently believe will help us as we continue to create new MOOCs as well as improve upon our initial two on digital storytelling and new technologies for teachers. Below are some of the most significant lessons we have learned from this process to date.

Converting Content from Text to Video. Although we had voluminous amounts of educational materials for the MOOCs, it took much longer than anticipated to select the appropriate amount of content for a five-week format. Converting our content into short videos, the preferred method for presenting content in a MOOC, also took significantly more time than we anticipated.

For example, in previous Webscape projects, we created large numbers of text-based Web pages with a selection of multimedia content. In this project, the emphasis is on developing large numbers of video clips that participants watch in place of simply reading text. Consequently, we were forced to re-format much of our educational content into a library of short video clips to be used in the MOOCs. This created a significant challenge since we needed to develop the scope and sequence for the videos, which involved determining which videos we would develop for each of the five weeks. Next, we needed to make decisions on several key issues, such as where videos would be shot, whether the instructors would appear in them, how long they would last, what format would be used, and what background music, if any, to include.

Many of our decisions were made after we shot the first set of videos early in the process. We had not fully understood the number of variables that were involved in video production. For example, we had not grasped the importance of writing a script in advance. As a result, in some early videos, the instructor began speaking extemporaneously. We had assumed that she was quite knowledgeable on the topic and did not need a script. Unfortunately, this proved to be a false assumption once we understood that speaking in front of a video camera and recording content that will be watched by perhaps thousands of students online is a much different experience than speaking to a relatively small number of students in a face-to-face class.

Universal Access to Technology. Crafting technology-based assignments for potentially thousands of online students from more than one hundred different countries requires both creativity and flexibility. For example, in the digital storytelling MOOC, we wanted students to be able to share audio and video files in order to obtain peer feedback on their work. However, sharing multimedia files online may work better for participants in some countries than in others. In the MOOC on new technology for teachers, it remains to be seen if access to free Web 2.0 tools is universally available to participants in all countries.

Using the Coursera Platform. We also spent considerable time exploring how Coursera affects the way a MOOC is structured and, consequently, how it is taught (Lane, 2009). We needed to spend more time than anticipated learning to use the Coursera platform. Of course, it would have been helpful to tackle this issue earlier. As much as we pride ourselves on being technologically proficient, learning to use a new content submission system was not as simple and intuitive as we had expected.

Support for MOOC Development. Since MOOC development is relatively new at our university, we found that there were few campus-wide systems in place at this time to support the creation of MOOCs. Consequently, we needed to do many things on our own, such as finding quiet locations to shoot videos and record audio narration, editing multimedia files, and tweaking the HTML code of Web pages that we had developed in Coursera. Of course, we were fortunate to have a group of talented and motivated Learning, Design and Technology graduate students who could assist us with these tasks.

Copyright Issues. Since Coursera is a for-profit company, we found that content we used in our MOOCs needed to be free of copyright restrictions. This copyright requirement differed somewhat from our campus-based courses, in which we occasionally use some materials under the guidelines of non-profit educational fair use. However, since some students may be from countries where educational fair use is much more restrictive, we felt that it was important to only include materials in our MOOCs that we had either created ourselves or had obtained permission to use.

Extended Timeframe. Our initial idea had been that students would spend the first half of the semester on the design process and the second half of the semester on the development aspect. However, the reality was that the design process took much longer than we expected. Not only did our students wrestle with design decisions throughout the entire semester, so did we. Discovering that we had an overly ambitious and optimistic timeline was not too surprising given that this was our first experience designing MOOCs as well as for most of our students. In fact, for our students, this was the first exposure to what a MOOC was and how one worked.

Design Decisions. We learned that it was easier and more productive for us to design one MOOC first, rather than two different MOOCs simultaneously. We focused most of our efforts on completing the development of the digital storytelling MOOC before we began developing the MOOC on new technologies for teachers. This made the development of the second MOOC easier since many important technical and pedagogical decisions about how to present content in a MOOC had already been made and we could apply lessons we learned from developing the first course.

In the final analysis, there were three significant choices we made in the design process that influenced the project. First, rather than just create one MOOC, we determined that it made more sense to develop a series of MOOCs. That way, we could use the knowledge and skills we learned in creating one MOOC to develop additional ones on a variety of educational technology topics suitable for teacher professional development. Next, we determined that since the scope of the MOOC project would be quite extensive, we should involve our graduate students in the process. We felt that this would be a great educational experience for them, and it would also benefit us since we would be learning how to create the MOOCs together. The design and development process provided the students with first-hand understanding of many key principles that faculty members often face in the design and delivery of instructional content. Finally, we strongly believed that the Webscape model could be adapted to guide the design of MOOCs since we had previously used it to design and develop several large-scale educational Web projects.

Concluding Thoughts

The Webscape model could be characterized as a design-based research project since it is focused on improving educational practices, promoting reflection, and encouraging collaboration between researchers and practitioners in real-world settings (Wang & Hannafin, 2005). The lessons we learned as faculty will set the foundation for a series of design-based research studies we plan to conduct that focus on the design, development, implementation, and evaluation of the entire six-course MOOC series.

Data we will gather during the implementation of the first two MOOCs will help us in multiple ways. First, it will enable us to improve the design and delivery of the curricula for extremely large numbers of students in a global online environment. Second, it will help us evaluate which technologies perform well and which ones need to be modified or replaced since the MOOC framework is radically different from typical online courses. Finally, the data will help us understand how to construct better guidelines for the design of authentic projects that use innovative technologies to enhance learning.

Although the topic for this project was significantly different from previous Webscape projects, the critical elements of the model were effective in structuring activities for the courses. The five components of the model, (1) small team collaboration, (2) variety of multimedia and technologies used, (3) real-world projects, (4) reflective, recursive instructional design, and (5) an extended timeline for development, provided a useful framework for designing the first two MOOCs. This project represents the latest iteration of our Webscape model that continues to evolve along with new technology-based teaching and learning methods such as MOOCs which will allow us to reach even larger and more diverse Web audiences.

Bernard Robin, Associate Professor of Learning, Design and Technology at the University of Houston, teaches traditional and online courses on the integration of technology into the curriculum, emphasizing educational uses of multimedia. He is a recognized leader in the educational uses of digital storytelling and has been teaching courses, conducting workshops, writing articles, and supervising student research on the subject for over a decade. His Educational Uses of Digital Storytelling website (http://digitalstorytelling.coe.uh.edu/) serves as a resource for educators and students interested in how digital storytelling can be integrated into a wide variety of educational activities.

Sara McNeil, Associate Professor of Learning, Design and Technology at the University of Houston, teaches courses in instructional design, the collaborative design and development of multimedia, and the visual representation of information. She also researches, publishes, and presents internationally about emerging technologies in educational environments. Her multimedia projects include the design and development of Digital History (http://www.digitalhistory.uh.edu), a comprehensive resource that provides teachers and students with a wealth of high quality, historical resources at no charge, and New Technologies & 21st Century Skills (http://newtech.coe.uh.edu), a website for K-16 teachers to help them select an appropriate Web 2.0 tool for a specific task.

References

Abramson, G. (2013). The newest disruptive technology—MOOCs. *Journal of Applied Learning Technology, 3*(1), 3–4.

Billington, P., & Fronmuller, M. (2013). MOOCs and the future of higher education. *Journal of Higher Education Theory and Practice, 13*(3/4), 36–43.

Bruff, D., Fisher, D., McEwen, K., & Smith, B. (2013). Wrapping a MOOC: Student perceptions of an experiment in blended learning. *MERLOT Journal of Online Learning and Teaching, 9*(2), 187–99.

Coursera. (2014). *Courses.* Retrieved from https://www.coursera.org/courses.

Daniel, J. (2012). Making sense of MOOCs: Musings in a maze of myth, paradox and possibility. *Journal of Interactive Media in Education.* Retrieved from http://jime.open.ac.uk/2012/18.

Dick, W., Carey, L., & Carey, J. (2011). *The systematic design of instruction.* Upper Saddle River, NJ: Pearson.

Dolan, V. (2014). Massive online obsessive compulsion: What are they saying out there about the latest phenomenon in higher education? *The International Review of Research in Open and Distance Learning, 15*(2), 268–81.

Franka, G., Meinel, C., Totschnig, M., & Willems, C. (2013). Designing MOOCs for the support of multiple learning styles. *Proceedings of the 8th European Conference on Technology Enhanced Learning (EC-TEL)*, Paphos, Cyprus: Springer Verlag.

Guàrdia, L., Maina, M., & Sangrà, A. (2013). MOOC design principles. A pedagogical approach from the learner's perspective. *eLearning Papers, 33*(May), 1–6.

Jordan, K. (2014). Initial trends in enrollment and completion of massive open online courses. *The International Review of Research in Open and Distance Learning, 15*(1), 133–59.

Kolowich, S. (2013). The professors who make the MOOCs. *Chronicle of Higher Education, 59*(28). Retrieved from http://chronicle.com/article/The-Professors-Behind-the-MOOC/137905/#id=overview.

Lane, L.M. (October, 2009). Insidious pedagogy: How course management systems affect teaching. *First Monday, 14*(10). Retrieved from: http://firstmonday.org/htbin/cgi-wrap/bin/ojs/index.php/fm/article/viewArticle/2530/2303.

Lee, H., & Lim, C. (2012). Peer evaluation in blended team project-based learning: What do students find important? *Journal of Educational Technology & Society, 15*(4), 214–24.

Liyanagunawardena, T., Adams, A., & Williams, S. (2013). MOOCs: A systematic study of the published literature 2008–2012. *International Review of Research in Open & Distance Learning, 14*(3), 202–27.

Lombardi, M. (2013). The inside story: Campus decision making in the wake of the latest MOOC tsunami. *MERLOT Journal of Online Learning and Teaching, 9*(2), 239–48.

Marshall, S. (2013). Evaluating the strategic and leadership challenges of MOOCs. *MERLOT Journal of Online Learning and Teaching, 9*(2), 216–27.

Martin, F. (2012). Will massive open online courses change how we teach? *Communications of the ACM, 55*(8), 26–8. Retrieved from http://dl.acm.org/citation.cfm?id=2240246.

McNeil, S., & Robin, B. (2013). Linked graduate courses in instructional technology: An innovative learning community model. In R. McBride & M. Searson (Eds.), *Proceedings of Society for Information Technology & Teacher Education International Conference 2013* (pp. 1373–80). Chesapeake, VA: AACE.

Rivard, R. (2013, July). Beyond MOOC hype. *Inside Higher Ed*. Retrieved from http://www.insidehighered.com/news/2013/07/09/higher-ed-leaders-urge-slow-down-mooc-train.

Robin, R., & McNeil, S. (1998). A theoretical framework for creating Webscapes: Educational information landscapes on the Web. In T. Ottmann & I. Tomek (Eds). *Educational Hypermedia and Multimedia*. Charlottesville, VA: Association for the Advancement of Computing in Education, pp. 1816–17.

Robin, B., & McNeil, S. (2015). Webscapes: An academic vision for digital humanities projects on the Web. *Book 2.0, 4*(1 + 2). pp. 123-143. doi:10.1386/btwo.4.1-2.123_1.

Sandeen, C. (2013). Assessment's place in the new MOOC world. *Research & Practice in Assessment, 8*(1), 5–12.

Schrire, S., & Levy, D. (2012). Troubleshooting MOOCs: The case of a massive open online course at a college of education. In T. Amiel & B. Wilson (Eds.), *Proceedings of World Conference on Educational Multimedia, Hypermedia and Telecommunications 2012* (pp. 761–6). Chesapeake, VA: AACE.

Thomas, J. (2000). *A review of research on project-based learning*. San Rafael, CA: Autodesk Foundation. Retrieved from http://www.bie.org/research/study/review_of_project_based_learning_2000.

Vega, A., & Brown, C. (2013). The implementation of project-based learning. *National Forum of Educational Administration & Supervision Journal, 30*(2), 4–29.

Wang, F., & Hannafin, M. J. (2005). Design-based research and technology-enhanced learning environments. *Educational Technology Research and Development, 53*(4), 5–23.

Willis, J. (1995). A recursive, reflective instructional design model based on constructivist-interpretivist theory. *Educational Technology, 35*(6), 5–23.

Yuan, L., & Powell, S. (2013). *MOOCs and open education: Implications for higher education*. Bolton: CETIS. Retrieved from http://publications.cetis.ac.uk/wp-content/uploads/2013/03/MOOCs-and-Open-Education.pdf.

17

FEMINIST ALTERNATIVES TO MASSIVE OPEN ONLINE COURSES (MOOCs)

The Inception of the Distributed Open Collaborative Course (DOCC)

Erika M. Behrmann, Radhika Gajjala, Elizabeth Losh, T.L. Cowan, Penelope Boyer, Jasmine Rault, Laura Wexler, and CL Cole

Protests, palace coups, and scandals involving vandalism and cheating students marked the academic year 2013. Interestingly, this pushback was not due to worldwide politics at the government level; instead it was in resistance to massive open online courses (MOOCs). Faculty feared losing their jobs, their traditional classroom dynamics, and their agency. Despite mounting faculty dismissal of this new form of educational delivery, school administrations still saw immense value in them and continued to push for their use. FemTechNet and the Distributed Open Collaborative Course (DOCC) were both formed to address the issues highlighted in this moment of faculty hesitation and skepticism.

A DOCC is a collaborative project motivated by feminist pedagogical insights. In utilizing recent advances in learning technology, it weaves those insights into collaborative possibilities enabled *and* limited by digital knowledge production. What is the collective obligation of a DOOC? For starters, there is intense reflexive engagement with process. Additionally, one will find a focus on the co-creation of knowledge, the recognition of distributed expertise, and the cooperative use of distributed resources. As such, a DOCC requires extensive labor over and above what is typically required to teach a course. Designing and implementing a DOCC requires collaboration between diverse platforms and pedagogical models adapted to distinct needs, strengths, and limitations of diverse local environments.

The authors of this chapter were part of the inception and the continuation of this DOCC. The 2013 DOCC network included 18 nodal sites and 27 instructors who represented different institutions, institutional positions, and disciplines. Our faculty were at Bowling Green State University, Brown University, Cal Poly San Luis Obispo, Colby College, Yale University, the New School, University of California San Diego, Pitzer College, the University of Illinois, the Ohio State University, Penn State University, Cal State Fullerton, Rutgers University, and Ontario College of Art + Design. We also had two community-based projects: one in San Antonio, Texas and another in Northampton, Massachusetts. Our faculty were located in departments such as Media Studies, Science and Technology Studies, Library Information Sciences, Fine and Applied Arts, American Studies, Gender & Women's Studies, and Ethnic Studies. In addition to being cross-disciplinary, the nodal classes varied in terms of both class size and level; they ranged from undergraduate general education and introductory courses to specialized undergraduate and graduate seminars. While most of the courses were a hybrid of online and offline courses, two of the DOCC courses were taught completely online and one course—at Ohio State University—was taught in Second Life. Across these 18 sites, there were more than 200 registered students involved, and 25 drop-in learners. Only two students were unable to complete the courses, giving us a 99 percent completion rate.

The Inception of FemTechNet

In Spring 2012, Anne Balsamo from the New School and Alexandra Juhasz from Pitzer College gathered with feminist scholars working on issues in technology to discuss developing pedagogical issues. Networking through listservs, such as those hosted by the Fembot Collective and through face-to-face meetings at conferences such as 4S, HASTAC, ICA, and other such venues, produced the FemTechNet: a network of scholars, artists, and students who work on, with, and at the borders of technology, science and feminism.

During the Fall 2012 semester, several of us worked on developing a beta course for the Distributed Open Collaborative Course (DOCC) structure. Much of this structure focused on cross-institutional collaboration. For instance, Radhika Gajjala of Bowling Green State University and Professor Juhasz connected students using online formats for collaboration on assignments and then posted them on our main server and website (see http://femtechnet.newschool.edu/) for others to share.

In the 2013–14 academic year, faculty members piloted their own large-scale experiments in networked learning framed around the subject of *Dialogues on Feminism and Technology*. The DOCC included several basic components—what we called *Shared Learning Tools* and *Shared Learning Activities*. Incorporating some of these tools or activities into your course—in ways best suited for your local conditions—was one of the few requirements to be a part of the DOCC. One major course tool was our Video Dialogue Series in which scholars around the world film a dialogue about the theme of the week. Students watch the videos, and, in turn, create their own videos, called "Keyword Videos." These videos were shared between nodes in the FemTechNet network and utilized based on the needs of each location. Three other major activities included: (1) "Object

Exchanges," where students became pen pals with other nodes in the network across the country; (2) "Teaching with Wikipedia" or "Wikipedia Storming," where students edit Wikipedia to reflect the learnings of their class; and (3) a "Feminist Mapping Project," in which students created a digital, interactive map that traces a topic's social history or location. Although each node adapted the aforementioned activities as desired, each activity selected centered on the major themes for the course.

The course themes for *Dialogues in Feminism and Technology* emerged through identifying scholarly, artistic, and activist work that has shaped the interdisciplinary fields of Feminist Science and Technology Studies (e.g., Body, Labor, Race, Gender, Machine, etc.). Collective efforts produced a series of video dialogues, featuring the work of innovative feminists such as Heather Cassils, Skawennati, Shu Lea Cheang, Wendy Chun, Maria Fernandez, Donna Haraway, Lynn Hershman, Alexandra Juhasz, Lisa Nakamura, Dorothy Roberts, Lucy Suchman, Judy Wajcman, and Faith Wilding. During the fall of 2013, a new video was released weekly; these videos were immediately made available to anyone who wanted to watch them. At the time of this writing, the video dialogues have been accessed more than 3,000 times.

Faculty also shared syllabi with readings related to each topic. These readings were often foundational texts by the feminist thinkers featured on that week's video. As a key component of these classes involved faculty and student commenting on these videos and using them as research prompts or supplemental resources. In the 2014–15 DOCC, *Collaborations in Feminism and Technology*, FemTechNet participants will continue to develop new themes while adding content to existing course resources.

Central to FemTechNet's DOCC are six core values. These six values comprise the balance of this chapter and are described below.

(1) Effective Pedagogy that Reflects Feminist Principles

Distributed, collaborative teaching requires a multidirectional, multinodal, flexible praxis of knowledge production and circulation. It also makes transparent the feminist pedagogy that recognizes complexity, difference, situated knowledge(s), and asymmetrical relations of power and access to resources, within classrooms. FemTechNet's DOCC forges connections between faculty and students rather than increasing individualism and isolation, and recognizes connection as a condition with politically transformative potential (Balsamo & Juhasz, 2012). It privileges distribution rather than a hoarding of resources, producing a network rather than a "brand." The interdisciplinary "Dialogues in Feminism and Technology" DOCC does not belong to a single institution—it was produced through a collaborative process across many campuses and community locales.

One of the core principles of the DOCC is that it matters *who you learn with*, not simply *what you learn*. One of the ways that DOCC faculty members have manifested this principle is through online office hours. Students can "drop in" to the office hours of someone who teaches across the globe, from their home campus or community. Online interactions during these office hours can occur either one on one or in an online group discussion. As a result of this type of networked teaching, students not only have the opportunity to discuss their ideas with many different faculty, but can also participate in a shared intellectual project with students they would otherwise be unlikely to meet.

Similar to the student participants, the DOCC faculty can benefit from the networked learning environment. Faculty have led sessions on important pedagogical skills like "Effective Blogging," "Feminist Online Pedagogy," "Grading Non-Traditional Assignments," and "Building Activities Across (International) Contexts." Through these sessions, faculty members experience the resource-sharing capacities of networked expertise and distributive pedagogies. In the contemporary institutional context in which faculty are competing for gutted resources and scarce meaningful affective support, these sessions are one of the ways in which the DOCC can be understood not simply as a course, but as a set of feminist world-making tactics.

In many ways, the DOCC reverses the logic of the MOOC. Rather than using digital technologies to increase the teacher-to-student ratio, a DOCC model operates through a network that seeks to subvert streamlined education. Unlike MOOCs that are structured by corporate learning management systems (commonly referred to as "xMOOCs"), such courses are often referred to as "cMOOCs." At their core, cMOOCs attempt to reflect connectivist principles and strive to distinguish themselves from branded "xMOOCs" that too often isolate learners and treat them as competitive autonomous entities (Losh, 2014). The DOCC foundationally parallels with aspects of the cMOOC in that it aims for student connections. Yet it is important to note that, unlike the cMOOCs, the DOCC is molded out of feminist pedagogy and strives to eliminate systems of power both at the micro level (the faculty student binary) and the macro level (systems of oppression).

By working across various forms of difference (i.e., location, institution type, level of education, knowledge base, etc.), we are resisting the individualist approach to professional development and learning success. Instead, we are designing a digital structure informed by both feminist educational innovations of the past and contemporary online pedagogical public spaces that continue to reshape what it means to "teach" and to "learn." The DOCC model offers an educational experience that recognizes the complexity not only of course materials, but also of the praxis of learning itself (Cowan, 2014; Cowan & Rault, 2014).

(2) Disrupting the Structural Status Quo of Educational Institutions

Much of the discussion in the DOCC initiative has focused on distributing tasks among participants, so that junior faculty, adjunct faculty, graduate students, instructional technologists, and librarians would see equitable rewards from their collaboration. While the MOOC model invokes a top-down way of pedagogy, the DOCC model strives for collegial respect between peers across job titles and honest acknowledgement of how vexed issues about power relationships could be. In this way, the infrastructure and process of community building became integral parts of the subject matter of the course, neither fetishized nor shunted offstage but substantially and critically engaged.

Feminists have been doing free and open learning for a long time now, starting even before the settlement movement at the turn of the previous century. From the Cambridge Women's School to the education projects of transnational cyberfeminism, pioneering feminist pedagogies have since become commonly accepted best practices—many of which are recognized by the Association of American Colleges and Universities in its current "high impact" inventory (Kuh & O'Donnell, 2013). These pedagogies often differ significantly from the standard operating procedures of college and university courses that MOOCs are merely tweaking. For instance, community-based groups in the DOCC initiative were able to push for even greater accessibility, while MOOCs—driven by the demands of venture capital—are hard-pressed to give community-based participants a voice. For instance, in the 2013 DOCC in which we participated, "at-large" self-organized groups that were unaffiliated with any educational institution met in three different locations.

(3) Challenging the Assumption that Access to Technology Guarantees Access to Knowledge, and Respecting the Investment of Labor in Education

Feminist scholarship has also taught us that technological innovations alone do not make structural changes—just as new cleaning technologies have not reduced the average amount of (vastly unequal) time that women spend on unpaid domestic labor (Bittman, Mahmud Rice, & Wajcman, 2004). Additionally, we know that the "freedom" of cyberspace is not free of racism or sexism (Nakamura, 2007). Moreover portable computers and phones that liberate us from the office do not free us (particularly women) from unremunerated overtime work (Gregg, 2011). Perhaps most recently, we have learned that the celebration of MOOCs (Pappano, 2012) obscures their high costs as well as the limited access to MOOCs by females, the less educated, and the underprivileged (Newman & Oh, 2014).

While these MOOCs may be free to non-tuition-paying students, they are not free to the universities or the people developing and teaching these courses. For example, Harvard and MIT each gave $30 million to create edX in 2012. In addition, universities across the US are paying anywhere from $2 million to $5 million to join, as well as $250,000 per (new) course and another $50,000 each time the course is run. University of Pennsylvania and California Institute of Technology invested $3.7 million in Coursera in 2013, with the University of Pennsylvania estimating an additional cost of $50,000 per course (Peterson, 2013). The most recent comprehensive study of costs associated with running MOOCs across any platform estimates $39,000 to $325,000 is spent per course. This report concludes that "MOOCs have, so far, proven to be a significant drain on time and money for institutions" (Hollands & Tirthali, 2014, p. 9).

Beyond these estimated expenditures for MOOCs, we are concerned by the more hidden or subtle costs related to the use of professors and instructional teams (often consisting of graduate students) for the creation and delivery of these MOOCs, as well as the various costs to tuition-paying students who could benefit from such resource allocation and attention. Given that all of the high-impact educational practices identified by the Association of American Colleges and Universities (AAC&U) rely on small class sizes and regular face-to-face contact hours with faculty and instructional teams (Kuh & O'Donnell, 2013), it seems that the resources going to the development, maintenance, and teaching of massive online courses could be better used to increase the number of faculty and graduate students (i.e., teaching assistants) working with smaller groups of students. As highlighted in this chapter, for example, such resources might support the development of existing feminist instructional infrastructures, like the network of DOCC professors, students, and instructional technology designers.

Moreover, with the presumed ubiquity of smartphones, all faculty are subject to the pressure of "professional presence bleed." The prevailing expectation is that faculty members will be digitally available for work at every hour every day, responding to emails, updating shared (Google) documents, posting on academic blogs, joining video meetings, and so on. However, when "the domestic division of labour by gender remains remarkably resistant to technological innovation" (Bittman et al., 2004), this pressure can be particularly hazardous for female faculty (Gregg, 2011). As a network of feminist scholars working with various non-academic organizations and academic institutions, and in a mix of conditions including unpaid, contingent, non-tenure-track, tenure-track, and tenured employment, the DOCC participants build on existing feminist pedagogical methods, technology studies, and labor studies to develop a feminist 'disruptive innovation' within current academic labor conditions.

(4) An Understanding That Technoscientific Choices Are Not Value-Neutral, and Building Infrastructure Is Not Simply About Choosing Components Among Consumer Products

The most compelling claim made about MOOCs, and the companies and organizations that facilitate them (Coursera, Udacity, Edx, FutureLearn, NovoEd, etc.), is the promise of "free"—and presumably, accessible—education. This promise is particularly striking for feminist scholars who have been advocating for and developing innovative and more accessible education methods for decades. We can think back to Jane Addams' work in the early part of the twentieth century to provide free university-level education for working poor and immigrant populations in Chicago (Addams & Lagemann, 1994), or to the Cambridge Women's School which taught hundreds of free feminist courses to thousands of students in Boston from 1971 to 1992 (Burgin, 2011).

Recently, feminist "bridging programs" throughout the United States have offered courses and university resources to encourage low-income (primarily women) students to start or continue their higher education (Biemiller, 2011; Conway, 2001). Ongoing practices of transformative feminist pedagogies have been developed as critical correctives to the economic, social, political, and physical inaccessibilities which continue to haunt higher education in the US (hooks, 2003; Rich, 1979). Indeed, the promise of free and accessible education appeals to no one more than feminist educators and scholars, who have been working towards these very goals for over a century.

(5) Recognition of Regional and Cultural Complexity

FemTechNet wants to effect a fundamental shift away from the basic concept and design of the MOOCs (often perpetuated throughout xMOOCs and sometimes cMOOCS) which claim to export first-world knowledge from elite North American universities to the so-called underprivileged citizens of the developing world. But in fact, most MOOC students already hold college degrees or are currently enrolled in college (Newman & Oh, 2014). Furthermore, the MOOC design is questionably conducive to the complexities of the global south.

If one visits campuses, think-tanks, and learning spaces in India, for instance, people express confusion about why the country's multilingual professors should be replaced by canned videos. Furthermore, even the most hardcore MOOC enthusiasts at places like the work-sharing space, "Jaaga," in Bangalore—in the heart of India's Silicon Valley—admit to being unable to finish online courses without human encouragement or community.

At a 2013 digital humanities symposium, Sritama, a Kolkata student enrolled at Presidency University, vented her frustration at being graded by culturally insensitive US peers unfamiliar not only with her linguistic Britishisms but also with the entire framework of her subcontinental knowledge (Chatterjee, 2013). Michael Roth, the president of Wesleyan University as well as the professor teaching her MOOC course on "The Modern and the Postmodern" (Roth, 2013), would have perhaps treated her with much more empathy if he had known her face to face as an individual among his thousands of students. Unfortunately, the efficiency of the course management system prohibited the personalized interactions that thousands of students long for. This is unfortunate because MOOC instructors are often nominated for their superior teaching abilities and instructional presence. Some of the most committed teachers one can meet are deeply engaged with the MOOC experiment. As an example of this commitment, whenever Berkeley instructor Armando Fox travels to a conference in a foreign city, he tries to meet as many of his MOOC students as possible during his trip. But this is no substitute for sustained two-way communication.

Feminists know that people's lived experiences matter. An Egyptian software engineer may enthuse about increased access to programming education resources, but he also knows from working with his own colleagues that it is the supposed "soft skills" of interpersonal interaction and the acquisition of tacit knowledge through activities such as in-person internships that really ensure more diverse workplaces and universities. Faculty within the FemTechNet DOCC wish to increase such contact. To such ends, academic institutions and self-directed learners in other countries have expressed interest in joining the DOCC to contribute their own video dialogues and learning projects.

(6) Innovative Experimentation That Enables Learning for Multiple Stakeholders

The 2013 FemTechNet DOCC emphasized community over content such that community took the course outside the computer and—in two locations— outside the academy, at *FemTechNet ¡Taller!* in San Antonio, TX and at *Mass FemTechNet* in Northampton, MA.

Notably, participants at these events were not matriculated students and instructors were not salaried faculty. They met in community spaces with free Wi-Fi and shared all the DOCC tools that the university-enrolled students used. Finally, there were no formal obligations to the project as there were no grades or responsibilities to the project. Self-directed learners tuned in globally and focused their attention to the FemTechNet Commons website for syllabi, readings, and videos.

For *FemTechNet ¡Taller!*, some thirty individuals met over the course of 12 weeks. Participants ranged from stay-at-home and working moms, to PhDs working at cultural non-profits or in academia, to practicing artists and undergrads from community colleges or local universities. They were a mix of Latinas and Anglos.

A Feminist Mapping Project about female public art parity in San Antonio was collaboratively conceived and conducted by *Taller* [workshop] participants. Another successful tactic was the invitation of local co-facilitators including theme-related artists, community leaders, and professors for about half of the sessions. Particularly memorable sessions included Dr. Merla Watson's presentation on "Place" and Dr. Cortez Walden presenting Gloria Anzaldua's theory of transformation during the final DOCC session.

Mass FemTechNet, held in Northampton, MA, met weekly with a core group of six participants ranging in age from 22 to 45. Of these six, two were recent college graduates, three were current PhD students, and one held a PhD. In addition, four worked as teachers, researchers, or librarians, five identified as women, one as trans, at least two identified as women of color, and at least five identified as queer. Everyone had significant experience with feminist theory, and interests in technologies including Tumblr, online surveillance and security, access and accessibility, library practice, film and media art, and sociological methods.

According to a report by Stephanie Rosen, the *Mass FemTechNet* facilitator:

"We had very productive conversations about Wikipedia-editing and feminist mapping . . . and one member of our group became interested in mapping the access barriers to FTN readings. For the final object-making project, we ended up creating a zine together." Rosen noted that *Mass FemTechNet* formed a solid intellectual community and applied their own experiences to their work within various FemTechNet committees. For example, they have pushed for greater accessibility of the FemTechNet videos and readings for all participants.

Community engagement continues to be central to FemTechNet. The DOCC's online and open to the public Town Hall meetings, Speaker's Bureau, Open Online Office Hours (OOOH), and FemTechNet Digest on Flipboard are all community engagement components now underway with pathways for self-directed learners provided on the FemTechNet website.

Future Frameworks

Future plans for the DOCC envision a broader, global community. Through drawing new liminal spaces between the academy and the broader community—an innovative paradigm for a community-based DOCC was formed. As the DOCC continues to expand, new ideas and theories are formed. In addition to the DOCC's six characteristics, namely, (1) a feminist pedagogical framework, (2) its push back on the status quo, (3) the assumptions about access to knowledge, (4) its focus on a value-neutral infrastructure that does not involve corporate consumerism, (5) its ability to understand cultural complexities, and (6) its ability to have many teaching moments for its students and non-students alike—the DOCC's mutable and ever-expanding nature is one of its major characteristics that separates it from other styles of MOOCs. From only a few individuals, the FemTechNet and the DOCC has now enlisted hundreds of participants worldwide. This initiative hopes to challenge the MOOC system and offer new, more equitable, ideas for everyone invested.

 **Erika M. Behrmann** is a doctoral student at Bowling Green State University. She has a MA in Women's and Gender Studies and is working towards a PhD in the School of Media and Communications. Her research focuses on feminist theory, postfeminism, pedagogy, postcolonialism, and their various intersections and materializations within digital media and gaming. Her work has been presented at several national conferences such as the National Women's Studies Association and National Communication Association.

 **Radhika Gajjala** is Professor of Media and Communication at Bowling Green State University. She is author of *Cyberculture and the Subaltern* (Lexington Press, 2012) and *Cyberselves: Feminist Ethnographies of South Asian Women* (Altamira, 2004). She has also co-edited books, including *Cyberfeminism 2.0* (2012), *Webbing Cyberfeminist Practice* (2008), and *South Asian Technospaces* (2008). She is a member of the Fembot Collective and FemTechnet (participating in the DOCC nodal teaching projects) and is co-editor (with Carol Stabile) of "ADA: Journal of Gender, New Media and Technology."

 **Elizabeth Losh** is Director of Academic Programs, Sixth College at the University of California, San Diego. She writes about gender and technology, the digital humanities, distance learning, connected learning, media literacy, and the rhetoric surrounding regulatory attempts to limit everyday digital practices. Liz is the author of *Virtualpolitik: An Electronic History of Government Media-Making in a Time of War, Scandal, Disaster, Miscommunication, and Mistakes* (MIT Press, 2009) and *The War on Learning: Gaining Ground in the Digital University* (MIT Press, 2014). She is the co-author of the comic book textbook *Understanding Rhetoric: A Graphic Guide to Writing* (Bedford/ St. Martin's, 2013) with Jonathan Alexander. She is currently working on a new monograph, tentatively entitled *Obama Online: Technology, Masculinity, and Democracy,* and a new edited collection from University of Chicago Press about MOOCs and other experiments in scale and access in higher education.

 **T.L. Cowan** is a writer, performer and professor currently living in Brooklyn, NY. She teaches at Eugene Lang College in Culture & Media, Gender Studies, and Integrated Arts and is the FemTechNet Chair of Experimental Pedagogies in the School of Media Studies at The New School. Across her various practices, T.L. is deeply committed to the knowledges and aesthetics of transformational media, performance, and subjects and scenes. Her homepage can be accessed at: http://tlcowan.net/.

 **Penelope Boyer** is involved in community-based work in San Antonio, TX. She conceived and directs the LHI Art-Sci Projects at Land Heritage Institute (LHI), 1200 acres of open space under development as a land museum. She holds a PhD from the European Graduate School (EGS) in Saas Fee, Switzerland. Her book, *My Great High-Roofed House: Homer's Penelope~Paradigm, Periphrasis, Periphron, Phenomenology, Poesis, Poludeukes and Praxis* (Atropos Press, 2012), treats the gynaeceum as a homosocial setting for early technology, among other things.

Jasmine Rault is an Assistant Professor in Culture and Media at Eugene Lang College at The New School in New York City. Rault works on themes of feminist and queer affective and cultural economies and has new work in *ephemera*, "The Labour of Being Studied in a Free Love Economy" (with T.L. Cowan, 2014); *Women's Studies Quarterly* on racialized queer debt and the politics of history-making (with Cowan, 2014); and *Ada: A Journal of Gender, New Media and Technology* on designing trans-feminist and queer online archives (with Cowan and Dayna McLeod, 2014). Rault's first book is *Eileen Gray and the Design of Sapphic Modernity: Staying In* (2011).

Laura Wexler is Professor of American Studies, Professor of Women's, Gender & Sexuality Studies, Director of The Photographic Memory Workshop, Principal Investigator of the Photogrammar Project, and Co-coordinator of the Public Humanities Program at Yale University. A scholar and theorist of visual culture, she authored the prize-winning book, *Tender Violence: Domestic Visions in an Age of US Imperialism*, and the book, *Pregnant Pictures*, with photographer Sandra Matthews, as well as many other publications. Currently she is working on the intergenerational transfer of historical memory in family photograph albums. She holds an MA, MPhil, and PhD in English and Comparative Literature from Columbia University.

CL Cole is Professor and Head of Media & Cinema Studies and Professor of Gender & Women's Studies, Criticism & Interpretive Theory, and the Information Trust Institute at the University of Illinois at Urbana-Champaign. Cole studies and teaches about sport, bodies and technology, media literacy, and digital technology and pedagogy.

References

Addams, J., & Lagemann, E. (1994). *On education*. New Brunswick, NJ: Transaction.

American Association of University Professors. (2012–13). *Annual Report on the Economic Status of the Profession*. Washington, DC.

Balsamo, A., & Juhasz, J. (2012). An idea whose time is here: FemTechNet—a distributed online collaborative course. *Ada: A Journal of Gender, New Media & Technology, 1*. http://adanewmedia.org/2012/11/issue1-juhasz/.

Biemiller, L. (2011, September 11). Women's colleges try new strategies for success. *Chronicle of Higher Education.* Retrieved from http://chronicle.com/article/Womens-Colleges-Try-New/128935/.

Bittman, M., Mahmud Rice, J., & Wajcman, J. (2004). Appliances and their impact: The ownership of domestic technology and time spent on household work. *The British Journal of Sociology*, *55*(3), 401–23.

Burgin, S. (2011). Coarse offerings: Lessons from the Cambridge Women's School for today's radical education alternatives. *Graduate Journal of Social Science, 8*(2), 21–40.

Chatterjee, S. (2013). *Digital humanities workshop 2013: Remediating texts and contexts.* Presidency University, Kolkata, India.

Conway, J.K. (2001). *A woman's education.* New York: A.A. Knopf.

Cowan, T.L. (2014, August 14). *FemTechNet—distributed digital pedagogies: Collaborating across difference.* Paper presented to the Digital Pedagogies Institute, University of Toronto at Scarborough, Ontario, Canada.

Cowan, T.L., & Rault, J. (2014, April 25). 'Haven't you ever heard of Tumblr?' Killjoy affects and online pedagogical publics. Paper presented to the HASTAC conference on the panel FemTechNet: Dialogues on feminism and technology rethinks the MOOC paradigm. Lima, Peru.

Downes, S. (2008). *MOOC—The resurgence of community in online learning.* Retrieved from http://halfanhour.blogspot.com/2013_05_01_archive.html.

Gregg, M. (2011). *Work's intimacy.* Cambridge, UK: Polity Press.

Hollands, F.M., & Tirthali, D. (2014). Why do institutions offer MOOCs? *Online Learning, 18*(3). Retrieved from http://olj.onlinelearningconsortium.org/index.php/jaln/article/download/464/116.

hooks, b. (2003). *Teaching community: A pedagogy of hope.* New York: Routledge.

Kuh, G.D., & O'Donnell, K. (2013). *Ensuring quality & taking high-impact practices to scale.* Association of American Colleges and Universities, Washington, DC.

Losh, E. (2014). *The war on learning: Gaining ground in the digital university.* Cambridge, MA: MIT Press.

Nakamura, L. (2007). *Digitizing race: Visual cultures of the Internet.* Minneapolis: University of Minnesota Press.

Newman, J., & Oh, S. (2014, June 13). 8 things you should know about MOOCs. *The Chronicle of Higher Education.* Retrieved from http://chronicle.com/article/MOOCs-EdX/146901/.

Pappano, L. (2012, November 2). The year of the MOOC. *New York Times.* Retrieved from http://www.nytimes.com/2012/11/04/education/edlife/massive-open-online-courses-are-multiplying-at-a-rapid-pace.html?pagewanted=all.

Peterson, R. (2013, September 17). What do MOOCs cost? *Minding The Campus.* Retrieved from http://www.mindingthecampus.com/2013/09/what_do_moocs_cost/.

Rich, A. (1979). Claiming an education. In A. Rich (1979). *On lies, secrets and silence: Selected prose, 1966–1978* (pp. 231–6). New York: W.W. Norton & Company.

Roth, M. (2013, April 29). My modern experience teaching and MOOC. *Chronicle of Higher Education.* Retrieved from http://chronicle.com/article/My-Modern-MOOC-Experience/138781/.

PART 6

MOOCs and Open Education in the Developing World

Part 6 is filled with news of many exciting courses, programs, and models for MOOCs and open education that enhance, extend, and, at times, even transform the learning experiences of millions of individuals in some of the most remote and least funded parts of the planet. Stated another way, this section specifically highlights the use of MOOCs and open education in developing parts of the world. As educational opportunities find their way into lands that were, in effect, previously shut off from the learning spigots of the world, it lends hope to the future of humanity. At the same time, from a developmental standpoint, much is still needed in terms of technology affordability and accessibility, policy development, quality control and course design standards, and professional development and training.

Chapter 18, by Balaji Venkataraman and Asha Kanwar of the Commonwealth of Learning (COL) in Vancouver, Canada, begins this part by describing unique ideas that they have developed and tested involving the use of MOOCs for human development. These authors accurately note that MOOCs originated in higher education, flourishing mostly in the milieu of top tier universities in North America, and are incorrectly perceived by many to be solely applicable to such settings. As a result, MOOCs are commonly associated with global brands and celebrated research institutions such as Stanford University, MIT, and Duke University. In response to this situation, these two COL leaders force us to reflect on whether MOOCs can make a contribution toward the advancement of human learning and development. In effect, can individuals and institutions in developing countries derive new advantages from the MOOC phenomenon? In responding to their own questions and concerns, in late 2013, the COL organized a MOOC on Mobiles for Development with approximately 2,200 participants from 116 countries. Both the course evaluation instruments and the related participant feedback received affirm the resounding success of this MOOC. Using their research results from the M4D MOOC, the authors present the outline of a model called MOOC for Development (MOOC4D). The authors also discuss one of their latest projects, "MOOC on MOOCs," which was offered in the summer of 2014 and targeted academics and government officials working in the area of human development as well as professionals and potential leaders of NGOs. This particular MOOC concerned how MOOCs might foster vital training and education in the developing world.

In Chapter 19, Sheila Jagannathan from the World Bank Institute details how open forms of learning offer exciting potentials for building capacity on a large scale in developing countries. Her chapter briefly describes the challenges of designing a knowledge-sharing and learning culture for eradicating poverty and sharing global prosperity. Importantly, Jagannathan provides rich examples of where online and blended learning can make a difference, including those of a farmer in Tanzania, a Skype entrepreneur in Bangladesh, an auto mechanic in Vietnam, and a civil servant in Bolivia. Jagannathan also describes how MOOCs, and digital learning in general, are reshaping the World Bank's capacity-building programs. Two quite useful examples of MOOCs from the World Bank are described in this chapter, including one on climate change and another on managing risk for development. Several key problems and issues are pointed out, including those related to feedback mechanisms that need to be put in place for course redesign, the technical training and peer support of MOOC participants, and the capability of tracking the reasons that development professionals fail to complete MOOCs. Jagannathan concludes with a discussion of the newly established Open Learning Campus and its emerging suite of tools and resources for addressing the needs of the World Bank staff, World Bank clients, and the general public. She also discusses the many challenges it faces in customizing program design to cater to the many languages and countries of the world.

In Chapter 20, Zoraini Wati Abas offers insights into the unique opportunities as well as recent implementation efforts related to MOOCs in two countries where she has recently worked—Malaysia and Indonesia. She contends that with the rapidly increasing access to the Internet, the rising demand for higher education, and the high-profile MOOC examples from Stanford University and other well-known Western universities, educators in Southeast Asia have become increasingly attracted to the idea of offering MOOCs. Although they have been comparatively slow to join the bandwagon, numerous institutions in Southeast Asia, both public and private, have begun to launch massive open online courses that attempt to meet local needs. Many of these massively open courses are being designed for the local students and, as such, are delivered in local languages. This chapter provides an overview of the development of MOOCs in Southeast Asia in general, and in Malaysia and Indonesia in particular. Importantly, Dr. Wati Abas discusses the "glocalization" of MOOCs within this region of the world and in these two countries. In effect, educators in Malaysia and Indonesia are taking the general concept of MOOCs and designing an educational experience for the local audience rather than having the local audience enroll in MOOCs from institutions overseas.

Chapter 21 is jointly written by Melinda dela Pena Bandalaria of the University of the Philippines Open University (UPOU) and UPOU Chancellor Grace Javier Alfonso. It is important to point out that Professor Bandalaria was a featured panel member at the pre-conference symposium at E-Learn 2013 in Las Vegas that led directly to the production of this book. This timely and engaging chapter discusses issues related to offering MOOCs in the context of a developing country like the Philippines. It also describes how a quality assurance framework that the UPOU was already using for open and distance e-learning was adapted to address the myriad issues and concerns challenging MOOCs and related forms of open education. According to Bandalaria and Alfonso, MOOC developments at the UPOU drew on various insights from its experiences in offering credit and non-credit courses that relied on e-learning for more than a decade. Bandalaria and Alfonso also highlight recommendations from experienced academics in the design of the learning management system that they ultimately employed for MOOCs. In addition, the resulting MOOC framework, MODeL (Massive Open Distance eLearning), is described.

In the final chapter of Part 6, Griff Richards and Bakary Diallo of the African Virtual University (AVU) document how open educational resources have provided accessible content for learning that is severely needed in Africa. At the same time, MOOCs have garnered unprecedented attention as a means of delivering courses to tens of thousands of African learners. Accordingly, their chapter outlines several partnerships and collaborative efforts related to OERs and MOOCs at the AVU. Among the discussions are strategies for the delivery of high-volume professional development in areas of critical need in Africa. Several examples of projects at the AVU are detailed, along with recent decisions related to MOOCs and open education and associated technology advances. Finally, the chapter ends with speculations about the overall potential for growth of these new forms of educational delivery within Africa; within that discussion, several key challenges are mentioned.

18

CHANGING THE TUNE: MOOCs FOR HUMAN DEVELOPMENT?

A Case Study

Balaji Venkataraman and Asha Kanwar

The Massive Open Online Course (MOOC) is covered in critical analysis as well as in popular media as a development exclusively bearing on the higher education sector (The Economist, 2014). This term has also acquired an informal brand connotation—it refers to a package of course offerings, platforms, and processes identified with three pioneering organizations, namely edX, Coursera, and Udacity, who tend to offer lecture and content-based MOOCs or "xMOOCs." A thoroughly informed analysis of MOOCs has tended to focus on their role and impact in higher education in North America (Hollands & Tirthali, 2014). In contrast, proponents of connectivist MOOCs or "cMOOCs" have focused on pedagogy and style (for example, see Siemens, 2014).

Relatively less attention, however, has been devoted to the relevance of different types of MOOCs for those in developing countries. Data from MOOC providers show that the number of learners or "joiners" from developing countries is significant. For example, about 13 percent of joiners in edX are from India (Ho et al., 2014). In the available literature, there is no explicit statement of the usefulness of branded MOOCs in global development beyond the number of participants from developing countries. At best, there is an implicit assumption that the delivery process in branded MOOCs, if not the content, constitutes a Global Public Good (GPG) (World Bank, 2011). Institutions and individuals in developing countries, in their own interest, could make use of such a public good.

A branded MOOC does not provide course credit as a matter of standard practice. For learners from developing countries, course participation, in real time or online, is expected to lead to credit. Given these expectations, is it sufficient to make a branded MOOC available without due credit and claim a contribution to global human development? MOOCs have the major advantage of scale. How can institutions in developing countries utilize MOOCs to increase access to learning materials and courses for very large numbers of people?

These and related questions were considered from a perspective of re-engineering the technological and process components of the MOOC to enhance learner experience. The Commonwealth of Learning (COL) built and offered a MOOC in partnership with a research university based in a developing country (i.e., Indian Institute of Technology—Kanpur, IITK) without involving the brand names usually associated with the MOOC. This online course on Mobiles for Development (M4D) (2013), offered in the last quarter of 2013, attracted 2,282 unique joiners from 116 countries. Of the more than 2,000 MOOC participants, 333 went on to receive certificates of competence or participation jointly issued by COL and IITK. Nearly 90 percent of the joiners were from developing countries. In addition, the proportion of developing country participants who received certificates was slightly higher than 90 percent, which is a sign of success in terms of original course goals and objectives. This MOOC was focused on the use of mobile devices in areas of development such as agriculture and food security. The content has been released as open education resources (OER) for anyone to use. What follows is a brief description of the course, and an analysis of the results that leads to an outline of a MOOC4D model.

Unbundling and Re-Engineering a Branded Practice: An Example

As detailed in various chapters of this book, OER have been published globally for free and unrestricted re-use for about 15 years, especially since 2002 when an internationally accepted definition of OER was formulated (UNESCO, 2002). In the earlier phase, almost all OER were published by universities located primarily in the Organisation for Economic Co-operation and Development (OECD) countries. There was an assumption that this high-quality content was a GPG produced in the developed world and that the developing world would re-use and create new local benefits.

A decade later, there are relatively fewer instances of such adaptation (Dhanarajan & Porter, 2012; McGreal, Kinuthia, Marshall, & McNamara, 2013). What has emerged is that developing countries are now significant publishers of OER. For example, in the Commonwealth, the total volume of OER published by the developing countries is larger than that from the developed countries (COL, 2014). Although the concept and practices of OER originated in the OECD countries, developing countries have been able to adapt and re-create them in their own contexts. The technology and processes in the OER paradigm have been de-linked from the content of developed countries; these were then re-combined with what was assessed to be good-quality content from developing countries. The initial assumption was that OER was a package; however, OER is now a basket of processes, procedures, and content, some or all of which can be substituted or changed, as required.

In a similar vein, we believe this re-engineering and unbundling would be a more practical approach to assess the relevance of MOOCs in development. For example, unbundle the MOOC, set aside the brand value, separate content from processes, procedures, and technology, and re-combine these components to suit the context and purpose at hand. Doing so would enable institutions in developing countries to harness MOOCs in order to contribute to local and national development needs.

COL-IITK MOOC on Mobiles for Development

During the year 2012, the COL commissioned a set of analyses on MOOCs with IITK (COL, 2013b). These analyses clearly showed that: (1) the unbundling of content, processes, and procedures of a typical MOOC was feasible, and that (2) offering a MOOC is best viewed as managing an event (especially a media event) such as a virtual conference, rather than as a virtual classroom. Reliability of access even at lower bandwidths to the materials and interaction space of the MOOC was a critical factor. The opportunity for learners to interact with instructors and mentors was also critical to the success of a MOOC experience. Grading and assessment processes needed to be simple to implement in technological terms. These insights were derived from our experience and expertise in open and distance learning (ODL) and formed the basis for the design of the MOOC on M4D.

The topic of the course was identified from a number of consultations organized by the COL (2013a). We were keenly aware that the spread and pace of mobile phones in developing countries had been phenomenal. Moreover, we also realized that this growth had created new opportunities for addressing the digital divide and beginning to reach the unreached. COL's consultations with learning for development partners revealed that a neutral forum to discuss key concepts and developments in mobile technology would be highly welcome to stakeholders in developing countries. COL then decided to test the MOOC approach against this background. Given IITK's expertise in mobiles in agriculture (Balaji & Prabhakar, 2014) and experience with MOOCs, combined with the COL's strength in ODL and Lifelong Learning for Farmers, there were genuine synergies and a sense of complementarity in this partnership. Certification was an important consideration. It was agreed that the COL and the Center for Continuing Education at IITK would co-sign the certificates.

The course was managed by Professor T.V. Prabhakar of IIT Kanpur (i.e., IITK) in India with marketing advice and support provided by COL. IITK took responsibility for the core content on technology and involved a number of faculty members and associates from various departments. Using an online knowledge repository for information related to agriculture, the agropedia/vKVK team at IITK provided content for the topics related to agriculture. The goal of the vKVK or "Virtual Krishi Vigyan Kendra" is to connect KVK experts and local farmers using the Internet as well as mobile technology to help speed the transfer of technology to the farmer's fields (Bagga, 2010). Professor Mohamed Ally from

Athabasca University in Canada led the m-learning portion of the MOOC, while faculty from the National Institute of Banking Management (NIBM) in India, handled the section on financial inclusion. COL coordinated the participation of all non-IITK faculty.

COL, with the approval of IITK, invited an external expert to conduct an ex post evaluation of the course, with a focus on its pedagogical aspects. A report of the course evaluation by David Porter, Executive Director of the BCcampus in British Columbia, was published as an open access document (Porter, 2014). In the following three sections, we quote extensively from the Porter Report.

Course Platform and Delivery

COL initially considered using Canvas as a course delivery platform for the MOOC on M4D but the costs of hosting turned out to be high. IITK, with much experience in the use of various learning management systems (LMS), proposed using Sakai, an open source LMS, as the online class site. In addition, video content would be deployed on YouTube and the course homepage would be employed to host assorted other documents (e.g., PowerPoint files, video transcripts, announcements, etc.) and valuable course information. Online registration was also linked to this page.

The screen layout for the course was designed for straightforward navigation to all components of the course. The features of the M4D course environment included the following: 1. Course header and student workspace; 2. Navigation menu for the course; 3. Topic list; 4. Weekly module dividers; 5. Colour-coded topics; 6. Login and course role graphic; 7. Colour-coded legend for topic; 8. Instructor for topic; 9. Video link for topic; 10. Slides and/or script link/s.

The primary instructional strategy for the M4D course was the use of instructional videos that varied in length from 2 to 25 minutes. In total, there were 92 videos produced by the development team for the course topics. The videos were organized over a six-week time period. Students were required to view 15 videos per week on average.

Most video lectures also included a supplementary PowerPoint slide deck. In some cases, a transcript was added to the video. In terms of resulting transcript benefits, student feedback indicated that scripts were helpful in dealing with unfamiliar accents or speech intonation.

There were two activity strategies employed during the course:

- Chat room
    - o   1,641 messages were exchanged in the chat room during the course.
- Discussion forums
    - o   General discussion forum with 398 messages across 76 topics.
    - o   Technical forum with 370 messages across 55 topics.
    - o   Technical support forum with 89 messages across 35 topics.

Online quizzes were employed as an evaluation strategy. There were three quizzes during the course:

- Test Quiz   324 students submitted quizzes for evaluation.
- Quiz 1   296 students submitted quizzes for evaluation.
- Final Quiz   261 students submitted quizzes for evaluation.

The quiz format used multiple choice questions.

Course Results

As indicated earlier, the course began with 2,282 course registrants, from which 1,441 registrants were considered active participants in the course during its six-week timeframe. Site statistics from the M4D course provide a snapshot of activity and participation.

- A total of 333 participants received either Certificates of Competence (244 participants) or Certificates of Participation (89).
- The top five countries in terms of registrants were India, Nepal, Mauritius, Grenada, and South Africa.
- About 500 registrants were from countries in the Africa-Caribbean-Pacific regions. About 200 registrants were from the OECD countries and from East Europe.

Course Costs

From documents provided to COL by IIT Kanpur the following conclusions were drawn:

- COL provided a total of 15,000 in Canadian dollars (roughly the same in US$ in 2013).
- The bulk of the course costs (just over 75 percent) were incurred in content development, including costs of recording and editing of instructional videos.
- The IITK team provided support for server management costs, which was actually a substantial contribution although they, as a public institution, had not placed a monetary value on IT support.

COL hosted the homepage of the course, http://m4d.colfinder.org on its server (hosting cost of CAD140). In addition, COL committed support expenses totaling CAD6,000.

The IITK team added to the course homepage a secure and reliable registration system from which they transferred data in a secure way to the online class site, www.m4d-mooc.org. The transfer process was developed exclusively for this course by IITK, since it involved transfer from Drupal to Sakai for which there were no known solutions. This task required software development and has not been assigned a cost by IITK.

The literature on MOOC development provides estimates of course development and delivery costs between US$50,000 and US$250,000 for a single instance of a large-scale MOOC (Porter, 2014). A recent report in the *Economist* (2014) contains a figure of US$70,000 as the average cost of a MOOC. These cost estimates suggest that the M4D MOOC was at the very low end of the cost scale for development and delivery.

Feedback from Students

An online student survey was conducted with students after the course was completed. A total of 208 responses to survey questions were received. For each question, students were provided with a five-point scale on which to record a numeric answer, with 1 being the lowest rating and 5 being highest. The key results are summarized in the paragraph below.

Overall, student satisfaction based on responses was 87 percent, indicating strong satisfaction with the instructors, course content, resources, and delivery format. Clearly, the survey respondents rated the course website easy to use (4.38 average rating; 208 respondents); the discussion on forums/chat sessions highly useful (4.06; 207 respondents); the quizzes relevant and well chosen (4.12; 205 respondents); the material clearly presented (4.30; 205 respondents); the course that was delivered was in line with stated objectives (4.40; 207 respondents); the students were highly satisfied with the overall quality of the course (4.45; 208 respondents); and the presenter had a good grasp of the course content (4.66; 206 respondents).

The student survey asked two questions requiring YES, NO, CAN'T SAY responses. First of all, around 71 percent of students indicated they would have taken the M4D course even without certification. Even more impressively, 201 of the 208 survey respondents (i.e., 97 percent) stated they would recommend the M4D course to others. In addition to questions requesting numeric ratings and Yes/No responses, students were provided four open-ended questions that requested a text-based response. The text-based responses from 208 students were coded and clustered as themes in the Porter (2014) report (see Table 18.1).

Discussion

The course description, cost analysis, and the results from participant surveys show that the M4D MOOC was an unqualified success. The online delivery arrangement of Sakai, YouTube, and Drupal specially put together for this course worked well. In contrast, a branded MOOC platform would have been a turn-key solution, but the costs would have been very high.

TABLE 18.1 Responses to questions requiring a text-based response (Porter, 2014)

Question	Emergent themes from responses
What did you like about this short course?	• Course content
	• Relevance of the topics and case studies
	• Flexibility of the design
What suggestions do you have on how we can improve?	• Video: Shorter and higher quality video and audio
	• Assessment: More quizzes
What did you NOT like about this course?	• Intensity of the course
	• Quizzes had too many technical questions
What other short courses would you be interested in for the future?	• Educational topics: instructional design applications of mobile technologies for teaching
	• Agricultural topics: expanded cases studies from other areas of the world
	• Wireless and network topics
	• Security: cyber-security
	• Management: knowledge management, technology transfer
	• Digital media
	• Entrepreneurship: small business development in rural settings
	• Health
	• Finance: micro-finance, cooperatives
	• Gender: gender equity, gender issues

During the MOOC, the course sites were accessible in a highly reliable way. They were secure against cyberattacks that could lead to denial of services. Except for a total of three hours of scheduled maintenance work, the class site was available uninterrupted throughout the duration of the course. This is part of the quality assurance that self-directed learners expect of any online offering and it was fully met. The schedules for real-time chat events, assignments, and assessments were strictly adhered to. While most learners accessed the course site and learning materials using PCs and laptops, a noticeable proportion (about 10 percent) used either tablets or smartphones. On three occasions, at the request of groups of learners who had difficulty accessing the videos on YouTube, the course managers dispatched the learning materials on DVDs to nodes in Nepal, Sierra Leone, and Zambia. These participants were able to access the assignments and quizzes and the discussion forum areas and eventually received their certificates.

Although originally not planned, tests in the form of online quizzes were introduced based on the demand for such that was raised in the discussions. Also based on opinions and views expressed in the discussions, a few topics were expanded or abridged. Four real-time chat sessions (one every week from the second week of the course) were organised with the instructors using the chat facility. Since participants were distributed in 18 time zones, the instructors located in three different time zones were able to support learners in real time. According to the survey results, the quality of content was judged as excellent. The competence of the instructors in their respective domains was also rated highly.

Given that MOOC pedagogy is still an emerging area, educators utilizing MOOCs have much to learn from the important insights and practices from the world of ODL and online learning (Sharples et al., 2012). Most of the instructors in this effort were from a research university where standard contact with learners was in the face-to-face mode. However, the instructors were able to adapt surprisingly quickly to the MOOC environment. The IITK course team had conducted a smaller MOOC earlier (Sodhi & Prabhakar, 2014), thereby enabling the team to use the experience for a pedagogically effective design. External evaluations revealed that it was compatible with good practices in online learning (Porter, 2014). Thus, in addition to delivering a highly rated MOOC to students, this effort also helped the faculty members of a research university in a developing country to enhance their skills in designing a MOOC-friendly framework in support of self-directed learning.

Towards a Model of MOOC for Development

From our experience, it is clear that the MOOC can be unbundled effectively and its components can be purposefully recombined to create an appropriate and highly functional learning space for thousands of learners. Branded MOOCs could become a source of effective practices and do not need to be the sole technology platforms. The elaborate discussion on styles of MOOCs (e.g., cMOOCs and xMOOCs) and pedagogy (e.g., Yuan & Powell, 2014), while academically interesting, is not that applicable to the context of learning for development. Our experience shows that a MOOC4D is a blend of styles and pedagogies dictated by context.

Intensive involvement of the core team of faculty members and support groups in mentoring is critical to the success of the MOOC. Data from learning analytics can be used to ensure that a learner in need of support will receive it in time. The selection of topics is best preceded by a close study of the needs in the milieu of development. The core team should be always prepared to engage learners using cross-media and blended approaches. For example, this team used courier services to deliver content to some learners who were facing challenges in connectivity and online access.

It is important to point out that this was only the first such MOOC for Development course. A few more iterations (COL and IITK, 2014) of this MOOC for Development course are necessary to provide a more detailed model. MOOC-as-event (not as just an online class) will continue to inform our approach and cross-media approaches to support local needs (for example, phone-in or Skype-in talk shows where feasible). It is also important to embed a research process into the course development and delivery process and identify the lessons learned.

More iterations needed? Well, we did just that. COL and IITK organized a *"MOOC on MOOCs: What you need to know about massive open online courses"* (four weeks in Sep.–Oct. 2014), where a number of insights and learning from the M4D MOOC were used in the design and delivery processes. The *"MOOC on MOOCs"* addressed the basics or nuts and bolts of designing and running a MOOC (Perris, 2014). Among the goals for this particular MOOC was to expose the participants to a MOOC as a means for them to see their potential and perhaps later pursue MOOC initiatives within their own areas of expertise or interest. Academics and government officials whose work involves human development issues were directly targeted as well as professionals working in the NGO space (Perris, 2014).

In terms of enrollments, there were 2,347 registrants (from 93 countries, with two-thirds being academics and college teachers, and 316 being eligible for certificates). As a sign of wide impact from this MOOC, the five countries with the highest enrollments were India, Nepal, Mauritius, South Africa, and Canada (i.e., the headquarters of the COL). Learners were interested in knowing more about MOOCs, with some interested in doing trials on their own. Taking advantage of the global possibilities for MOOCs, guest experts were solicited from around the world to augment and enhance the *MOOC on MOOCs* course. Besides IIT-Kanpur and COL faculty, there were talks by Sir John Daniel (former President of COL), Dr Sanjay Sarma (Director of Digital Learning at MIT), and Professor Russell Beale (University of Birmingham and Future Learn, UK; plus education sector leads from Google and Microsoft. In addition, the IITK team designed and built a new MOOC platform called *MOOKIT*. As with the M4D MOOC, participant surveys showed that the course was highly effective while the new platform received a strongly positive rating.

As of time of this writing in late November 2014, COL and IITK are engaged in a new trial of deploying MOOC technology to train semi-skilled gardeners in the basics of modern horticultural production techniques through the *delivery of an audio-only course* (four weeks). Given the modest level of literacy of the intended audience and the known inability to make use of the Web to access learning materials, a platform to deliver materials in an audio format (in this case, Hindi) and to receive queries and responses has been developed and deployed. There were 1,075 registrants in this course at the time it started, almost 90 percent of whom were gardeners and subsistence farmers. Suffice to say, with such response and participation, many of key goals for MOOCs for human development are being more than met.

It is important to point out that many development institutions and national governments accept skills development as a policy priority (Aggarwal & Gasskov, 2013). Rather than immediately influencing the higher education sector, MOOC for Development as a support technology is likely to be useful in faster diffusion of intermediate skills on a mass scale (COL, 2013c). A series of trials and prototypes are necessary to determine the nature and extent of blending MOOCs with existing approaches related to quality assurance, assessment, certification, and credentialing.

In MOOC for Development practice, online educational materials and resources are likely to be a core technology rather than the sole technology (similar to e-commerce practices in many developing countries where it is possible to place an order online and make the payment at a bank counter or through a post office). Inadequacies in pedagogy in MOOCs need to be addressed through specially designed trials. In all these matters, open and distance learning organizations, COL's primary constituency, would be able to contribute effective strategies from years of well-established practices.

There is a rising interest of political leadership in MOOCs, including places like India (Prime Minister's Office, 2014). Government offices are interested in how MOOCs might enhance literacy skills, health awareness, and economic development as well as serve as a channel for youth engagement. As such interests result in success stories, we should expect to see wider and faster development of MOOC for Development models.

Balaji Venkataraman is the Director for Technology and Knowledge Management at the Commonwealth of Learning (COL), Vancouver, Canada. He is a worker in the area of IT applied to rural development and learning. His recent work relates to applications of semantic Web technologies in agriculture. His current interests are in deploying new-generation mobile devices in rural learning and in examining the advantages of MOOCs in support of skill development. Balaji received his master's and doctoral degrees from the Indian Institute of Technology and the University of Madras.

Asha Kanwar is the President and CEO of the Commonwealth of Learning (COL), Vancouver, Canada. She is an internationally renowned Distance Educator who is also known for her pioneering contributions in the area of learning for development. She has made significant contributions to gender studies, especially the impact of distance education on the lives of Asian women. A recipient of several awards, fellowships and honorary doctorates, Professor Kanwar has studied and worked in different contexts, both developing and developed. She received her master's and MPhil degrees from the Panjab University in India and DPhil from Sussex.

References

Aggarwal, A., & Gasskov, V. (2013). *Comparative analysis of national skills development policies: A guide for policy makers.* Retrieved from International Labour Organization website: http://www.ilo.org/wcmsp5/groups/public/---africa/documents/publication/wcms_224559.pdf.

Bagga, M. (2010, October). vKVK—A way to empower Krishi Vigyan Kendra. *Information Technology in Developing Countries*, 20(3). Retrieved from http://www.iimahd.ernet. in/egov/ifip/oct2010/meeta-bagga.htm.

Balaji, V., & Prabhakar, T.V. (2014). Changing the tunes from Bollywood's to rural livelihoods. In M. Ally & A. Tsinakos (Eds.). *Perspectives on open and distance learning: Increasing access through mobile learning* (pp. 205–16). Retrieved from Commonwealth of Learning website: http://www.col.org/resources/publications/Pages/detail.aspx?PID=466.

Commonwealth of Learning (COL). (2013a). *Mobiles for Development (M4D)*. Retrieved from Commonwealth of Learning website: http://www.col.org/progServ/pro grammes/KM/Pages/M4D.aspx.

Commonwealth of Learning (COL). (2013b). *MOOC for Development (MOOC4D)*. Retrieved from Commonwealth of Learning website: http://www.col.org/progServ/ programmes/KM/Pages/MOOC4D.aspx.

Commonwealth of Learning (COL). (2013c). *Events*. Retrieved from Commonwealth of Learning website: http://www.col.org/news/Connections/2014Mar/Pages/Events.aspx.

Commonwealth of Learning (COL). (2014). *DOER Infographic*. Retrieved from Piktochart website: https://magic.piktochart.com/output/1834969-doer-infographic.

Commonwealth of Learning and IIT Kanpur (COL and IITK). (2014). *MOOC on MOOC*. Retrieved from http://mooconmooc.org/.

Dhanarajan, G., & Porter, D. (Eds.). (2013). *Perspectives on open and distance learning: Open educational resources: An Asian perspective*. Retrieved from Commonwealth of Learning website http://www.col.org/resources/publications/Pages/detail.aspx?PID=441.

Economist, The. (2014, June 28). The future of universities: The digital degree. *The Economist*. Retrieved from http://www.economist.com/news/briefing/21605899-staid-higher-education-business-about-experience-welcome-earthquake-digital.

Ho, A.D., Reich, J., Nesterko, S., Seaton, D.T., Mullaney, T., Waldo, J., & Chuang, I. (2014). *HarvardX and MITx: The first year of open online courses, fall 2012–summer 2013* (HarvardX and MITx Working Paper No. 1). SSRN-id 2381263. Retrieved from http://papers.ssrn.com/sol3/papers.cfm?abstract_id=2381263.

Hollands, F.M., & Tirthali, D. (2014, May). *MOOCs: Expectations and reality. Full report*. Retrieved from Center for Benefit–Cost Studies of Education, Teachers College, Columbia University, NY website: http://cbcse.org/wordpress/wp-content/ uploads/2014/05/MOOCs_Expectations_and_Reality.pdf.

McGreal, R., Kinuthia, W., Marshall, S., & McNamara, T. (Eds.). (2013). *Perspectives on open and distance learning: Open educational resources: Innovation, research and practice*. Retrieved from Commonwealth of Learning website: http://www.col.org/resources/ publications/Pages/detail.aspx?PID=446.

MOOCs for development: A massive open online course (MOOC) by IIT Kanpur and COL (2014). Retrieved from http://m4d.colfinder.org/.

Perris, K. (2014, September 12). MOOC on MOOCs? A novel yet pragmatic approach. *University World News*. Retrieved from http://www.universityworldnews.com/article. php?story=20140903154113518.

Porter, D. (2014). *MOOC on mobiles for development report*. Retrieved from Commonwealth of Learning website: http://www.col.org/resources/publications/Pages/detail. aspx?PID=483.

Prime Minister's Office. (2014). *Text of Prime Minister's statement in the 6th BRICS Summit on the Agenda: Sustainable Development & Inclusive Growth*. Narendra Modi, Prime Minister's Office, India. Retrieved from http://pmindia.nic.in/details156.php.

Sharples, M., McAndrew, P., Weller, M., Ferguson, R., FitzGerald, E., Hirst, T., et al. (2012). *Innovating Pedagogy 2012.* Retrieved from the Institute of Educational Technology, The Open University website: http://www.open.ac.uk/personalpages/mike.sharples/Reports/Innovating_Pedagogy_report_July_2012.pdf.

Siemens, G. (2014, May 6). Multiple pathways: Blending xMOOCs & cMOOCs. eLearnSpace. Retrieved from http://www.elearnspace.org/blog/2014/05/06/multiple-pathways-blending-xmoocs-cmoocs/.

Sodhi, B., & Prabhakar, T.V. (2014). Architecting software for the cloud: An online course on building cloud based applications. *About the course.* Department of Computer Science and Engineering at IIT Ropar (Punjab), India. Retrieved from http://www.iitrpr.ac.in/class/a4c/.

UNESCO. (2002, July 8). *UNESCO promotes new initiative for free educational resources on the Internet.* Retrieved from UNESCO. Education News website: http://www.unesco.org/education/news_en/080702_free_edu_ress.shtml.

World Bank. (2011). What are global public goods? Retrieved from World Bank website http://go.worldbank.org/JKZLIHR2B0.

Yuan, L., & Powell, S. (2013). MOOCs and open education: Implications for higher education. A White Paper. Retrieved from JISC CETIS website: http://publications.cetis.ac.uk/wp-content/uploads/2013/03/MOOCs-and-Open-Education.pdf.

19

HARNESSING THE POWER OF OPEN LEARNING TO SHARE GLOBAL PROSPERITY AND ERADICATE POVERTY

Sheila Jagannathan

Significance of Open Learning in Developing Countries

Among the yet to be exploited potentials of emerging educational technologies, including the Internet, are their leveraging effects on learning and capacity building. Universities, think-tanks, and the corporate sector in developed countries and regions of the world are already engaged in disrupting traditional notions of training and capacity building. Can these learning strategies be transferred to developing parts of the world, so that poverty is eradicated and economic prosperity shared by 2030?

Consider this: in 2010, 1.2 billion people tried to feed and clothe their families, put roofs over their heads, and pay for healthcare and other essential services with incomes less than $1.25 a day. Another 3 billion people lived on less than $4 a day (World Bank, 2013a) (see Figure 19.1). Many of these people, in China, India, and the rest of the developing world, are young parents, often not yet adults, with boundless energy but relatively inadequate education. The key point is that many of these individuals have not acquired the competencies and skills to prepare themselves for better-paying jobs that the globalizing economy is creating even within their countries, towns, and villages. As such, their life aspirations are lowered or all together diminished.

In many developing countries, the educational infrastructure of "bricks and mortar" institutions is inadequate in terms of serving the needs of citizens. Consequently, the desire to learn often does not get translated into the actual acquisition of knowledge. The learning infrastructure from schools, colleges, and training institutions does not function either efficiently or equitably for a number of reasons.

First, the sheer number of individuals wanting to learn puts enormous pressure on the educational system. And when educational opportunities are available, those

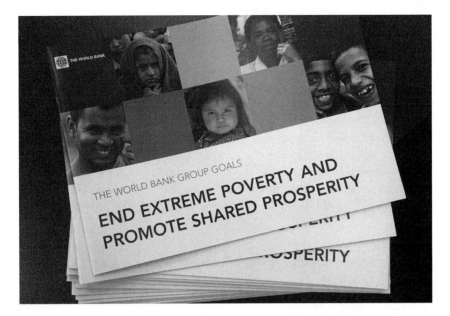

FIGURE 19.1   World Bank Group twin goals

living in rural areas and remote communities typically do not get access to instruction of the same quality as their peers living in the large cities where the premier institutions are located. Second, the lack of resources in the educational institutions that they attend combined with the low level of motivation among their instructors further inhibits classroom learning for many students in public schools and colleges. Third, there has been a fundamental "cascading" effect on the ability to learn—a student who does not receive a decent education at the primary school level ceases to aspire for jobs that require a high school diploma. Likewise, a student who was discouraged at the high school level does not aspire for jobs that require a college-level education and so on. As a direct consequence of this process of stunted aspirations, hundreds of millions of youth are unable to take advantage of the income and employment prospects of the globalized economy.

All is not lost, however. Exciting opportunities await in the land of open learning, including those related to acquiring basic education, customized training, and re-skilling themselves to meet the competencies required for better-paying jobs that already exist as well as those which are emerging. It is the premise of this chapter that the forms of education available from various virtual learning platforms and online resources have the potential to open up opportunities to share prosperity and reduce poverty (Hewlett Foundation, 2011).

The solution now available from different online delivery mechanisms and platforms envisages leveraging technology to globally scale up knowledge and learning of what works, why it works, and under what circumstances. For example:

- the Tanzanian farmer who is an elementary school dropout learns through her mobile phone how to combine her on-the-ground experiences growing crops with how to make a lot more money by managing food spoilage better;
- the young woman in Bangladesh, who has invested in a mobile Internet connection, can provide long-distance Skype services between villagers and the family wage earners in the Middle East;
- the Vietnamese auto mechanic who is a high school graduate learns though the Internet how to repair cars and motorcycles that are constantly becoming more sophisticated in terms of electronic components;
- the Bolivian city official, who is a college graduate, and learns through a blended learning course on the "why and the how to" respond to questions and concerns of citizens on improving delivery of basic services (such as clean water, trash removal, health, and education).

Capacity Development at the e-Institute

In order to achieve the above transformations, the codification and packaging of tacit knowledge and lessons into digestible learning is critical (in the above examples, customized to the needs of the farmer, the Skype entrepreneur, the auto mechanic, and the civil servant, respectively). Equally important is the ability of the learning platform infrastructure to constantly renew and enrich the knowledge base through feedback loops from the learning process itself—based on what worked well and what did not work well.

Digital and online learning opportunities can scale up and reach thousands of people who are eager to learn and apply new knowledge, while continuing to learn as they face new challenges in earning livelihoods and incomes. This democratization of learning helps citizens fully realize their economic aspirations, particularly when the required information is available at our fingertips, just-in-time, and just-enough (bite sizes). Furthermore, continuous cost-reducing innovations in learning technology make future prospects much more cost effective than in the past.

This educational approach is in sharp contrast to traditional capacity-building approaches that focused on publishing research reports, policy briefs, and technical guidelines as paper-based knowledge products. The World Bank Group (WBG), for example, invests large amounts of resources on such knowledge products. Internal evaluations indicate that barely 2 percent have direct practical learning impacts on the intended audience. Similarly, capacity building through face-to-face courses has been the staple of the Bank's knowledge-sharing and learning efforts. Unfortunately, besides being expensive and resource intensive to deliver, they reach only a small fraction of select clients.

This new approach to capacity development recognizes the challenges developing countries are still facing in ensuring that their many stakeholders (farmers, youth, disempowered women, civil servants, political leaders, etc.) are able to access high-quality and up-to-date knowledge and learning products, which can help in their achieving the twin goals of ending poverty and sharing prosperity. Explicit and tacit development knowledge can be fed into the learning design that curates, customizes, and transfers knowledge on how to achieve specific results that matter to concerned stakeholder groups.

An open learning platform, called the e-Institute, was established by the World Bank Group on a pilot basis in 2011. The e-Institute was a means of delivering high-quality, critical learning products that focused on self-paced and virtually facilitated e-courses. Taking advantage of new technologies, learning experiences of the e-Institute have been cost effective, innovative, and practitioner-focused.

During the past four years this pilot has grown substantially. In fact, over 200 courses have already been delivered in a wide variety of development themes (such as Urban Development, Climate Change, Governance, Innovation, and Competitiveness) by inducting expertise, learning, and knowledge from across the World Bank Group (WBG) and its partners. The courses have included the "how to" of policy reform and proven good practices across the world on the delivery of a variety of services—ranging from accountable governance to better toilets as well as from improved nutrition to "smart city" planning. Importantly, many courses offered were customized to fit the local needs. In addition, monthly webinars, online learning communities, interviews, and various forms of multi-media support practitioners on their "learning journeys" on a continuous and just-in-time basis.

The e-Institute was able to reach out directly to policy makers, civil society organizations, members of the media, government officials and parliaments, different key players in the private sector, a range of academics, and, of course, the youth and future leaders. Each of these targeted groups, of course, are the key stakeholders for change. The e-Institute also successfully built collaboration models with key partners, including national and regional training institutes, networks, think tanks, and universities.

MOOCs as Global Classrooms to Raise Awareness and Engage Citizens Anywhere, Any Time: An Opportunity to Deliver Learning at Scale

The e-Institute pilot was taking place fortuitously at a time when learning was being disrupted on a global scale by the emergence of massive open online courses (MOOCs). There was interest on both sides—the emerging MOOC providers and the WBG—to collaborate and explore how this new instrument could leverage global learning for development. In the past six months, two MOOCs have been successfully launched by the WBG in collaboration with Coursera. This particular section summarizes the preliminary lessons learned through the process of offering these initial MOOCs.

MOOCs have the potential to scale up and advance the development agenda. At the same time, they can effectively spread the reach and impact of high-quality education. In the development context, they enable capacity-building programs to reach beyond traditional clients and services. Moreover, MOOCs can engage large and diverse sets of people globally to learn about how other countries and communities might have reduced poverty, created jobs, lowered inequality, and empowered their citizens to demand corruption-free governance. As such, these initial MOOCs are providing a dynamic and interactive space for practitioners and the general public to have live discussions and debates as well as share ideas, tools, and resources on development topics. Fortunately, we have seen a high level of engagement and interaction among the MOOC participants. As a result, we are beginning to realize that this process represents a groundbreaking option for the WBG to convene participants to share knowledge that leads to innovative and tangible actions on the ground.

In January 2014, the first WBG MOOC, titled "Turn Down the Heat: Why a 4 °C Warmer World Must be Avoided," was launched (World Bank, 2012a, 2013b, 2013c). This MOOC repackaged content from a major scientific report with the same title prepared jointly by WBG and the Potsdam Institute for Climate Impact Research and Climate Analytics.

By repackaging the content into a comprehensive, open access, free, and interactive learning tool, the MOOC provided a platform to enhance scientific understanding of the risks and devastating effects of climate change (World Bank, 2012b). It simultaneously launched global discussions in both developed and developing countries on the key policy implications for climate action. By sharing examples of key mitigation and adaptation actions across sectors, along with a discussion on how individuals and countries can act now, act together, and act differently on the climate challenge, the MOOC inspired practitioners as well as the general public to obtain valuable information on how to take action on this important development challenge. We were able to reach 20,000 participants who amassed over 100,000 video downloads.

The course was structured around four key themes (World Bank, 2012a) which corresponded to the following four weeks of the course:

Week 1 focused on observed climate changes and impacts through a sweep of history, from 650,000 years ago until today.

Week 2 had experts take participants through a range of emissions and subsequent climate change scenarios, as well as projected climate impacts and risks associated with a warming of 2 °C to 4 °C expected by the end of this century.

Week 3 introduced how our very life, including essentials such as agriculture, water resources, human health, biodiversity, and ecosystem services, become impacted by a changing climate (Figure 19.2).

Week 4, which was in many ways the most important week, enabled learners to bring their learning together by giving an information base on which to act. Activities this week provoked learners to think of possible ways of making a difference, including options on how to prepare for the probable impacts of climate change.

FIGURE 19.2 Impacts of climate change on farmland

In June 2014, we launched a second MOOC, based on the World Development Report 2014: Risk and Opportunity—Managing Risk for Development (World Bank, 2013d). As with the first MOOC on climate change, this one was also available as open source educational resource. In addition, a report upon which this MOOC was based is available with overviews in seven languages (i.e., English, Spanish, French, Portuguese, Russian, Arabic, and Chinese) (World

Bank, 2013d). The Risk and Opportunity course highlighted the importance of risk management for development—stressing how the lack of preparation can often contribute to crises and development setbacks. At the same time, the fear of risk may also prevent people from taking on risk in pursuit of opportunities (see Figure 19.3). The discussion and debate of such issues encourages participants to think about what changes are needed in their own communities and countries. The 34,500 participants for this course came from some 145 countries, with good coverage of all the WBG's regions (including the Middle East and North Africa, South Asia, East Asia and the Pacific, Europe and Central Asia, Africa, and Latin America and the Caribbean) (Berniyazova & Kyla, 2014).

Pedagogical Approaches Followed

The MOOC design blends contemporary MOOC pedagogical approaches that have been customized for developing country audiences with low-bandwidth constraints. Some highlights are discussed next (Berniyazova & Kyla, 2014).

Dual tracks. To reach a broad target audience, the MOOCs were offered in two tracks: (1) a Generalist or a Champion track; and (2) a Policy and Leadership track. The two tracks enabled us to reach both development practitioners, who constituted 80 percent of participants, and the general public who are showing increasing interest in these topics. For example, in the Heat MOOC, the generalists were interested in tracking their carbon footprint, and exploring ways of reducing it.

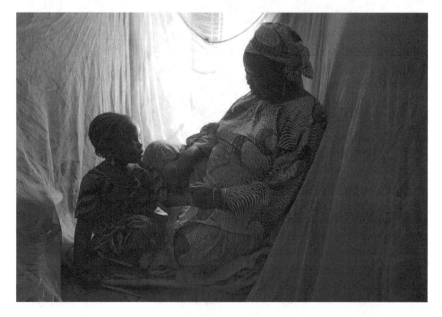

FIGURE 19.3 Reducing the risk of child mortality

For policy makers, the course offered discussions on key policy instruments. In addition, an (optional) geographic dissemination was enabled by the platform's "Map Yourself" function that allowed participants to identify their organization/city/country/continent, which subsequently led to the formation of sub-groups based on thematic areas as well as geographic or other personal interests.

Hybrid of xMOOC and cMOOC approaches. To achieve the learning outcomes of both communicating evidence-based lessons on development challenges and solutions as well as facilitating networks of learning and collaboration, this approach blends the two models of MOOC design—connectivist cMOOCs and instructionist xMOOCs.

For example, in the Heat MOOC, at one level, the course design relies on traditional instructivist tools, associated with xMOOCs, such as interactive, short video lectures by 17 world-renowned experts. These video resources were coupled with a set of core readings, online resources, quizzes, and focused assignments. At another level, the course caters to climate change professionals and policy makers who might want to expand existing knowledge and develop networks of learning and collaboration. In effect, these two World Bank MOOCs were designed around the cMOOC idea of learning as knowledge co-creation with the participant playing an active role with the xMOOC concept of specific content delivery from experts to awaiting learners.

Experiential learning via game-based simulation: In the Risk MOOC we included game-based simulation and cartoon animations as means of encouraging learners to think deeply about assumptions and relationships underlying risks.

Beyond the examples discussed in the expert videos, a new game, called the "Risk Horizon" game, was developed for the course participants to make their personal risk management choices, while animated cartoons (World Bank, 2013e) illustrated the course's key ideas in a fun, engaging way (see Figure 19.4). The game, which was developed by Engagement Labs in collaboration with the World Bank, allowed learners to experience the process of having to make risk management choices for themselves. While the game is highly stylized, it reflected the dilemma of making choices in the real world. Initially, the game received mixed reviews from players which the Game team plans to address.

While some players immediately took to the game, and could see its broader relevance for the MOOC, others were frustrated that they did not fully understand all of the components of the game, and could not easily progress between levels. Given that course facilitators were geographically removed from participants, a key learning point for the game design team was to have a very clear illustration of how the game worked. A detailed tutorial of the game was an immense help in improving its accessibility.

Busy social media channels: Social media provided dynamic and interactive spaces for practitioners and the general public to have live discussions and debates as well as share ideas, tools, and resources to respond to current development challenges (e.g., climate change). The high level of engagement and interaction

FIGURE 19.4 Risk Horizon game interface

between practitioners represented a groundbreaking option for the WBG to convene participants to share knowledge that would be followed up by innovative and tangible action on the ground. For example, in the case of the Heat MOOC, the busy Twitter hashtag #wbheat, generated over 800 tweets and counting. Other innovative tools used included Google+ Hangouts, which was used in conjunction with Twitter and YouTube to engage in real-time dialog and discussions with world-renowned experts and course participants.

Digital artifact: To further promote global awareness on issues raised during the MOOC, participants were assigned to produce "digital artifacts," or creative online resources that would convey some of the important takeaways from the course. Among the most interesting outcomes were the final projects, in which participants displayed a wealth of creativity and a wide spectrum of interests and perspectives. This creativity was reflected by the diversity of projects including presentations, blogs, videos, comics, info graphics and even a song (Quismundo, 2014) that gently asserted the course's main refrain: *Time to change . . . got to change . . . time we change the world . . .*

Overall, the two early MOOCs proved to be fulfilling experiences for participants, as evidenced in feedback at the conclusion of the course. Evaluations from the voluntary end of course survey showed that the MOOCs were highly appreciated: most learners could be described as *active participants* (see Figure 19.5). The majority of survey participants viewed all videos and took all quizzes (≈80 percent),

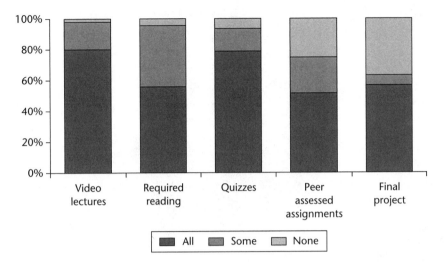

FIGURE 19.5   Completed elements of the course

as well as completed all required readings, peer-assessments and submitted the final project (>50 percent in each case). The assessment of the participants regarding the readings and assignments was either very good or excellent; where there was a drop in assessment was in peer-to-peer assessments—reflecting the continued challenge of virtually developing a community of practice. The pie chart displayed in Figure 19.6 summarizes the satisfaction of the whole process. While only a small percent rated the experience as "poor" or "fair," these responses, nevertheless, reflect the continued challenges of building high-quality peer-to-peer interactions. Moreover, since peer-assessed assignments and the final project required them to generate what could be considered as new course content, the majority of surveyed learners can be recognized as not only *active participants*, but, in fact, *community contributors*. Fortunately, an overwhelming majority (92 percent) of respondents rated their learning experience as *excellent, very good*, or *good* (see Figure 19.6).

Emerging Challenges

Rather than typical college students enrolling in MOOCs to earn university credentials and certificates, MOOCs focusing on development topics are of interest to a different set of learners, namely, development practitioners. These development practitioners are usually mid-career officials, NGOs, and other stakeholders who are interested to not only learn specific topics, but also network with peers. When such workforce professionals drop out of a MOOC, we need to have a tracking system that is able to report back on whether they left because they received the "bite-sized" learning they were seeking or whether they dropped out because of a lack of interest.

The availability of MOOC content in local languages is also another consistent request from many developing countries. The challenge for us has been to invest in translation in the "right" amount. For example, languages such as

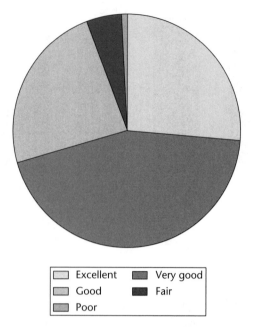

FIGURE 19.6 Participant rating of experience with the course

Mongolian and Khmer are spoken in relatively small countries, but these are also the countries where the potential for achieving reach with impact are among the highest because the educational system is highly inadequate and the desire to learn is extremely great among the people living there.

Another significant lesson is that the feedback mechanisms need to provide adequate real-time data for designers to modify course content if and when necessary. For example, the climate change MOOC has recommended some generalizable policies for building resilience among herders in pastoral societies. Such policies can help herders to adapt their strategies of owning large herds. The real-time feedback from these communities is quite important in order to ensure that the messages that they are sent via the MOOC and other online content are relevant to their specific concerns.

Technical Challenge and Peer-Support

A large number of participants were not initially comfortable enough to engage in producing a digital artifact due to the lack of necessary technical skills and hesitation about posting one's own work on a public domain. However, by the beginning of the second week of this peer assignment, the MOOC team witnessed a truly special phenomenon—some of the participants who had already managed to produce their own creative artifacts were "zooming" over the course's discussion forums and sharing suggestions and ideas with their online peers on how to accomplish the task at hand. As a result, many participants who were initially skeptical were motivated to produce something meaningful and eager to share their artifacts and ideas.

A Single Destination for Learning with Three "Schools"		
WBx *Talks* *Just-in-time Learning*	**WBa** *Academy* *Structured Learning*	**WBc** *Connect* *Communities of Learning*
WBx is the space for podcasts, video talks by external and internal experts, story telling, bite-sized talks on hot topics e-mentoring	Explore deep learning on development issues and solutions: e-Learning courses, MOOCs, bite-sized modules for customized and tailored learning	Connect with experts and peers for solutions to development challenges faced by practitioners
Live participation and broadcast of WBG talks and conferences, e.g. Knowledge Talks, Chief Economist's Series	Face-to-face facilitated learning sessions, course and workshops	South–South Knowledge Exchange & Solution Hubs Solutions Labs Communities of Practice
Modeled on TED, Aspen Institute, WEF	Modeled on Khan Academy, Coursera, and GE Crotonville	Modeled on Quora, Google Hangout, and Dartmouth Collaboratory on HealthCare

FIGURE 19.7 Open Learning Campus Structure

The Open Learning Campus

The WBG experience with implementing e-courses through the e-Institute and later through the two pilot MOOCs have been significant milestones in introducing learning and innovation in its capacity-building programs. These new educational delivery mechanisms have enabled the WBG to reach beyond traditional audiences who read its reports and attend its face-to-face training sessions. This journey has led us to build an Open Learning Campus which will be launched in Spring 2015 (see Figure 19.7).

The Open Learning Campus will be a single destination for learning, where World Bank clients, the general public, and World Bank staff can access real-time, relevant, world-class learning. It will feature online and face-to-face learning. More specifically, the three "schools" envisaged include:

- **WBx—Talks.** With a focus on bite-sized learning, featuring short focused podcasts, webinars, games, and talks by leading development experts.
- **WBa—Academy.** A destination for deep learning related to development issues and execution offering e-Learning courses, MOOCs, bite-sized lessons. It also includes face-to-face facilitated learning sessions, courses, and workshops.

- **WBc—Connect.** This is a virtual space for connecting with experts and peers toward getting answers to development challenges faced by practitioners. This space includes the South–South Knowledge Exchange, Solution Labs, and Communities of Practice.

The Open Learning Campus is a logical sequel to changes that are ongoing in our own internal learning processes and training programs. In addition, it taps into a wide array of global trends in disruptive learning. The Open Learning Campus recognizes the fact that knowledge, learning, and innovation are key ingredients of any development process. It also highlights the fact that the prospects of delivering educational programs and events on a massive scale with impact are getting progressively better with the spread of the Internet and mobile telephony throughout the world. The information detailed in this chapter is just the beginning. The WBG sees the Open Learning Campus as a way to shape new learning activities and experiences that can have a major impact around the globe. We view MOOCs and other online and blended learning courses and experiences, as well as the online communities of learners built around them, as a way to exchange knowledge and foster practical skills.

To sum up, the impact of the body of development knowledge becomes considerable when we transform it into customizable learning for stakeholders, be they policy makers, civil servants, farmers, auto mechanics, academics, or the World Bank staff itself. The good news is that learning aspirations do not have to be stunted to anyone or anywhere in the world in the future. Open learning provides a much more inexpensive and nuanced platform that can be customized to realize the aspirations of hundreds of millions of persons in the developing countries. We truly hope that The Open Learning Campus will play a significant role in connecting, sharing, and supporting a community of learners throughout the world.

Acknowledgements

We wish to acknowledge the guidance on MOOC pedagogy provided to us on our first set of MOOCs by Jen Ross, Hamish Macleod, and their team from the University of Edinburgh, School of Education.

 **Sheila Jagannathan** is Lead Learning Specialist and Program Manager of the e-Institute, at the World Bank Institute in Washington DC. She has over 28 years of experience in designing and managing distance learning programs and transforming the use of online and classroom pedagogies and technology. Sheila also provides policy advice and technical assistance to World Bank country-level capacity-building programs in East Asia, China, the Middle East and North Africa, Africa, and South Asia. Her interest areas include MOOCs, experiential pedagogy, online and hybrid or blended learning strategies, the development of

rich multimodal and social learning environments, big data and learning analytics, learning management systems, and learning ecosystems.

References

Berniyazova, A., & Kyla, R. (2014). Internal consulting notes. World Bank's e-Institute. Washington, DC.

Hewlett Foundation (2011, November 23). *Quality education in developing countries.* Retrieved from http://www.hewlett.org/library/hewlett-foundation-publication/qedc-overview.

Quismundo, E. (2014, February 19). *YouTube: Turn down the heat (an environmental song).* Retrieved from https://www.youtube.com/watch?v=jXq2TlfkJ6E&feature=youtu.be.

World Bank (2012a, November 1). *Turn down the heat: Why a 4 °C warmer world must be avoided.* Retrieved from http://documents.worldbank.org/curated/en/2012/11/17097815/turn-down-heat-4%C2%B0c-warmer-world-must-avoided#.

World Bank (2012b, November 18). *Climate change report warns of dramatically warmer world this century.* Retrieved from http://www.worldbank.org/en/news/feature/2012/11/18/Climate-change-report-warns-dramatically-warmer-world-this-century.

World Bank (2013a, January 1). *End extreme poverty and promote shared prosperity.* Retrieved from http://www.worldbank.org/content/dam/Worldbank/document/WB-goals2013.pdf.

World Bank (2013b, June 19). *Publication on turn down the heat: Climate extremes, regional impacts, and the case for resilience.* A Report for the World Bank by the Potsdam Institute for Climate Impact Research and Climate Analytics. The World Bank, Washington, DC. Retrieved from http://www.worldbank.org/en/topic/climatechange/publication/turn-down-the-heat-climate-extremes-regional-impacts-resilience.

World Bank (2013c, June 19). *Turn down the heat: Climate extremes, regional impacts, and the case for resilience.* Retrieved from http://www-wds.worldbank.org/external/default/WDSContentServer/WDSP/IB/2013/06/14/000445729_20130614145941/Rendered/PDF/784240WP0Full00D0CONF0to0June19090L.pdf.

World Bank (2013d, October 6). *World Development Report 2014, risk and opportunity, managing risk for development.* Retrieved from http://econ.worldbank.org/WBSITE/EXTERNAL/EXTDEC/EXTRESEARCH/EXTWDRS/EXTNWDR2013/0,,contentMDK:23459971~pagePK:8261309~piPK:8258028~theSitePK:8258025,00.html.

World Bank (2013e, March 19). *YouTube: The Gomez family: A modern tale of risk and opportunity.* Retrieved from https://www.youtube.com/watch?v=-Ri0jG6dPe8.

20

THE GLOCALIZATION OF MOOCs IN SOUTHEAST ASIA

Zoraini Wati Abas

Introduction

Southeast Asia is a group of independent countries in a region of Asia bounded roughly by the Indian subcontinent on the west, China in the north, and the Pacific Ocean in the east. It comprises eleven countries: Brunei Darussalam, Cambodia, East Timor, Indonesia, Laos, Malaysia, Myanmar, the Philippines, Singapore, Thailand, and Vietnam. Like all their Asian counterparts, each is striving to increase opportunities for access to higher education. In short, the aim is to democratize education or to provide education for all, by way of increasing the number of places and the number of higher education institutions (HEIs), or by offering distance learning such as venturing into online learning.

According to Economy Watch, the top six countries in this region in terms of GDP per capita are:

1. Singapore (US$64,832.62)
2. Brunei Darussalam (US$58,695.77)
3. Malaysia (US$18,752.92)
4. Timor-Leste (US$11,821.22)
5. Thailand (US$11,481.60), and
6. Indonesia (US$5,672.59).

According to Economy Watch, Singapore and Brunei Darussalam rank 3rd and 4th highest in terms of GDP per capita in the world, just below Qatar (1st) and Luxembourg (2nd) and ahead of the United States of America (6th) (Economy Watch, 2014).

Singapore, Timor-Leste (or East Timor), and Brunei are the smallest among the Southeast Asian countries with populations of 5.6 million, 1.2 million, and

423,000, respectively. The most populous country in Southeast Asia is Indonesia with 253.6 million people, making it the fourth-largest country in the world in terms of population. It comprises over 1,700 islands. In terms of similarities across countries, Malaysia (with a population of 30.1 million), Indonesia, and Brunei border each other geographically, share a similar national language, and have populations that are majority Muslim. Other Southeast Asian countries are again unique in terms of the main or national language spoken, cultural practices, history, and targets for the education of the local population.

A recent UNESCO (2014) report highlighted that many countries in Southeast Asia have, over the course of the past two decades, seen their HEIs moving from previously catering to the elites to now catering for the masses. The next phase will likely see higher education being offered universally in terms of the percentage of enrolment in higher education.

Interestingly, both Malaysia and Singapore have become education hubs, each attracting a sizeable number of international students from various countries. International students in the 20 public HEIs in Malaysia make up just slightly over 5 percent (28,837 students) of the total campus population of 560,359 students (Ministry of Education, Malaysia, 2014). Malaysia is reported to have more than 100 nationalities represented among its international student population. In addition, Malaysia has more female students (approximately 61 percent) than male students (about 39 percent) enrolled in its public universities.

As part of the objective of being education hubs, both countries have attracted foreign universities to establish branch campuses. Today, Singapore has 16 branch campuses and Malaysia has nine. Each country has also set targets to increase international student enrolment and are in the process of bringing in expatriate staff to help out.

It is interesting to note that five of the Southeast Asian countries are among the ten highest Internet-using Asian countries. Combined they have a total of 180.4 million Internet subscribers (see Figure 20.1). According to the Internet World Statistics (Miniwatts Marketing Group, 2014), Malaysia's Internet penetration rate is 67 percent with 20.1 million users, whereas Indonesia is less than half that rate at 28.1 percent (which amounts to roughly 71 million users). The development of MOOCs would not have been possible had the requisite Internet infrastructure not been in place. Indonesia, however, is quickly growing given the number of mobile Internet service providers in Indonesia as well as the 4.3 million smartphones and six million tablets owned by Indonesians.

MOOCs in Southeast Asia

As of October 2014, MOOCs have been launched in Indonesia, Malaysia, Singapore, and the Philippines. Thailand is expected to launch its first MOOCs in December 2014. However, to date it is only in Malaysia and Indonesia that MOOCs have become strategic government initiatives. MOOCs from these two countries were launched within a month of each other in September and October, 2014, respectively.

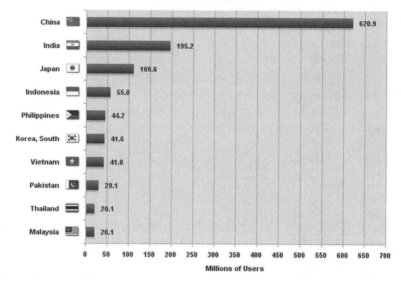

Asia Top Internet Countries
December 31, 2013

FIGURE 20.1 Five Southeast Asian countries among Asia's top ten Internet countries
Source: Miniwatts Marketing Group, 2013; http://www.internetworldstats.com/stats3.htm

As stated earlier, Malaysia has more than enough HEIs for its local students. As a result, it has become an education hub that attracts nearly 30,000 additional students from abroad. In contrast, Indonesia, being such a huge and populous country, only 30 percent of Indonesian school leavers are currently able to enroll in higher education despite the country having about 4,000 HEIs serving 5.4 million students. Moreover, most of the HEIs are concentrated on the island of Java and in the major cities, especially Jakarta and Yogyakarta. Indonesia has not intended to attract significant numbers of international students, nor international faculty for that matter, as it has a more urgent agenda to educate more of its own people, largely making use of the Indonesian language for its course delivery. Hence, the purpose of offering MOOCs in each of the two countries was expected to be somewhat different.

MOOCs in Malaysia

The first MOOC involving a Malaysian instructor took place when I was invited to be a guest presenter in a MOOC on major contributions being made to the field of instructional technology that was facilitated by Canadian educators, Dave Cormier, George Siemens, and Stephen Downes (from September 2011 to May 2012) (for more details, see http://change.mooc.ca/about.htm). I presented my research on mobile learning at the Open University Malaysia during one of the

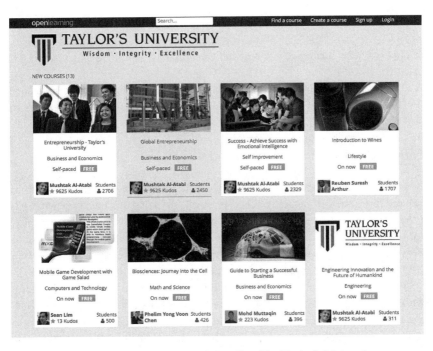

FIGURE 20.2 Eight of the thirteen MOOCs offered by Taylor's University

Source: https://www.openlearning.com/taylorsuniversity.

designated weeks. It was at about that time that MOOCs became an exciting trend made popular in the news media and that they began to attract the attention of both educators and the general public.

In March 2013, Taylor's University, a private Malaysian institution, experimented by offering its first MOOC on the subject of "Entrepreneurship." It was possibly the first MOOC by a HEI in Malaysia. This MOOC attracted students from 115 different countries. Following the success of this initial MOOC, the university launched its second MOOC, "Achieving Success With Emotional Intelligence" in July 2013. Next, it offered 14 MOOCs on the OpenLearning site (see Figure 20.2). One of the objectives of OpenLearning was to create a Web presence for Taylor's University. Simply put, the OpenLearning website allows an institution to "brand" itself by having its logo on the landing page for a subscription fee.

Through its Ministry of Education, the Malaysian government made plans to further develop e-learning between 2011 and 2015. Among its objectives were: to provide equal educational opportunities through e-learning, to provide the necessary infrastructure, to develop online contents to enhance learning and teaching, to enhance professional development through e-learning, to build a repository and directory of online resources, and to support the development of an e-learning community.

The development of MOOCs is seen as a way to:

1. increase the quality of learning and teaching;
2. save costs;
3. promote the country's niche in areas such as tropical diseases, Islamic finance and business, halal industry, and biodiversity for higher education institutions to go global;
4. create global visibility and branding; and
5. provide lifelong learning opportunities.

Universiti Putra Malaysia is the first public institution to offer MOOCs to its students and the general public. In April 2013 it launched two MOOCs ("Agriculture and Man" and a course titled "Malay Arts") on its own platform (Ismail, 2014). The MOOCs were combined with face-to-face sessions to provide a form of blended learning to the students. The contents of these two MOOCs contributed up to 30 percent of the content of the blended courses.

The next move of the Ministry of Education was to launch its first set of MOOCs on 18 September 2014. The objective of the initiative was to encourage the implementation of online learning in the public universities as well as to reduce face-to-face class sessions. The first semester of the 2014 academic year saw the launch of four MOOCs: (1) Islamic Civilisation and Asian Civilisations, (2) Ethnic Relations, (3) Entrepreneurship, and (4) ICT Competencies (see Figure 20.3). These four courses were developed by four different public universities. While two courses were offered in English, the other two were in Malay,

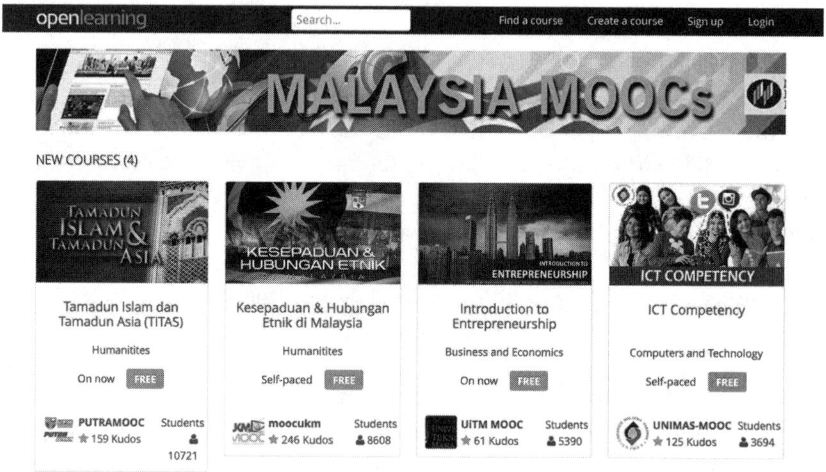

FIGURE 20.3 The first four MOOCs offered by Malaysian public universities

Source: https://www.openlearning.com/malaysiamoocs.

Malaysia's national language. At the time of this writing, after a mere two weeks of launching, about 33,500 people have enrolled in the four MOOCs. The ministry expects to have 15 percent of learning in the public universities offered through MOOCs by 2015, and increasing to 30 percent in 2020. It is important to point out that the ministry recently adopted OpenLearning as its national MOOC platform (Brimo, 2014).

In the midst of these MOOC initiatives, Shawn Tan (2014) shared his hopes for the improvement of Malaysian MOOCs. For example, he advocated that they should be more learner-friendly and easy to navigate. He also recommended that they have standard layouts in terms of quality and structure. The size of the videos in these courses needed to be reconsidered since not everyone has access to large bandwidth capabilities. It appears that views like Tan's are similar to the criticisms and comments made about MOOCs offered by more renowned universities and found in more developed countries; as they, too, often suffer from a lack of expertise in course or learning design. So while the potential of MOOCs is enormous, the provider needs to ensure that such open courses are of a certain quality before making them public.

MOOCs in Indonesia

Indonesia today is the 16th-largest economy, but could be the seventh-largest economy in the world by 2030, overtaking Germany and the United Kingdom (Oberman, Dobbs, Budiman, Thompson, & Rosse, 2012). This rapid economic growth will require some 113 million skilled workers (Oberman et al., 2012). Although there are about 4,000 HEIs at present, places exist for only 30 percent of its school leavers. MOOCs are seen to be one way of increasing the percentage of enrolment or one way of reaching out to those in faraway places.

Indonesia's first MOOC on Entrepreneurship Ciputra Way was launched by Universitas Ciputra Entrepreneurship Online in August 2013 (Darmawan, 2014). The course was delivered through the medium of Indonesian. The Universitas Terbuka (UT) (also known as the Open University of Indonesia) launched several MOOCs as part of its 30th anniversary celebrations on 24 March 2014 (see Figure 20.4). The five MOOCs offered by UT were: (1) Public Speaking, (2) English for Children, (3) Marketing Management, (4) Distance Learning, and (5) Various Food Technologies. Only the first two courses were in English whereas the others were offered in Indonesian.

Additional MOOCs were later launched by the Ministry of Education and Culture on 15 October 2014. The first five HEIs (public and private) to offer a total of 23 MOOCs were Institut Teknologi Bandung, Institut Teknologi Sepuluh Nopember, Universitas Gadjah Mada, Universitas Indonesia, Universitas Bina Nusantara, and STMIK AMIKOM Yogyakarta. It is important to point out that the development and implementation of MOOCS is funded by the ministry as part of a trial run.

FIGURE 20.4 Indonesia MOOCs being offered at Universitas Terbuka

Source: http://moocs.ut.ac.id/

According to Prof. Paulina Pannen, the head of Indonesia's MOOC development initiative at the Director-General's Office, Ministry of Education and Culture, MOOCs are a way for the Indonesian government to:

1. Improve the distribution of quality education (equity and quality) so as to reach those living in areas outside Java (where universities are concentrated).
2. Widen the access to quality education to more than the current 30 percent of school leavers enrolled in about 5,000 higher education institutions.

Indonesia's online learning program, including MOOCs in its HEIs, would have providers (institutions or individuals) contribute MOOCs and these will be aggregated by the Ministry of Education and Culture (see Figure 20.5). Other than MOOCs, students, lecturers, and members of the public will be able to access open content, open courses, and online courses (Pannen & Abas, 2014) from the links provided at the ministry portal (see http://pditt.belajar.kemdik bud.go.id).

The ministry is the gatekeeper and provides quality assurance. Each institution would determine how best to make their MOOCs available to the public. MOOCs developed by institutions would be hosted on the platform of the respective institution. MOOCs developed by individuals would be directly hosted at the ministry through its learning management system.

The ministry's plan is to first offer a trial run of its MOOCs to those interested. Course participants will receive a certificate of completion upon meeting the requirements of the course. The next phase is to offer study programs by way of MOOCs, thereby enabling participants to obtain a degree if they so choose. While currently free, those who will enroll in the upcoming study programs will be charged minimal fees.

It is expected that 25 HEIs will contribute MOOCs within the first five years. The total number of courses expected to be offered by these institutions would be around 800 courses for eight study programs. The target is to see 300,000 or more students benefit from the ministry's MOOC initiative.

The Way Forward

Each of these two countries, Malaysia and Indonesia, have launched MOOCs in a combination of individual and institutional efforts, both government and private. Whereas Malaysia aims to promote its institutions overseas and increase online learning for its students through its MOOCs as part of a policy of blended learning, Indonesia hopes to increase higher education opportunities in order for its people to obtain degrees through study programs in the form of MOOCs. Hence, while Malaysia launched its MOOCs on an international platform, Indonesia makes its MOOCs available on the platforms of the institution or of the education and culture ministry.

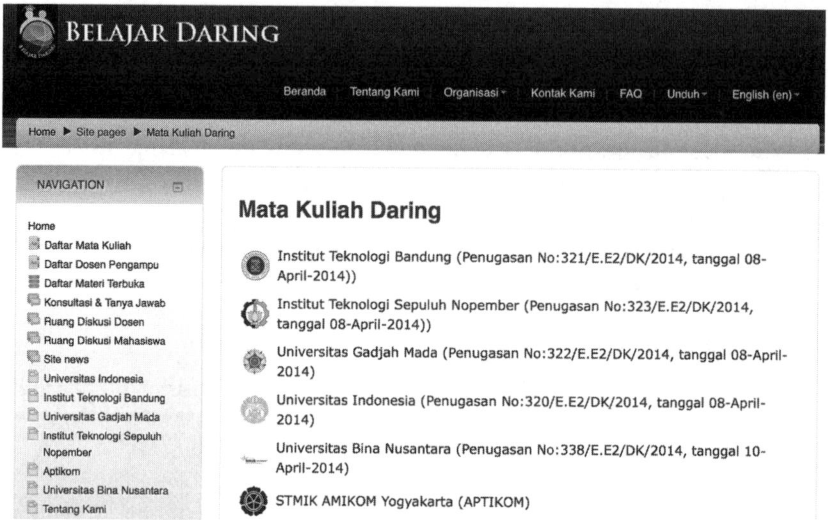

FIGURE 20.5   The list of higher education institutions offering MOOCs in Indonesia at the Ministry of Education and Culture portal

Source: http://pditt.belajar.kemdikbud.go.id

It is also expected that high-quality MOOCs will go a long way toward providing lifelong learning opportunities to the general public, especially for those who are not fluent in English and would prefer to access courses in Malay or Indonesian. With effectively designed MOOCs, it is possible that corporations will empower their staff to take ownership over their own professional development by taking selected MOOCs. It is also highly likely that high school students will enrol in MOOCs that they have an interest in for self-knowledge. Additionally, many such teenage learners will enrol in MOOCs as a means to help them determine whether they would actually be interested in majoring in a certain field by completing one or more MOOCs in the target major. Students enrolled in HEIs may also browse or more fully participate a MOOC to supplement courses currently being taken as a means to enhance their understanding of the content.

At the KMOOC symposium recently held in Seoul in September 2014, Professor Tom Reeves from the University of Georgia reported that MOOCs in Asia may take on at least three perspectives (Reeves, personal communication, September 22, 2014). The first view is that each Asian country will need to develop its own MOOCs in the local language(s) and reflect the local culture and developmental needs. The second view is that there could be an ASEAN-wide MOOC model developed with help from a group like UNESCO. And the third view is that Asian countries should primarily utilize the MOOC courses and OER emerging from the USA and the UK, and build support services for their own students around these free and open resources.

Conclusion

MOOCs can take on a few perspectives such as those offered at the recent KMOOC symposium in Seoul, Korea, mentioned above. While these views and other valuable perspectives may be taken into account in the long term, the ultimate approach or delivery method selected depends on what the intentions or purposes of the MOOC(s) are in each country. MOOCs should be glocalized ("think globally but act locally"). This term, glocalization, means taking the general concept of MOOCs and designing an educational experience for the local audience rather than having the local audience enrol in MOOCs from institutions overseas since not all MOOCs will be suitable or useful for their particular context or livelihood. In effect, MOOCs should be designed and developed for the local audience in the preferred language of instruction. They should also provide meaningful and relevant examples that the local audience can easily relate to. In other words, the design of MOOCs should consider the local cultural elements, religious values, and social norms.

As indicated, the goals of offering MOOCs in Malaysia and Indonesia vary somewhat from each other. However, the goals of these two countries differ even more strikingly from the intentions of those offering MOOCs in the more developed countries which experiment far and wide while often promoting the MOOC instructor as well as the institution. In contrast, the goals of the Malaysian government for its MOOCs include creating an international presence (via the OpenLearning platform) as one means to attract and increase international student enrolment. Another such objective pertains to having MOOCs become part of a blended learning experience (30 percent online) for students in the public universities. In the case of Indonesia, it is important for the government to be able to provide entire study programs made up of MOOCs for which students will be awarded a degree upon completion. This objective is a means to increase access to higher education as well as success within it. Indeed, the latter is what Indonesia needs most as it prepares its people to reach higher levels of education and to achieve greater economic progress in the next few years.

 **Zoraini Wati Abas** is a professor in the field of instructional technology. She has worked in both government and private universities in Malaysia and Indonesia. She is now Acting Vice-Rector, Academic and Student Affairs as well as Director, Center for Learning, Teaching and Curriculum Development at USBI-The Sampoerna University in Jakarta. Zoraini is an e-learning pioneer and has played a key role in open and distance learning, mobile learning, and in designing learning with appropriate learning technologies. In 2014, she received the Education Leadership Award from the World Corporate Universities Congress in Mumbai, India and was named second of 14 influential higher educational technology leaders in Southeast Asia.

References

Brimo, A. (2014, September 26). *OpenLearning selected as Malaysia's MOOC platform.* Retrieved from: https://www.openlearning.com/blog.

Darmawan, A. (2014, February 17). *Sekolah wirausaha tanpa biaya ala Ir Ciputra.* [*Entrepreneurial school without fees the Ir Ciputra way*]. Retrieved from http://tinyurl.com/ko4f59v.

Economy Watch. (2014). GDP per capita (PPP), US dollars data for all countries. Retrieved from http://www.economywatch.com/economic-statistics/economic-indicators/GDP_Per_Capita_PPP_US_Dollars/2014/.

Ismail, A. (2014). *Malaysia MOOC: Leveraging on blended learning at Malaysia public universities.* Paper presented at the ASEAN-ROK Workshop on Models of Teaching e-learning/blended learning in higher education, Seoul, Korea.

Ministry of Education, Malaysia. (2014, July). *Quick facts 2014: Malaysia educational statistics.* Retrieved from http://tinyurl.com/mb853gp.

Miniwatts Marketing Group. (2014). *Internet World Stats: Usage and population statistics.* Retrieved from http://www.internetworldstats.com/stats3.htm#asia.

Oberman, R., Dobbs, R., Budiman, A., Thompson, F., & Rosse, M. (2012). *The archipelago economy: Unleashing Indonesia's potential.* McKinsey Global Institute. Retrieved from http://www.mckinsey.com/insights/asia-pacific/the_archipelago_economy.

Pannen, P., & Abas, Z. W. (2014). *E-learning models in Indonesia.* Paper presented at ASEAN-ROK e-Learning Workshop: Best Practices in Higher Education, Seoul, Korea.

Tan, S. (2014, September 29). *On blended learning and Malaysian MOOCs.* Digital News Asia. Retrieved from http://www.digitalnewsasia.com/insights/on-blended-learning-and-malaysian-moocs.

UNESCO. (2014). *Higher education in Asia: Expanding out, expanding up. The rise of graduate education and university research.* UNESCO Institute for Statistics. Retrieved from http://tinyurl.com/ox5tjuf.

21

SITUATING MOOCs IN THE DEVELOPING WORLD CONTEXT

The Philippines Case Study

Melinda dela Pena Bandalaria and Grace Javier Alfonso

Introduction

MOOCs have been regarded "as the biggest revolution in higher education since Plato opened his academy" (Drake, 2014). Although there are still a myriad of questions and concerns about the wisdom of developing and offering MOOCs, many academic institutions have found it to their advantage to offer their own version of MOOCs or MOOC-like courses. Two of the most cited reasons to try MOOCs are to (1) "increase institution visibility" or market the institution, and (2) "drive student recruitment" or increase enrollment (Blake, 2014; Drake, 2014).

As implemented, the MOOC concept is simple:

> A highly qualified professor offers an online noncredit "class" free to any-one willing to listen. The system allows students from around the globe to learn from renowned academics, who in turn are able to reach many more people than could ever fit inside a traditional classroom. (Drake, 2014)

There are numerous criticisms and assessments that MOOCs have not fulfilled their promise and that their real deficiency is *"more fundamental than just the dropout problem"* (Wetterstrom, 2014). Nevertheless, there remains much hope that MOOCs can offer valuable learning opportunities, especially in a context where the lack of access to education has become an impediment to progress and growth, as in the case of developing countries.

The Context of Developing Countries: Philippines in Focus

Development-oriented organizations use different terms to refer to the con-text or description of developing countries. Hence, it is not unusual to hear of "less-developed countries," "least developed countries," "small island developing states," and "landlocked developing countries" (Library of Congress Collections Policy Statements, 2008). The United Nations uses three criteria to determine whether a country can be classified as developing or least developed: (1) Gross National Income (GNI) per capita; (2) Human Assets Index (HAI); and (3) the Economic Vulnerability Index (EVI) (United Nations, 2013).

Education has a direct impact on the second criteria, HAI, which consists of four components, each contributing an equal weight (25 percent) to the overall measure. These components are: (1) the percentage of population that is under-nourished; (2) the mortality rate of children aged 5 years and under; (3) gross secondary enrollment ratio; and (4) adult literacy rate. On the other hand, education has an indirect impact on GNI per capita given that this is the measure of the income status of a country or the value of the products and services produced by that country (World Bank, 2014).

In the case of the Philippines, in 2013, the country registered a GNI of US$3,270 comparable only with Egypt (US$3,160), Vanuatu (US$3,130), and Guatemala (US$3,340). It is substantially higher than Vietnam (US$1,730) and Lao PDR (US$1,460), but lags substantially behind many of its other neighbors in the Asian region: Thailand (US$5,370), Singapore (US$54,040), Malaysia (US$10,400), and Hong Kong (US$38,420). The GNI of the Philippines is demonstrably lower than that experienced in highly developed countries such as the US (US$53,670), Japan (US$46,140), France (US$42,250), Germany (US$46,100), and the UK (US$39,110) (World Bank, 2014).

The Philippines GNI is a reflection of the educational situation in the Philippines as follows:

> High drop out rates of 6% for elementary and almost 8% for secondary mean many students do not complete their education and do not acquire skills needed for jobs in a modern middle-income economy. From 1,000 students who begin schooling at Grade 1, only 650 complete elementary school. Of these, only 430 graduate from high school, and 230 enter college, but only 120 will get a degree (12% of the number who started). Most who drop out are among the poorest and cannot afford the costs associated even with free basic education and college. Like their parents, the drop outs are destined for low-skill jobs and unemployment, repeating the cycle of a life of poverty. (Arangkada Philippines, 2014)

This situation in education is also reflected in the labor sector in the Philippines where unemployment and underemployment have become the dominant characteristics.

> Unemployment Rate in Philippines averaged 9.01 percent from 1994 until 2013, reaching an all time high of 13.90 percent in the first quarter of 2000 and a record low of 6.30 percent in the third quarter of 2007. Among the unemployed persons in April of 2014, 61.7 percent were males. Of the

total unemployed, the age group 25 to 34 comprised 30.5 percent. By educational attainment, one-fifth (22.4 percent) of the unemployed were college graduates, 14.5 percent were college undergraduates, and 32.7 percent were high school graduates. (Lopez, June 2014)

The Department of Labor and Employment (DOLE) cited job mismatch as one of the top factors in explaining why there are many unemployed Filipinos today. While "there are many jobs available for jobless Filipinos, many of them, unfortunately, are not qualified" (Waga, 2014).

MOOCs for the Philippines

The University of the Philippines Open University (UPOU) has always been an advocate of openness in education. The MOOC model of delivering instructional content has provided the opportunity to push this advocacy further and make quality education accessible for the Filipino learners all over the world. The connectivist and constructivist pedagogy of teaching and learning in the digital age that characterizes the UPOU online courses was also integrated into its MOOC offerings. The university has adapted ICT and maximized Web 2.0 affordances as it has turned to learner-centered and highly flexible elearning and distributed learning as key components of its operations. Closely aligned with its guiding philosophy of learning and knowledge, this push for an online constructivist pedagogy embraces the notion that learners and teachers are co-creators of academic texts.

The UPOU is one of the constituent units of the premier university in the Philippines; namely, the University of the Philippines. Established in 1995 to further democratize access to higher-quality education by offering degree and non-degree programs through distance education, the university now offers 27 degree programs, including two programs at the doctoral level. In 2001, the university started offering its courses online and in 2007 it became 100 percent online with the digitized course materials and the use of Moodle for its learning management system (LMS). In 2013, the uLearn Project was established to serve as umbrella project for all MOOC initiatives that the university undertakes and to emphasize the integration of research into these initiatives.

MODeLing MOOC

In developing its own MOOCs, UPOU came face to face with the many concerns and issues surrounding this form of instruction. Some of the most pressing issues and challenges are:

1. The quality of education, which covers the issue of cheating and plagiarism (Anders, 2012), and appropriate assessment mechanisms, considering the massive enrollment.
2. The initial investment and sustainability model.

3. Appropriate learner support model or framework and whether the university can provide it, considering the massive course enrollment.
4. Recognition and accreditation by the industry and other academic institutions. Significant potential resistance among educational institutions is anticipated considering the possible impact of this development to their revenue model.

Added to these assorted issues and challenges, which became major concerns in the Philippines setting, are the global experiences and perspectives related to MOOCs, which include the perceived intellectual neocolonialism resulting from the one-way transfer of educational materials from the rich North to the much poorer South (Rivard, 2013), and the widely reported low course completion rates of MOOC participants (Quillen, 2013).

In the Philippines, the specific discourse on openness in education and involvement in areas of openness such as MOOCs revolves around three inter-related issues: (1) access, (2) quality, and (3) transnational education. Drawing upon its more than ten years of experience in being a distance elearning institution, UPOU designed its MOOCs to address most if not all of the above listed challenges in a holistic manner.

Quality of Instruction through the QA for ODeL Framework

To address the concern about the quality of instruction in MOOCs, UPOU adopted the Quality Assurance (QA) for Open and Distance eLearning (ODeL) framework that it had been already using for its regular distance elearning courses. This quality framework incorporated domains or benchmarks of quality in open and distance elearning usually discussed in literature. These benchmarks, which comprise UPOU's *I Teach IDEA* quality framework, include: institutional support or commitment (I), teaching, support staff, and the teaching learning environment or hub (Teach); IT infrastructure (I); design of learning and instruction (D); evaluation or continuous research and monitoring of the initiative (E); and the assessment of and for learning (A) (Frydenberg, 2002; Phipps, & Merisotis, 2000; Jung, Wong, Li, Baigaltugs, & Belawati 2011). By adapting this *I Teach IDEA* framework, several other common concerns which challenge MOOCs have also been addressed.

MOOC offerings are developed by the UPOU, which is known for its quality standard. It is, therefore, anticipated that the same quality standards will be applied to all of its course offerings. The "Teach" component of the framework includes how teaching will be conducted in a MOOC, including the teaching–learning environment or the LMS which will be used for MOOCs. Through a process dubbed as MOOCathon, the university academics started the "unending conversation" on MOOCs to try to come up with mechanisms to address the Teach component. For instance, part of the MOOCathon is a design thinking workshop to come up with the specifics of a desirable LMS for MOOCs.

Designing the LMS for UPOU's MOOCs was done through crowd sourcing and the full use of open source courseware. The first LMS to be tested was powered by Moodle with various free and open plug-ins. The LMS features took into consideration a number of aspects of the design of the teaching and learning design of their courses such as allowing direct instructions from the teachers, academic discussions and interaction among learners, automated assessments or quizzes to facilitate assessment for learning, blogging, and peer assessment. Providing the opportunity for learners to interact with one another aims to provide a sense of belongingness which distance learners often look for and the lack of which could result in course dropouts.

In designing the assessments, extra measures were taken to minimize, if not totally eliminate the possibility of cheating and plagiarism. Most of the assessments developed would require learners to engage in contextualized case analysis, and providing the answer within a given duration, e.g., five minutes by video capture using the plug-in YouTube Anywhere. Students' responses to assessments questions were uploaded to YouTube for marking by the teacher or assigned marker. Learners were instructed to set their YouTube account to private, thereby allowing only those who know the requisite Web link to access the material.

Such security measures prevent other learners from copying the responses of their peers in the course. Moreover, a student's entire assembly of coursework will be uploaded in the learner's ePortfolio which can be used when applying for jobs and when assessing student's learning for certification purposes. Hopefully, these assessment mechanisms will address the issue of certification and recognition of Certificates of Accomplishment as well as cheating and plagiarism, which has become a common concern in online courses.

Partnership with Industry

Offering MOOCs in partnership with industry can address the following concerns based on the experience of UPOU: the initial capital investment; sustainability; industry recognition of the Certificate of Accomplishment; and even quality of content. In the Android Apps Development MOOC, UPOU fortuitously partnered with one of the leading telecommunication companies in the country and with an association of business processing companies for MOOCs that provide skills and knowledge to those who desire to be part of this industry. For these MOOCs, industry practitioners became the subject matter experts who have developed course content as well as the industry-accepted rubrics to evaluate learners' progress and responses to assessments. The involvement of the industry in the development of teaching materials, co-teaching these MOOCs, and in marking the assessment associated with certification of MOOC learners is intended, in part, to make the industry more confident of the relevance of the content while simultaneously becoming aware of the integration of industry practices in evaluating knowledge and skills for their manpower requirements.

Learner Support

Two factors became major considerations in the development of the learner support framework for MOOCs at the UPOU: the massive enrollment in the courses which implies that there will be a diverse set of background, skills, and the context of learners; and the fact that the potential learners lack extensive experience in distance elearning. In the initial MOOC offerings, learner support was provided during pre-course enrollment, while taking the course, and post-course completion.

The pre-course enrollment support consisted of detailed text announcements about the course itself like the schedule of offering, link to the course site, how to sign up or register to the course, and specific technical requirements e.g., Android gadget, camera, etc. In addition, there were video orientations about the university, instructions on how to use the LMS, and a Distance Education Readiness module which gave learners some preparation about how to go about distance elearning, including posting on discussion forums, replying to posts by fellow learners, taking quizzes, and uploading files/assignments.

After course sign up, learners were also provided with a Course Guide that contained their course requirements, their schedule, and other policies that the learners have to consider. Support during or while taking the course consisted of email announcements when new files were uploaded or a new activity was about to start—as well as reminders of an upcoming quiz or deadline related to the submission of course requirements. Learners who had been inactive for some considerable time (e.g., three weeks), were also sent mass email reminders that they could still complete the course requirements and get the Certificate of Accomplishment. Assessment for learning, such as automated quizzes with immediate feedback to students, could also be considered learner support since they provide learners with information regarding their learning progress concerning the course content. Finally, post-course completion support deals with assessment for certification concerns.

It should be noted that asynchronous technical support in the form of Help Tickets was integrated into the learner support framework before, during, and after completing the course. A technical team was tasked to address the requests for assistance forwarded through these Help Tickets.

The learner support component of MOOC offering was envisioned to address the low completion rate of MOOCs as well as it being one of the benchmarks or domains of quality in distance elearning.

Recognition by Academic Institutions or MOOC for Credits

Ideally, completed MOOCs should be credited towards a degree under the Accreditation of Prior Learning (APL) framework. This aspect has been considered in the MOOCs for the business process management industry. These courses have been integrated into the tertiary education curriculum on information technology and management through a memorandum circular from the Philippines Commission on Higher Education (CHED). Academic institutions offering these courses can have their students enrolled in UPOU MOOCs, get the Certificate of Accomplishment, and apply for the transfer of equivalent credits so that these courses can fulfill the partial requirements of their degree. MOOC completion and the associated learning which is supposed to occur as a result of taking the course is attested by the Certificate of Accomplishment, the branding for which implies passing the standard set by the university (e.g., passing the assessments—both formative and summative). This branding is designed to address the recognition and accreditation for MOOCs and to differentiate it from the usual Statement of Accomplishment usually given by MOOC providers.

Sustainability Model

Courses are free, but there are costs associated with offering a MOOC—such as assessing students, the hosting of LMS, and providing learner support. The sustainability model considered for UPOU MOOCs consists of certification for a fee (to cover the cost of assessment), grants and industry support, and work credit for extension/community work for university personnel.

The process by which UPOU planned, designed, and delivered its own MOOCs involved active search and evaluation of an appropriate model that could be adapted for its own MOOC. Referred to as Massive Open Distance eLearning (or MODeL for short), courses under this framework also exhibit a "coherent academic engagement with a defined set of learning outcomes" (Youell, 2011), are shorter than the usual degree or credit course offerings of the university running for eight weeks at the most, are maximizing the use of learning tools such as an LMS with the desired plug-ins, and the primary distinguishing factor which is openness to anyone who is interested in being a part of this unique teaching and learning environment.

UPOU's move to offer its MOOCs can be considered an effort to address the concern of intellectual neocolonialism which, as noted earlier, is also happening in the MOOC movement. MOOCs are often associated with well-known universities or branded names (e.g., UPenn, Duke, the University of Michigan, Korea Advanced Institute of Science and Technology (KAIST), Nanyang Technological University in Singapore, the University of Edinburgh, etc.). This connection to the elite institutions is not too surprising given that the two professors who started Coursera (www.coursera.org) were from Stanford University. Similarly, edX (www.edx.org) emerged from a partnership between Harvard and the Massachusetts Institute of Technology and now includes such partners as the University of Tokyo, Rice University, Tsinghua University, the University of Toronto, and Berkeley. In contrast to Coursera and edX, the UPOU MOOC can be considered as a form of South to South cooperation.

Profile of MOOC Learners in the Philippines

There was some concern about whether the first few UPOU MOOCs were able to fulfill their promise of making education more widely available, especially to the marginalized sectors of society. In the first MOOC on Android Apps Development, 91 percent of the learners were based in the Philippines and these came mostly from the metropolitan areas. This figure closely matched the geographical profile of UPOU students enrolled in the degree programs probably because this particular MOOC was advertised only through the university website. In the succeeding MOOCs, there was a slight increase in the proportion of learners based outside the country due to the wider dissemination of information about the MOOC offerings but the proportion of those coming from the rural areas remained low.

In terms of the gender profile, initial observations revealed the significant influence of the nature of the course. In the Android Apps MOOC, the majority (63 percent) of the learners were male—something which was anticipated given the technical nature of the course. The profile for the Service Management MOOC, in contrast, was dramatically different—with 62 percent of the learners being female. For the age profile, 75 percent of the students were in the 20–40 age bracket or those who were born and grew up during the rise of the Information Age, the Internet (dot.com) bubble, and a time of intense digital globalization (see Isacosta's Site, n.d.). The age range of MOOC learners, 15 as the youngest and 57 as the oldest, is indicative of the lifelong learning opportunities that MOOCs can provide. Those with college degrees comprised 48 percent, indicating an interest from working professionals to learn something new that is aligned to their interests or current job requirements. The competencies acquired could also be additional credentials for future employment.

Insights from the Philippine Experience

1. A MOOC is just like any other distance elearning course. The only substantive difference is that it is open, and, therefore, that it can enroll as many students as possible. Consequently, the principles and processes that determine quality in distance elearning can also be considered in the case of MOOCs.
2. The learning design and assessment mechanics of a MOOC are very much dependent on the learning goals. Therefore, a MOOC could be implemented from a direct instruction or a connectivist perspective, or from a combination of both. The pedagogical aspect of the MOOC should always take precedence in addressing the learning perspective intended.
3. In selecting courses that can be offered as a MOOC, a major consideration is the set of skills that the participants will acquire at the end of the course. This set of skills should be market-driven and in accordance with what is desired by major industries.

4. Partnership with industry can directly address concerns related to the initial capital investment required, the recognition of certification, and the model selected for sustainability.
5. A state-funded academic institution may be able to sustain the offering of a MOOC given its mandate of being a public service institution.
6. National-level policies and directives are essential to address the quality of education that will be made available through distance education and MOOCs.

Situating MOOCs in Developing Countries: Options and Directions

Almost two years after the declared "Year of the MOOC" (Pappano, 2012), the future of MOOCs in higher education institutions around the world is still highly uncertain and widely debated (Drake, 2014). Many believe that MOOCs are not a threat to residential campuses. In fact, they argue that the low completion rate of MOOCs highlights the importance and the value of residential instruction. MOOC advocates, in contrast, argue that any type of education—face-to-face, online, or blended—is worthwhile if it can benefit learners who previously lacked access or who were disadvantaged in some way. While there are already talks of "MOOC for credit" and "MOOC towards a degree," the conservative view that MOOCs are not at par with the kind of education delivered face-to-face still predominates.

However, there is also the view that MOOCs are challenging residential instruction in many ways and they may find niche areas in which significant impact will be felt, such as teacher professional development.

MOOCs in developing countries are making an impact. The following mechanisms might be considered in planning for MOOCs and MOOC-related ideas in the context of developing countries and regions of the world.

1. Plan for a blended delivery mode that takes into consideration issues related to the digital divide. Aside from implementing MOOCs directly to the learners, a blended approach can be incorporated as noted below.

    a. Higher education institutions (HEIs) use the materials made available in MOOCs as additional course resources (i.e., open educational resources (OERs)) for their own teaching as a means to enhance the quality of instruction in their respective institutions.
    b. HEIs enroll their students in MOOCs that are similar to the courses they are offering, thereby maximizing the learning opportunities provided by MOOCs and supplementing them with residential instruction and assessment mechanisms being practiced by the academic institution.

    c.   HEIs directly credit the MOOCs taken by the students towards a degree. The academic institution may opt to give challenge exams to validate the learning of the students seeking credits for MOOCs completed.

2.   Bridge the education–industry requirement gaps and mismatches. For instance, MOOCs can be offered as short training courses designed to provide specific sets of skills and knowledge to the talent pool of targeted industries. The corollary to this is the provision of opportunities to early school leavers or those who have yet to complete tertiary education, to acquire relevant knowledge and skills for employment or even to earn credits towards a degree.

3.   Provide lifelong learning opportunities, especially to the industry workforce as a means to provide a competitive skill base amidst the fast-changing skill requirements of most jobs. Such learning opportunities are especially vital for teacher professional development.

Specific to the Philippines, while there is an opportunity for academic institutions to offer online courses and even MOOCs, not all HEIs are allowed to do so. There are government policies and regulations which specify the guidelines and requirements for curriculum and delivery systems, instructional materials development, delivery mode and strategies, and student support services. As a result of these requirements, only a few institutions have been able to adopt flexible modes of instructional delivery. There are also government guidelines regarding Transnational Education (TNE) engagements, particularly in terms of capacities of institutions, legality, equivalency, accreditation, and transparency. These are government efforts to promote greater openness in education and at the same time address the quality of education that impacts not only the Filipinos but those learners located outside the country and enrolled in such courses.

Summary

Despite some progress in terms of MOOC design and delivery at the UPOU, there are many issues and concerns that surround MOOC deployment in its current format. The development and implementation of various MOOC-related teaching and learning initiatives continue to unfold as institutions engage in using different frameworks designed to address an assortment of issues and concerns. The important role of MOOCs in developing countries cannot be overemphasized as this new form of instructional delivery offers an opportunity for open access to education and the continuous acquisition of knowledge and skills. However, there should be efforts on the part of both academic institutions and governmental agencies to maximize the potential of MOOCs for them to genuinely serve lifelong learners and effect the overall development of the country and its people.

Melinda dela Pena Bandalaria is a professor at the University of the Philippines Open University where she also serves as Dean of the Faculty of Information and Communication studies. She handles distance elearning courses at both the undergraduate and graduate levels and is actively involved in research and community development projects. Mel has helped coordinate international conferences on open education and written extensively on elearning in the Philippines. She was a panelist and key participant in the preconference symposium at E-Learn 2013 in Las Vegas which led to this book.

Grace Javier Alfonso is a professor of Film and Mass Communication. She has been the University of the Philippines Open University Chancellor since 2007 and is now serving her third term. She is the current President of the Philippine Society for Distance Learning. She is also Chair of the Philippine Commission on Higher Education (CHED) Technical Panel for Transnational and Distance Education.

References

Anders, G. (2012). Are they learning or cheating? Online teaching's dilemma. *Forbes*. Retrieved from http://www.forbes.com/sites/georgeanders/2012/08/16/are-they-learning-or-cheating-online-teachings-dilemma/?&_suid=141087518605007.

Arangkada Philippines. (2014). *Education*. Retrieved from http://www.investphilippines.info/arangkada/climate/education/.

Blake, D. (2014). New data on online education, MOOCs. *MOOC Musings*. Retrieved from http://moocs.com/index.php/new-data-on-online-education/.

Drake, M. (2014, February 9). Old School rules! Wisdom of massive open online courses now in doubt. *The Washington Times*. Retrieved from http://www.washingtontimes.com/news/2014/feb/9/big-plan-on-campus-is-dropping-out/?page=all.

Frydenberg, J. (2002). Quality standards in e-learning: A matrix of analysis. *International Review of Research on Open and Distance Learning*, 3(2). Retrieved from http://www.irrodl.org/index.php/irrodl/article/view/109/551.

The Institute for Higher Education Policy. (2000). *Quality on the line. Benchmarks for the success in Internet-based distance education*. Retrieved from http://www.americanbar.org/content/dam/aba/migrated/legaled/distanceeducation/QualityOnTheLine.authcheckdam.pdf.

Isacosta's site (n.d.). *List of generations chart*. Retrieved from http://www.esds1.pt/site/images/stories/isacosta/secondary_pages/10%C2%BA_block1/Generations%20Chart.pdf.

Jung, I., Wong, T. M., Li, C., Baigaltugs, S., & Belawati, T. (2011). Quality assurance in Asian distance education: Diverse approaches and common culture. *International Review of Research on Open and Distance Learning, 12*(6). Retrieved from http://www.irrodl. org/index.php/irrodl/article/view/991/1953.

Library of Congress Collections Policy Statements. (2008, November). Retrieved from http://www.loc.gov/acq/devpol/devcountry.pdf.

Lopez, E. (2014, June 10). Unemployment rate eases to 7% in April. *Manila Bulletin.* Retrieved from http://www.mb.com.ph/unemployment-rate-eases-to-7-in-april/.

Pappano, L. (2012, November 2). The year of the MOOC. *New York Times.* Retrieved from http://www.nytimes.com/2012/11/04/education/edlife/massive-open-online-courses-are-multiplying-at-a-rapid-pace.html?pagewanted=all&_r=0.

Phipps, R., & Merisotis, J. (2000, April). *Quality on the line: Benchmarks for success in Internet-based/distance education.* Institute for Higher Education Policy. Washington, DC. Retrieved from http://www.nea.org/assets/docs/HE/QualityOnTheLine.pdf.

Quillen, I. (2013, April 5). Why do students enroll in (but don't complete) MOOC courses? *Mind/Shift.* Retrieved from http://blogs.kqed.org/mindshift/2013/04/why-do-students-enroll-in-but-dont-complete-mooc-courses/.

Rivard, R. (2013, April 25). The world is not flat. *Inside Higher Education.* Retrieved from https://www.insidehighered.com/news/2013/04/25/moocs-may-eye-world-market-does-world-want-them.

Tabonda, J. (2014, September 10). Philippines unemployment rate. National Statistics Office. Retrieved from http://www.tradingeconomics.com/philippines/unemployment-rate.

United Nations. (2013, August). *LDC information: The criteria for identifying least developed countries.* Department of Economics and Social Affairs (DESA). Development Policy and Analysis Division. Retrieved from http://www.un.org/en/development/desa/policy/cdp/ldc/ldc_criteria.shtml.

Waga, B. (2014). Job mismatch causes unemployment problems—DOLE. *Kicker Daily News.* Retrieved from http://kickerdaily.com/job-mismatch-causes-unemployment-problems-dole/.

Wetterstrom, L. (2014, January 28). The year after the year of MOOC. *The Gate.* Retrieved from http://uchicagogate.com/2014/01/28/years-after-mooc/.

World Bank (2014). *GNI per capita, Atlas method (current US$).* Retrieved from http://data.worldbank.org/indicator/NY.GNP.PCAP.CD).

Youell, A. (2011, December). *What is a course?* London: Higher Education Statistics Agency. Retrieved from http://www.hesa.ac.uk/dox/publications/The_Course_Report.pdf.

22

OER AND MOOCs IN AFRICA

The AVU Experience

Griff Richards and Bakary Diallo

It is estimated that only 6 percent of Africans can access post-secondary education. The development goal is set at 12 percent, even though the figures for North America and Europe are somewhere around 45 percent. The gap is huge. This is not to say that African nations are not investing in post-secondary education. For example, Nigeria has been steadily building universities during the past couple of decades and it now has 102 universities with over one million places (Aluede, Idogho, & Imonikhe, 2012). However, Okeke (2008) notes that roughly 85 percent of qualified Nigerian applicants still cannot find places in these universities since the population continues to grow faster than campuses can be built and faculty recruited.

Building Capacity through Distance Learning

The African Virtual University (AVU), with funding from the African Development Bank for the Multi-National Project Phase II (MNP II), seeks to encourage sub-Saharan universities to build capacity to deliver education through open, distance, and e-learning (ODeL). Open means anyone can try the courses, thereby enabling access to those who were not in the top 5 percent in their university entrance exams and those who can afford to pay tuition. Distance means the learners seldom have to attend campus—they can complete the better part of their study at home or in a rural setting. Finally, elearning increases the scalability of courses; more courses can be offered to more students by leveraging Africa's rapidly developing Internet capabilities as well as the wide use of mobile devices. In short, elearning has the potential to increase capacity faster than the construction of traditional face-to-face campuses.

Building capacity for elearning faces many barriers in Africa (Diallo, 2014), including the following:

1. The ICT infrastructures of African countries are much less extensive than those in the developed world. Only in the last two years have the transoceanic fiber networks connected major African seaports with the rest of the world. From the coast, high bandwidth cabling now runs inland to major cities, and telecommunications providers are busy digging up urban streets to install dark fiber. Most rural areas have little or no high-bandwidth Internet. Where there is access, this is generally provided via satellites or the increasing spread of mobile networks. Although there is much interest in cloud computing, little affordable infrastructure has developed. Furthermore, electrical power is neither ubiquitous nor stable. Some major cities such as Lagos (population 17 million) rely on private power generators for a few hours each day. Many in rural areas are expanding their use of solar energy for lighting as well as for charging mobile phones.
2. There are few personal computers. A recent World Bank report (Crandall, Otieno, Mutuku & Colaço, 2012) notes that 80 percent of Africans who access the Internet do so via their mobile phones, but they note smartphone uptake is still primarily limited to professionals and students in urban areas.
3. There is a shortage of skilled ICT professionals, especially outside the major centers. At a recent AVU stakeholders meeting, it was noted that the shortage of up-to-date equipment in universities means that most computer scientists graduate with extensive theoretical knowledge but only limited practical experience.
4. There is limited experience with distance education or elearning within the traditional face-to-face universities.

As a result, tackling elearning as an educational delivery mechanism means having strategies for several fronts (Diallo & Richards, 2014), including one or more of the following:

1. Where there is weak infrastructure, enhance whatever connectivity exists. AVU's MNPII, mentioned earlier, provides each participating institution with equipment and connectivity. In some cases, the enabling technologies still mean providing satellite dishes and power generators.
2. Computers can be provided to set up ODeL Centres for participating institutions. However, the elearning materials need to be optimized for the possibility for mobile learning.
3. AVU and 18 participating institutions are developing a new ODeL Applied Computer Science Program.
4. AVU is updating and expanding the materials in its ODeL Teacher Education programs with 12 universities.

5. AVU is coordinating the development of faculty skills through the creation of modules for online learning as well as through a faculty professional development program for ODeL.
6. Short-term projects need to be reinforced with support for the creation and facilitation of sustainable communities of practice for elearning.

Key to the AVU strategy is the collaborative development of distance learning modules involving faculty from 27 participating universities in 21 countries. Since the majority of the African population simply cannot afford most textbooks, it is critical to ensure relevant content is embedded in the modules. Given that our goal is to disseminate educational content in English, French, and Portuguese, we make an attempt to engage faculty in each language as translations have proven expensive, and in many instances lacking in attention to scientific jargon, secondary references, and graphics. Next, the modules are peer-reviewed for content and organizational quality. If translations are necessary, these are also peer-reviewed. Dissemination under a Creative Commons license (CC-BY-SA) as open educational resources (OER) means educators can freely adopt or adapt the materials for local use.

To date, the AVU has left the delivery of academic programs to the 27 participating institutions. It has been considered that they are best placed to tailor course content and delivery to meet local needs. However, AVU is involved with the professional development of academics to develop, manage, and deliver ODeL programs. A significant deliverable of our multinational project involves the professional development of ODeL faculty and staff in the participating institutions. Each trained group can work as a team to plan, launch, and support ODeL at their institution. They also can provide workshops ("cascade training") to other interested faculty on their campuses. Always looking for better ways to implement this "cascade training," we recently started to examine the potential of MOOCs for this purpose.

MOOCs in the African Context

The massive online open course (MOOC) phenomenon has now arrived in Africa and many Africans have enrolled in the free online courses offered by American, European, and Indian universities. These courses tend to stick to the 13-week academic formula and have enrolments in the thousands or tens of thousands. However, only about 5 percent of learners actually finish these massive courses.

The learner completion statistic is interesting given that approximately 83 percent of MOOC enrollees, including those from developing countries, already hold university degrees (Christensen, Steinmetz, Alcorn, Bennett, Woods, & Emanuel, 2013). Presumably these experienced learners are not finding the MOOCs sufficiently engaging to hold their attention. Although massive amounts of data have been analyzed about learner engagement in MOOCs (see, among others, Christensen et al., 2013; Perna, Ruby, Boruch, Wang, Scull, Evans, & Ahmad, 2013), engagement usually is defined as watching videos, accessing questions, or completing assignments, rather than probing for intellectual engagement as discussed by Richards (2011). Since half of MOOC registrants enroll out of simple curiosity, it is unsurprising that many will drop out when the course becomes less entertaining, or requires some active participation.

Short, focused non-academic courses seem to have higher completion rates. For example, a six-week course in perinatal care in Africa reported some 35,000 participants and completion rates of around 65 percent (S. Einarson, personal communication, 2013). Similar high success rates were reported in a short three-week management skills program by the African Management Initiative (R. Harrison, personal communication, 2014). These experiences suggest that MOOCs may be better focused on professional development topics than on full-term academic courses. AVU will start by using a MOOC-type approach for focused faculty development activities as well as courses for the general public such as peace management and conflict resolution. Even with a 50 percent drop-out rate, such a MOOC would be successful in raising awareness about these issues. In addition, if the content were left open and available, faculty could return to it whenever additional information is needed.

In the case of faculty development, faculty members might benefit greatly by discussing and sharing promising practices. Consequently, a constructivist-style course site would enable AVU to deliver high-quality faculty development courses across Africa. Given there are about 640 universities in Africa, if one hundred faculty members were to be trained in ODeL methods at each university, then that would yield 64,000 potential enrolments.

However, our strategy is to start with smaller numbers (a "mini-MOOC"?) and allow the offerings to scale up as we gain experience and smooth out the delivery of our courses. Working collaboratively, AVU also hopes to enlist the assistance of faculty developers in participating institutions to help deliver the program, thereby strengthening local support networks in each institution. Familiarity with the platform would, in turn, increase the likelihood that the faculty development facilitators develop and deliver additional topics. AVU is also considering a similar constructivist approach for a potential series of public seminars in peace building where there may be advantages to interacting with and becoming part of a larger network of peace workers.

Regardless of the type of MOOC deployed, our focus will be on quality of the learning experience rather than the quantity of enrolments. The MOOC approach may be seen to be most appropriate when it enables the scalable delivery of courses at a distance and avoids access barriers imposed by on-campus delivery. At the same time, the MOOC structure could also be used with small numbers of learners in ready-to-go templated courses that could be easily capitalized on by our partnering institutions.

North American MOOCs on the Coursera and edX platforms made exten-sive use of digital video to deliver introductions, captured lectures, or provided Khan Academy-style tutorials. While bandwidth and connectivity are improving in Africa, this heavy use of video is not realistic for African learners located in rural areas. This is probably just as well given that recent analysis of over six mil-lion edX video interactions by Guo, Kim, and Rubin (2014) noted that even in bandwidth-rich areas, viewers have a low tolerance for anything that drones on for more than a few minutes. As a result, they recommend keeping videos under six minutes in length as well as anchoring clips with the occasional head shot and utilizing an informal or conversational style of language. Importantly, Guo et al. (2014) found learners more engaged with the single-topic Khan-style tutorials than in listening to lectures that covered a wider range of topics.

Indeed, perhaps part of the reason why MOOCs have failed to engage learn-ers is that many have attempted to reproduce the classroom lecture experience rather than to take advantage of the high-engagement opportunities possible with the use of new media. Problems encountered with such an approach serve as a reminder that thoughtfully crafted instructional design can make any course more effective simply by ensuring an alignment of content, media, and formative assessments with the intended learning outcomes. In the design of any media for MOOCs in Africa, those on the design team need to be careful to ensure that glitz does not get in the way of learning, and that the core presentation of con-tent, be it text or video, is available in multiple formats to accommodate those in low-bandwidth areas as well as diverse learners. Along these same lines, MOOC designers need to add captions for easier understanding and utilize brief videos to optimize viewing times while reducing potential file transfer problems. Clearly, there is still a lot to be said for the instructional advantages of text, especially on the African continent and in other parts of the globe with limited bandwidth.

Realizing the Potential

For post-secondary educators, these are interesting times. Never before has so much educational content been available for free to so many potential learners. However, given completion rates, perhaps we should not get too excited just yet about the potential for academic MOOCs. In Africa, the attrition of learn-ers from primary education through secondary to post-secondary education is already high. Africa also has a significant urban–rural divide in terms of basic infrastructure such as dependable electrical power and broadband access to the Internet. Basic literacy remains a challenge and, in some countries, there is a size-able gender gap with significantly fewer females accessing all levels of education compared to males. MOOCs may offer interesting learning opportunities but there are many other access issues for basic education that are calling for attention.

Open Distance and eLearning from organizations like the AVU has much potential to improve or elevate the educational opportunities and attainments of learners across the continent. However, ODeL must build on the success of primary and secondary education as well as the existing initiatives related to adult literacy. eLearners also need to learn about information and communications technology (ICT) and how to learn in their new online environment. The potential rewards are tremendous for the emergent "global learner" to truly become free to learn anything anywhere. With access to post-secondary education soaring beyond the current levels, there is hope that economic and social development will follow.

As with any seed, growth depends upon careful nurturing. AVU's teacher education materials were particularly successful in Senegal where the alignment of effort among government, university, and school authorities resulted in the training of some 13,000 previously unqualified teachers—an improvement for both educational quality and teacher retention rates, especially in rural areas (B. Diallo—personal communication, 2014). In another example, the University of Nairobi, a partner of the AVU, has developed 23 learning centers across Kenya capable of providing administration, examinations, and access for up to 7,000 learners annually (H. Kidombo—personal communication, 2014). In the period 2010 to 2012, AVU has logged over two million accesses to its online repositories—almost 25 percent of them from Brazil. In addition, we have learned of a university in Sri Lanka implementing a program based on our open curriculum.

Clearly, developing OER for Africa not only builds capacity in the continent, but also provides a benefit to the rest of the world. While we are still at the initial stages of the development and evaluation of MOOCs, open education in its various forms is an important initiative. With the support of the African Development Bank, the AVU and its institutional partners in 22 countries are taking a leadership role in improving educational access in Africa in the hopes that this investment will trigger social and economic improvement for generations to come.

 **Griff Richards** is a Canadian e-learning researcher and an advocate of open education. Griff received his doctorate in educational technology from Concordia University. Among his many accomplishments, Griff set up British Columbia's online francophone high school and designed distance courses for Thompson Rivers University, Open Learning. In addition, he has participated in several European research projects, was Foreign Research Fellow at the Open University of Japan, and has designed open education modules in Africa. Griff Richards is an Honored Professor in the Institute of Social Sciences and Humanities in Kazan, Tatarstan. Griff currently teaches Instructional Design at Athabasca University where he is Fellow of the Technology Enhanced Knowledge Research Institute (TEKRI). He can be contacted at griff@sfu.ca and his portfolio is at: athabascau.academia.edu/GriffRichards.

Bakary Diallo earned a PhD in Educational Administration from the University of Ottawa, Canada. He joined the African Virtual University in 2005 and was appointed Rector in 2007. His latest research activities promote the use of ICT in higher educational institutions with a focus on the development and delivery of open education resources. He is fully bilingual in French and English.

References

Aluede, O., Idogho, P.O., & Imonikhe, J.S. (2012). Increasing access to university education in Nigeria: Present challengers and suggestions for the future. *The African Symposium, 12*(1), 3–13. Retrieved from http://www.ncsu.edu/aern/TAS12.1/TAS12.1.pdf.

Christensen, G., Steinmetz, A., Alcorn, B., Bennett, A., Woods, D., & Emanuel, E.J. (2013). The MOOC phenomenon: Who takes massive open online courses and why? [Working Paper]. Retrieved from http://ssrn.com/abstract=2350964.

Crandall, A., Otieno, A., Mutuku, L., Colaço, J., Grosskurth, J. & Otieno, P. (2012). Mobile Usage at the base of the pyramid in Kenya [World Bank Report]. Retrieved from https://blogs.worldbank.org/ic4d/files/ic4d/mobile_phone_usage_kenyan_base_pyramid.pdf.

Diallo, B. (2014). Pragmatism before popularity: The African Virtual University's approach to MOOCs. In D. Wagner & J. Sun (Eds.), MOOCs4D: Potential at the bottom of the pyramid. [Conference Report], April 10–11, University of Pennsylvania. http://www.gse.upenn.edu/pdf/moocs4d/moocs_pragmatism.pdf.

Diallo, B., & Richards, G. (2014). Pragmatism before popularity: The African Virtual University's approach to MOOCs. In D. Wagner, & J. Sun (Eds.), *MOOCs4D: Potential at the bottom of the pyramid.* [Conference Report], April 10–11, University of Pennsylvania http://nebula.wsimg.com/832d31b1a1e95f24bb2a8d0b1086fc15?AccessKeyId=A8CECD67C777CBD7A503&disposition=0&alloworigin=1.

Guo, P., Kim, J., & Rubin, R. (2014). How video production affects student engagement: An empirical study of MOOC videos. *Proceedings of the L&S Conference*, March 4–5, Atlanta, GA. Retrieved from http://groups.csail.mit.edu/uid/other-pubs/las2014-pguo-engagement.pdf.

Okeke, E.A.C. (2008). Access in Nigerian education. In B.G. Nworgu & E.I. Eke (Eds.) *Access, quality and cost in Nigerian education.* Proceedings of the 23rd Annual Congress of the Nigerian Academy of Education, pp. 20–34. University of Nigeria, Nsukka, Nigeria.

Perna, L., Ruby, A., Boruch, R., Wang, N., Scull, N., Evans, C., & Ahmad, S. (2013). *The life cycle of a million MOOC users.* Presentation at the MOOC Research Initiative Conference. December 4–5, University of Texas, Arlington, Arlington, Texas. Retrieved from http://www.gse.upenn.edu/pdf/ahead/perna_ruby_boruch_moocs_dec2013.pdf.

Richards, G. (2011). Measuring engagement: Learning analytics in online learning. *Electronic Kazan 2011*. Kazan, Tatarstan, Russian Federation. Retrieved from http://www.academia.edu/779650/Measuring_Engagement_Learning_Analytics_in_Online_Learning.

PART 7

MOOCs and Open Learning Alternatives in Corporate Settings

This recent embrace of MOOCs and open education around the world is not just taking place in higher education settings. While stymied for several years after MOOCs emerged as a viable form of education, corporations and professional organizations are finally beginning to tap into MOOCs and other open forms of learning in a wide array of ways. Many examples of the impact of MOOCs and open education in the workplace are emerging. Interestingly, corporate MOOC provider Udacity has formed the Open Education Alliance to help educate the workforce of tomorrow by providing "nanodegrees" in areas like Web design, coding, interactive 3D graphics, and data analysis. Similarly, Aquent Gymnasium offers free technology courses for creative professionals in Web design, Coding, JavaScript, and similar skill areas. It appears that the corporate world is swiftly moving from a closed world, in terms of education and training practices, to a much more open one. The three chapters in Part 7 help to inform the reader of what is currently happening in this space.

In Chapter 23, Elliot Masie, corporate learning guru, explores the meaning of "open" in the context of corporate learning. The open concept is controversial in the corporate sector where profits and "return on investment" are major goals. In fact, in terms of traditional ways in which corporate learning occurred in the past, such as in face-to-face settings from experts and utilizing e-learning from established context providers, this notion of openness in corporate learning is highly disruptive. As Masie points out, since 2010, content is increasingly being "harvested" from open and public repositories for use in corporate training. Content and access are two important issues that cut both ways with corporations drawing content from public resources such as TED talks and releasing their own content for use in higher education and by individuals. In terms of TED talks and other forms of shared online video, Masie provides the results of a poll he conducted with chief learning officers as to why the use of such video is popular as well as several recommended best practices related to its use. This is just a start. As Masie notes, based on recent trends, the corporate open movement will significantly grow and evolve in the years to come.

In the next chapter, Mike Feerick discusses ALISON, an online learning community that offered what some consider the original MOOC back in 2007 and, to date, has had more than 500,000 graduates worldwide. Feerick, CEO and Founder of ALISON, informs us how learning and upskilling one's competencies within the workplace and beyond is about to become far more dynamic, personalized, and, above all, free. As an example, ALISON.com provides free online learning through 600 openly available courses at Certificate and Diploma levels to over four million learners worldwide. In contrast to MOOCs found at the post-secondary level, ALISON's focus is on workplace knowledge and skills development. Interestingly, the clientele of ALISON has changed significantly since its first course back in 2007. This chapter describes the evolution of the site from early ALISON users such as the librarians, the unemployed, the elderly, and newly arrived immigrants, to more recent use by multinational corporations for technology and leadership training as well as language education. ALISON's system of assessment is also described in this chapter as is the potential for free online learning certification.

Chapter 25 was written by Ray Schroeder and his colleagues at the University of Illinois, Springfield (UIS) where online and blended forms of learning have played pivotal roles for nearly two decades. As part of these efforts, Schroeder is widely known for his daily blogging of current news involving online education as well as his own experimentations with emerging online technologies. As described in this chapter, in fact, he was the first to offer a professional development type of MOOC in the summer of 2011 related to online learning. In this MOOC, more than 2,700 people enrolled from 70 countries; it was the largest MOOC that had ever been offered to that point. Since that time, the UIS Center for Online Learning, Research and Service (COLRS) has been engaged in studying and offering MOOCs in higher education. COLRS has found huge potential in MOOCs as venues for training, professional development, information sharing, and collaboration as well as vehicles for discussions and debates of key public interest topics. In this chapter, Schroeder, and his UIS colleagues, Vickie Cook, Carrie Levin, and Michele Gribbins, discuss various alternative models related to MOOCs, most of them related to corporate settings and professional associations. Schroeder and his colleagues argue that we could be entering a MOOC-enabled future that may play a key role in the transformation of traditional higher education as well as corporate forms of training and education.

23

OPEN LEARNING IN THE CORPORATE SETTING

Elliot Masie

"Open" is an interesting and disruptive word to use about a corporate setting. Yet Open Learning is one of the most provocative and rapidly changing elements of how corporate learning is being harvested, delivered, and packaged. This chapter explores the word "Open" in corporate training settings as applied to content and even access.

Reflecting back, in 2010, there was hardly any open content used in corporate learning environments. Organizations offered face-to-face classroom and e-learning programs with content from two sources: (1) internal expertise or (2) external providers of services or curriculum, such as publishers or universities.

Now, a few short years later, in 2014, we find an enormous and often quiet shift in content sources. More and more content is being "harvested" from open and public repositories. Below are two examples of how this harvesting is making an impact in corporate training settings.

TED Video Disrupts: Almost every major corporation in the United States is making use of a wide range of TED video clips, from both TED's global conferences and TEDx events. TED video content is assigned or leveraged in classroom curriculum where a 6–18-minute video is a substitute for hiring an external expert. Additionally, organizations are using TED videos as part of eLearning programs— from traditional modules to extended viewing elements in development programs.

I polled a series of Chief Learning Officers recently about their use of TED videos and there was an overwhelming sense that these open (e.g., free and clear) segments work for the corporate space since they are:

- **Short in Segment Length:** The TED model supports compression, rehearsal, flow, and repetition.
- **Topically Focused:** Unlike other video clips, TED offers very focused segments on single key topics.

- **Best Online:** The TED video segments that are offered online are already selected as high value and high interest.
- **Branded Credibility:** The TED name adds a stamp of approval for a video segment, indicating that this is important and perhaps a provocative and growing perspective.
- **Access and Rights Are Clear:** The company is clear about TED's rights and access options for use of the video, which makes it cleaner for the company to integrate the video into a segment.

YouTube Video Segments: At the same time, organizations are going wider to look at video segments that they can locate via a Web search, often ending up at YouTube. There is a growing use of YouTube videos in corporate learning offerings, but with a number of key constraints and research requirements. A few of these are listed below.

- **Clearance and Rights:** Just because it is on YouTube does not mean that the organization feels comfortable with corporate use. In many instances, the company does some background checking and affirming that they have the right to leverage a video, particularly if used in-house or as an embedded part of an eLearning program. There is a stated need for better coding or tagging of content rights for these uses.
- **Time Code Selection:** Some YouTube segments go long!!! Organizations are experimenting with using time code selections to have the viewer watch the segment from a specific starting point, like 2 minutes 5 seconds into the video, to a specific end point, like 11 minutes 8 seconds into the video. One tool for segmenting YouTube videos is called TubeChop. Time code selection helps the organization achieve the brevity and focus that is desired.
- **Updating and Framing:** In some instances, a YouTube video segment might have been shot in 2009 and needs to be updated or at least framed for context. Such updating and contextualization can be performed by adding a window for the segment in the middle of a Web page with context and dates included.

There are other versions of open content that are also emerging in the corporate learning space. Four types of open content are noted below.

1. **Association Content:** In the early days of eLearning, many associations naively thought they would get significant revenue for industry-wide content. Now, we are seeing more segment-specific open content for use by member companies in segment-oriented associations like National Retail or National Swimming Pool non-profit entities.
2. **Shared Collections of Content:** In some instances, a number of companies have agreed to create a content-sharing collaboration where each organization shares the best of its knowledge segments for use by other groups.

3. **Higher Education MOOCs and Content:** Some companies are integrating content from MOOCs or other higher education sources as part of their curricula. Depending on the circumstance, this content might be in an open source model or come with an affiliation charge, but it is viewed more as an open content version.

4. **Curated Content:** Corporations are also leveraging content that flows from the learners and users themselves. Learning design is being opened up to both learner-contributed content during or after a course as well as a crowd source design model where content is curated from an expanded set of sources both inside and outside of corporate walls.

Finally, corporations are realizing the upside for sharing their content in a more open form for others outside the organization. This practice might include:

*   Corporate content placed on a public access server for use by individuals who are not employees. Such content might be focused on their main or growing product areas as well as developmental content that future employees might want added to their knowledge base before applying.

*   Sourcing content to higher education: A number of accounting companies have placed their content in a format that can be used by business faculty members and departments in colleges and universities. This approach is seen as a service and also as a branding element that could help with downstream recruitment of students exposed to their curricula.

The world of Open Learning in corporate workplaces is a disrupter in several ways:

*   Downsizing the amount of content that is purchased from external content providers.

*   Reducing the number of days for hired expert speakers. One technology firm informed me that they did not need to hire me anymore for their development programs since my good content was available on the Web. I agreed!

*   Learners have access to wider sets of perspectives, beyond just in-house approved sages on the stage.

*   Learner personalization is enabled by facilitating learners gaining access to content that has relevant context. A learner working with customers in Dubai may gain more knowledge by viewing Emirate faculty members talking about compliance and negotiation. This discussion can include language, background, geography, and even professional history.

*   Content is becoming shorter as it goes "Open." At the Masie Center, we have been tracking a reduction in the duration of content that companies are accessing and using from open sources. The delivered segments are increasingly shorter and more focused.

The other side of open learning in corporate settings is access. Many companies have decided to open access to their learning programs to a wider set of populations. This expanded access might include audiences such as:

- Employees
- Customers
- Distributors
- Providers to the company
- Regulators
- Higher education and technical school Students
- The general public
- Other partners.

Likewise, some companies are removing the approval process before an individual can gain access to a program. For example, a company with a leadership program that is primarily delivered online and in a MOOC-like format made a decision to open it up to all of their employees—not just the ones selected for promotion. They shifted leadership from a promotion to a skill set and opened up their assets to the entire enterprise.

Finally, as alluded to in the opening of this chapter, the word "Open" is not a particularly easy word for those in for-profit settings. Many corporate cultures are not very open in deed or even in language. Clearly, the use of Open Learning, in modest as well as more substantive ways, is both disruptive and interesting. Nonetheless, it continues to happen, grow, and evolve.

 **Elliott Masie** is a leading researcher, analyst, thought leader and futurist in the fields of learning, collaboration, and workforce effectiveness. Elliott is the Chair of the Learning CONSORTIUM, a collaboration of 200 global companies, focused on the future of learning and knowledge. In addition, he is the host of the annual Learning Conference in Orlando, Florida as well as the CEO of the MASIE Center—a think-tank focused on the intersection of learning, education, and technology. He is the author of 12 books, including *Big Learning Data*. He has presented to over two million professionals around the world. He has served on a wide range of corporate and non-profit boards, including Skidmore College, the CIA University Board, and FIRST Robotics. In addition, he is a Broadway producer (*Kinky Boots* and *Allegiance*). His website is http://www.masie.com.

24

ALISON

A New World of Free Certified Learning

Mike Feerick

When you last booked a hotel, did you first it look up online to check whether the hotel was a accredited member of the National Association of Hotels, or did you simply look up its profile on TripAdvisor? If you did the latter, you are among the millions of people worldwide bypassing traditional models of quality assessment and buying into the concept of free non-formal accreditation. Harnessing the power of the crowd via the Internet is enabling society to assess quality without having to refer to paid traditional third parties to assess how good products and services really are.

From a practical point of view, people don't want to rely on a hotel association to discover whether a hotel is good or not. They want to hear directly from customers who potentially, like themselves, will have already experienced the services offered and have an unbiased view—experience-based rather than fee-based. Via the Internet, more immediate and accurate assessment is now available to us in all walks of life, making old forms of accreditation redundant.

This dynamic is about to profoundly impact how we learn. For the first time in human civilization, we are coming to a point when not only can everyone be a learner, but everyone can be a teacher also. As free, easy-to-use self-publishing platforms like ALISON develop, the old barriers that held back the free sharing of knowledge and skills are being broken down forever.

This disruption is the result of the emergence and confluence of new technologies and economic models that support these changes. As education underpins all social progress, these dynamics will completely change our world. The following are some of the key ALISON concepts that will surely come to dominate a new world of free certified learning.

All Fact-Based Education and Training Will Be Free

As free self-publishing platforms provide the ability for teachers and experts of all kinds to share what they know, it is clear that almost all fact-based education will be freely accessible online. These changes will affect every level of education, from grade school to adult education. At grade school through to high school level, it must be said that fact-based education is less of a focus than the overall social development of the child. However, in the workplace, these changes will be profoundly evidenced. The quality control capability of the crowd is key to the development of this new education model. The crowd we are referring to is an army of experts and concerned adults determined to see quality delivery of education in areas that matter to them.

For those of you who doubt the capability of free crowd-sourced quality control, consider for a moment the development of the crowd-control capabilities or services beyond TripAdvisor which are dependent on this dynamic; from authorship of Wikipedia, to reviews of Amazon books online, and even to how Apple efficiently reviews new apps for distribution with minimal intercession. What we are seeing is the advent of highly automated, self-correcting and sustainable educational systems that have the capacity to grow to enormous and sustainable scale.

Courses for Everything

As a consequence of free publishing platforms, the breath of free learning content through the development of self-paced interactive multimedia courseware will become unlimited. It will, for instance, only take a few short years before full free turnkey grade and high school curriculum in every language will be accessible via the Web. If this seems alarmingly simplistic, consider how few unique hours of learning content are actually required at grade school or high school level worldwide.

The workplace, in contrast, is becoming infinitely more diverse and unique in terms of each individual's job tasks and responsbilities. Long gone are the Victorian images of countless bookkeepers row by row. Every worker will soon have the ability to have set for them, or indeed set by themselves, a distinctive learning path specifically suited for the role in which they wish to optimally perform. Workplaces and industries will form and develop their own crowd-driven workplace learning ecologies where traditional third party suppliers of education and training services will become increasingly redundant. Quite simply, you need only one expert on any subject to publish what he or she knows and from there onwards the knowledge is free.

If you think that people will not share what they know openly and freely, the MOOC movement of recent years provides ample evidence to the contrary. Similarly, the success of Wikipedia is a powerful example. At ALISON, we offer revenue sharing and lead generation to our publishers and these attractions are compelling for many. However, there exist many other motivations to freely publish one's work or ideas, including: personal altruism, for the benefit of the public interest, and simply showing off what you know. All of these reasons are equally powerful incentives. At ALISON, we call this movement towards unlimited free structured learning the "Long Tail of Learning" although, clearly, it's a tail that has the potential to never end.

In contrast with MOOCs found at the post-secondary level, ALISON's focus is on workplace knowledge and skills development. The earliest adopters were librarians who sought free online skills development opportunities for their clients, many of whom were marginalized and could ill afford to pay, including students, the elderly, the unemployed, and newly landed immigrants to largely English-speaking countries. As the size and sophistication of the ALISON course portfolio has grown, organizations of all kinds and sizes, from start-ups to multinational corporations, have begun to use the ALISON platform to upskill their staff, from English language training to Six Sigma management. ALISON aims to offer its learners a progressive learning path. For instance, once a learner is familiar with a keyboard and controls, we can then introduce basic desktop applications. After that, we can teach about how to build a website, and later help them create an online business where they can even consider self-employment. We see no limit in what type of workplace learning might be provided on the platform.

Suffice to say, ALISON learners come from a diverse range of countries and backgrounds. The online platform, which offers free courses in more than 600 subjects, breaks down many of the barriers to traditional education (see Figure 24.1). It is worth noting that ALISON has been fortunate to receive much positive feedback about the skills that we are helping to develop. On our website, we have over 20,000 testimonials from thankful learners across the world. Occasionally, we have attracted the celebrity endorsements such as in 2011 when Professor Clayton Christensen of the Harvard Business School tweeted: "ALISON is what a fundamental re-think—a disruption—of the education system might look like." As a Harvard graduate and admirer of his work myself, such encouragement is greatly appreciated.

Certification for Everything

The system of assessment introduced by ALISON needs to be considered more widely worldwide. ALISON Testing or "Flash" Testing is a simple process whereby anyone who has graduated from an ALISON course can be tested on that course at any time in the future to make sure they retain the standard that they once achieved. Many of us possess degrees of learning from various universities and colleges, but how many among us would like to be tested on the course material tomorrow morning to see if we remember it all? Very few of us indeed. We are complicit in a charade here, one wilfully engaged in by us all for years.

Perhaps to be kind to ourselves, we might say that there seemed no alternative. Now, however, we have an alternative. Harnessing the Web, anyone can be tested (and educated) on any subject, anywhere, at any time. The continuing

FIGURE 24.1 ALISON learners represent a range of countries and backgrounds

innovation and ubiquity of smartphones has enormously helped to universalize this solution. On my iPhone, I can test anyone on any ALISON course once we have a Web connection. All that is needed is a bank of questions which the likes of ALISON can arrange and provide.

Two points must be considered: firstly, the world is getting connected online at an extremely rapid pace—and ever increasingly in areas of the world where you might not expect it. ALISON, for example, now has one million online learners across the continent of Africa, and substantial numbers of learners across the Middle East and North Africa (MENA) region as a whole. There is also extensive use in the Indian subcontinent and Southeast Asia. ALISON learners, in fact, are located in every country worldwide (see Figure 24.2 for a geographical profile of ALISON learners).

Secondly, it should be understood that the traditional certification systems we have grown to rely on within developed societies have limited relevance in developing countries. Traditional frameworks of certification and quality assurance of education have limited traction in non-developed economies. In some cases, they hardly exist. Remember, only two billion of the seven billion people in the world are currently online. The systems of learning and certification that developing countries will adopt in the future will be ones that suit their times, needs, and circumstances; not what we grew up with in the developed world, or what suits us to sell to the developing world!

Finally, the concept of certification itself is going to change. The idea that a credential is tied to the concept that the candidate "once knew something" is

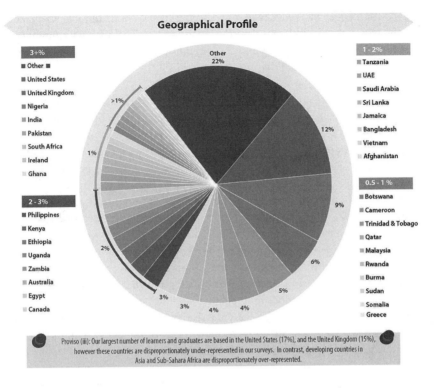

FIGURE 24.2 A geographical profile of the distribution of ALISON learners, worldwide (ALISON, 2014).

heading to extinction. The concept of certification is going to focus much more around what you know now. At ALISON, we call this "Dynamic Certification" where the form and substance of what you know and what you declare you know will always be changing. For instance, certifications in the future will always be time stamped. If you have completed a Diploma in Project Management on ALISON in 2015, it is important that you recertify in that course or learning experience in a couple of years or sooner. Similarly, employers will want to see increased recency and relevancy in educational or training accomplishments you present, simply because they can.

Social Impact of Free Certified Learning

The potential of free online learning certification to change society was made all the more clear to us at ALISON following a worldwide survey of our graduates and learners in February 2014 to which nearly 40,000 people replied (ALISON, 2014). Among the most thought-provoking result was that 90 percent of ALISON graduates indicated that free study had encouraged them to learn further. In addition, 88 percent of these graduates said that free learning on ALISON had increased their overall confidence. And, thirdly, 76 percent of them noted that such free learning made them feel more self-empowered (ALISON, 2014). Perhaps the most important statistic for us was that 14 percent of ALISON graduates said that studying on ALISON for free helped them get a new job, promotion, or new college placement.

Such results remind us how much traditional cost barriers to education and training have been holding back society worldwide in terms of restraining the natural ambition of people to learn and to better themselves. What if everyone could feel more confident and empowered in their lives and were eager to learn further? There is a message of hope for all of us to take note of, including politicians as well as everyone else concerned with better use of limited public resources.

We all have our part to play in making this revolution in education and training happen. We should not underestimate what people and organizations who gain from the current status quo in education and training will do to protect their own self-interests and perceived "territory." Those of us who understand the potential of this opportunity must support and have confidence in new ways of doing things and encourage their adoption in many forms. Just as we have embraced new methods to decide which hotel we will stay in, we need to embrace new ways of learning. Everyone reading this chapter needs to decide for themselves whether they are going to remain part of the old system, or embrace the new opportunity to its full and glorious extreme.

Free universal certified education and training has enormous potential to positively transform the world around us. As Nelson Mandela once said: "Education is the most powerful weapon which you can use to change the world." Free certified learning of the manner in which ALISON is pioneering is surely one of the great opportunities of our time.

Mike Feerick is Founder and CEO of ALISON.com, a global leader in free online certified learning. ALISON has five million learners and 500,000 graduates worldwide. Founded in 2007, ALISON is widely recognized as the first MOOC (Massive Open Online Course) provider. Mike is an internationally distinguished social entrepreneur receiving a WISE Award from the Qatar Foundation (2013), an Arthur Guinness Funding Award (2012), and an Ashoka Globaliser Fellowship (2011). He was presented with a Diploma Award from UNESCO (2010) for making access to education and skills training more accessible to all.

References

Alison (2014). *ALISON Learner and Graduate Survey Results 2014*. ALISON. Retrieved from http://www.advancelearning.com/wp-content/uploads/2014/07/ALISON_Survey_2014_Infographic.pdf.

25

ALTERNATIVE MODELS OF MOOCs

Ray Schroeder, Vickie S. Cook, Carrie Levin,
and Michele Gribbins

Introduction

The most important impact of MOOCs may be in uses focused outside of subject-based higher education. At the University of Illinois Springfield, the Center for Online Learning, Research and Service (COLRS) has been examining the potential of massive open online learning for segments of society outside formal course-based higher education. Looking at MOOCs as a vehicle for training, information, collaboration, and public issue discussion, COLRS has found significant potential.

Drawing upon leaders in learning at multiple levels around the world, COLRS led one of the last pre-xMOOC offerings in the summer of 2011. Through edu-MOOC, COLRS offered an eight-week connectivist MOOC on the present and future of online learning. Attracting education leaders and students from 70 different countries among the 2,700 registered in this particular MOOC, edu-MOOC created a forum for discussion and engagement related to preparing for the future of online learning.

It may be that professional associations and corporations will find MOOCs an effective way to reach the general public, dispersed members of their profession, and those in related fields. In this chapter, we will examine a MOOC in development that brings together two professional associations in the field of healthcare seeking to inform their field about issues in access to palliative care for end-of-life hospice patients, and also the trend for corporations to employ MOOCs as a means of staff training.

COLRS is tracking the advent of business and corporate use of MOOCs for the training and professional development of employees. These uses are fast emerging outside the higher education realm. Needs of corporations and associations are focused on employees and the efficiency of delivery of training for skills, procedures, and practices that can be rolled out in a timely fashion to a nationwide or worldwide employee base. Higher education remains behind in developing continuing and professional education related to specific industry needs. Several factors play into this lag, but perhaps the most significant are concerned with the limitation of budgets related to innovation and research, the lack of providing a just-in-time educational model for employee training, and the need for portability of credentialing for a transient workforce (Blair, 2010; Christensen & Horn, 2011; Oshita, 2012; Ross-Grodon, 2011).

COLRS continues to track the development of a rich variety of alternative uses of MOOCs as vehicles to learning. The business industry is taking the initiative of providing training related to entry-level skills and competencies to eager students who have been unable to find such types of learning opportunities in higher education.

One example is the "nanodegree" offered by Udacity and its corporate partners (Udacity, 2014), recently launched with 6- to 12-month programs. Among the initial clients for nanodegrees are those individuals wanting to learn front- and back-end Web development, IOS development, and data analysis. These are worldwide programs designed and offered by businesses on an unprecedented scale. Nanodegree programs, unlike many other Udacity initiatives, are not developed in collaboration with any higher education institution.

Unlike the Udacity facilitated Georgia Tech online master's in Computer Science degree program, these programs are developed directly with corporate, rather than university, partners. Udacity advertises them as "credentials built and recognized by industry leaders to advance your career" (Udacity, 2014). The initial partners are AT&T, Cloudera, Salesforce, and Autodesk. Udacity describes the advantage to students, "Leading technology companies design and teach nanodegrees with our help, and also endorse them. They know what technical skills they need to hire for and which new skills their employees need. Because they use the technologies and skills they teach, they teach them in a concrete applicable way" (Udacity, 2014). This statement hints at the future of education for career fields—a MOOC-enabled future, or some derivative of it, that may chip away at traditional higher education institutions, programs, and experiences.

eduMOOC: A Connectivist International Collaboration on the Future of Online Learning

In the spring of 2011, Ray Schroeder, founding Director of COLRS, called together his staff to share a bold idea. Having recently presented a keynote address on "The Open Digital University" at the eCornucopia conference at Oakland University in Michigan, Schroeder had become aware of the growing MOOC movement and felt it was time for UIS (an institution known for innovation in online learning) to dive in. The COLRS staff began pulling together ideas and materials for a MOOC on a topic they knew well—Online Learning—Today and Tomorrow.

This early MOOC was conceived of and designed as a connectivist MOOC or "c-MOOC." COLRS staff realized that George Siemens and Stephen Downes (Downes, 2012; Siemens, 2005) had designed and advocated for a new theory named connectivism that related specifically to learning in a digital society. In a c-MOOC, the learning occurs within a network of participants using such technologies as blogs, wikis, and social media to connect both with the course content and each other (Yeager & Bliss, 2013).

As materials were gathered and ideas shared, Schroeder and his staff decided that the UIS MOOC would offer weekly modules for eight consecutive weeks, beginning the week of June 27, 2011 and ending the week of August 15, 2011. Each module would include links to articles of interest on a given topic, related discussion questions, and a live, synchronous panel discussion led by top professionals in the field of online learning. The materials developed for the MOOC were shared using free, cloud-based technologies and social media sites, including Google Sites, Google Groups, Wikispaces, Twitter and Twitterfall, Google Hangouts, and Facebook (eduMOOC OERu Planning Group, 2013).

The following topics and panelists were chosen for the weekly modules: (1) *Online Learning Today*—Ray Schroeder (UIS), Bruce Chaloux (SREB), Robert Hansen (UPCEA), and Witt Salley (MoDLA); (2) *What the Research Tells Us*—Karen Swan (UIS), Phil Ice (APUS), and Ben Arbaugh (UWOSH); (3) *Online Technologies Today and Tomorrow*—Michael Cheney (UIS), Alexandra Pickett (SUNY), Bethany Bovard (NMSU), and Nic Bongers (Oakland U); (4) *Online Learning Apps and Mobile Learning*—Glenda Morgan (UIUC), David Middleton (Seton Hall), and Patricia McGee (University of Texas San Antonio); (5) *Public, Private and Open Online Learning*—Ray Schroeder, Cable Green (Creative Commons), Larry Ragan (PSU World Campus), and Jeff Newell (IL Community College Board); (6) *Personal Online Learning Networks*—Shari McCurdy Smith (UIS), George Siemens (Athabasca), Jason Rhode (NIU), and Nancy Rubin (Learning Objects); (7) *Collaboratives, Collectives and Clouds*—Shari McCurdy Smith, Karen Vignare (MSU), and Linda C. Smith (UIUC); (8) *Online Learning Tomorrow: 2011–2021*—Ray Schroeder, Cable Green, Curt Bonk (IU), Bruce Chaloux, and Seb Schmoller (ALT UK).

Having developed a devoted following with his many blogs and Twitter personae, Schroeder began using his social media muscle to promote eduMOOC. Initial enrollments trickled in slowly but steadily.

Marc Parry and others from the *Chronicle of Higher Education* learned of the event. On June 21, 2011, just days before the MOOC was set to launch, Parry (2011) published an online article for the *Chronicle* titled "U. of Illinois at Springfield Offers New 'Massive Open Online Course.'" This article opened with the question "What happens when you invite the whole world to join an online class?" Enrollments quickly skyrocketed—in fact, staff members at

COLRS struggled to keep up with the enrollment requests. On the day edu-MOOC commenced, enrollments had grown to over 2,700 participants from 70 countries. That made eduMOOC the largest MOOC, in terms of enrollments, that had ever been offered up to that time. (These numbers would soon be significantly eclipsed by Sebastian Thrun's MOOC from Stanford University on artificial intelligence in the fall of 2011. His course enrolled 160,000 students from more than 190 countries.)

In 2011, the University of Illinois Springfield was using Elluminate (now Blackboard Collaborate) to conduct synchronous online learning sessions. The largest webinar "room" owned by UIS accommodated 100 people. With edu-MOOC enrollments soaring over the 2,000 mark, the COLRS staff looked for a way to include all who wanted to view the live sessions and question the panelists. A website that offered a streaming version of the Elluminate session—complete with slides and audio as well as a panel showing the live Twitter feed—was developed quickly by the Information Technology staff at UIS. Additionally, during the live sessions, COLRS staff monitored questions submitted via Twitter to share with the speakers. All live sessions were recorded and made available to participants unable to attend the event. Importantly, these recordings remain available today on the course website: https://sites.google.com/site/edumooc/home.

As eduMOOC progressed, participants found creative ways to expand their own personal learning networks. Feeling frustrated with the technological limitations of the Google Group community employed for this course, several participants launched a Wikispaces group that, over time, became the most popular site for asynchronous eduMOOC discussions. Schroeder chronicled his own experiences with convening eduMOOC in a personal blog: http://edumooc.blogspot.com/. In addition, eduMOOC participants created Twitter groups, hosted weekly Google Hangouts reflection activities to discuss the live sessions, created an eduMOOC online newspaper (using Paper.li), and began a Facebook group. In a striking demonstration of the reach of open online learning, a group of edu-MOOC participants in Christchurch, New Zealand began weekly, face-to-face meetings at a local McDonald's restaurant to view and discuss the recordings of the live sessions.

The success of eduMOOC as an initial experiment led the staff of COLRS to begin to research additional types and variations on the MOOC initiative. One such initiative is the partnership discussed in the following section with two state associations and two universities.

Associations and Corporations Take MOOCs Outside the Course-Based Models

Building a strong partnership on a foundation of a shared vision and trust will ensure that a partnership model can be successful in the world of MOOCs. In partnership with the Illinois Hospital Association, the Illinois Home Healthcare and Hospice Association, and the Southern Illinois University Medical School, the University of Illinois at Springfield is currently assisting with the creation of a professional development MOOC to promote excellence in palliative care. This partnership will provide both healthcare professionals and home healthcare providers access to palliative care experts around the country with information that will help assist with the quality of care offered to patients.

This MOOC is being funded through a variety of grant and association funds. The anticipated costs are less than $35,000 with administrative costs being absorbed by the partners. While the timeline remains somewhat fluid, based as it is upon the availability of experts and other scheduling challenges, the anticipated MOOC launch date is late 2014.

This MOOC is being built on the same foundation as the eduMOOC— as a c-MOOC. Drawing upon the theory of connectivism, the Palliative Care MOOC partners will connect with each other and with organizations and global experts to provide a high-quality experience for learners in locations around the country. This topic must be handled responsibly to ensure substantial learning takes place while recognizing the sensitivity surrounding the issue. Building a strong partnership where ideas can be presented, discussed, and discarded without threat to any one organization has been key to providing the best possible scenario for this work to be presented. The process of developing a strong partnership was necessary to provide an excellent product.

As with any partnership, there are several key areas that must be considered and significant attention given to ensure success. As detailed below, in this particular case, there were seven primary ones that needed to be in place.

1. A strong, written document that outlines each partner's responsibilities.
2. Expertise in content areas that complement each partner.
3. Shared mission and vision for a final product.
4. Open and effective communication processes.
5. Ability to consider the gains available for each partner.
6. Consideration of social ethics and the place of the MOOC within the social environment.
7. Firm deadlines for producing deliverables.

Each of these areas is critical to a highly operational or functional MOOC delivery model that is developed through a shared, collaborative approach. Each of these areas is needed to lay the groundwork for the success of the MOOC participants. These practices also become the foundation for future MOOC content areas that might be developed by the partners. By developing a strong partnership among the collaborating associations, built upon a shared vision and trust, this alternative model for MOOC delivery is achievable. Like associations, corporate organizations are looking for ways to decrease costs and increase visibility.

Corporate MOOCs

With employee training expenditures reaching more than $150 billion per year (Meister, 2013), companies are turning to MOOCs as a way to decrease costs and increase the relevancy and availability of employee training. MOOC providers are connecting with companies to help them train their employees by providing content development services, learning platforms, and content licensing (Bersin, 2013). Furthermore, companies are customizing open courses to develop training specific to their needs.

According to the Udemy website for Organizations, the MOOC model, when used internally for corporate training, helps companies unify their learning experiences. Such a model also allows for tacit knowledge from employees to be better documented. For example, Pitney Bowes uses the MOOC model to train information technology developers on business skills and the latest programming languages. Google's g2g Program is helping its employees collaborate and learn from each other's rich set of experiences (Hughes, 2013a).

For many companies, a MOOC often remains open and available to all employees long after it has officially ended or any synchronous events have concluded. As a result, it serves as a repository of resources for future reference. This repository of prior MOOC content can be especially useful for newly hired employees of a company who are able to access such training content upon their arrival. Such course reuse and content-sharing opportunities are often not possible with in-person training. For instance, both McAfee and Intel are using the MOOC model to increase the efficiency and consistency of new-hire training (Hughes, 2013a).

In addition to internally developed MOOCs, companies are looking at externally created MOOCs as a substitute for company-sponsored training. As noted in the book chapter from DeMillo (this volume), AT&T partnered with Georgia Tech and Udacity to provide a computer science master's degree program to its employees, in addition to other applicants accepted by the university (Bersin, 2013). Naturally, when MOOCs focus on a specific topic area—such as the ones in the master's program from Georgia Tech and Udacity—employees have a classroom full of people with similar interests or work experiences who can help answer questions, provide recommendations, or build network connections to those within their field. That is what also happened for MOOCs that UIS has developed, including the eduMOOC and the MOOC to assist with palliative care professional development. Those in the corporate training world have quickly realized the benefits of such types of focused MOOCs. For instance, companies, such as Yahoo, are reimbursing employees for the cost of course-completion certificates when participating in an externally created MOOC, a cost that is much less than that of in-person training (Bersin, 2013).

Companies are also using MOOCs to provide training and build better relations with business partners, customers, potential employees, and consumers in general (Bersin, 2013; Hughes, 2013a). SAP, for instance, developed openSAP (https://open.sap.com/) to educate both developers and users of SAP. Along these same lines, Oracle has developed a MOOC to introduce Java developers to embedded applications (McGinn, Caicedo, Weaver, Ritter, & Chin, 2014). As a third example, 1-800-FLOWERS uses MOOC technology to educate independent florists on various business and floral design topics. Fourth, Bank of America and Khan Academy have partnered to provide personal finance education to consumers (http://www.bettermoneyhabits.com/), an effort to help Bank of America build brand marketing. Finally, companies, such as Google, Amazon, and Facebook, are using MOOCs for candidate screening and to build talent pipelines for their companies.

Given the five examples above, clearly, the benefits of MOOCs for corporate training are plentiful. MOOCs help employees maintain relevant skills and knowledge in an ever-changing work environment (Carson, 2014). Because MOOCs save time and money in relationship to in-person training, and are not confined to the limitations of a physical size of a room, more employees are able to benefit from the training. In addition, the learning is self-paced and modular, which is beneficial to employees who find it difficult to devote entire workdays to in-person training (Hughes, 2013b). MOOCs also improve the learning experience for employees who find in-person training to be too fast or too slow for their learning needs. With MOOCs, such individuals can now adapt their pace as needed to better consume the content (Abbasi, 2014).

An additional benefit for the use of MOOCs is that competency in content, as well as engagement with materials, can be more easily assessed on an individual basis than can traditional, in-person training where presence does not always equate to comprehension or engagement in activities. Through the use of certificates of completion or badges that are only made available after the completion of a series of activities, employees can provide evidence of their participation. Documenting the completion of MOOCs and other online learning programs is such an important part of the employee training process that LinkedIn has partnered with numerous MOOC and online learning providers to create "Direct-to-Profile" certifications that will appear in an employee's LinkedIn profile with just a few clicks after participants successfully have completed a class (Baird, 2013).

Udemy offers several considerations when using the MOOC model to develop corporate training (Hughes, 2013b). First, the platform should be user-friendly. Second, training content should be designed and delivered in a way to reach different types of learners and various generations of workers. Third, corporate leaders should be involved in the development, and ideally, some of the delivery of content. Lastly, managers should have tools available to track employee participation.

Emerging New Models Outside Higher Education

In 2008, a unique form of instruction—that might be considered the infancy of MOOCs—began to be tested and soon was considered highly relevant for learners. Then, in 2012, MOOCs became fledgling adolescents as universities began to explore how to make use of the MOOC delivery model.

Today, new models of learning delivery are emerging in many fields outside of higher education that will significantly impact the evolution of the MOOC. As Erin Carson (2014) notes, "Apart from big name MOOC platforms, companies are taking the idea and often the structure of this next iteration of online learning, and creating their own MOOCs, both internal and external facing." To make her case, she cites, Jenny Dearborn, chief learning officer at SAP, who believes that this new trend in corporate education to develop MOOCs related to specific job training will more effectively empower employees within the organization. Carson (2014) also points out that the MOOCs developed and led by the SAP team feature a variety of topics, including product understanding, soft skills, and leadership development.

German companies such as SAP are not the only corporations building MOOCs for industry use. Other corporations such as TELUS, a Canadian-based communication company, are also using MOOCs to deliver employee training. In February 2011, TELUS launched a six-week training program to include all 40,000 employees of the company. That particular MOOC utilized a high level of media content through use of videos, webcasts, and various social media (Nielsen, 2013). As a sign of commitment to such efforts, Dan Pontefract, Head of Learning and Collaboration at TELUS, argued "We're not afraid of the MOOC; we're demonstrating it has benefit inside the corporate ranks as it does in the academic ranks through ventures like Coursera, Udacity and edX" (Nielsen, 2013). Undoubtedly, Pontefract will not be the last voicing such commitments. In fact, in a popular *New York Times* piece in the fall of 2013, Clayton Christensen and Michael Horn (2013) used the analogy of a steamship when writing about MOOCs. We can see the impact the use of technology in learning is having on continuing education and lifelong learning just as the steamship impacted transportation and the far reaches of our physical journeys.

In 2012, many media outlets began to consider 2012 the year of the MOOC (Pappano, 2012). Higher education institutions were utilizing MOOCs in new ways to reach new audiences and many were incorporating this new delivery mechanism into their online learning platforms. Now, two years later, 2014 is being heralded as the year of the Corporate MOOC. Business leaders and others are making predictions that corporations will soon innovate and evolve MOOCs into new platforms of learning that will enhance corporate learning opportunities. Increased employee engagement is anticipated as part of the evolution of the MOOC. Not too surprisingly, new and more effective training methods are anticipated to be in development. Predictions are that corporations will increase the use of MOOCs and that employees are more likely to engage in completing MOOCs offered for specific skills and certification related to employment (Bersin, 2014).

A review of the McAfee Corporation's use of MOOCs to reinvent the company's corporate training model indicates that the use of MOOCs in initial training has significantly saved the company time, as well as added to the profitability of their sales force (Meister, 2013). The use of MOOCs in this way has a vital impact on the innovation of corporations in their adoption and adaptation of different MOOC models to build the human talent required in today's economy and job market.

The advent of learning hubs located in libraries and other support sites enables students to gather in a physical location to participate in group learning and discussion (Coursera, 2014). Coursera and the US State Department provide tutoring in hub sites around the world that support students with tutoring and related services. In effect, these learning hubs turn MOOCs into a "blended learning" experience for these students. This unique government–university collaboration is yet another way in which MOOCs are evolving outside the traditional university model.

MOOC ideas, models, and applications continue to emerge and develop. By the time this book is published, many more new MOOC models will have been designed and implemented as we build upon the research and experiences of the initial years of MOOCs. Hopefully, innovation and creativity surrounding this mode of learning will continue to grow to the mass benefit of educators and learners alike.

Ray Schroeder is Associate Vice Chancellor for Online Learning at the University of Illinois Springfield. He is also Director of the Center for Online Leadership and Strategy at the University Continuing and Professional Education Association (UPCEA). Ray has published the popular Online Learning Update and Educational Technology blogs for the past decade. Ray Schroeder was named the inaugural 2010 recipient of the Sloan Consortium's highest Individual award—the A. Frank Mayadas Leadership Award. In addition, he received the 2011 University of Illinois Distinguished Service Award. Finally, Ray Schroeder is an inaugural Sloan Consortium Fellow and the 2012 Innovation Fellow for Digital Learning by the UPCEA. He can be contacted at Schroeder.ray@uis.edu.

Vickie S. Cook is the Director of the Center for Online Learning, Research and Service at the University of Illinois Springfield. She holds a dual appointment as an Associate Research Professor in the Department of Educational Leadership. Her research focus in in leadership in online education. Dr. Cook may be reached at cook.vickie@uis.edu.

Carrie Levin has been working in the field of online learning since 2005. She serves as the Assistant Director for the Center for Online Learning, Research and Service (COLRS) at the University of Illinois Springfield. She has presented numerous workshops and trainings on many aspects of online learning. Carrie has authored and co-authored several proceedings papers and journal articles. She earned her BFA degree in Theatre at UIUC and her Master's in Dance-Movement Therapy/Counseling at Columbia College. In addition to her work with COLRS, Carrie is an adjunct instructor at UIS in the Computer Science department.

Michele Gribbins is an Online Learning and Faculty Development Specialist for the Center for Online Learning, Research & Service at the University of Illinois Springfield. She is also an Adjunct Lecturer for the Department of Management Information Systems. She has presented at many national and international conferences in the areas of online learning and information systems. Her research has been published in the *Journal of Information Technology*, the *Communications of the Association for Information Systems*, *Electronic Markets*, and the *International Journal of Management Theory and Practices*.

References

Abbasi, S. (2014, May 29). The business benefits of adopting a corporate MOOC in your organization. *Udemy for Organizations*. Retrieved from http://www.udemy.com/organizations/blog/2014/05/29/the-business-benefits-of-adopting-a-corporate-mooc-in-your-organization/.

Baird, A. (2013, November 14). Introducing a new way to add certifications to your LinkedIn profile. *LinkedIn Blog*. Retrieved from http://blog.linkedin.com/2013/11/14/introducing-a-new-way-to-add-certifications-to-your-linkedin-profile/.

Bersin, J. (2013, November 30). The MOOC martketplace takes off. *Forbes*. Retrieved from http://www.forbes.com/sites/joshbersin/2013/11/30/the-mooc-marketplace-takes-off/.

Bersin, J. (2014, February 4). Spending on corporate training soars: Employee capabilities now a priority. *Forbes*. Retrieved from http://www.forbes.com/sites/joshbersin/2014/02/04/the-recovery-arrives-corporate-training-spend-skyrockets/.

Blair, A. (2010). In from the margins: The essential role of faculty in transforming a professional studies unit into an academic department. *Journal of Continuing Higher Education*, 58(1), 31–9.

Carson, E. (2014, June 20). How MOOCs are flattening corporate training and education. *TechRepublic*. from http://www.techrepublic.com/article/how-moocs-are-flattening-corporate-training-and-education/.

Christensen, C., & Horn, M. (2011, July/August). College in crisis: Disruptive change comes to American higher education. *Harvard Magazine*. Retrieved from: http://harvardmagazine.com/2011/07/colleges-in-crisis.

Christensen, C.M., & Horn, M.B. (2013, November 1). Innovation imperative: Change everything. *New York Times*. Retrieved http://www.nytimes.com/2013/11/03/education/edlife/online-education-as-an-agent-of-transformation.html?_r=0.

Coursera. (2014). *Coursera learning hubs*. Retrieved from http://www.coursera.org/about/programs/learningHubs.

Downes, S. (2012). *Connectivism and connective knowledge: Essays on meaning and learning networks*. Retrieved from http://www.downes.ca/files/books/Connective_Knowledge-19May2012.pdf.

eduMOOC OERu Planning Group. (2013). WikiEducator. Retrieved from http://wikieducator.org/OERu/eduMOOC_planning_group/MOOC_comparison.

Hughes, S. (2013a, December 23). Seven ways to corporate MOOC. *Udemy for Organizations*. Retrieved from http://www.udemy.com/organizations/blog/2013/12/23/seven-ways-to-corporate-mooc/.

Hughes, S. (2013b, June 24). What are the lessons of massive open online courses (MOOCs) for corporate learning and training? *Udemy for Organizations*. Retrieved from http://www.udemy.com/organizations/blog/2013/06/24/what-are-the-lessons-of-massive-open-online-courses-moocs-for-corporate-learning-and-training/.

McGinn, T., Caicedo, A., Weaver, J., Ritter, S., & Chin, S. (2014). Oracle massive open online course: Develop Java embedded applications using a Raspberry Pi. *Oracle Learning Library*. Retrieved from https://apex.oracle.com/pls/apex/f?p=44785:145:0::::P145_EVENT_ID,P145_PREV_PAGE:861,143.

Meister, J. (2013, August 13). How MOOCs will revolutionize corporate learning and development. *Forbes*. Retrieved from http://www.forbes.com/sites/jeannemeister/2013/08/13/how-moocs-will-revolutionize-corporate-learning-development/.

Nielsen, B. (2013, April 29). MOOCs: From the classroom to the conference room. *Your Training Edge*. Retrieved from http://www.yourtrainingedge.com/moocs-from-the-classroom-to-the-conference-room/.

Oshita, Y. (2012). Committed to continuing higher education in the workplace. *The Evolllution*. Retrieved from http://www.evolllution.com/corporate_partnerships/committing-to-continuing-higher-education-in-the-workplace/.

Pappano, L. (2012, November 2). The year of the MOOC. *New York Times*. Retrieved from http://www.nytimes.com/2012/11/04/education/edlife/massive-open-online-courses-are-multiplying-at-a-rapid-pace.html?pagewanted=all&_r=0.

Parry, M. (2011, June 21). U. of Illinois at Springfeld offers new 'Massive Open Online Course'. *Chronicle of Higher Education*. Retrieved from http://chronicle.com/blogs/wiredcampus/u-of-illinois-at-springfield-offers-new-massive-open-online-course/31853 - http://chronicle.com/blogs/wiredcampus/u-of-illinois-at-springfield-offers-new-massive-open-online-course/31853.

Ross-Grodon, J. M. (2011). Research on adult learners: Supporting the needs of a student populations that is no longer nontraditional. *Peer Review*, *13*(1), 26–9.

Siemens, G. (2005). Connectivism: Learning as network-creation. *ASTD: eLearnSpace*, 1–28.

Udacity. (2014). *Nanodegrees: A new kind of credential for jobs in technology—Udacity*. Retrieved from http://www.udacity.com/nanodegrees.

Yeager, C., Betty, H.-D., & Bliss, C.A. (2013). cMOOCs and global learning: An authentic alternative. *Journal of Asynchronous Learning Networks*, *17*(2), 133–47. Retrieved from http://onlinelearningconsortium.org/jaln/v17n2/cmoocs-and-global-learning-authentic-alternative.

PART 8
Future Glimpses and Open Options

Anyone who has been following the evolution of learning technology and open education during the past few decades will readily admit that it is extremely difficult to attempt to predict what might happen next. Oftentimes, such forecasts and proclamations about the technologies and opportunities on the educational horizon are extremely conservative compared to what actually transpires. Other times, of course, it is quite the reverse and bold claims are made that are never seen or heard about again.

What we do know is that open and online education will evolve in the coming decade to new forms of learning delivery with massively more participants than what exists today. MOOCs and other MOOC-like derivatives, ideas, and formats will play extremely vital roles in further opening access to education to many millions of individuals who previously lacked it. At the same time, as can be seen from the emergence of MOOCs in top tier universities, these new open forms of distance education will play a significant role in reshaping, or at the very least augmenting, traditional higher education as well. As this occurs, open education policies, quality standards, and the overall level of use and acceptance of MOOCs and open education will also evolve during the next few years and beyond. Lifelong learning will no longer simply be a slogan or goal; it will be seamlessly and ubiquitously part of all human functioning on this planet.

In Chapter 26, Michael Keppell from the Australian Digital Futures Institute (ADFI) at the University of Southern Queensland in Australia focuses on the knowledge, skills, and attitudes of learners who need to navigate the "chaos" of an ambiguous learning landscape. As he points out, in this learning future, resilient personalized learners will seek solutions for problems, issues, and challenges on a daily basis as lifelong learners. Personalized learners will need a toolkit encompassing six dimensions, namely: (1) digital literacies, (2) seamless learning,

(3) self-regulated learning, (4) learning-oriented assessment, (5) lifelong learning, and (6) flexible learning pathways. According to Keppell, this toolkit will enable the learner to tackle the complexities of the learning landscape that is becoming increasingly digital, connected, and ambiguous. In this chapter, Keppell describes each of the six dimensions as well as three levels of progression within each one as a roadmap for lifelong personalized learning in the coming decade. As such, it offers a highly useful lens through which to envision the future of learning in this highly technological and increasingly open learning age.

In the ensuing chapter, Rita Kop and Hélène Fournier in Canada argue that MOOCs are perfectly positioned to contribute to the "Knowledge Commons." Importantly, Figure 27.1 offers a way to visualize their ideas about the Knowledge Commons. According to Kop and Fournier, MOOCs exist at the cusp of formal and informal learning as prime examples of open networked learning events wherein participants can contribute to the knowledge commons. All is not rosy, however. As discussed by David Wiley in Chapter 1 of this volume, Kop and Fournier also contend that too often MOOCS are not fully open. In addition, despite recent shifts toward learner-centered instruction across educational sectors, there is mounting concern that active learning—such as the creation of digital artefacts—is not at the heart of the learning experiences or activities typically felt by most MOOC participants. What is worse, the immense scale of MOOCs forces developers to use data-driven techniques, rather than people-driven and connectivist technologies, to advance the learning process. This focus on data-driven and top-down approaches is a significant problem when developers of learning environments intend to create a place that enriches the commons of openly available information and knowledge to all. In response, Kop and Fournier suggest several solutions to the current shortcomings of MOOCs by drawing on the literature related to open, networked learning and MOOCs.

In Chapter 28, Rebecca Ferguson, Mike Sharples, and Russell Beale from the UK look ahead to the year 2030. They consider several ways in which current visions of massive open online courses may develop into realities. Their vision is shaped by the "Technology-Enhanced Learning Complex," which is an interlocking system of technologies, people, and practices. It is also shaped by the ideas and mission of FutureLearn; a corporation that has evolved from the Open University in the UK to offer MOOCs. To reach these visions, this chapter considers the changes in pedagogy, technology, and the wider environment that will be necessary in order for MOOCs to flourish. The authors of this chapter argue that, by 2030, the systems that develop from MOOCs will be meeting the needs of society by educating millions of digital citizens. If this occurs, such systems will have opened up access to education to enable people from all over the world to enjoy the benefits of learning at scale. In order for this to happen, MOOC providers, policy makers, and educators will all need to proceed with such a vision in mind. In effect, if MOOCs are to make a difference and truly open up education while enhancing learning, the pedagogies in place by 2030 must take into account entirely new groups of learners as well as vastly new roles that will emerge for educators. Such pedagogical approaches must also utilize innovative approaches to the design of that learning, whether it be MOOCs or some other form of learning delivery at scale.

In Chapter 29, the final chapter of this book, the four editors of this volume offer a recap of the various contributions and ideas embedded in this comprehensive book on MOOCs and Open Education Around the World. As part of these efforts, we provide an overview of the book themes related to MOOCs and OER, including a review of the different ways in which MOOCs are currently being used. There is also a discussion of the unique contributions found in this book and the potential audiences and values to which it serves. Near the end of the chapter, we take a brief look at the future of learning in this increasingly open educational world. We surmise that in this new age of learning there are many "open options" for each of us. In closing, we offer hope that the ideas in this book serve not only the highly inquisitive, informal, and nontraditional learners who are already engaged in some form of open, online, or blended learning (including from MOOCs, OCW, and OER), but also the needs of the educationally disadvantaged, underprivileged, and at-risk learners around the world. Such marginalized learners are in dire need of new skills, competencies, and educational opportunities that can now be provided through MOOCs and open education as well as other forms of learning at a distance that will evolve in the coming decades.

26

THE LEARNING FUTURE

Personalised Learning in an Open World

Michael Keppell

Introduction

In this chapter, I will examine key concepts for learning in the future. I will focus on the knowledge, skills, and attitudes of learners who need to navigate the "chaos" of an ambiguous learning landscape. As part of this discussion, I will describe how they may need to continually refine their knowledge, skills, and attitudes as resilient learners to thrive in a rapidly changing world.

In this learning future, resilient personalised learners will need to adapt and seek solutions for problems, issues, and challenges on a daily basis. The future will also require learners to be lifelong learners whose ability to learn will be an essential survival skill set to thrive in this changing world. Resilient and adaptable learners will become the "norm" in the learning future, particularly as open education becomes more prevalent as an acceptable and viable means of learning in higher education. The chapter will begin by defining personalised learning and then examining a roadmap for personalised learning in an open world.

Defining Personalised Learning

I define personalised learning as the knowledge, skills and attitudes that enable learning and act as a catalyst to empower the learner to continue to learn.

In this definition, knowledge is now co-created, disseminated via networks, and personalised. It has moved from being described as "explaining some part of the world" and "used in some type of action" to involving ecologies and networks (Siemens, 2006, p. vi). Skills enable us to do certain tasks, whereas attitudes influence beliefs and behaviours. Clustered together, they may enable or constrain a learner's ability to learn. In addition, by focusing on specific dimensions of knowledge, skills, and attitudes in relation to personalised learning, we may be able to encourage and empower the learner to continue to learn.

Personalised learning is no longer about what the learner knows now, but concerns how the learner can learn more. I envisage a future where we will be unceasing learners, acting on feedback that we feed-forward to our next application of knowledge. Learners will need to adopt a "growth mindset" as opposed to a "fixed mindset" (Dweck, 2006). When a learner adopts a growth mindset, they openly seek challenge and thrive on challenge. They exhibit purposive engagement that is a key to learning. Growth mindset learners progress by cultivation of their efforts and they have a passion for stretching themselves as opposed to limiting themselves (Dweck, 2006). However, "growth mindset learners" also need a toolkit to tackle the complexities of the learning landscape that is becoming increasingly digital, connected, and ambiguous. This toolkit encompasses digital literacies, seamless learning, self-regulated learning, learning-oriented assessment, lifelong/life-wide learning, and flexible learning pathways.

Roadmap of Personalised Learning

Recently, I wrote about personalised learning strategies for higher education and how learners customise and personalise their own physical and virtual learning spaces as they traverse their learning journey (Keppell, 2014). In that chapter, I laid out how seven principles of learning space design are adapted for use by the personalised learner. In the present chapter, I provide a roadmap for personalised learning across six dimensions: (1) digital literacies, (2) seamless learning, (3) self-regulated learning, (4) learning-oriented assessment, (5) lifelong learning, and (6) learning pathways. As detailed in Table 26.1, each dimension contains three levels of progression for lifelong personalised learners. This roadmap examines the growth and progression of the personalised learner that could provide a framework for future adoption.

I will now focus on each of these six dimensions of personalised learning and describe a suggested progression through the three levels.

1 Digital Literacies

The first dimension of personalised learning is in the area of digital literacy. Digital literacies encompass the knowledge, skills, and attitudes that will enable individuals to learn, work, live, play, and interact more effectively in a digital age (Johnson, Adams, Cummins, & Estrada, 2012). I use the plural version of literacies as opposed to literacy as it provides a framework for integrating other literacies which include meaning making and other cognitive skills (Lankshear & Knobel, 2008). In addition, it is important that we focus on "literacies of the

TABLE 26.1 Levels of personalised learning

Personalised learning	Level 1	Level 2	Level 3
1. Digital literacies	**Digital competence** Precursor to digital Literacy (Martin, 2008). Knowing how to use digital tools and devices. This would include the use of computers, tablets, smartphones, and word processing or internet searching.	**Digital fluency** Comfort with digital technology to apply knowledge and skills for a specific purpose in learning, teaching, or practice. Beetham (2010) focused on personal, academic, and professional use of digital technologies; e.g., developing a solution or solving a problem.	**Digital design** Subsumes competencies and fluency and examines the concept of 'learner as designer'. Learner-generated content could include the design of media; e.g., video. Learner-generated content is a viable resource for open education.
2. Seamless learning	**On-campus** Learner is comfortable with: On-campus learning in formal and informal learning spaces; e.g., classroom or café.	**Virtual campus** Learner is comfortable with: Online learning, Blended learning, Social media.	**Anywhere** Learner is comfortable learning anywhere; e.g., trains, cafes, teleworking spaces. Learner will require learning space literacies (Keppell, 2014).
3. Self-regulated learning	**Scaffolded learners** Teacher supports self-regulated learning through scaffolding and devolving learning to the learner. Teacher empowers students to take ownership of their own learning. Learners begin to set learning goals.	**Strategic learners** Learners begin to manage their own learning. Learners adopt strategies to advance learning.	**Autonomous learners** Learners are able to evaluate performance on learning task and adapt their own learning. Learners make strategic decisions about their learning needs. Learners become autonomous learners.

4. Learning-oriented assessment	**Authentic assessment** Teachers support authentic assessment through scaffolding. Learners participate in authentic assessment.	**Negotiated assessment** Learner negotiates assessment with teacher. Learner negotiates role in peer assessment activities or group work.	**Self-Assessment** Acts on 'feedback as feed-forward.' Learner choice of submission format; e.g., written, media, etc. Learners self-assess their own learning.
5. Lifelong learning	**Short-term** Focussed on current courses. Teacher provides connection of learning to future job.	**Future-oriented** Relates individual courses to future job. Identifies gaps in knowledge and undertakes learning to address.	**Being a learner** Learning becomes a customary practice. Life-wide learning is emphasised.
6. Learning pathways	**Prescribed** Learner follows a prescribed learning pathway.	**Flexible** Learner has some choice in courses through electives.	**Open education** Learner has freedom to construct a learning pathway that meets their learning needs.

digital" (Martin, 2008, p. 156). Such literacies range from "functional" (e.g., simple skills) to "social engagement" in a specific context (e.g., socio-cultural practice) to "transformation" of thinking and "empowerment" of the learner (Belisle, 2006; Martin, 2008).

Level 1: Digital Competence

Martin (2008) described digital competence as a precursor to digital literacies. He suggested that before a learner can engage in the digital environment, the learner needs to know how to use digital tools and devices before they can apply this knowledge in the learning environment. For example, the learner will need basic skills and competencies in how to use the computer, tablets, and smartphones. In addition, the learner will need to learn software such as word processing, spreadsheets, presentation software, and Internet searching to be competent in the digital environment.

Level 2: Digital Fluency

I have chosen digital fluency as the next stage of digital literacies learning for the personalised learner. The concept of "fluency" suggests a familiarity and comfort with the digital technology that translates into applying knowledge and skills for a specific purpose in learning, teaching, or practice. Beetham (2010) focused on personal, academic, and professional use of digital technologies. By focussing on the context, the learner is able to develop a solution or solve a problem specific to the learning context.

Level 3: Digital Design

Digital design subsumes competencies and fluency and examines the concept of "learner as designer-producer model" (Lockyer & Kerr, 2000). It is suggested that when the learner is engaged in design and production of digital resources, she will be deeply engaged in applying digital literacies to create new artefacts and create new knowledge. User-generated learning often involves curation, reflection, and the creation of an artefact (Swanson, 2013). This learner-generated content could include the design of media such as a video that can also be shared as an open educational resource (OER) for open education.

2 Seamless Learning

Conole (2014) suggested that we are entering a third generation of learning environments. She proposed that we have moved from virtual learning environments through personal learning environments to a third phase that encompasses the "Internet of Things," and seamless learning. Seamless learning is about "connecting learning across settings, technologies and activities" (Sharples et al., 2012, 2013). Kuh (1996) contended that "the word seamless suggests that what was once believed to be separate, distinct parts (e.g., in-class and out-of-class, academic and non-academic, curricular and co-curricular, or on-campus and off-campus experiences) are now of one piece, bound together so as to appear whole or continuous" (p. 136).

Level 1: On-Campus Learning

Traditional on-campus learning involves the learner in formal learning spaces such as lecture rooms, tutorial rooms, and labs as well as informal learning spaces that would include areas like a library, learning commons, cafés, and other informal spaces for learning. The learner may also use laptop computers, tablets, and smartphone technology in each of these environments. It is typified by being a predominantly campus-based experience.

Level 2: Virtual Campus Learning

At this level, the personalised learner is comfortable with learning via the virtual campus which may include a blended learning approach that requires the learner to participate in the online environment, by accessing content, interacting in forums, or completing online assessment. The blurring of face-to-face learning and teaching and online learning is a significant shift for both learners and teachers in universities. It also has implications for learners who desire flexible learning, teaching, and assessment options without losing the fidelity of face-to-face interactions. The learner may also undertake fully online courses and utilise social media to interact in the virtual campus.

Level 3: Anywhere Learning

Anywhere learning means that the personalised learner is comfortable learning anywhere and at any time. This learner is comfortable interacting in a variety of learning spaces that may include formal and informal on-campus spaces and online learning environments. It might also include accessing learning while on the move such as from trains, cafés, and teleworking spaces. Bonk (2009) suggested that "the routes we take to the local school, college, university, or government or corporate training centre are no longer just paved in concrete; our learning journeys might now take place aboard ships or planes, high up in the mountains, at the bottom of the Grand Canyon, or when standing on thinning sea ice. The world is wide open from sea, land, and ice views as well as from spaceships hovering hundreds of miles above or beyond."

Learners in this more open educational world are comfortable using a variety of technologies to connect to their learning. To be fully empowered, they also need to have a knowledge of learning space literacies (Keppell, 2014). Flexible learning provides opportunities to improve the student learning experience through flexibility in time, pace, place (physical, virtual, on-campus, off-campus, etc.), mode of study (print-based, face-to-face, blended, online, etc.), teaching approach (collaborative, independent, etc.), forms of assessment and staffing. It may utilize a wide range of media, environments, learning spaces, and technologies for learning and teaching. However, seamless learning requires the learner to take responsibility for their own learning journey. Self-regulated learning is the next dimension that we will explore that examines the role of the learner in personalised learning.

3 Self-Regulated Learning

"Self-regulated learning is a process that assists students in managing their thoughts, behaviors, and emotions in order to successfully navigate their learning experiences" (Zumbrunn, Tadlock, & Roberts, 2011, p. 4). It involves three phases: (1) forethought and planning, (2) performance monitoring, and (3) reflection. It requires the learner to take ownership for their own learning. Self-regulated learning is a key dimension of personalised learning that requires teachers to mentor and scaffold learning in order to encourage students to become autonomous learners.

Level 1: Scaffolding Learners

At this level, the learner needs to be mentored into adopting self-regulated learning strategies by the teacher. The teacher will support self-regulated learning through scaffolding and devolving learning to the learner. Scaffolding involves encouraging deep learning and a focus on encouraging the learner to achieve their goals through individualised support. As part of these efforts, the teacher empowers learners to take ownership of their own learning and assists them to begin to set learning goals.

Level 2: Strategic Learners

The goal of this level is to become a strategic learner where learners begin to manage their own learning. It is here at Level 2 that they need to take ownership, plan goals, and monitor their own performance. In addition, they begin to adopt a range of strategies to advance their own learning to a higher level.

Level 3: Autonomous Learners

At the third level, learners are able to evaluate performance on learning tasks and adapt their own learning. In effect, they have become reflective learners who make strategic decisions about their learning needs. Such learners independently determine appropriate learning goals and are becoming autonomous learners. They seek and explore learning options to achieve their goals.

4 Learning-Oriented Assessment

Learning-oriented assessment is about putting learning at the centre of assessment and reconfiguring assessment design so that the learning function is emphasised. Learning-oriented assessment has three core aspects: (1) *Assessment tasks as learning tasks*, (2) *Student involvement in the assessment processes*, and (2) *Forward-looking feedback* (Carless, Joughin, Liu, & Associates, 2006). Because all assessment leads to some form of learning, it is important to thoughtfully design assessment in order to encourage the types of learning outcomes that we value and desire (Boud, 1995; Carless, 2007, 2014; Keppell & Carless, 2006). I am particularly keen to reduce the common practice of teachers providing most of their feedback after a course has been completed which means that the learner is unable to act upon this feedback to enhance their learning (Keppell & Carless, 2006). Assessment should be relevant to the learner and provide exciting opportunities to solve learner-generated topics via authentic assessment.

Level 1: Authentic Assessment

First of all, authentic assessment focuses on real-world application, and involves problems, issues, etc., that should have direct relevance to the learner. At this level, assessment should be focussed on providing a context for the learning participants to see the value of assessment. For this to be effective, teachers need to develop authentic assessment tasks that have relevance and allow the application of student prior knowledge. They need to support authentic assessment through scaffolding and guiding the learner to fully participate in authentic assessment.

Level 2: Negotiated Assessment

At this level, the personalised learner is involved in negotiated assessment. Such negotiations may take the form of having input into the assessment rubric or other types of involvement which promotes a co-design of assessment in order to optimise relevance for the learner. Within group projects or peer assessment activities, learners will need to negotiate their role in ways that begin to mirror real-life interactions.

Level 3: Self-Assessment

A personalised learner at this level reflects on their performance and begins to choreograph their own learning through "feedback as feed-forward"

(Keppell, 2014). Those accomplished in self-assessment have the ability to act on this feedback to improve their learning. In addition, the learner should have a choice in the submission format of assessment. For a formal assignment, they will take responsibility for choosing a medium of presentation (e.g., written, audio, video, photographs, blog, etc.) that best suits the learning and assessment goals. Self-assessment as a customary practice means that the learner is always learning by acting on feedback on an iterative basis.

5 Lifelong Learning

Personalised learning requires a certain attitude and motivation. To be self-motivated to learn is both fun and a necessity for learners in the digital age. Personalised learners need to embrace the concept of lifelong learning due to the changing nature and fluidity of the job market where workers no longer have one job throughout their lifetime. Lifelong learners are self-regulated learners who seek challenge and act on feedback-as-feed-forward.

Level 1: Learning in the Short Term

At this level, learners are focussed on short-term goals of progressing through a course or a semester. Teachers have a responsibility to remind learners of the "bigger picture". It is essential for teachers to provide the relevance of their learning for future learning and the connection of their learning to a future career.

Level 2: Future-Oriented Learning

At this level, learners begin to take responsibility for their own learning and relate their current course focus to their future courses. They also begin to relate what they are doing to their future career aspirations and examine what is next in their learning to achieve these goals. As they begin to reflect on their learning, they also identify gaps in knowledge and undertake learning to address these gaps. In effect, they are becoming lifelong learners.

Level 3: Being a Learner

The final level of lifelong learning focuses on learning becoming a habit or a customary practice. This type of learner cannot imagine a day when they are not learning something new. In addition, this type of learner seeks life-wide learning experiences (Jackson, 2010) that stretch themselves to include areas that are not within their comfort zone. The forms of such lifelong learning may involve experiences in musical–rhythmic, visual–spatial, verbal–linguistic, logical–mathematical, bodily–kinesthetic, interpersonal, intrapersonal, and naturalistic intelligence (Gardner, 2000). Simply put, "beingness as a learner" is a distinct characteristic of this level.

6 Learning Pathways

This dimension of personalised learning focuses on gradually relinquishing control of the learning pathway to the learner. It begins with a structured learning pathway and aspires to a time when courses can be assembled by the learner to achieve their own learning goals. "Personalised learners will need to continually refine their learning journey by considering their desire paths at different stages of their learning journey" (Keppell, 2014).

Level 1: Prescribed Learning Pathway

The prescribed learning pathway, as its name suggests, focuses on a predetermined learning pathway for a specific purpose. Restrictive pathways provide minimal choice for the learner. It is important that teachers provide learner choice in authentic assessment, and foster self-regulated learning in this context.

Level 2: Flexible Learning Pathway

At this level, the learner has choice in terms of determining their electives and must rationalise their choice based on their future learning needs. It is essential that the learner begins to construct their own learning pathways in order to learn how to adjust learning pathways throughout their life.

Level 3: Open Education Pathway

At this level, the learner has the freedom to construct their own learning pathway to meet their learning needs. In the formal education setting, this freedom to construct one's learning pathway would involve learners assembling building block courses into a program of study. In addition, this may involve assembling open education resources (OER) or micro-courses.

Implications for Open Education

With the demand for tertiary education forecasted to significantly increase in the coming decades, personalised learning will be an essential component of success in a learning future. Gibney (2013), for instance, predicts that there will be an increase of 98 million students that will be undertaking tertiary education by 2025 and that "four major universities of 30,000+ students would need to open every week for the next 15 years." To accommodate such extraordinary numbers, open education will need to be more prevalent and new models of credentialing developed and tested. The Open Education Consortium suggests that open education "combines the traditions of knowledge sharing and creation with 21st century technology to create a vast pool of openly shared educational resources, while harnessing today's collaborative spirit to develop educational approaches that are more responsive to learners' needs" (Open Education Consortium, 2015).

The Open Education Resources university (OERu) is a consortium of 35 institutions focussed on developing open education courses that are equivalent to formal courses offered by universities. The courses are developed from open educational resources, thereby allowing learners to undertake self-directed learning and formal assessment of the course for credit (http://wikieducator.org/OERu). The OERu suggests that open education should "provide authentic opportunities for students to gain academic credit across a variety of disciplines at a range of accredited institutions as a result of active student-centred participation in online education experiences of the highest quality" (Jim Taylor, quoted in Mackintosh, 2014).

Conclusion

This chapter has explored a roadmap for personalised learning. Learning in the 21st century increasingly occurs outside of formal school or university settings; in this new age, there is a ubiquity of learning across a wide range of contexts, including work, home, and within the community: "The challenge for individuals in the dissolving social order of late modernity is to maintain, or regain, some control of their own destinies, to retain involvement in the creation of meaning" (Martin, 2008, p. 155).

I argue that personalised learners will need to have a rich range of knowledge, skills, and attitudes to learn in a changing and ambiguous learning environment. Learners need digital literacies, an understanding of seamless learning, and also need to be aware of their own learning through self-regulated learning. "Gaining a literacy of the digital is thus one means by which the individual can retain a hold on the shape of his/her life in an era of increasing uncertainty" (Martin, 2008, p. 156). In addition, learners need to be involved in assessment, embrace lifelong learning, and have a say in their learning pathways. Learners will need to be "chaos pilots" to navigate the changing learning landscape.

The roadmap detailed in this chapter is an aspirational framework that provides both teachers and learners with guidelines for promoting personalised learning. Digital technology has enabled access to learning that was previously not possible. However, without appropriate knowledge, skills, and attitudes, full participation will be quite limited.

Michael Keppell is Pro-Vice Chancellor (Learning Transformations) at Swinburne University of Technology in Melbourne. Previously, he was Executive Director, Australian Digital Futures Institute at the University of Southern Queensland and Director of the Digital Futures Collaborative Research Network (DF-CRN). He was also Project Director, Regional Universities Network (RUN) Maths and Science Digital Classroom project at University of the Southern Queensland.

Mike has a long professional history in higher education in Australia, Canada, and Hong Kong. His research focuses on digital futures, learning spaces, blended learning, learning-oriented assessment, authentic learning, leadership, and transformative learning using design-based research. He is an avid photographer and adventurer and has summited Mounts Kilimanjaro, Kenya and Kinabalu.

References

Beetham, H. (2010). *Digital literacy*. Lecture at Greenwich University. Retrieved from http://www.jiscinfonet.ac.uk/infokits/collaborative-tools/digital-literacy.

Belisle, C. (2006). Literacy and the digital knowledge revolution. In A. Martin & D. Madigan (Eds.). (2006). *Digital literacies for learning* (pp. 51–67), London: Facet.

Bonk, C. J. (2009, October 19). *The wide open learning world: Sea, land, and ice views*. Association for Learning Technology (ALT) Online Newsletter, Issue 17. Retrieved from http://archive.alt.ac.uk/newsletter.alt.ac.uk/newsletter.alt.ac.uk/1h7kpy8fa5s.html.

Boud, D. (1995). *Enhancing learning through self-assessment*. London: Kogan Page.

Carless, D. (2007). Learning-oriented assessment: Conceptual basis and practical implications. *Innovations in Education and Teaching International, 44*(1), 57–66.

Carless, D. (2014). *Exploring learning-oriented assessment processes. Higher Education*. DOI 10.1007/s10734-014-9816-z.

Carless, D., Joughin, G., Liu, N. F., & Associates. (2006). *How assessment supports learning: Learning-oriented assessment in action*. Hong Kong: Hong Kong University Press.

Conole, G. (2014). *Disruptive innovation and the emergence of the PLE+*. Retrieved from: http://e4innovation.com/?m=201408.

Dweck, C. (2006). *Mindset: How you can fulfil your potential*. London: Constable and Robinson, Ltd.

Gardner, H. (2000). *Intelligence reframed: Multiple intelligences for the 21st century*. New York: Basic Books Inc.

Gibney, E. (2013, January 13). A different world. *Times Higher Education*. Retrieved from: http://www.timeshighereducation.co.uk/features/a-different-world/2001128.article.

Jackson, N. J. (2010). From a curriculum that integrates work to a curriculum that integrates life: Changing a university's conceptions of curriculum. *Higher Education Research & Development, 29*(5), 491–505. doi:10.1080/07294360.2010.502218.

Johnson, L., Adams, S., Cummins, M., & Estrada, V. (2012). *Technology outlook for STEM+ education 2012_2017: An NMC horizon report sector analysis*. Austin, TX: The NewMedia Consortium.

Keppell, M. (2014). Personalised learning strategies for higher education. In K. Fraser (Ed.), *The future of learning and teaching in next generation learning spaces*. International Perspectives on Higher Education Research, Volume 12 (pp. 3–21). Bingley, UK: Emerald Group Publishing Limited.

Keppell, M. J. (2010). *Blended and flexible learning standards*. Charles Sturt University. Unpublished report.

Keppell, M., & Carless, D. (2006). Learning-oriented assessment: A technology-based case study. *Assessment in Education, 13*(2), 153–65.

Kuh, G. D. (1996). Guiding principles for creating seamless learning environments for undergraduates. *Journal of College Student Development, 37*(2), 135–48.

Lankshear, C., & Knobel, M. (Eds.) (2008). *Digital literacies: Concepts, policies and practices*. New York: Peter Lang.

Lockyer, L., & Kerr, Y. (2000). *Learner as designer-producer: Physical and health education students experience of Web-based learning resource development.* (pp. 591–5) World Conference on Educational Multimedia, Hypermedia and Telecommunications, Chesapeake, VA: Association for the Advancement of Computing in Education (AACE).

Mackintosh, W. (2014, May 11). *OERu launches strategic planning consultation.* Retrieved from http://oeru.org/news/oeru-launches-strategic-planning-consultation/.

Martin, A. (2008). Digital literacy and the "digital society." In C. Lankshear and M. Knobel (Eds.), *Digital literacies: Concepts, policies and practices.* New York: Peter Lang (pp. 151–76).

Open Education Consortium (2015). *About the Open Education Consortium.* Retrieved from http://www.oeconsortium.org/about-oec/.

Sharples, M., McAndrew, P., Weller, M., Ferguson, R., FitzGerald, E., Hirst, T., & Gaved, M. (2013). *Innovating pedagogy 2013: Open University Innovation Report 2.* Milton Keynes: The Open University.

Sharples, M., McAndrew, P., Weller, M., Ferguson, R., FitzGerald, E., Hirst, T., & Whitelock, D. (2012). *Innovating pedagogy 2012: Open University Innovation Report 1.* Milton Keynes: The Open University.

Siemens, G. (2006). *Knowing knowledge.* Creative commons. Retrieved from http://www.elearnspace.org/KnowingKnowledge_LowRes.pdf.

Swanson, K. (2013). *Professional learning in the digital age: The educator's guide to user-generated learning.* Larchmont, NY: Eye On Education, Inc.

Wikieducator. (2014). *OERu.* Retrieved from http://wikieducator.org/OERu.

Zumbrunn, S., Tadlock, J., & Roberts, E. D. (2011). *Encouraging self-regulated learning in the classroom: A review of the literature.* Metropolitan Educational Research Consortium (MERC). Virginia Commonwealth University. Retrieved from: http://www.self-regulation.ca/download/pdf_documents/Self Regulated Learning.pdf.

27

PEER2PEER AND OPEN PEDAGOGY OF MOOCs TO SUPPORT THE KNOWLEDGE COMMONS

Rita Kop and Hélène Fournier

Connectivist massive open online courses (cMOOCs) represent a new pedagogical approach in the network age. cMOOCs focus on knowledge creation and generation. In cMOOCs, the learners take a role in shaping their learning experiences, while facilitators focus on fostering a space for learning connections to occur. When in a cMOOC, students are empowered to make their own learning decisions. This self-reliance is the basis for a re-emergence of the promising paradigms in educational practice of informal, autonomous learning, self-directed learning, and self-managed learning within personal learning environments.

Loosely organized learning networks such as MOOCs can be placed in the category of non-formal learning where learning does not necessary lead to an academic or technical credential (Bouchard, 2014). In the earliest cMOOCs, which first emerged in 2008 and 2009, certain students received credits through the University of Manitoba, whereas others located across the world participated informally at no cost. Indeed, enrollment was open to anybody interested in the subject who had an Internet connection. Other models of participation were also arranged with one student undertaking the activities at her own pace but still being evaluated by her own institution (Fini, 2009).

Such approaches lead to the questioning of the role of formal institutions in light of the growth of MOOCs and options for engaging in informal learning. While institutions still play an important role in providing credentials for acquired knowledge, the current move towards openness of knowledge means that their role may be changing in an era of networked knowledge where people share their expertise for free (Bouchard, 2014; Weller, 2013). Not only is a form of open scholarship developing, but informally acquired knowledge is being valued at a higher level than ever before (Irvine, Code, & Richards, 2013). Moreover, research on self-directed learners in MOOCs and other open educational environments underscores the point that it is vital to understand the specific types of resources that learners find valuable to their changing learning needs. In addition, if learners find resources informally on the Web network on which cMOOCs are positioned, it is important to contemplate the role of the network itself.

Some researchers see structural problems with online networks that might prevent learners from having access to the best resources for their learning needs. For example, Bouchard's research revealed that "The natural tendency within the 'perfectly' democratic network is to organize itself, over time, in a hierarchical system composed of leaders and followers. The social organization of networked learning on a personal learning environment has been described as resembling the 'outside' world of government and commerce, with the difference that the currency of exchange in the network is not money or power, but reputation and popularity" (Bouchard, 2011, p. 296).

As we have observed in monitoring and evaluating several cMOOCs, the reputation and popularity of facilitators such as George Siemens, who wrote the foreword to this volume, and Stephen Downes, from the Canadian Research Council, often accounts for much of the motivation to register and attend the first few live sessions. Reputation and popularity, however, cannot counter what Graham (2006), in his work on blended learning that predated MOOCs by a couple of years, has identified as persistent barriers or challenges in self-directed environments. The barriers he identified included the lack of feedback and support, lack of personalization, and overwhelming amounts of resources.

Research also highlights that the changes and ease of access to information and knowledge that technology provides means that information behaviour of learners is dramatically changing, as is learner or participant relationships with "knowledgeable others" (Bouchard, 2014; Mott & Wiley, 2009; Pardo & Kloos, 2011). Why would learners, for instance, rely on university professors for access to resources and articles as they are openly and freely available to anyone with access to a computational device?

To add to the complexity, our understanding of the intricacies of the network is still limited, especially in terms of the knowledge that is vital for learners to negotiate the Web structure effectively while learning. Kop and Bouchard (2011) posited that it is the presence and involvement of knowledgeable others in an environment characterized by many technological variables and contexts that help learners make sense and be critical of the multitude of resources offered on the Web. As part of our human social nature we communicate, reflect on activities and information, and make connections with what we already know. Information and knowledge is validated in the process.

The developing online networks are promising places for such novel or generative connections and knowledge to occur as they offer possibilities to receive information not just from one information broker, or the mass media, but from a multitude of people. Social media could facilitate the transformation from an educational model structured around courses, controlled by institutions using a "broadcasting" model in an enclosed environment, to a model that is adapted to learners' needs and owned by individuals using an aggregation model in a personalized open learning environment that provides a fluid extension of the wider informal personal space.

Open and Active Learning

If technology facilitates the transfer of power from institutions to learners, this will put the onus on the learner to not be passive and wait for the transfer of knowledge from an instructor. A certain level of autonomy and activity will be required to move her learning forward.

For decades, numerous educationalists have advocated the move from a pedagogical approach to an andragogical one in education and learning (Knowles, 1970; Tough, 1971). This educational trend entailed a shift from dependency by the learner to higher levels of self-direction. It also marked a distinct shift in emphasis from subject-based learning towards problem-based learning. Finally, it involved a shift from teaching towards facilitating. At the same time, there were strong voices calling for the reduction of the influence of institutions in our everyday life (Foucault, 1977; Illich, 1971).

Illich's vision was to see people take ownership of the learning process, rather than rely on institutions to control education. He called for "the possible use of technology to create institutions which serve personal, creative and autonomous interaction and the emergence of values which cannot be substantially controlled by technocrats" (1971, p. 2). He perceived that the alternative to "scholastic funnels," as he called educational institutions, would be true communication webs. In his work, Illich discussed the restriction on freedom, the "enclosure of the commons," the increased policing, and surveillance of everyday life from traditional educational institutions (Illich, 1992, p. 51), and the stifling effect all this has on people's creativity. Interestingly, these are the same issues that are increasingly discussed today in education (Benkler, 2006; Bouchard, 2014; Willis, Spiers, & Gettings, 2013). Under the influence of emerging technologies, the development of "open education" (e.g., MOOCs) seems promising as an avenue for moving Illich's ideas into reality. In the words of Willis et al.:

> MOOCs tread on the utopia of education, the promise of knowledge, power, and social mobility vis-à-vis traditional or even online platforms, thereby marking out space that undermines the monetary value of education all the while elevating the value of disseminating the potentiality of knowledge for those who otherwise may not be participants. (Willis et al., 2013, p. 2)

New technologies make it possible to connect with other people and exchange information and create knowledge on an unprecedented scale; they facilitate the creation of an open knowledge commons.

The Knowledge Commons: Challenges of Learning on the Network

We have spoken about the abundance of information on the Web, and how learner information behaviour might change under the influence of technology. The wealth of information means that choices need to be made about what information and resources are valuable and what not, while the low level of teacher presence on open online networks increases the self-directed nature of this task for learners. Some researchers advocate for online services that stimulate human filtering to help Web users with this information abundance, whereas others are working on automated information filtering systems (Boyd, 2010; Duval, 2011).

The challenge is that access to information on the Web is influenced by inherent power relations and the distinctive ways in which networks develop (Barabasi, 2003). It is also clear that commercial interests influence what information individuals can access easily and what they have to work harder for to find or have to pay for (Bouchard, 2014; Ingram, 2014). Such issues raise not only educational questions and concerns, but also societal ones about the need for open and free access to information. Harvard Law School Professor Yocahi Benkler formulated this well:

> How a society produces its information environment goes to the very core of freedom. Who gets to say what, to whom? What is the state of the world? What counts as credible information? How will different forms of action affect the way the world can become? These questions go to the foundations of effective human action. (Benkler, 2006, p. 1)

Such questions and concerns are at the heart of the development of the "Knowledge Commons." The Web is a place where information is stored, in addition to being a place where people come together and actively do something with this information and the available resources (perhaps to produce multimedia, share, remix, or build on information). It is not only access to information that is at stake but also public access to knowledge. According to Hess and Ostrom, this situation requires "a new way of looking at knowledge as a shared resource, a complex ecosystem that is a commons—a resource shared by a group of people that is subject to social dilemmas" (Hess & Ostrom, 2006, p. 3). The commons might also be a place at which different disciplines come together and solve joint problems related to that knowledge.

Increasingly, countries aim at developing a "knowledge economy" dependent on free flows of and free access to information. Individuals are also increasingly "do-it-yourself" learners, which means that access to free and open content will increase their potential to find valuable, relevant information in their searches. As most current knowledge has been produced by publicly funded universities, it is important to grasp who actually owns that knowledge as well as the yet to be developed future knowledge (Bouchard, 2014).

The research agenda related to free and open education and open online knowledge has to a large extent been owned by the US and Europe, or, in effect, the more developed portions of the Northern hemisphere. At the same time, the actual research results have, until recently, been mainly published by commercial publishers. As a result, copyright of the publications has been transferred to these publishers. There are intense debates about such copyright and intellectual property rights today. Data for research have also been largely proprietary and owned by the producer. This has led to a worldwide billion-dollar intellectual property (IP) control industry (Bouchard, 2014; Weller, 2011). However, IP laws and practices were developed in a time of scarcity of resources. As we have moved into an era of abundance of resources, the old IP control systems no longer seem to work.

Some serious challenges against the closed knowledge situation are developing, especially as innovative and open alternatives are available. The scientific community and governments, such as the European Union, are all advocating for openness in data (including their own government data), as well as unprocessed Big Data and research publications so that data-mining and other forms of analysis and knowledge development might be made achievable (UNESCO, 2014; OECD, 2013).

Big and Open Data to Enhance Learning

The majority of e-learning design models are currently founded on the development of positive learning outcomes under the influence of effective teaching practice in institutions of higher education. Without a doubt, new and emerging learning technologies make different models possible. Some research groups are currently working on data-driven learner support structures and learning environments such as MOOCs. The European Union as well as the National Research Council of Canada are each separately funding several large research projects to develop personal learning environments by using data (as well as visualizing traces of data) that learners have left behind in their online activities to support their learning (Downes, 2013; Duval, 2011). At the same time, the Open University in the UK is working on discourse analysis techniques to enhance learning (Ferguson, Wei, He, & Buckingham Shum, 2013). Moreover, a research group at Carnegie Mellon University is just starting to work on using machine-learning techniques to personalize the learning experience (Spice, 2014).

Clearly, researchers of the 21st century have access to massive amounts of data that capture the entire digital experience in a constant stream of inputs and outputs.

Given such massive data inputs, the key challenge is the analysis of such "Big" data. Big Data poses new difficulties in terms of incredible diversity and abundance of data as well as the complexity and uncertainty in deciphering any meaning from it. There are also challenges related to determining important contextual cues or information from the data, and in the overall interpretation of results (Kitchin, 2014).

What all of these projects have in common is that they attempt to use learner data to enhance future learning. However, there is intense debate around the ethical use of data gathered from online learners. There are also myriad issues around informed consent in conducting research. As shown in the recently published Facebook experiment on emotional contagion (Authur, 2014), such ethical issues and concerns may or may not influence or affect users of social media.

The problem, of course, is that it is not the learner who is in charge of these projects, but technologists and researchers. In some cases, the research is even funded by corporations and it is unclear how this might affect the research. For instance, if corporations such as Google fund educational research projects, we have to question the research results as Google has a vested interest in the findings; accordingly, the results can impact its bottom line. Such corporate embedded search practices stand in stark contrast to those who advocate for open learning and an open knowledge commons. Moreover, sociologists argue that "any form of digital data is an evolving entity that the original sources often have little or no control over" (Selwyn, 2014, p. 7). Furthermore, those data are not only shaped but also shape our everyday lives. This means that we should be cautious about how data are being used in an educational context as the different layers of data might make it non-transparent how they have been manipulated and who controls them.

Open Access to Knowledge and Education

Of course, there are many questions to ask in relation to opening up education and knowledge. Weller (2011) insightfully revealed how digital and open scholarship can be fostered through the current technological changes. He also pointed out how openness of academic publication might positively impact on public engagement. In 2013, Weller highlighted a variety of motivations for providers to offer MOOCs, including opening access, experimenting with pedagogy, and marketing their courses (Weller, 2013).

These motivations pose a challenge for MOOC providers and instructors. For instance, it is difficult to filter and streamline the abundance of information made available to learners as well as the resources and data generated by these same learners and other MOOC participants. Kop, Fournier, and Mak (2011) argued for the need of a human face to the pedagogy in an open learning environment, not just an automated one. When a human touch is added, there is a sense of trust in the validity of the information and any knowledge that emerges or develops later. Kop et al. also posit that active engagement in the learning process by the learner is at the heart of a quality learning experience.

This emphasis on active and engaging learning resonates with the views of Stephen Downes, one of the founders of the MOOC. Downes (2013) suggested that to harness the potential of emerging technologies in connectivist MOOCs, four principles are paramount to foster learning, namely: (1) the autonomy of participants, (2) connectivity, (3) the diversity of participants, and (4) openness. Moreover, Siemens (2011) and Bell (2011) have highlighted the importance of human agency and the necessity of active participation in connectivist learning. Facilitators in a cMOOC promote a learning organization whereby there is not a body of knowledge to be transferred from educator to learner and where learning does not take place in a single environment. Instead, Connectivism promotes an environment in which participants contribute resources and technologies peer to peer to the network and are active participants on networks around a particular topic of interest. In doing so, they contribute to the Knowledge Commons.

One of the challenges that all MOOCs have in common, however, is that participants use them as they do other Web resources. For instance, at times they dip in and out to select and mix resources and technologies to complement their own learning needs. Such behavior is atypical of learners in university courses. As a result, this Web as a resource mentality by many MOOC participants has been perceived as contributing to the exceedingly high dropout rates in MOOC-related learning opportunities. Our research in cMOOCs has shown that for participants to remain engaged in MOOCs, it is necessary to create a learning environment with a high level of activity and presence of participants. If this is achieved, the open educational MOOC network is a good place for contemporary learners to find their information, make connections with others, and be challenged to learn.

How Could MOOCs Contribute to the Knowledge Commons?

The MOOC concept at its inception seemed promising to achieve an open learning environment that creates networks of people learning from each other and contributing to a common good, which we label a "Knowledge Commons." In such a knowledge commons, MOOCs are positioned on the cusp of formal and informal education. In this gray space between formal and informal education, MOOCs are open and they are not necessarily controlled by educational institutions; in fact, they could be controlled by the learners or participants.

As noted earlier, MOOCs have been around since 2008. Initially, they were based on connectivist principles. Connectivist experimentations were suddenly possible, since, at the time, emerging technologies increasingly facilitated peer-to-peer interaction, collaboration, and knowledge and resource sharing on an unimaginable scale. People were invited to explore, reach out, evaluate, create, connect, negotiate, share, and control their learning environment.

More recently, however, the name MOOC has been repurposed by several higher education institutions to mean something different. In effect, technological platforms have allowed for the scalability and replication of traditional university courses with a top-down pedagogy in an online environment. This development has allowed higher education institutions to market their course offerings by opening up tasters to the wider public. At the same time, it has also allowed for the creation of for-profit spin-out companies. Providers of these MOOCs (sometimes referred to as xMOOCs) have so far closed the courses after they end, which highly restricts their contribution to an open knowledge commons. The connectivist MOOCs, in contrast, leave open their learning environments and make the student contributions and resources produced by knowledgeable invitees freely available, which also contributes to the commons.

Conclusion

The generation, accumulation, processing, and analysis of digital data is now being touted as a potential solution for many prevailing educational problems. Researchers are currently working on using data to enhance the learning experience and to personalize learner searches. However, researchers call for caution in how data are being used in an educational context. This leads us to believe that, at least at the present time, the validation of data and information might still require the involvement of humans, perhaps through the use of social media.

We propose a learning design model that not only uses data, but also technologies, such as social media. The learning design model would allow the support of learners in a one-off event, such as the participation in a MOOC. Perhaps more importantly, it would also keep the resources and communications channels available after the event to contribute to the open knowledge commons. We have tentatively produced a model for the purposes of this chapter (see Figure 27.1).

It is clear from the model that we value human involvement. What also is noticeable in this model is that we want to ensure MOOCs contribute not only to learners' own learning process and that of their peers during an open learning event, but also to the Knowledge Commons. For this to occur, MOOCs should be open and make available all resources. Moreover, learners' active involvement in knowledge production, and in creating and contributing to knowledge, should be fostered. This viewpoint requires a pedagogical model that is based not just on the traditional transfer of knowledge, but that also involves active participation in the learning process, through which learners produce something of relevance. It involves communication with (knowledgeable) others to advance their learning as well as guidance on how to contribute to the Knowledge Commons. It is toward such ends that we are proceeding in promoting a philosophy of sharing across any and all learning environments We invite you to meet us there!

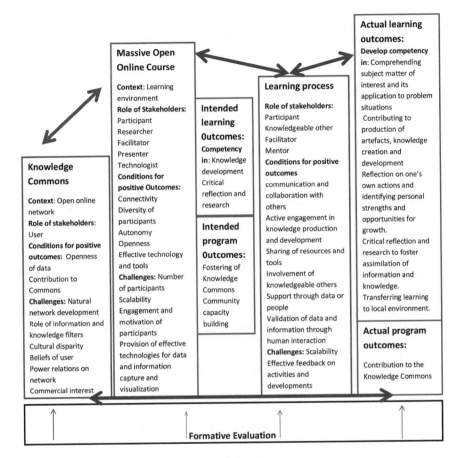

FIGURE 27.1 MOOC model of the Knowledge Commons

Rita Kop is Dean of the Faculty of Education at fully online Yorkville University. She has been a researcher at the National Research Council of Canada and holds a PhD in Adult Continuing Education. Her current research focuses on learning in advanced networked learning environments. Before she joined the NRC, she was an assistant professor at Swansea University in the UK. At Swansea, Rita worked with community groups and universities contributing to community-based and online services for adults in some of the most deprived areas of the UK. Dr Kop is originally from the Netherlands, where she spent ten years as teacher and headteacher in elementary education. Additional information on Dr Kop can be found at: http://www.you-learn.org. She can be contacted at rkop@yorkvilleu.ca.

 **Hélène Fournier** has been a Research Officer at the National Research Council Canada's Institute for Information Technology since 2002 and holds a PhD in Educational Psychology from McGill University. The primary focus of her research is in education and technology. She has participated in several research projects focused on the application and evaluation of advanced technologies in the training sector, in distance education, and, more recently, in the learner-centered research and development of Connectivist Massive Open Online Courses (cMOOCs) and Learning and Performance Support Systems. Dr Fournier has contributed to the advancement of research in the field of distance education, online learning, and adult learning. She has also been engaged in the study of informal learning experiences in the context of cMOOCs. She has published widely in peer-reviewed journals and at international conferences.

References

Authur, C. (June, 2014). Facebook emotion study breached ethical guidelines, researchers say. *The Guardian*. Retrieved from http://www.theguardian.com/technology/2014/jun/30/facebook-emotion-study-breached-ethical-guidelines-researchers-say.

Barabasi, A. (2003). *Linked: How everything is connected to everything else and what it means*. New York: Penguin Books.

Bell, F. (2011). Connectivism: Its place in theory-informed research and innovation in technology-enabled learning. *International Review of Research in Open and Distance Learning*. Retrieved from http://www.irrodl.org/index.php/irrodl/article/view/902/1664.

Benkler, Y. (2006) *The wealth of networks: How social production transforms markets and Freedom*. New Haven and London: Yale University Press.

Bouchard, P. (2011). Network promises & their implications. In The impact of social networks on teaching & learning. *Revista de Universidad y Sociedad del Conocimiento (RUSC)*, *8*(1), 288–302. University Of Catalunya. Retrieved from http://rusc.uoc.edu/ojs/index.php/rusc/article/view/v8n1-bouchard/v8n1-bouchard-eng.

Bouchard, P. (2014, June). The problem of learner control in networked learning environments. *Journal of Literacy and Technology*, *15*(2), 80–110. Retrieved from http://www.literacyandtechnology.org/uploads/1/3/6/8/136889/pb_3.pdf.

Boyd, D. (2010, September/October). Streams of content, limited attention: The flow of information through social media. *EDUCAUSE Review*, *45*(5), 26–36.

Downes, S. (2013, December 4). Learning and performance support systems. *Half an Hour*. Retrieved from http://halfanhour.blogspot.com.es/2013/12/learning-and-performance-support-systems.html.

Duval, E. (2011, February). Attention please! Learning analytics for visualization and recommendation. *Proceedings of 1st International Conference on Learning Analytics and Knowledge*, Banff, Alberta, Canada.

Ferguson, R., Wei, Z., He, Y., & Buckingham Shum, S. (2013, April). An evaluation of learning analytics to identify exploratory dialogue in online discussions. *Proceedings of the Third Conference on Learning Analytics and Knowledge (LAK 2013)*, CAN, pp. 85–93, Leuven, Belgium.

Fini, A. (2009). The technological dimension of a massive open online course: The case of the CCK08 course tools. *The International Review of Research in Open and Distance Learning, 10*(5). Retrieved from http://www.irrodl.org/index.php/irrodl/article/view/643/1402.

Foucault, M. (1977) *Discipline and punish: The birth of the prison*. London: Peregrine Press.

Graham, C. R. (2006). Blended learning systems: Definition, current trends, future directions. In C. J. Bonk & C. R. Graham (Eds.), *The handbook of blended learning: Global perspectives, local designs* (pp. 3–21). San Francisco, CA: Pfeiffer Publishing.

Hess, C., & Ostrom, E. (2006) *Understanding knowledge as a commons: From theory to practice*. Cambridge, MA: The MIT Press.

Illich, I. (1971). *Deschooling society*. Reprinted in 1978 by Marion Boyars, London.

Illich, I. (1992). *In the mirror of the past*. New York and London: Marion Boyars Publishers.

Ingram, M. (2014, May 23). Giants behaving badly: Google, Facebook and Amazon show us the downside of monopolies and black-box algorithms. *Gigaom*. Retrieved from http://gigaom.com/2014/05/23/giants-behaving-badly-google-facebook-and-amazon-show-us-the-downside-of-monopolies-and-black-box-algorithms/.

Irvine, V., Code, J. & Richards, L. (2013). Realigning higher education for the 21st century learner through multi-access learning. *MERLOT Journal of Online Learning and Teaching, 9*(2), 172–86. Retrieved from http://jolt.merlot.org/vol9no2/irvine_0613.pdf.

Kitchin, R. (2014, April–June). Big data, new epistemologies and paradigm shifts. *Big Data & Society. 1*(1). Retrieved from http://bds.sagepub.com/content/1/1/2053951714528481.full.pdf+html.

Knowles, M. (1970). *The modern practice of adult education: Andragogy versus pedagogy*. New York: Cambridge Book Co.

Kop, R., & Bouchard, P. (2011). The role of adult educators in the age of social media. In M. Thomas (Ed.), *Digital education*. London: Palgrave Macmillan.

Kop, R., Fournier, H., & Mak, S. F. J. (2011). A pedagogy of abundance or a pedagogy to support human beings? Participant support on massive open online courses. *International Review of Research in Open and Distance Learning, 12*(7), 74–93. Retrieved from http://www.irrodl.org/index.php/irrodl/article/view/1041/2025.

Mott, J., & Wiley, D. (2009). Open or learning: The CMS and the open learning network. *E in Education: Exploring our connective educational landscape, 15*(2), 3–22. Retrieved from http://ineducation.ca/index.php/ineducation/article/view/53/529.

OECD (2013). *Commercialising public research: New trends and strategies*. OECD Directorate for Science, Technology and Industry. Retrieved from http://www.oecd.org/science/sci-tech/commercialising-public-research.pdf.

Pardo, A., & Kloos, C.D. (2011, February/March). Stepping out of the box. Towards analytics outside the Learning Management System. *Proceedings of the 1st International Conference on Learning Analytics and Knowledge* (pp. 163–7), ACM, Banff, Alberta, Canada.

Selwyn, N. (2014). Data entry: Towards the critical study of digital data and education. *Learning, Media and Technology*. Retrieved from https://www.academia.edu/7187672/Data_entry_towards_the_critical_study_of_digital_data_and_education.

Siemens, G. (2011). Moving beyond self-directed learning: Network-directed learning. *Connectivism*. Retrieved from http://www.connectivism.ca/?p=307.

Spice, B. (2014, June 24) Paying attention to how people learn promises to enhance MOOCs. *Carnegie Mellon News*. Retrieved from http://www.cmu.edu/news/stories/archives/2014/june/june24_improvingmoocs.html.

Tough, A. (1971). *The adult learning projects: A fresh approach to theory and practice in adult learning.* Toronto: Ontario Institute for Studies in Education.

UNESCO (2014, June 1). UNESCO publications now freely available through a new open access repository. *UNESCO Media Services.* Retrieved from http://www.unesco.org/new/en/media-services/single-view/news/unesco_publications_now_freely_available_through_a_new_open_access_repository/#.U7_q5Wcg_EU.

Weller, M. (2011). *The digital scholar: How technology is transforming scholarly practice.* Bloomsbury Academic, London, UK. Retrieved from http://www.bloomsburycollections.com/book/the-digital-scholar-how-technology-is-transforming-scholarly-practice/.

Weller, M. (2013). The battle for open—a perspective. *Journal for the Interactive Media in Education, 15.* Retrieved from http://jime.open.ac.uk/article/2013-15/pdf.

Willis, J.E., Spiers, E.L., & Gettings, P. (2013). MOOCs and Foucault's heterotopia: On community and self-efficacy. *Proceedings LINC 2013 Conference,* MIT, Cambridge, MA. Retrieved from http://jime.open.ac.uk/jime/index.

28

MOOCs 2030

A Future for Massive Online Learning

Rebecca Ferguson, Mike Sharples, and Russell Beale

Introduction

In this chapter, we look ahead to the year 2030 and consider the ways in which current visions of massive open online courses may develop into realities. We also look at the changes in pedagogy, technology, and the wider environment that will be necessary in order for them to flourish.

MOOCs are a form of technology-enhanced learning (TEL). Like other successful TEL innovations, we can expect them to mature and transform over a period of many years. Like other such innovations, MOOCs are based on a core vision—of massive-scale open learning—that will keep them focused during this period of extended development. This vision is shaped in relation to the 'TEL Complex' (Scanlon et al., 2013), an interlocking system of technologies, peoples, and practices (see Figure 28.1).

The TEL innovations that flourish are those that engage with every element of the complex. As shown in Figure 28.1, these elements include the wider context of policy, funding, and environment, as well as the different communities and practices that exist within that context. They also include the developments in pedagogy and technology associated with this vision of learning.

For an innovation in TEL to succeed, a persistent vision of educational change is required. This vision gives the innovation a purpose, a direction, and a base. In the case of MOOCs, the vision has three elements: (1) meeting global society's need for education, (2) opening up education, and (3) benefiting from education at scale. In other words, today's societies need massive open education for their citizens to develop and prosper.

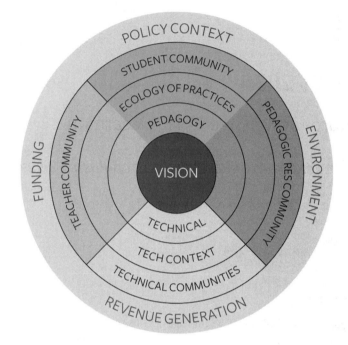

FIGURE 28.1   The Beyond Prototypes model of the TEL Complex

The MOOC Vision: Meeting Society's Needs

Almost 20 years ago, Sir John Daniel, the former Vice Chancellor of The Open University, observed that "a sizeable new university would now be needed every week merely to sustain current participation rates in higher education" (Daniel, 1996, p. 4). More recently, at the opening of the FutureLearn MOOC platform, the British Minister of State for Universities and Science noted that "MOOCs provide the opportunity to widen access to our world-class universities and to meet the global demand for higher education" (quoted in Clifton, 2013). This increasing demand for education is partly due to population growth, with the world population forecast to increase by almost one billion people over the next 12 years (United Nations, 2013). It is also partly due to the increasing number of people worldwide who are trying to access the benefits associated with post-secondary education and training.

The first MOOCs, known as "connectivist MOOCs," were developed as collections of online resources for individuals to develop skills, knowledge, and attitudes needed to thrive in a digital economy. Because a connectivist MOOC encourages people to create networks across local, regional, and national boundaries, it aims to increase participation in the lifelong learning and collaborative practices needed by digital citizens (McAuley, Stewart, Siemens, & Cormier, 2010).

More recently, MOOC platforms, including Coursera and Udacity, have also addressed these issues of participation and empowerment. The Udacity website states that "education should empower students to succeed not just in school but in life [. . .] Udacians are curious and engaged world citizens" (https://www. udacity.com/us). The introduction by Udacity of "Nanodegrees" is intended to provide a compact way for employees to develop the skills they need to advance their careers. Meanwhile, Coursera's mission states "We aim to empower people with education that will improve their lives, the lives of their families, and the communities they live in" (https://www.coursera.org/about/).

The MOOC Vision: Opening Up Education

In order to educate and empower citizens worldwide, MOOCs need to make education accessible. Anderson (2013) identifies four ways in which they can do that: (1) opening courses up to learners from other areas and countries, (2) opening courses up in terms of academic freedom and free speech, (3) opening up content by providing it as open source software and open educational resources, and (4) opening up enrolment to everyone without regard to demographic data or to previous experience.

Sebastian Thrun, co-founder of Udacity, originally expressed his vision of openness as: "I am against education that is only available to the top one per cent of all students. I am against tens of thousands of dollars of tuition expenses. I am against the imbalance that the present system brings to the world. I want to empower the 99 per cent" (Leckhart & Cheshire, 2012).

In order to match this ambition, learners will need a range of tools, skills, and resources, including:

- access to personal computing devices and the Internet;
- unrestricted access to key sites;
- MOOCs available in a language they understand well, designed with accessibility in mind as well as to support progression;
- safe environments for young learners;
- enough basic knowledge to be able to begin learning;
- skills in digital literacy, online study, and social networking; and
- high motivation and self-efficacy.

Some of these are essential in order to access online learning. Some are necessary for continuing to engage with courses. Others are prerequisites for a productive learning experience. It is already apparent that MOOCs cannot empower everyone. They can, at best, offer a safe, engaging, and informative environment for learning. The necessary technology, infrastructure, and learning skills must be developed by societies that value online higher education and can equip their citizens to engage with it.

The MOOC Vision: Education at Scale

"Massive" provides more than a route to opening up education. For learners, scale offers access to support from a wide range of other learners, to resources provided by those learners, and to a range of perspectives. For educators, scale offers a positive and enjoyable experience, opportunities for increased access to resources, and a motivation to develop teaching practices. For society, scale offers the potential to develop tools and resources for use in other contexts, to change professional practice, to increase access to education and to achieve global impact by solving large-scale problems (Ferguson & Sharples, 2014).

Putting these elements of the MOOC vision together suggests that:

> by 2030, the systems that develop from MOOCs will be meeting needs of societies by educating millions of digital citizens worldwide. They will open up access to education and enable people all over the world to enjoy the benefits of learning at scale. This can only happen if there is persistent intent not only from MOOC providers, but also from policy makers and educators.

In order to achieve this, all elements of the TEL Complex (see Figure 28.1) need to be taken into account. Changes to practices in pedagogy, technology, and the wider environment will be essential. The following sections examine the changes that will be required in these areas.

Pedagogy: Approaches to Learning and Teaching

If MOOCs are to meet societies' needs, open up education, and reap the benefits of learning at scale, by 2030 our pedagogies must take into account new groups of learners, new roles for educators, and new approaches to learning design.

Learners

MOOCs emerged from universities, where academics had the time and resources to develop them, but this may not prove to be their natural habitat. Recent surveys of MOOC participants show that many learners are already well educated. When the University of Edinburgh analysed data from their initial MOOCs, offered using Coursera, over 70 percent of respondents stated they had a first degree, and 40 percent had a postgraduate degree (University of Edinburgh, 2013). Although thousands who are unemployed or who have never attended university are registering for MOOCs, the scales are weighted in favour of those who already possess the skills necessary for study at this level.

Changes are beginning to take place as MOOC providers offer courses introducing essential online study skills. Currently, most education above primary level proceeds on the assumption that learners know how to be students and where to focus their attention. At the same time, there is an assumption that they know what to expect in a learning environment and what is expected of them. However, this knowledge has typically been gained in a face-to-face environment. Future learners will need to know how to take responsibility for aspects of their learning journey, how to function as self-directed online learners, and how to make the most of the possibilities offered by open online learning at scale.

Educators

Educators also need to know how to make the most of these possibilities, and how they can support learners effectively when opportunities for one-to-one contact are very limited. In many cases, content production and presentation will be split up to a greater extent than in face-to-face environments, especially when the same course is presented on many occasions or adapted for different platforms. Educators will spend less time lecturing and more time within discussion forums, where they will be involved in motivating and socialising learners. They will also foster the promotion of information exchange, knowledge construction, and learning development.

John Daniel's view is that opening up teaching to the public view will encourage many institutions to improve their provision.

> MOOCs will create popular and public indices of teaching quality. This may expose the teaching weaknesses in some elite institutions. The publicity and scale of the format will oblige institutions to do more than pay lip service to the importance of teaching and put it at the core their missions. This is the real revolution of MOOCs. (John Daniel, quoted in Haggard, 2013)

This view presents the role of the teacher as being the same in MOOCs and classrooms. In reality, there will be multiple roles for educators within the systems that develop from MOOCs. Those trained as teachers and lecturers will apply their skills and widen their repertoire to include online presentation, facilitation, and mentoring. Some may choose to specialise in one of these areas, or in learning design. Others will work on content production, together with media producers, animators, social media specialists, and others. Librarians will help learners to acquire digital literacy skills, access resources, and evaluate sources. All this activity will draw on the work of researchers whose findings are based on tests and observations related to thousands of learners. By 2030, a MOOC educator will be a member of a skilled team that works together to build on the subject knowledge and professional expertise of all team members.

Learning Design

A key role for those whose professional expertise is in education will be the design of courses for effective learning. These designs will take into account the needs of those who could not previously access education due to physical, financial, or technical limitations. They will also be aligned with the needs of society, and make use of the benefits of education within massive communities of social learners.

Early evidence from analysis of MOOC activity shows that learners' appetite is typically satisfied with small learning chunks in short-period courses. Today's MOOCs are usually individual units with no clear progression path unless learners are willing to take the leap from a short, free, and informal course to a long and expensive formal course. In the future, many highly modular, self-contained courses will be available. These will be based on focused, refined materials. Increased use of learning design and metadata will mean that these courses are used as steps in coherent and personalised learning journeys.

We are already seeing increased interest in MOOCs as a form of continuing professional development. MOOCs can be used to train worldwide networks of specialists, or to share practice across different workplaces. They also offer a way of addressing "wicked problems"—problems such as climate change or access to safe drinking water—that cannot be solved by individuals or even by small groups.

These possibilities suggest that the systems that develop from MOOCs will move away from the university sector, or perhaps the university sector will reshape itself to include learning and development in new areas. In order for these developments to take place, innovations in technology will be required.

Technology

There are many technological changes under development that will impact on MOOCs and open education in general. As information and communication technology expands its reach, the possibility of ubiquitous access to information is becoming a reality. Web 2.0, or the "read/write Web," is giving way to Web 3.0, also known as the "semantic Web," in which every object is associated with metadata. Beyond Web 3.0, visions of a future in which the Web and the human body are united are already on the horizon (Kurzweil, 2005). In the future it will make no sense to talk of mobile technology or mobile learning, because these will be the norm. Technology and the possibility of learning will always be with us.

However, technology does not exist in isolation. Just as possibilities appear on the horizon, so do barriers. Firewalls and paywalls cut many potential learners off from tools and resources. Ethical considerations prompt us to reflect on how much data we should collect and analyse about learners and teachers. We will need to work hard to avoid a digital divide that restricts educational access to only those individuals and countries that can afford both the technology and the infrastructure to support it. Our vision for MOOCs can only be attained if we take these considerations into account as we develop and deploy our technology.

MOOCs are already making use of emergent learning technologies, including:

- learning analytics to improve feedback;
- adaptive learning that offers personalised pathways;
- social network analysis tools that highlight connections;

- discourse analytics that support automated assessment;
- semantic Web technologies that provide customised support; and
- virtual problem-based learning that allows learners to develop their skills within immersive environments (Haggard, 2013).

Together, the development of these various technologies will provide learners and educators with automated support and feedback, thereby allowing them to focus their attention on problem areas.

These technologies alone will not be sufficient. A transferable credit system, agreed internationally, will allow learners to take badges and qualifications with them as they move between institutions and platforms. For a qualification system to be workable, we need improved authentication technology that will establish firm links between the registered learner, the learning activity, and the badge or qualification. Technology will be used to detect plagiarism; this will be a growing challenge if increasing numbers of learners are assessed from limited question banks. There will also be increasing demand for a lifelong learning portfolio that gathers evidence of learning from different platforms, stores them safely, and makes them available on demand.

From the perspective of accessibility, resources will need to be available in many languages. The technological solution here may draw on the power of the crowd to carry out crowd-sourced translations. For this to work, MOOC creators will need to pay careful consideration to the Creative Commons and open educational resources. At the same time, learners whose physical restrictions have limited their access to face-to-face learning will be expecting accessible online options. Challenges such as providing mathematical notation for those with restricted vision will have to be overcome. These cannot be seen simply as technological challenges; they will also require changes in environments and attitudes.

Wider Environment

The changes necessary to achieve the MOOC vision cannot be confined to universities, learners, and educators. These changes will be associated with a shift in our understanding of what higher education is and who should be able to access it. These dramatically changing times will also require an increased willingness to learn collaboratively online and to make use of social media in this context. They will also require changes to policy in order to support and drive change.

Changing Higher Education

For many students, the university experience is focused on obtaining a degree qualification. This focus has been intensified by rising university fees in many countries and the subsequent self-identification of learners as customers. Financial constraints mean that both universities and learners are looking for ways to make savings. MOOCs offer a way of unbundling the services provided by higher education institutions (Anderson, 2013). The traditional package of teaching, student experience, and credentials will become less stable as students study online, institutions take into account learning that has taken place elsewhere, and students mix and match courses from different institutions. Just as lecturers have provided pathways through excellent resources in the past, in the future they will have the option of providing pathways through excellent courses.

Many universities run Web-based learning environments for their students to access learning and administration resources. Some traditional universities use these environments as a means to offer online degree programmes. This extension of campus courses into online environments is accompanied by a merging of MOOC materials into the campus offering, so that campus students have the benefit of accessing high-quality video presentations and engaging in online discussion.

Without a doubt, the blending of online and campus learning will develop further. Pre-university MOOC courses are being designed to prepare students for academic writing or university-level mathematics. Universities are realising that it is not cost-effective for each faculty or institution to offer a campus course on introductory statistics or study skills. Such courses will increasingly be offered as multi-institution MOOCs, perhaps with additional support on campus. Higher-level classes are being converted to the "flipped classroom" model where students access core teaching materials online, engage in online discussion and testing, and use campus time for academic discussion and problem solving.

Technologies are also being blended, with virtual learning environments providing sites for MOOCs, and MOOC platforms such as OpenEdx being adopted for campus learning. By 2030, the distinction between a MOOC platform and a virtual learning environment is likely to have disappeared. Students will do the majority of their learning online, visiting the campus primarily for group workshops, intensive discussions, lab classes, and invigilated exams. In some universities, these campus sessions may become optional, premium offerings.

Post-school education will no longer be seen as an intensive experience, because lifelong learning will be taken for granted. Learning journeys will offer people different routes through education. An individual might move from just-in-time learning such as watching a video about an immediate concern, to a series of MOOCs about related issues or topics, to a full-time degree, a part-time postgraduate course, and career-spanning workplace training. Such learning journeys will intersect with many others. Learners on many different pathways will use the same resources. During their learning journeys, learners will create resources of their own, which may be taken up by others. At the same time, they are likely to develop skills in collaborating with and mentoring others.

As MOOCs proliferate, the importance of constructing and accrediting learning journeys will grow in importance. Successful universities will be active in these areas, and will include them in their business strategy. They will build learner communities that maintain engagement with the institution over time. The divide between students and alumni will be reduced; those who have finished one course will be encouraged to take others over their lifetime. Cohorts will carry on communicating, with MOOC platforms forming a hub for social media and community building. People who have studied together will be able to continue their conversations, sharing experiences as they put their learning into practice. Importantly, these conversations will feed into the next iterations of the courses.

MOOCS already model and build capacity for collaborative networks that transcend both time and space (McAuley et al., 2010). By 2030, the top universities will be those with learner communities that function as effective think-tanks. Their learners, whether in student- or alumni-mode, will enjoy discussing the big issues of the day with a large worldwide community. As this occurs, these debates and the universities' expert knowledge will be combined to produce reports and recommendations that go far beyond what was possible for smaller, national groups.

Policy: Quality Assurance and Regulation

In order for such large-scale change to take place, changes in policy will be necessary, particularly with regard to quality assurance and regulation. Currently, MOOCs are largely unregulated and quality is highly variable. This situation will offer an increasing challenge as MOOCs become more closely linked with formal education, workplace training, and accreditation.

Daniel points out that quality assurance agencies around the world very seriously consider the rate of course and degree completion. As he states, "They take the view that students seek not merely access, but access to success, which the institution should do everything to facilitate while maintaining standards" (Daniel, 2012). Consequently, the media are delighted to report concerns about dropout rates from MOOCs. However, it is increasingly clear that course completion is a highly limiting measure of success. As with other forms of informal learning, learners set their own goals, and these do not necessarily align with the outcomes set out by the educator. People may primarily register to gain access to a single piece of content, or to a series of discussions, or to find out more about open learning. Their paths are multiple and expectations diverse; hence, traditional criteria are unlikely to prove sufficient.

Just as MOOCs prompt higher education institutions to consider and unbundle their offerings, they prompt quality assurance agencies to consider the needs of different user groups. Learners are investing time in education and will be looking for a reliable assessment of what they can expect. A crowd-sourced ratings site, like the TripAdvisor site currently used for rating travel experiences, will be more useful and up to date than a series of formal reports. Employers, on the other hand, will be investing in MOOCs by allocating staff time to them and by hiring on the basis of the credentials gained. They will be looking to quality assurance agencies to provide unbiased assessments of course design, educators, and outcomes. Overall retention may not be an issue, but employers will want to know that learners on particular learning pathways complete courses and programmes successfully.

Government-approved organisations will also have an important role to play in the qualification system. MOOCs represent an international form of education, so the credits that can be gained should be recognised worldwide. Some of these credentials will be associated with professional bodies, but countries will need a way of ensuring that qualifications are consistent, that they are assessed rigorously, and that the potential for cheating and misconduct is reduced as far as possible.

Governments will have an important role in agreeing, regulating, and funding quality assurance and qualification systems. They may also have a role in ensuring that sufficient MOOC educators are trained, and that school curricula prepare children to be lifelong learners. Governments will also be able to take a lead in encouraging the development of open educational resources and the sharing of publicly funded research. They will ensure that MOOC providers take a responsible attitude to child protection, to the curation and analysis of personal data, and to the moderation of online debate. Through funding, legislation, and research, they can enable the development of MOOCs that open up education, meet society's needs, and make use of the benefits of learning at scale.

By 2030, it is unlikely that we will still be using the term MOOC. What MOOCs have initiated is an understanding of how higher learning can be offered online at massive scale. As universities, companies, governments, and non-government organisations enter this world of massive online learning, they will encounter not only economies of scale, opportunities to enter new education markets, and ways to disseminate their ideas worldwide, but also the traditional education issues of teacher education, course design, quality assurance, examination, and accreditation, recast for a global body of students. The roles of universities will change as they seek to expand their programmes for online learning, with all the issues associated with students from many locations and cultures engaging in learning at a distance. Nevertheless, the university will have a place in this new mix, leading research into innovative pedagogy, providing a site for premium campus services and acting as a trusted examining body. They will have a key role in ensuring the systems that develop from MOOCs meet the needs of societies by educating millions of digital citizens worldwide, open up access to education, and enable people all over the world to enjoy the benefits of learning at scale.

Rebecca Ferguson is a lecturer at The Open University, focused on educational futures, learning analytics, MOOCs, augmented learning and online social learning. Her most recent book is *Augmented Education: Bringing Real and Virtual Learning Together*, which was published by Palgrave in 2014.

Mike Sharples is Professor of Educational Technology in the Institute of Educational Technology at The Open University, UK. He also has a post as Academic Lead for the FutureLearn company. His research involves human-centred design of new technologies and environments for learning. He inaugurated the mLearn conference series and was Founding President of the International Association for Mobile Learning and is also Associate Editor in Chief of *IEEE Transactions on Learning Technologies*. He is the author of over 300 papers in the areas of educational technology, science education, human-centred design of personal technologies, artificial intelligence, and cognitive science.

Russell Beale is Director of the Human–Computer Interaction Centre in the School of Computer Science at the University of Birmingham, UK, and a Professor of Human-Computer Interaction (HCI). Russell has been involved with FutureLearn from the beginning, firstly as a critical friend and now as a researcher. In addition to his work on pedagogies and interaction design for MOOCs, he has conducted research on user-centred knowledge discovery, on intelligent support for browsing and on optimum information presentation in complex situations. His current interests are in how users can interact with complex information; ubiquitous, pervasive, and mobile computing; and how technology impacts and affects our social structures and activities.

References

Anderson, T. (2013). *Promise and/or peril: MOOCs and open and distance education*. Retrieved from http://www.col.org/SiteCollectionDocuments/MOOCsPromisePeril_Anderson. pdf.

Clifton, B. (2013). *FutureLearn to launch unique social online learning experience, delivering free university courses to learners around the world*. Retrieved from http://www3.open.ac.uk/media/fullstory.aspx?id=26322.

Daniel, J. (1996). *Mega-universities and knowledge media: Technology strategies for higher education*. London: Kogan Page.

Daniel, J. (2012). Making sense of MOOCs: Musings in a maze of myth, paradox and possibility. *Journal of Interactive Media in Education, 18*. Retrieved from http://www-jime. open.ac.uk/jime/article/view/2012-18.

Ferguson, R., & Sharples, M. (2014). *Innovative pedagogy at massive scale: Teaching and learning in MOOCs.* Proceedings of ECTEL 2014, Graz, Austria.

Haggard, S. (2013). *The maturing of the MOOC.* London: Department for Business Innovation and Skills.

Kurzweil, R. (2005). *The singularity is near.* London: Duckworth.

Leckhart, S., & Cheshire, T. (2012). University just got flipped: How online video is opening up knowledge to the world. *Wired,* 5: May 2012. Retrieved from http://www.wired.co.uk/magazine/archive/2012/05/features/university-just-got-flipped?page=all.

McAuley, A., Stewart, B., Siemens, G., & Cormier, D. (2010). *The MOOC model for digital practice.* Retrieved from http://davecormier.com/edblog/wp-content/uploads/MOOC_Final.pdf.

Scanlon, E., Sharples, M., Fenton-O'Creevy, M., Fleck, J., Cooban, C., Ferguson, R., Cross, S., & Waterhouse, P. (2013). *Beyond prototypes: Enabling innovation in technology-enhanced learning.* London: Technology-Enhanced Learning Research Programme.

United Nations. (2013). *World population prospects, the 2012 revision: Highlights and advance tables.* Retrieved from http://esa.un.org/unpd/wpp/Documentation/pdf/WPP2012_HIGHLIGHTS.pdf.

University of Edinburgh. (2013). *MOOCs@Edinburgh 2013 – Report#1.* Retrieved from http://hdl.handle.net/1842/6683.

29

OPEN OPTIONS

Recapping This Book with Eyes on the Future

Thomas H. Reynolds, Thomas C. Reeves, Mimi M. Lee, and Curtis J. Bonk

Voices Included

We appreciate you finding your way to this closing chapter. It has been a long, and, we hope, informative and inspiring journey through the current state of *MOOCs and Open Education Around the World*. Capping such a journey is not particularly easy, as there are sixty-four contributors in the thirty-two articles found in this volume (i.e., two insightfully written forewords, one introductory preface and this closing chapter from us, and 28 other chapters from dozens of leaders in the fields of MOOCs and open education addressing a wide gamut of vital issues and topics today). However, even with this extensive compilation of views and experiences, there remains so much more that we would have liked to have included. For instance, you did not find chapters from those in Russia, Mexico, China, Korea, or Finland, or anywhere in the Middle East or Central or South America.

You did, however, hear from advocates of this emerging field of MOOCs and open education representing 14 countries as well as many groundbreaking stories from MOOC and open education implementation efforts directly impacting people in numerous other countries and settings. And, as mentioned in the Preface, the MOOCs and various forms of OER designed, delivered, or evaluated by the various authors of this book were taken by people spanning the globe. As such, this truly was a collective effort of what is happening in this fast emerging field around the world.

Among those included in this book are critical views and voices from some who have expressed legitimate concerns about the potential of open education to resolve current and projected educational problems. Several of the contributors also raise cautionary flags about whether Western-dominated MOOCs delivered only in English can adequately address the diverse needs of learners around the world. Innovative ideas, as well as an array of apprehensions and concerns, were also put forth by those involved in corporate training, open universities, and non-profit organizations.

As such, it is clear that the purpose of this volume was not to identify and select contributors such that a consensus about the global status of MOOCs and OERs could be reached from a single book. Rather, we undertook this effort to provide a sample of the various perspectives, projects, and possibilities that characterize current MOOC and OER endeavors around the planet. We invited a wide range of contributors, and, as expected, we were rewarded with a spectrum of unique and divergent views. In effect, this volume, in chronicling some of the leading OER and MOOC efforts that innovative educators are carrying out on behalf of learners around the world, acknowledges that the OER/MOOC movement is characterized in as much by its departures from standard educational practices as it is by how it serves common educational business practices.

So, in recognition of the useful tensions between opening up education and keeping to its current management, the goal of this closing chapter is to briefly point out some of the consistent perspectives, unique observations, and open options encouraged by the contributors to this volume. As you read through it, we recommend that you keep your options open too as you and your colleagues look ahead to a highly exciting future of education and educational delivery with us.

Recapping This Book

In this volume you have read from some of the foremost leaders in open education, MOOCs, and distance learning in general. We were fortunate to have the opening foreword written by the person who is known for teaching the first MOOC (i.e., George Siemens), while the other foreword was penned by the UNESCO Chair in Open Educational Resources at the Open University of the Netherlands (i.e., Fred Mulder). Both Siemens and Mulder offered a sense of the historical foundations of what is currently happening in this field (i.e., MOOCs did not just spring up overnight) as well as projections toward the future. We were delighted to include their pieces given that they each have been key leaders in this emerging field for some time.

The first part of the book was intended to foster discussion of several key issues and concerns. We began with a contribution from one of the foremost voices in open education, David Wiley. In his historical account of the field, Wiley calls into question the true openness of MOOCs. His cautions should be earnestly reflected upon, given that he played a major role early on in the formation of the field. Wiley's current work at Lumen Learning is creating new forms of open education at lower costs. The second chapter, from Karen Head at the Georgia Institute of Technology, expands upon such concerns about MOOCs, including the potential problems of the exclusivity of such courses and the privileging of certain dominant voices, especially those from particular regions of the world and *socioeconomic status* (SES) levels. According to Head, single-provider models must give way to greater consideration of the highly diverse nature of MOOCs and potential open education participants. Among the chapters you may have read or perused with some interest is the one on the historical unfolding of distance, open, and online education in Japan (see Chapter 3 from Kumiko Aoki). Those who have read it are likely alarmed by the fact that technology adoption and integration in educational contexts in Japan has likely been much slower than most people would have predicted given that country's pre-eminent role in the development of consumer electronics and computing technology.

In the Part 2 of this book, you will have read about the evolution of policies addressing the quality, feasibility, acceptance, and growth of open educational resources and open scholarship from thought leaders in the United States (see Chapter 4 on MERLOT from Gerard Hanley), Australia and Ireland (see Chapter 5 from Carina Bossu and her colleagues), and South Africa (see Chapter 6 from Laura Czerniewicz and her colleagues at the University of Cape Town). Undoubtedly, the unique historical development of MERLOT, as well as the impact of tens of thousands of freely available learning objects and resources found there, is definitely worth pondering. When viewed on a continuum of open education, Hanley accurately makes the case that MOOCs are part of a natural progression or evolution of the field. In Chapter 5, Bossu, Bull, and Brown extend this evolution by showcasing their feasibility protocol for open educational resources (OERs) and offering guidelines for their use. In the next chapter, Czerniewicz et al. highlight the large and increasing impact of digital scholarship and open access to content in higher education. As they suggest, there must be a concerted effort and commitment to open education for it to truly make its mark in higher education. Taking these three chapters together one quickly realizes that there is much to contemplate and work on related to open education right now, as well as in the coming decades. Given the newness of the field and the many interesting changes, or, in fact, transformations, occurring around us in terms of what a scholar is or does today in higher education, one can easily build a research career studying digital scholarship.

Whereas the first two sections provide an historical tone for the book, the next section addresses research and evaluation related to MOOCs and open education. As you will have noted, many chapters from the book originate from North America, wherein much has unfolded in this space since the initial MOOC from George Siemens and Stephen Downes back in 2008. At the same time, we made a concerted effort to gather perspectives from other parts of the world. For instance, in Part 3 of the book, you will have read about early research on MOOCs from Germany (Chapter 7), New Zealand (Chapter 8), and Scotland (Chapter 9). While these authors document quite promising results, there are many issues left to sort out regarding socially responsible research goals and questions, specific learning variables, and reliable and valid measurement instruments, among others.

The fourth part of the book focuses on issues of quality assurance and standards of openness. Authors in this section come from not only the US but also Canada, India, and the Netherlands. These authors offer unique guidelines, frameworks, and advice related to MOOCs and open education. Whereas Karen Swan and her research team at the University of Illinois at Springfield detail a useful scheme for understanding the pedagogical approaches of MOOCs (Chapter 10), Sanjaya Mishra and Asha Kanwar from the Commonwealth of Learning provided quality guidelines and "TIPS" for OERs (see Chapter 11 for details on their framework). In the third and final chapter of this part, Fred Mulder and Darco Jansen offer a means to score or evaluate the true "openness" of different MOOC initiatives according to the potential barriers, issues, and incentives related to a massively open online course. Their pan-European OpenupEd initiative holds much promise as a standard of open education that others may attempt to match or expand upon in the coming decade. These three chapters, of course, are not the final word on quality; nevertheless, we hope that they stimulate serious conversations about it in institutions and organizations across education and training sectors.

Next up was a section on innovative MOOC courses, programs, and models of instruction. Naturally, many of those who open this book are concerned with finding out about the design, implementation, and evaluation of innovative and cost-effective degree-granting programs offered via MOOCs. One such example is the low-cost master's degree in computer science at the Georgia Institute of Technology described in Chapter 13 by Richard DeMillo from the Georgia Institute of Technology.

At the same time, many readers may be curious about how to foster spontaneous communities or ecosystems within MOOCs, wherein peer support is extensive. This approach is explained in Chapter 14 from Kim and Chung—just one example of the many cutting-edge projects currently being developed by Paul Kim at Stanford University. If you become energized by the ideas found in his chapter, we highly recommend that you explore some of the other projects Kim has spearheaded. That exhortation applies, in fact, to the work of all the contributors to this volume.

Similarly, you can turn to the next chapter and read about the novel pedagogical approach to office hours for MOOCs that has been piloted and refined by Charles Severance from the University of Michigan. Severance is a longtime proponent of open source software and online education. In fact, he played a major role in the development and implementation of the well-known Sakai open source course management system. As detailed in his chapter, Severance has developed his ideas of office hours in hotel lobbies and cafés all over the world as a means to personalize the MOOC experience for his students as well as for himself. If you would like to find out more details of how he conducted these meetings in Los Angeles, Boston, Austin, Washington, DC, and Chicago in the

United States as well as Amsterdam, Perth, Paris, Puebla (Mexico), Maribour (Slovenia), and other international locations, we recommend that you watch the videos that he and his MOOC participants have posted to YouTube (see http://www.dr-chuck.com/). Clearly, Severance has designed a highly vibrant and growing community that epitomizes the title that we have chosen for this book.

In the next chapter, you will find information on how graduate students in instructional technology at the University of Houston are helping faculty members to co-design and develop MOOCs for the professional development of K-16 teachers as part of their postgraduate studies (see Chapter 16). In this particular chapter, Bernard Robin and Sara McNeil offer many highly important and replicable MOOC development guidelines to others. Their Webscape design model is likely one of the first insights into how small teams of students can work with faculty and other instructional experts during the entire instructional design process for a MOOC. As such, as with the prior chapter from Severance, this is a key contribution to this emerging field that others may want to replicate and extend as a means toward improving the quality of the MOOC experience.

Capping off Part 5 of this book is a chapter on a highly unique initiative called FemTechNet. This groundbreaking project evolved over several years from a network of scholars, artists, and students who were interested in the intersection of technology, science, and feminism. As perhaps the most collaborative open education project documented in this book, eight scholars teamed up to author Chapter 17. In it, they describe how instructors in multiple universities and institutions across the United States (and eventually around the world) are collaborating to provide common course experiences and content within individually directed courses in a MOOC derivative called a "Distributed Open Collaborative Course," or DOCC. Of course, DOCCs are but one of the many MOOC-like spin-offs or derivatives which are currently being piloted and researched today; and undoubtedly many others will arise in the coming decade.

Part 6 of this book focuses on the varied and fast-emerging uses of MOOCs and open education in the developing world. For example, in Chapter 18 Balaji Venkataraman and Asha Kanwar from the Commonwealth of Learning document how MOOCs can play a huge role in educating people in the developing world on the benefits of mobile technology and other training-specific skills as well as value of MOOCs themselves. Similarly, in the following chapter Sheila Jagannathan from the World Bank Institute explains how more open forms of learning are being provided by the World Bank with the goal of sharing global forms of prosperity and eradicating poverty. These chapters were followed up with explanations of how MOOCs and open education are impacting Southeast Asia and, in particular Malaysia and Indonesia (see Chapter 20 from Zoraini Wait Abas) as well as the evolution of MOOCs and online learning in the Philippines (Chapter 21 from Melinda Bandalari and Grace Javier Alfonso). Across Southeast Asia, MOOCs and open education are being explored, piloted, and evaluated as key prongs in educating the populace, and, thereby, enhancing the economy of the region. In taking a westward migration, Chapter 22 details what is happening in Africa in relation to MOOCs and open education from the vantage point of the African Virtual University (AVU). In this particularly significant contribution, Griff Richards and Bakary Diallo discuss many exciting projects that are currently underway at the AVU in the midst of significant infrastructure issues.

The seventh part of the book considered the current state of open learning in corporate settings. In this section, the learning and technology guru Elliott Masie discusses recent open education inroads and trends in the context of corporate training and learning (see Chapter 23). He accurately points out that open content portals, such as TED and YouTube, are increasingly being mined and harvested for corporate training initiatives. Next, in Chapter 24, Mike Feerick, the Founder of ALISON, describes the ascendance of free online learning for millions of learners worldwide who need specific skills development (e.g., leadership training, computer programming, management, etc.) for the workplace and other settings. In that chapter, Feerick discusses issues surrounding the free online assessment and certification of such skills. In the final contribution to this part, in Chapter 25, Ray Schroeder and his colleagues at the University of Illinois at Springfield describe various ways in which MOOCs have already made an impact in corporate training and professional organizations as a means to reach employees around the globe. In particular, they have been designing MOOCs for healthcare settings and professional development. Given that this is a fast-emerging area, a recap of some of the ideas in Chapter 25, as well as additional corporate training ideas and examples, can be found later in this chapter.

In the eighth and final part, Michael Keppell from the Australian Digital Futures Institute at the University of Southern Queensland in Australia raises awareness of different aspects of what he deems will be a much more personalized learning environment in the near future across six learning and skill dimensions. His multidimensional vision and roadmap in Chapter 26 starts with (1) an important list of digital literacies. After that, he discusses (2) opportunities for highly seamless learning, (3) the need for learners to be more self-directed, (4) the transformation from curriculum-oriented assessment toward more learner-oriented ones, (5) the realization of a lifelong learning society, and (6) the evolution of more flexible learning paths to make all of this possible. Clearly, each dimension is increasingly vital in the evolutionary process of humanity in the 21st century, especially in terms of learning and education. As such, we recommend that you first conduct a quick scan or read through of this chapter as a means to gain an overall sense of what Keppell is attempting to accomplish. Then go back through it and make notes on the ideas and insights that link to initiatives that you and your colleagues might be engaged in within your own organization or institution.

There are two other chapters in this section, in addition to the one you are presently reading. In Chapter 27, Canadians Rita Kop and Hélène Fournier indicate that the forms of personalized learning that Keppell and others now advocate will require an evolving knowledge commons to emerge at the intersection of formal and informal learning. As pioneers in the research and evaluation of MOOCs, especially constructivist types of MOOCs, Kop and Fournier have many unique insights into current and future possibilities of MOOCs and open education around the world.

Finally, in Chapter 28, those involved with FutureLearn and the Open University in the UK contemplate changes in technology, pedagogy, and society as a whole that are needed to allow MOOC and open education visions and hopes to flourish. In this chapter, Rebecca Ferguson, Mike Sharples, and Russell Beale argue that we need vision. Accordingly, they gaze out 15 years into the future to the year 2030 and ask how online learning, including MOOCs and other forms of open education, might educate millions of digital citizens, most of whom, until recently, have lacked such educational opportunities. Those wondering how this is possible might also want to read one or more of the highly timely, informative, and comprehensive reports from Mike Sharples and his colleagues at the Open University and FutureLearn (e.g., Scanlon et al., 2013; Sharples et al., 2014).

Themes and Values

As is clear by now, there are a wide range of innovative ideas and contributions presented in this volume. That is not to say that the volume has not coalesced along certain recurrent themes and ideas or that leading indicators cannot be gleaned from it. They definitely can. For example, despite the premature predictions about the demise of MOOCs back in the spring and summer of 2013, this volume clearly supports the view that the OER movement, of which MOOCs are now a key part, is being vigorously discussed, piloted, researched, and utilized. In fact, the various chapters in this book confirm that educators—from administrators, managers, and policy analysts to instructors, instructional consultants, and instructional designers as well as numerous other stakeholders—perceive MOOCs and other forms or OER as effective ways to resolve various educational resource and delivery issues. However, as an intended goal of this book, we hope that the divergent perspectives supported within this book foster fruitful discussions in educational, political, corporate, non-profit, and military settings about the applicability of MOOCs and open education. We also intend for the book to lend assistance to those developing strategic plans and planning for future directions in this area.

Another dominant takeaway, and possibly the most emphasized idea contained in this book, is that MOOCs and OERs are increasingly becoming part of local, regional, and global educational strategies and solutions for early 21st-century university educators. In addition, they are becoming an important component of the educational infrastructure in a wide range of organizational contexts and situations. They facilitate cross-border relationships among countries and regions of the world that result in forms of global education that previously were deemed highly utopian or not even fathomed. However, as is apparent here, today they are increasingly common.

What is also clear from this volume—and from the numerous articles and reports that the four of us read, shared, and discussed during its compilation—is that MOOC-specific efforts and MOOC derivatives are being carried out in at least four distinct ways: (1) via loosely formed collaborative groups where participants are linked by common curriculum ideals but are free to use a variety of platforms and instructional approaches (e.g., the DOCC as described in Chapter 17); (2) in designed distributed networks wherein curriculum, instructional design and delivery, and some administrative control is centralized (see xMOOCs and most courses from Coursera, edX, and Udacity); (3) by individual institutional efforts that conform to specific purposes and processes (see Chapter 13 from DeMillo for what is happening at Georgia Tech); and (4) by individual faculty or groups of faculty where student and instructor roles as well as other aspects of curriculum and instruction are controlled at the individual or group levels (see Chapter 14 from Kim and Chung, Chapter 15 from Severance, and Chapter 16 from Robin and McNeil).

In addition, as one would expect, the above models can be located along a continuum of curricular approaches from the behaviorally bound to the cognitively unbound, from instances where instruction is managed and assessed in predictably standardized ways to areas where instruction is a shared learning experience involving the creation and expansion of various social space connections. Two chapters ago, Kop and Fournier (Chapter 27, this volume) noted that some refer to the differences between cMOOCs and xMOOCs as one way to explain these models. At the same time, as described in Chapter 14 by Kim and Chung, a MOOC that is designed as a shared social space is complex and requires much foresight and planning as well as extensive instructional design skills and technological savvy. It also entails much patience, risk taking, and the ability to deal with ambiguity. Such traits, while vital in face-to-face forms of instruction, seem pivotal where MOOCs and open education are concerned.

Given the breadth of MOOC and open education approaches described above, there is a need to discuss a few key considerations involved in the various projects and initiatives described in this book and some of their underlying purposes and values. As such, this volume makes very clear that higher educational institutions, non-profit organizations, and corporations that pursue MOOC and OER ends are concerned with a wide range of potential benefits and outcomes. For instance, they are interested in the utility of such enterprises and the potential role that they can play in favorably impacting institutional or organizational budgets, institutional branding, student recruitment and retention, and faculty member research and development. They are also drawn to numerous other practical concerns such as accreditation, course articulation, quality assurance, and faculty roles and responsibilities. However, in all fairness, many of those same institutions also realize that MOOCs and OERs are an effective means for addressing humanitarian and global educational equity issues, and they include these value affirmations in operational plans and resource allocations.

Another key contribution of this volume is that it helps frame and extend the conversation on openness—its history, parameters, societal roles, and moral directives. To these ends, this volume clearly establishes the potentially impactful role that the OER and MOOC movement can have on ideals related to creating more open and productive societies across the globe. Whether institutions of higher education and other organizations in more developed countries are morally bound to participate and promote openness as a means of advancing social justice and equity is not uniformly answered in this volume—nor was it intended to be. We believe that any interpretations of who benefits, how they benefit, and for what purpose a MOOC or open education initiative comes to fruition will depend on a diverse array of factors that are highly contextualized and specific to the populations or situations they are intended to serve. Each such project or course will have its own goals, audiences, stakeholders, values, biases, etc. Accordingly, yours will undoubtedly vary to some degree from every project mentioned in this book.

At the same time, the volume does contain advice and assistance as to how to negotiate the broad instructional landscapes one encounters when thousands of diverse learners participate in common activities—the various MOOC and open education contributors must consider the pitfalls and benefits of having such varied personal and social histories that coexist for a brief moment in time in common instructional conversations. Without doubt, any course offered at any level encompasses a unique compilation of talents, interests, and experiences of those who enroll and participate in it. When considering a MOOC with thousands or even tens of thousands of participants, the complexity and diversity of human experiences and histories are most assuredly amplified and extended.

As we have personally discovered from some of our own MOOC experiences, there is a rich bounty of humanness that one enjoys when participating in a massively open course. Global peers that one meets in a MOOC often become permanent friends and colleagues. In fact, when an instructor goes "on stage" in a MOOC or enters as a participant, there is often a feeling that one is truly connected with peers and learners reaching across all parts of the globe. As shown in Chapter 14 from Kim and Chung and Chapter 15 from Severance, these are highly interesting and unique times to be a college instructor or educator in any sector; when effectively planned and designed, a MOOC can quickly evolve to activities that engage participants in innovative cross-institutional and cross-continent collaboration and resource sharing. Test scores and retention rates be damned; there are burgeoning new connections and partnerships occurring every day. And there are enhanced meetings of the minds.

As with many of you, we remember back to the dawn the first MOOC, when our friends George Siemens and Stephen Downes were making headlines by allowing their course to be open for thousands of "free range learners"

(Cobb, 2013). At that time, the four editors of this volume, as instructional designers, researchers, and college instructors, read with keen interest about the ways in which MOOCs were being designed and taught. Like many others, we devoured news stories and infographics about MOOCs and MOOC-like derivatives. We also read and shared dozens of book chapters, journal articles, technical reports, and white papers related to research and evaluation efforts on MOOCs and open education that were undertaken to ensure consistency and quality in their design and instruction. Fortunately, those early efforts resulted in personal lists of scores of potential contributors to this volume.

With the above backdrop, we were delighted that many of the unique efforts that we have been reading about and discussing since 2008 are now chronicled in this text for they include highly innovative and progressive approaches to MOOC design and teaching that others need to learn about and potentially refashion for their own organizations and institutions. Such piloting of the ideas in this book might evolve into a follow-up volume of educators who put into practice instructional models grounded in visionary ecological and connectivist principles. Or perhaps it will result in a special journal issue related to some learning approach or variation that is yet to be discovered. Whatever transpires, we hope that others will add their own stories and insights to the accounts of those of this book as a means to help establish quality assurance standards and best practices for MOOCs and OERs around the globe.

However, in all fairness, we also acknowledge that much of the criticism leveled at the MOOC movement correctly identifies the irony that, as the 21st century's first technologically-inspired mass educational movement, OER/MOOC-based instructional designs and teaching approaches are still predominantly characterized by 20th-century instructional theories, philosophies, and designs (Hollands & Tirthali, 2014; Reeves & Hedberg, 2014). Additionally, they too often come from the Western and English-dominant world. Clearly, there is a mismatch between what educators envision as essential new millennium literacy skills and the reductive approaches found in most of the current slate of MOOC offerings.

Another key contribution of this text is that it clearly advances the notion that the OER/MOOC world contains numerous "open options" for those who desire to participate, as learners, designers, administrators, or educators. We hope, too, that our readers can now envision the utility and potential benefit of opening up educational resources to populations seeking learning opportunities related to a vast array of topics and skills—not limited to formalized educational content and procedures or prepackaged approaches to instruction; instead, we encourage a more powerful and exciting instructional future involving ad hoc and entrepreneurial ventures like the recent MOOC developed by ALISON in response to the lack of clear information on the Ebola virus and its transmissions and treatments (Coughlin, 2014; Feerick, 2014; for more on ALISON, see also Chapter 24, this volume).

Such social entrepreneurship and innovation could place OERs and MOOCs at center stage of worldwide service centers in which communities of learners can access resources in response to local, regional, and global needs. As with the Ebola MOOC and other global public health initiatives designed by ALISON, the University of Edinburgh recently employed a MOOC as a means of responding to a pressing and high-profile current global issue; namely, whether Scotland should secede from the rest of the United Kingdom (BBC, 2014; see also Chapter 9, this volume). The role that this MOOC played in the Scottish independence campaign is not clear but it likely provided timely and vital content to tens of thousands of people who were seeking it.

In such situations, access to educational resources by masses of people is vital, whether it is from the radio or print media or via MOOCs and other forms of online or blended education. We expect such forms of education to proliferate in the coming decades; so much so that the questions about the viability, sustainability, quality, and learning outcomes from MOOCs and open education, while still vital, will be replaced by questions of life change and impact. Instead of "do MOOCs and other forms of open education replace teachers or traditional courses?," we will be asking where, when, and how open education can play major, and, simultaneously, more modest roles in society. We hope that you can join us in such efforts.

Eyes on the Future

As editors of this volume, we owe a debt of gratitude to the volume's contributors. We want them to know that we endeavored to produce a unified text that also promoted individual values and perspectives. In addition, we should mention that there have been many benefits to the collaborative editing process carried out by the four of us. During the past couple of years, there has been much task structuring, discussion, debate, and coming together of joint minds to help us filter through a plethora of momentous and highly engaging research reports as well as a never-ending supply of hype related to this field. We hope that the final selections in this book implicitly or explicitly exhibit the complementary purposes we envisioned in attempting to put together a text that both exemplified the field today while simultaneously indicating where it might lead in the near future. We will let you and time be the judge of our performance.

As we noted in the Preface, this comprehensive volume is instrumentally linked to a pre-conference symposium held just prior to the International E-Learn 2013 conference in Las Vegas sponsored by our good friends at the Association for the Advancement of Computing in Education (AACE). That one-day event served as the stimulus not only to pursue this project, but also to immerse ourselves in the vast array of ideas percolating around the OER/MOOC topic. Without a doubt, it widened our perspectives on how MOOCs and other forms of open education (e.g., OER, OCW, open educational services (OES), open universities, etc.) were contributing to efforts to improve educational opportunities around the planet. It was clear from that meeting in Las Vegas that the emerging field of open education, and in particular MOOCs and its associated spin-offs and derivatives, had attained more than a foothold in higher education as well as in government, military, and corporate training settings. Consequently, we embarked upon this book project, feeling strongly that it would advance the idea that MOOCs and OERs are an essential part of any educational response undertaken to enable globally engaged learners to build trust and understanding between nations across all regions of world.

What remains difficult is predicting the next steps, where the field of MOOCs and open education might eventually settle, and what impact they will make during the next few years; even more difficult is predicting their contributions in the coming decades. We duly note that each chapter contributor as well as each reader of this book likely has a vision of what he or she expects as well as what he or she would ideally prefer to unfold in this new age of massive open online learning. We take the safe road here by not providing specific or verifiable predictions. Many readers of this book undoubtedly feel that they are walking into an enlightened age of openness; an era of education for all, from all, and for all times. Others are undoubtedly not so sure. We fall somewhere in between such views, although we readily admit that even among the four of us there are distinct differences in our expectations for the future of MOOCs and open education. Keeping one's options open seems to be vital; at least at the moment.

What is certain is that we are living in the midst a vastly transformative time that is extremely difficult to describe and explain because it is so unusual, so enticing, and so filled with hope and brimming with potential. It goes without saying that at this time, learning from MOOCs and open education is nowhere near maximized or fully tested. In fact, quite to the contrary, many of our colleagues who hold key responsibility in the identification and selection of educational resources and technologies know little about even well-established OER repositories (Allen & Seaman, 2014), whereas others indicate that they often use OERs to get new ideas and inspiration and that their students are more satisfied when OER-based instruction is implemented (de los Arcos, Farrow, Perryman, Pitt, & Weller, 2014). Suffice to say, much education is still needed about open education, including its inherent goals, potential benefits, numerous barriers, and endless supply of resources.

So as we move forward in our discovery of the edges to which we can push the OER- and MOOC-related opportunities for diverse and disadvantaged learners, we must also devise ways of successfully inviting the many who struggle with rudimentary understandings of the movement and its utility. We also admittedly do not know what lifelong learning will look like in a few years; let alone in a quarter century or in 2115 or in the decades or centuries that will come after. We do know, however, that distance learning will play an increasingly vital role with each passing year.

What is better known by the four of us is that the world of MOOCs and open education is simultaneously wondrous and yet filled with many twists, turns, and transformations. In such a world, an array of new challenges, opportunities, and success stories are inevitable. For our part, we hope that this book provides some guidance toward an educational future where options and access are open for all learners—the highly inquisitive, informal, and nontraditional learners as well as the educationally disadvantaged, underprivileged, and at-risk. If each person reading this book or this particular chapter finds the means to answer to the problems, needs, and interests of one, two, or even a more "massive" number of these learners, the world will become a better place in which to live and learn. MOOCs and Open Education Around the World!

References

Allen, E., & Seaman, J. (2014, October). *Opening up the curriculum: Open educational resources in U.S. Higher Education, 2014.* Babson Survey Research Group. Retrieved from http://www.onlinelearningsurvey.com/reports/openingthecurriculum2014.pdf.

BBC. (2014, August 24). Scottish independence: Edinburgh University runs online referendum course. *BBC News.* Retrieved from http://www.bbc.com/news/uk-scotland-scotland-politics-28917876.

Cobb, J. (2013, January 22). What's it take to be an effective free range learner? *Mission to Learn.* Retrieved from http://www.missiontolearn.com/2013/01/free-range-learner/.

Coughlin, S. (2014, October 7). Online MOOC courses deliver Ebola health advice. *BBC News.* Retrieved from http://www.bbc.com/news/education-29521360.

de los Arcos, B., Farrow, R., Perryman, L.-A., Pitt, R., & Weller, M. (2014). OER evidence Report 2013–2014: Building understanding of open education. OER Research Hub. The Open University (OU) Institute of Educational Technology. Retrieved from http://oerresearchhub.files.wordpress.com/2014/11/oerrh-evidence-report-2014.pdf.

Feerick, M. (2014, October 7). Why wait for others to fight Ebola? ALISON *Blog.* Retrieved from http://www.advancelearning.com/why-wait-for-others-to-fight-ebola.

Hollands, F.M., & Tirthali, D. (2014). *MOOCs: Expectations and reality.* New York: Center for Benefit–Cost Studies of Education, Teachers College, Columbia University. Retrieved from: http://www.academicpartnerships.com/sites/default/files/MOOCs_Expectations_and_Reality.pdf.

Reeves, T.C., & Hedberg, J.G. (2014). MOOCs: Let's get REAL. *Educational Technology, 54*(1), 3–8.

Scanlon, E., Sharples, M., Fenton-O'Creevy, M., Fleck, J., Cooban, C., Ferguson, R., Cross, S., & Waterhouse, P. (2013). *Beyond prototypes: Enabling innovation in technology-enhanced learning.* University of London, Technology-Enhanced Learning Research Programme, London, UK. Retrieved from http://tel.ioe.ac.uk/wp-content/uploads/2013/11/BeyondPrototypes.pdf.

Sharples, M., Adams, A., Ferguson, R., Gaved, M., McAndrew, P., Rienties, B., Weller, M., & Whitelock, D. (2014). *Innovating pedagogy 2014: Open University innovation report 3.* Milton Keynes: The Open University. Retrieved from http://www.open.ac.uk/iet/main/files/iet-web/file/ecms/web-content/Innovating_Pedagogy_2014.pdf and http://www.open.ac.uk/blogs/innovating/.

INDEX